THE ASIAN JOURNAL
OF THOMAS MERTON

Thomas Merton

THE ASIAN JOURNAL
OF THOMAS MERTON

Edited from his original notebooks
by Naomi Burton, Brother Patrick Hart & James Laughlin
Consulting Editor: Amiya Chakravarty

A NEW DIRECTIONS BOOK

ACKNOWLEDGMENTS

Grateful acknowledgment is made to the publishers, authors, and copyright
owners of works quoted in this book for permission to reprint excerpted material: from Nancy Wilson Ross, *Three Ways of Asian Wisdom* (Copyright ©
1966 by Nancy Wilson Ross); from *The Columbia Encyclopedia,* Second Edition (Copyright 1950 by Columbia University Press); from Edward Conze,
Buddhist Thought in India (Copyright © 1962 by George Allen & Unwin
Ltd.); from Arnaud Desjardins, *The Message of the Tibetans* (Copyright ©
1969 by Vincent Stuart & John M. Watkins Ltd.); from Edward C. Dimock,
Jr. and Denise Levertov, *In Praise of Krishna* (Copyright © 1967 by the Asia
Society, Inc.); from Dom Aelred Graham, *Conversations: Christian and Bud-
dhist* (Copyright © 1968 by Aelred Graham); from Thomas Merton and John
Howard Griffin, *A Hidden Wholeness* (Copyright © 1970 by John Howard
Griffin; Copyright © 1970 by The Trustees of The Merton Legacy Trust);
from T. R. V. Murti, *The Central Philosophy of Buddhism* (Copyright ©
1960 by George Allen & Unwin Ltd.); from Anaïs Nin, *Under a Glass Bell*
(Copyright 1948 by Anaïs Nin); from Giuseppe Tucci, *The Theory and Prac-
tice of the Mandala* (Copyright © 1961 by Rider & Company); from Shankara
(Swami Prabhavananda and Christopher Isherwood, trans.), *The Crest-Jewel
of Discrimination* (Copyright 1947 by Vedanta Press); from *Webster's New
International Dictionary,* Second Edition (Copyright © 1959 by G. & C.
Merriam Co.) and *Webster's Third New International Dictionary* (Copyright
© 1971 by G. & C. Merriam Co.); from Finley Peter Dunne, Jr., ed., *The
World Religions Speak* (Copyright © 1970 by The Temple of Understanding,
Inc.); John Moffitt, ed., *A New Charter for Monasticism* (Copyright © 1970
by University of Notre Dame Press).

Manufactured in the United States of America.
First published clothbound (ISBN: 0–8112–0464–2) in 1973
and as New Directions Paperbook 394 (ISBN: 0–8112–0570–3) in 1975.
Published simultaneously in Canada by McClelland & Stewart, Ltd.
Design by Gertrude Huston

New Directions Books are published for James Laughlin
by New Directions Publishing Corporation,
333 Sixth Avenue, New York 10014

CONTENTS

PREFACE

Readers of Thomas Merton know that his openness to man's spiritual horizons came from a rootedness of faith; and inner security led him to explore, experience, and interpret the affinities and differences between religions in the light of his own religion. That light was Christianity. For him it was the supreme historical fact and the perfect revelation, but affirmations in many lands and traditions and, as St. Paul indicated, the "witnesses," were there; the witnessing continues. Merton sought fullness of man's inheritance; this inclusive view made it impossible for him to deny any authentic scripture or any man of faith. Indeed, he discovered new aspects of truth in Hinduism, in the Madhyamika system, which stood halfway between Hinduism and Buddhism, in Zen, and in Sufi mysticism. His lifelong search for meditative silence and prayer was found not only in his monastic experience but also in his late Tibetan inspiration. His major devotional interests converged in what he called "constantia" where "all notes in their perfect distinctness, are yet blended in one." Believing in ecumenicity, he went further and explored new avenues of interfaith understanding, encouraged by the open spirit of Vatican II.

Not only in religion and in religious philosophy but in art, creative writing, music, and international relations—particularly in a possible world renunciation of violence—he knew the challenge of reality. Intellectual illumination and phases of doubt enhanced the religious process; therefore, in a sense, he never withdrew from the world. Sometimes a bright idea would capture his imagination, and he might tend to overvalue it in the context of conformity. Perhaps it might even be said that he had carried over an experimental attitude from his secular days and made concessions to a social culture to which, he thought on entering the monastery, he no longer belonged. But he adjusted this impulsive quality to his acceptance of the rituals and basic dogmas of his life as a monk and a priest. The search for diversities is never free from an element of risk. But his long years of arduous discipline and his insights produced a deep religious maturity, and his encounters with other religions and religious cultures never found him unresponsive, nor irresponsible in regard to his own commitment. The monk of Gethsemani did not desert his own indwelling heights when he climbed to meet the Dalai Lama in the Himalayan mountains. In a way his discipleship of Jesus grew as he gained the perspective of divine faith; in Asia, he felt the need to return to his monastery in Kentucky with newly affirmed experiences.

Thomas Merton never quite accepted a fixed medieval line between the sacred and the profane. In this he was a modern Christian thinker and believer who had to redefine, or leave undefined, the subtle balance of the religious life.

The richness of this book, with its hurried jottings, referrals, notes on conversations, shifts in scenic travels along with profound insights—interspersed with light lyrics and humor—posed many problems. The editorial board had to consult Merton's friends and acquaintances in far-flung Asian and Western continents; even then some doubts remained as to the exact text and context. The author's erudition and phenomenal memory, as well as his capacity to absorb and reciprocate ideas, sometimes turned his pages into lists of terms and even cryptic puzzles (where the right order could not be traced)—but the editorial collaboration with many authors and correspondents, as the reader will find, led to very satisfactory results. The book is richly cohesive. Without changing the original, as Merton would surely have done in revision, every sentence has been scrutinized and notes (and appendixes and glossary) provided. Where the indigenous words were spelt differently, the variations have been preserved; sometimes the mutational changes of words—from Sanskrit to Pali, for instance—had to be kept as they were quoted or interpreted by the author. No uniformity brought about by diacritical marks has been imposed, the words appear as they were originally written down in the journal, and also as they are still mostly known to the "general public." This meant some sacrifice of academic levels but also an avoidance of stiffness which would have turned the book into a treatise. The improvised nature of the book, where fancy as well as an artist's composition may fling a Tamil word, a French quote, and a Tibetan mandala together, where excerpts from the local paper and a metaphysical discourse are juxtaposed, seemed to go well with the varied and incidental spelling and diction. This does not affect the high seriousness of the book, while it provides color to the rocklike structure and the skies of an unusual pilgrimage.

These pages reveal the character and circumstances of a rare and beloved person. It is a book which seemingly ends in tragedy: but the tragic element, which is a part of life, is transcended by his vibrant humanity.

New Paltz, N.Y.
August 1971

AMIYA CHAKRAVARTY
Consulting Editor

EDITORS' NOTES

The preparation of a publishable text of Thomas Merton's *Asian Journal* was a complicated process. A glance at one of the facsimile reproductions of typical pages from the holograph diaries (see pages xii–xiii) will show how rapidly Merton wrote them, often making it difficult, even for those of us who had known his handwriting for many years, to decipher certain words, particularly Asian names or terms with which we were not familiar. A second problem was that Merton spelled many of these Asian words "phonetically," that is, by as close a guess as he could make to how they had sounded in the day's conversations; some of these words were easy to check in reference works, but for others we were obliged to locate and correspond with some of the many friends whom he had made in his travels. The prompt help which these persons gave us bore witness to the devotion and esteem which even a brief encounter with Merton could inspire.

Related to this difficulty with spellings was the whole problem of transliteration into English from Pali, Sanskrit, Tibetan, and other Asian languages. Few authorities agree on systems for transliteration, this being especially true of Tibetan. Modern scholarship, to be sure, has evolved a complex system of diacritical marks for the English rendering of most of these languages, but since Merton himself almost never used the diacriticals in the *Journal,* we decided against an attempt to supply them. Nor did we try to make his spellings consistent in cases where he had used the Pali spelling of a term at one point and the Sanskrit spelling of its cognate version in another, or to make his spell-

Conversations

Madam my action
Thankyo.

I am your Enrico
Don't you remembraen?
~~thanky~~

Madam it is my turn

(M.m.u.m.mio.)

I am your Traure

Thankyo.

Madam Herr Traure
ready in a moment.

Thankyo.
You are my lifetime pigeon
~~Say~~ I am your ~~—————————~~ dreaming flight
(To stop is a better mistake)

Madam my action
Thankyo
(Sent from Enrico).
(Interception by T. Mustons).

a little to one side
(Be my Traure)

M.m.m.a.m.
should we wait?

I am your Euro.

Do you forget? Is Mustons?

a little to one side

"Not too diplomatic!"

a little to one side
(M' action!)

remained awake until dawn—rather than light a candle & so trying to read by candlelight & as I have a myself told I thought I'd stay under the good blankets. As soon as it was a little light outside the window I put on my clothes & went out—up the hill to the temple on top with all its prayer-flags & incense. The children meanwhile were chanting down at the tibetan school—joyous, lusty chanting that fitted in with the mountains) And there was Kanchenjunga — dim in the dawn & in haze (not colored by the sun but dove-like in its blue-grey — a lovely sight but hard to photograph). I went back after breakfast when the light was better. The view of this mountain is incomparable. I need to go back for more.

+

Seeing the Loreto College next to the hotel I went in to inquire about saying mass. Mother Damian nearly swooned, then pulled herself together & sent me down to the Loreto convent (no chapel at the college — it is a girls' school). I said mass in the big 19th century English type convent-school chapel. a few nuns on one side, a few little girls in uniform, hastily rounded up, on the other It was about 10:15. Then coffee & talk with the nuns, who are nearly old, all in the regular habit (no experimenting with other 'clothes here'!) The two daughters of the Queen of Bhutan are in the convent school here — & one of them was information about an interesting book concerning freemasons that is in Bhutan. I have not met any of the students yet. writing to hear from Mr Thondup at the Tibetan centre.

+

Added information on his G.T. — the Tibetan know them — "they have a reputation for playing very dirty football (in tibetan politics)

+

Nov 14   Providence — not a Tibetan know here & is very nice indeed — took me to the Tibetan Refugee center today & it seemed (relatively) a happy & busy place — she is a warm & active person. This afternoon — Tempa, a Tibetan monk who is teaching with the Jesuits, will come & will talk about interpreting. To Sherboune also.

+

"The self is not different from the states nor identical with them there is no self without the states nor is it to be considered non existent" Nagarjuna

+

"The fluctive consciousness is necessarily the consciousness of the false" Murti. 209.
"The essence of Madhyamika ... not allowing oneself to be entangled in views & theories but free to observe the nature of things without standpoints."   Murti 209.

+

Facing pages from Merton's Asian diary, entries dated November 13–14, 1968

ings, as long as there was authority for them, agree with those in source books from which he quoted. In what is intended as a spirit of ecumenism, we did not italicize foreign-language words except in quotations from other books. We capitalized only the names of religions, their major sects, and divinities.

So much for the minor problems of orthography. A far larger decision had to be made in the matter of editing for style. If, as was true for many of his earlier books, Merton had composed directly on the typewriter, this issue would have been minimized; practically no style changes had ever been required on the typewritten texts of other books he had sent to New Directions for publication. But in the haste of composing in hand, and often late at night or in odd moments snatched from a busy schedule of meetings and sightseeing, he wrote the *Journal* almost stenographically, omitting many verbs and small connective words, often indeed describing a scene or event with a series of phrases separated by dashes. Knowing that he would certainly have polished the style if he had lived to prepare a final version himself, we took the risk, which we felt to be a duty, of attempting to edit the text into sentences. Readers will judge for themselves our degree of success or failure in this effort to identify and reproduce a known style by comparison with such earlier journals as *The Sign of Jonas* or *Conjectures of a Guilty Bystander*.

But at least we can affirm that no substantive changes were made in the text, save in the following instances: certain short passages from the conversations with the Dalai Lama which were marked by Merton as "off the record" (probably because of the Dalai Lama's delicate political situation as an exile-guest in India) were deleted, as were half a dozen sentences about other persons in which the diarist's slightly irreverent sense of humor might have wounded feelings.

If little was subtracted from the text, it must be noted that there were a number of, we hope, useful additions. It should be explained that the editors worked from three separate notebooks: "A," the "public" journal, a spiral-bound school notebook that Merton intended for publication; "B," a black, cloth-bound, ledgerlike volume, the "private" journal, which in large part duplicates the "A" text, but contains as well an occasional intimate note of conscience or spiritual self-analysis; and, "C," the "pocket notebook," a small spiral-bound school notebook that was evidently carried in a coat pocket and used for quick, immediate notes during a conversation, drafts for suddenly-inspired poems, names and addresses of persons met or to be met, times and flight numbers of airline schedules, and other hasty jottings, a few of which were later elaborated in "A."

According to the terms of Merton's will and the indenture of the Merton Legacy Trust, which he had created in 1967 to act as his literary executor and to administer his copyrights for the benefit of the Abbey of Gethsemani, the "private" journal ("B"), as with other earlier journals of a similarly personal nature, is not to be published, or to be made available to scholars (other than his authorized biographer, John Howard Griffin) at the present time. However, permission was granted by the Trustees to supplement the text of the "public" journal ("A") with a few purely descriptive passages that gave information or detail not included in "A."

Little was taken from "C," the pocket notebook, because most of its entries are so fragmentary, but the editors could not resist the slightly surrealist charm of the poem "Kandy Express" (see pages 222–28), which was composed on the train ride between Colombo and Kandy in Ceylon, even though, unfortunately, in a hand so joggled by a rough roadbed that some words are quite indecipherable. There was also a legibility problem with the important notes on the conversation on "mindfulness" with Bhikkhu Khantipalo in Bangkok on October 17, 1968, but here, thanks to the Reverend Bhikkhu's kindness and excellent memory, we have been able to give (see Appendix II, page 297) Khantipalo's summary of the doctrines which were discussed.

Other appendixes provide the texts of the major lectures Merton gave in Asia and the account sent to Abbot Flavian Burns of Gethsemani from the leading Trappist participants at the

Bangkok Conference of the circumstances of Merton's accidental death on December 10, 1968. The *Journal* begins with an entry made on October 15 and ends with one for December 8, just two days before his death. It was fitting that Merton's friend and secretary at Gethsemani, Brother Patrick Hart, should sketch, in a foreword, the background for the Asian journey, and, in a postscript, recount the sad events of the return to the place which was Father Louis' chosen, and never forsaken, home.

Some additions were also made in a few of the quotations from source books on various Asian religions Merton was reading during his journey and from which he digested or paraphrased passages that, it was felt, would be clearer to the reader if given in their complete original form without ellipses. For the most part, these citations were copied out on the left-hand pages of notebook "A," while the right-hand pages were reserved for the main diaristic account and for comment on points of philosophy or religion as they bore directly on Merton's own beliefs. It would have been possible to present the story with the right-hand pages of "A" alone, omitting the quotations from other books. But it was decided early on that one of the most valuable assets of the *Journal* would thus be lost, the record of what Merton found particularly interesting in his reading or selected as relevant for further and future reference and study. Thus the quotations from left-hand pages of "A" were incorporated in the main narrative, being placed as nearly as possible to their facing location in the notebook. However, some pages of quotations and rather abstruse commentary that seemed to impede the flow of the "story," or not to relate directly to it, were segregated and will be found under the heading "Complementary Reading," beginning on page 261.

Most copious, and perhaps most "un-Mertonian," for with a humility that was not false modesty he seemed to assume in his readers, if not a knowledge, at least a spirit of inquiry as great as his own, are the footnotes to the main text. For these the publisher-editor must take full blame. He justified his own combination of ignorance with curiosity by hoping that Catholic readers might want to know more about matters Asian, and that readers already informed about Asia might need some help on Catholicism. In any case, the notes are safely hidden at the end of each narrative section, where they may be easily ignored. In general, persons (including deities) and places are covered by these notes, while Asian religious and philosophical terms are dealt with in a glossary that begins on page 363.

For the reader who, with this book, comes first to Asian thought, a perplexing feature will undoubtedly be the rapidity with which Merton, in the quotations from his reading, jumps from one religion, or sect, to another. His ecumenism was total, and we find him ranging from Tantric Buddhism to Zen, and from Islam and Sufism to Vedanta. If an unwarned reader were to proceed on the assumption that the quotations, as they follow each other in the text, were from the same religion, he would end up with a conglomeration of conflicting doctrines that would be baffling indeed. Accordingly, it may be helpful to point out that the book by Dom Aelred Graham deals particularly with the schools of Buddhism which flourish in Japan, those by Edward Conze with various sects of Buddhism, Murti's *Central Philosophy of Buddhism* with the Madhyamika tradition in Mahayana Buddhism, and the little book about King Rama IV of Thailand with Theravada Buddhism. Tibetan Buddhism and its elements of Tantrism are the only subject of the essays of Marco Pallis and the books by Evans-Wentz, Tucci, Desjardins, and S. B. Dasgupta, as well as the material drawn from the poetry of Milarepa. Surendranath Dasgupta treats both of Buddhism and Hinduism in his *Indian Idealism,* while the works cited by Esnoul, Dimock and Levertov, Mohan, the 8th-century Sankaracharya, and the contemporary Sankaracharya of Kanchi are concerned with various aspects and doctrines of Hinduism.

For the reader who wishes to approach the religions of Asia more systematically, to gain some historical perspective on how one set of beliefs gradually led to others, and how, geographically, they moved, there are perhaps few better general introductions than Nancy Wilson Ross's *Three Ways of Asian Wisdom,* though it does not go as deeply into Tibetan Buddhism as Marco Pallis, Christmas Humphrey's *Buddhism* in the Pelican paperback edition, or the excellent collections edited by Kenneth W. Morgan, *The Religion of the Hindus* and *The Path of the Buddha.*

The editors, the publisher and the Trustees of the Merton Legacy Trust wish to record here their deep gratitude to the many friends and admirers of Thomas Merton who have so generously assisted in the preparation of the text for publication by their research, suggestions, and answers to letters of inquiry. We would mention especially High Commissioner and Mrs. James George, Harold Talbott, Sonam T. Kazi, Professor V. Raghavan, Mother Myriam Dardenne, Phra Khantipalo, Gary Snyder, Lobsang P. Lhalungpa, George Zournas, Barbara S. Miller, Finley Peter Dunne, Jr., Victor Stier, Marco Pallis, Irving L. Sablosky, John Howard Griffin, Rev. A. M. Allchin, Suzanne Dale, Professor P. Lal, Dr. Kenneth W. Morgan, Fr. M. Augustine, O.C.S.O., Gunther Stuhlmann, Kay Bierwiler, Charlaine Hays, Patricia Marron, Peter Leek, Richard T. Stone, Professor Lucy Frost, John Blofeld, Lionel Landry, Kenneth J. MacCormac, Blaise Alain, Dr. F. Warren Roberts, Kathy De Vico, Dr. Malcolm Pitt, Alain Daniélou, Eleanor O'Dwyer, Professor Edward C. Dimock, Jr., M. Jansen-Borremans, Dorothy McKittrick Harris, Diana Eck, Rev. Richard Sherburne, S.J., Professor Huston Smith, R. Gordon Wasson, W. H. Ferry, Professeur Jean Filliozat, Rev. Abbé Marie de Floris, O.S.B., Fr. Maurice J. Stanford, S.J., A. Oswin Silva, Dom Aelred Graham, Professor S. Vahiduddin, Leila and Daniel Javitch, Professor Lokesh Chandra, Rev. Daniel C. Walsh, Robert M. MacGregor, Paul Laughlin, Tsering Yangdon, Emmett Williams, Sister Thérèse Lentfoehr, John Moffitt, Peter Glassgold, Michael Baldwin, Betty Delius and the staff of the Bellarmine Library.

Most grateful acknowledgment is also made to the publishers and copyright owners of works from which Father Merton quoted in his text and notes, or from which the editors have quoted in notes or glossary, and especially to Nancy Wilson Ross for permission to reproduce entries from the glossary in her *Three Ways of Asian Wisdom* (Simon and Schuster); to Columbia University Press for *The Columbia Encyclopedia;* to The University of Michigan Press and Allen & Unwin Ltd. (London) for *Buddhist Thought in India* by Edward Conze; to Vincent Stuart and John M. Watkins Ltd. (London) for *The Message of the Tibetans* by Arnaud Desjardins; to Doubleday & Co. for *In Praise of Krishna* by Edward C. Dimock, Jr. and Denise Levertov; to Dom Aelred Graham for *Conversations: Christian and Buddhist* (Harcourt, Brace & World); to Houghton Mifflin Company for photographs from *A Hidden Wholeness* by Thomas Merton and John Howard Griffin; to Allen & Unwin Ltd. (London) for *The Central Philosophy of Buddhism* by T. R. V. Murti, as well as for other books first published in England by Allen & Unwin; to Gunther Stuhlmann for Anaïs Nin's *Under a Glass Bell* (E.P. Dutton & Co., Inc.); to Hutchinson Publishing Group Ltd. (London) for Giuseppe Tucci's *The Theory and Practice of the Mandala* (Rider & Company), as well as other books first published in England by Rider; to The Vedanta Society of Southern California for *The Crest-Jewel of Discrimination* by Shankara [Sankaracharya], translated by Swami Prabhavananda & Christopher Isherwood; and to G. C. Merriam Company for definitions from *Webster's International Dictionaries.*

J.L.

FOREWORD

When I was asked to contribute a foreword and postscript to the *Asian Journal,* I remembered a talk I had with Thomas Merton (or Father Louis as he was known in the monastery) several weeks before he left Gethsemani on his Asian trip. It is still quite vivid in my memory, and I hope I can put down the essence of our conversation as we walked through the woods, and later as we sat inside his hermitage enjoying a cool drink.

Upon my return to Gethsemani in the summer of 1968 after a two-year stint at our General's House in Rome, the newly elected Abbot asked me to be secretary to Father Merton. As secretary to the former Abbot for ten years, his manuscripts had usually passed through my hands, either to the censors (now simply called "readers") or to his publishers, so I was well acquainted with his writings and with publishing procedures in general.

As I approached the hermitage that warm summer afternoon, I found Father walking slowly on a shady, well-beaten path at the edge of the woods overlooking the quiet valley, reading Dom Aelred Graham's new book on his Asian experiences: *Conversations: Christian and Buddhist.* I never saw him looking so healthy and happy as on that day. After I had given him a personal message and gift (a beautiful bronze cross) from Pope Paul, with whom I had an audience shortly before leaving Rome, we discussed his proposed trip to Asia, and what my work as his secretary during his absence would entail.

First, he explained to me the genesis of the trip: an international Benedictine group, organized to help implement monastic renewal throughout the world *(Aide à l'Implantation Monastique)*, was sponsoring a conference of all Asian monastic leaders (including Benedictines and Cistercians) to be held at Bangkok, Thailand, in the middle of December 1968, and that he was asked to deliver one of the principal addresses. Dom Jean Leclercq, a Benedictine scholar and old friend, had suggested the invitation, and was planning to meet him in Bangkok.

He told me how pleased he was that the Abbot had approved his acceptance of the invitation, and that he was allowed to plan the details of his itinerary to include visits to a great many Buddhist monasteries before and after the Bangkok meeting. Then, too, he had accepted another invitation to speak at the Spiritual Summit Conference, sponsored by the Temple of Understanding, which was to be held in Calcutta a few weeks prior to the Bangkok meeting. This was to be an interfaith meeting, which he describes in the pages of this book.

Several monasteries of our own Cistercian Order had asked him to come to preach retreats to their communities. He had accepted the invitation of the community at Rawa Seneng, Indonesia, where he planned to be at Christmastime. He had also tentatively arranged to give some talks at our Trappist

Brother Patrick Hart, Thomas Merton, and Brother Maurice Flood

Monastery on Lantao Island in Hong Kong Harbor early in January. As he explained to his friends in the last mimeographed circular letter he asked me to type for him shortly before leaving Gethsemani: "Considering the crucial importance of the time, the need for monastic renewal, the isolation of our Asian monasteries, their constant appeals for help, I feel it a duty to respond. And I hope this will enable me to get in contact with Buddhist monasticism and see something of it firsthand."[1] He was going to Asia not only to give of himself, but also to receive from their rich monastic tradition.

Thomas Merton's pilgrimage to Asia was an effort on his part to deepen his own religious and monastic commitment. This is evident from the prepared remarks for the interfaith meeting held in Calcutta in mid-November: "I speak as a Western monk who is pre-eminently concerned with his own monastic calling and dedication. I have left my monastery to come here not just as a research scholar or even as an author (which I also happen to be). I come as a pilgrim who is anxious to obtain not just information, not just facts about other monastic traditions, but to drink from ancient sources of monastic vision and experience. I seek not only to learn more (quantitatively) about religion and monastic life, but to become a better and more enlightened monk (qualitatively) myself."[2]

In the same context Merton continued: "I need not add that I think we have now reached a stage (long overdue) of religious maturity at which it may be possible for someone to remain perfectly faithful to a Christian and Western monastic commitment, and yet to learn in depth from, say, a Buddhist discipline and experience. I believe that some of us need to do this in order to improve the quality of our own monastic life and even to help in the task of monastic renewal which has been undertaken within the Western Church."

[1] See Appendix I for the full text of this "September 1968 Circular Letter to Friends."

[2] See Appendix IV.

In addressing the Asian monastic leaders at Bangkok a few weeks later, on the subject of "Marxism and Monastic Perspectives," Father Merton concluded his remarks with a frank appreciation of the monastic values of the East as a complement to our Western Christian monasticism: "I believe that by openness to Buddhism, to Hinduism, and to these great Asian traditions, we stand a wonderful chance of learning more about the potentiality of our own traditions. . . . The combination of the natural techniques and the graces and the other things that have been manifested in Asia, and the Christian liberty of the gospel should bring us all at last to that full and transcendent liberty which is beyond mere cultural differences and mere externals. . . ."[3]

His hopes were not in vain, for as he wrote to me in a letter dated October 21st from Calcutta: "Thailand and India have been wonderful experiences; utterly different in so many ways from Europe and America, in spite of Westernization. They are still totally religious cultures—with plenty of good and bad mixed up together. The Thai monasteries are very thriving and there is a minority very proficient in meditation and contemplation. . . ." A few days later, he was to write of his fruitful experience with the lamas near Darjeeling where he made a retreat in the guest bungalow of a tea plantation with a fantastic view of Kanchenjunga, the mysterious mountain which he felt impelled repeatedly to photograph: "I met also many new lamas in the Darjeeling area. My contact with all of them has been excellent because I have had the good fortune to have first-rate translators. The best lamas are extraordinary people and some of them real mystics. They have a very austere and I think effective approach to meditation and contemplation. . . ."

But these contacts were still hidden in the future as we sat in the cool front room of the hermitage that August afternoon. He spoke of his great desire to visit the Dalai Lama, and told me that a mutual friend was making the arrangements for

[3] See Appendix VII.

The Hermitage

the meeting. He did indeed have three audiences with the Dalai Lama at his monastic refuge near Dharamsala, about a month before the Bangkok Conference, which are described in this book. Other friends were busy making contacts to expedite his entrance into Burma and Nepal. Japan, too, was on his itinerary, but he was reserving this long-awaited joy until after the New Year before his return to America.

While listening to Father explain so enthusiastically the plans for his Asian trip, it became evident to me that his long interest in the East had been a providential preparation. Although his initial preoccupation with things Eastern can be traced to his college days at Cambridge and Columbia, he had begun to study the Zen Masters seriously in the late fifties.

Through the stimulus of such an eminent scholar as Dr. John C. H. Wu, he even made an attempt to learn the Chinese language, although he had to abandon it later because of the pressure of other work. Dr. Paul K. T. Sih of the Institute of Asian Studies at St. John's University in Jamaica had provided him with the Legge translation of the *Chinese Classics,* which he pondered deeply during these early years. His own book, *The Way of Chuang Tzu,* which he admitted frankly was one of his favorites, developed out of these readings in 1965.

His librarian friends, especially Mrs. Victor Hammer of the

Thomas Merton in the Hermitage

King Library at the University of Kentucky in Lexington, and Fr. Brendan Connolly, S.J., of Boston College, were inexhaustible sources of Asian books on loan, of which he availed himself at frequent intervals. Besides, there were the local Louisville libraries which he visited each time he went to Louisville for a medical appointment, a rather frequent occurrence during these years. He studied all these books thoroughly, reading and taking copious notes, and absorbed them completely. Even while he was traveling through Asia, he was still reading and making notes, as can be seen from the quotations and paraphrases from books by authorities such as Tucci, the Dasguptas, Evans-Wentz, and Murti, in this journal.

Doubtless Merton received the most encouragement in his Eastern studies from the great Zen authority, the late Dr. Daisetz T. Suzuki, with whom he had corresponded over the years, and with whom he had several conversations on Dr. Suzuki's last visit to America. Dr. Suzuki felt that Thomas Merton was one of the few Westerners who really understood what Zen was all about. (An interesting exchange of correspondence between Suzuki and Merton appeared in *Zen and the Birds of Appetite*, New Directions, 1968.)

While Father Merton's main concern was his Asian contacts, he was also taking advantage of his travels to explore the various possibilities for greater solitude in places like New Mexico, Alaska, and along the California coast before leaving for Asia. The Abbot had suggested to him that he be on the watch for a more solitary spot in which to live after his return from Asia, since his present hermitage was becoming more and more invaded by visitors, noisy hunters, and friendly neighbors. There was also the possibility that such a place could be used by others at Gethsemani, either permanently or for a time. Due to the monastic *aggiornamento* in the last few years, more flexibility was now allowed in making provision for a proper measure of solitude according to the needs of each individual monk.

However, he assured me very definitely as we talked that afternoon in the hermitage that it was his intention to remain always a monk of Gethsemani. If it turned out that he found a more solitary place in which to live, he would continue having his mail come to Gethsemani and expect me to act as his secretary. In fact, he was quite sensitive on this point of remaining a monk of Gethsemani, since a number of irresponsible rumors were circulating about his abandonment of the monastic commitment. In one of the earliest letters I received from him after his departure, he referred to some rumors which had already reached him: "Give my regards to all the gang and I hope there are not too many crazy rumors. Keep telling everyone that I am a monk of Gethsemani and intend to remain one all my days. . . ." Later, in a letter from New Delhi, dated November 9, 1968, just a month before his death, Thomas Merton wrote in part: "I hope I can bring back to my monastery something of the Asian wisdom with which I am fortunate to be in contact. . . ."

Toward the end of November, he made the following entry in his journal which reveals his continued determination to remain a monk of Gethsemani: "On the other hand, though the Jesuits at St. Joseph's have repeatedly dropped hints about the need for contemplative Catholic foundations in India, I do not get any impression of being called to come here and settle down . . . I do not think I ought to separate myself completely from Gethsemani, even while maintaining an official residence there, legally only. I suppose I ought to end my days there. I do in many ways miss it. There is no problem of my wanting simply to 'leave Gethsemani.' It is my monastery and being away has helped me see it in perspective and love it more."

The present journal makes many references to his continuous search for greater solitude, and indeed it is something of a leitmotif in all the writings of Thomas Merton—especially his journals.[4] Although he never abandoned the idea of finding a more perfect haven of physical silence and seclusion, he realized that the heart of the matter was on a deeper level, as he

[4] *The Sign of Jonas*, Harcourt, Brace, 1953, and *Conjectures of a Guilty Bystander*, Doubleday, 1966.

wrote in the closing paragraph of the circular letter quoted above: "Our real journey in life is interior; it is a matter of growth, deepening, and of an ever greater surrender to the creative action of love and grace in our hearts. Never was it more necessary for us to respond to that action." ("September 1968 Circular Letter to Friends")

Abbey of Gethsemani, Ky.　　　　BROTHER PATRICK HART
January 1971

View from the monastery of Gethsemani

THE ASIAN JOURNAL
OF THOMAS MERTON

Part One

THE EASTWARD FLIGHT
October 15–18

October 15

The Pacific is very blue. Many small white clouds are floating over it, several thousand feet below us. It is seven o'clock in Honolulu toward which we are flying. We—the planeload of people on Pan American: the silent Hawaiian soldier, the talking secretaries, the Australians, the others who like myself had to pay for excess baggage. Lesson: not to travel with so many books. I bought more yesterday, unable to resist the bookstores of San Francisco.

Yesterday I got my Indonesian visa in the World Trade Center, on the Embarcadero, and said Tierce[1] standing on a fire escape looking out over the Bay, the Bay Bridge, the island, the ships. Then I realized I had apparently lost the letter with addresses of the people I was to meet. However, I did jot down an address in Djakarta.

There was a delay getting off the ground at San Francisco: the slow ballet of big tailfins in the sun. Now here. Now there. A quadrille of planes jockeying for place on the runway.

The moment of take-off was ecstatic. The dewy wing was suddenly covered with rivers of cold sweat running backward. The window wept jagged shining courses of tears. Joy. We left the ground—I with Christian mantras and a great sense of destiny, of being at last on my true way after years of waiting and wondering and fooling around.

May I not come back without having settled the great affair. And found also the great compassion, mahakaruna. We tilted east over the shining city. There was no mist this morning. All the big buildings went by. The green parks. The big red bridge over the Golden Gate. Muir Woods, Bodega Bay,

Point Reyes, and then two tiny rock islands. And then nothing. Only blue sea.

I am going home, to the home where I have never been in this body, where I have never been in this washable suit (washed by Sister Gerarda[2] the other day at the Redwoods),[3] where I have never been with these suitcases, (in Bangkok there must be a katharsis of the suitcases!), where I have never been with these particular books, Evans-Wentz's *Tibetan Yoga and Secret Doctrines* and the others.

The smell of one of the Australians' cheroot. And, in the diffuse din of the plane, bird cries, waterfalls, announcements, and the pretty stewardess comes along handing out green mimeographed sheets of paper, or small blue cards, invitations to parties with the King of the Islands, perhaps. Someone holds high the San Francisco *Chronicle* with a big gray picture of a tiger skin.

⌘

Last week I had a dream about planes. It was at Yakutat,[4] one of the small airstrips to which I had been flown in Alaska. There is a low ceiling and we are waiting to take off in a small plane. But a large plane, a commercial prop plane, is about to land. It comes down, and then I hear it leave again. The way is clear. Why don't we take off now? The other plane is never seen, though it lands and takes off nearby.

⌘

Not long ago I was thinking about the level of communication —as a problem to be studied on this trip—with its many aspects. And the level of communion—problems resolved beforehand by the acceptance of "words," which cannot be understood until after they have been accepted and their power experienced.

Hrishikesa, destroyer of Titans, ogres and canailles,[5]
Slaves flee the old group, embracing the feet of Hrishikesa,
   flying from Wallace,
Free champagne is distributed to certain air passengers
"Ad multos annos,"[6] sings the airline destroyer of ogres
   and canailles
In the sanctuary of the lucky wheel
Blazing red circle in the fire
We are signed between the eyes with this noble crim-
Son element this Asia,
The lucky wheel spins over the macadam forts
Showering them with blood and spirits
The thousand bleeding arms of Bana
Whirl in the alcohol sky
Magic war! Many armies of fiery stars!
Smash the great rock fort in the Mathura forest
Baby Krishna plays on his pan-flute
And dances on the five heads
Of the registered brass cobra
Provided free by a loving line of governments.

✳

Berceuse: to end the sorrow of mortals: talelo, riding the bull.
Talelo. Riding the great blue buffalo. Talelo! They kill swine.
They break the bone, eat the marrow of sorrow. The Tamil[7]
page cures in the dry wind, the inner aviation. You striding
baby, you three-step world surveyor.

     Weep not. Talelo.
     Love has lotus feet
     Like the new blossoms
     Bells are on her ankles.
     Talelo.

You who came to drink on earth
Poisoned milk
Weep no more. Talelo?
The carp is leaping
In the red-rice. Talelo.
And in the open lotus
Stays the blackgold bee
The slow cows come
Heavy with milk
(Come, doll. Talelo.)
Kiss kiss one sandy sparrow
And coins tinkle on the wrist
Bells on the ankles of girls at the churns.
Talelo.

You little thundercloud
With red eyes
Lotus buds
Lion cub of yasoda
The girls go
To wash in the river
But for you
They do not pencil
Their eyes

⌘

The Lion Baby. He got rid of all the athletes.

⌘

After Honolulu

The very loud tour got out and Honolulu was hot. The airport
was at times like Whitestone, Long Island in 1929, and at times
heavenly with the scent of flowers. Hawaii could be so beauti-

ful—the dark green mountains rising up into the clouds! And I thought: "O Wise Gauguin!" But there is no longer any place for a Gauguin!

In the airport bar I met some people heading for New York via Las Vegas—no harm to be done. Then back in my waiting room, to get on Flight 7 to Tokyo, Hong Kong and Bangkok, and there was a whole new set. They were Asians, small anonymous types of no calculable age, and the sweet little Japanese girl—or Chinese?—poor, with a lei of colored plastic. When the stewardess began the routine announcement in Chinese I thought I was hearing the language of Heaven. Seven hours to Tokyo!

The stewardess hands out newspapers and I get the Hong Kong *Standard*. Stocks are up in heavy Hong Kong buying, and the astronauts have colds. And the Indonesians have released a Hong Kong freighter flying a Panamanian flag, which they thought was involved in a "multimillion dollar trade fraud," which maybe it was. It was held at Jambok six weeks.

✼

Ramanuja[8] was anointing the head of his guru when the latter asserted that the eyes of the Lord were red as the ass of a mandrill. A red hot tear fell from the eyes of the disciple on the face of the master. When requested to explain his grief, Ramanuja said the eyes of the Lord were in reality as red as a delicately red lotus. The master then gathered the other disciples in secret and intimated that Ramanuja was an enemy of the true faith. They all decided to take him on pilgrimage and drown him in the river Ganges.[9] Ramanuja took a side road and wandered off into the jungle. He met Vishnu[10] and his spouse disguised as birdcatchers. They led him to a more reliable master.

> —See A.-M. Esnoul: *Ramanuja et la mystique vishnouite,* Paris, Editions du Seuil, 1964, page 67. See also Part Two of this volume, "Complementary Reading," page 266, for additional passages from Esnoul.

"Mr. Feresko wants to see you, Captain."
"You mean he's conscious!" (Dr. Kildare in the comic strip)

"You born today are an ambitious leader, efficient promoter and a reasoner. You are a powerful friend and with your active disposition can be an equally potent enemy." That's for today in the astrology column, syndicated in the Hong Kong *Standard*. And the ocean is empty and deep, deep, blue. A Nixon victory will be bullish for the market, they think. They think. They think. They think too that Mr. Feresko is conscious.

⌘

I am over a wing and see only a lovely distant garden of delicate Pacific clouds, like coral, like rich and delicately formed full white and pink flowers, small enough for plenty of gaps over an ocean that has to be forever sunny.

It is 8 A.M. tomorrow in Tokyo toward which we are flying. It is 1:15 Honolulu time and we are about to have supper. In San Francisco it is nearly 5.

Hong Kong beats Singapore to retain the Ho Ho Soccer Cup.

Offerings of flowers, water and fire· they please Vishnu. A soldier heading for Vietnam studies his Bible. But in the airport he was chuckling at a joke in the *Reader's Digest*. God protect him!

On this flight—no complimentary champagne.

The utter happiness of life in a plane—quiet, time to read. But long, long. Endless noon. Tuesday afternoon turns into Wednesday afternoon, and no matter how hard we try we won't get much past 3 o'clock until after Tokyo, when we swing south, and the night will finally fall on us.

A Japanese (nisci) stewardess comes over and looks at this notebook and asks, "What is *that*?" I explain.

Long, long noon. Endless noon. Like Alaska in midsummer. In San Francisco it has long been dark. It is nearly 10 at night there. Here, endless sun. I have done everything. Sleep. Prayers. And I finished Hesse's *Siddhartha*.[11] Nothing changes the endless sunlight. And in this light the stewardesses come with questionnaires that we must all fill in. Why do we travel?, etc.

✼

October 17 / Bangkok

Last evening, the plane was late taking off and we did not leave Tokyo until after dark. I unknowingly broke the rules of the airline at Hong Kong where I walked up and down in the dark warm sea wind under the plane's huge tail, looking at the lights of Kowloon.[12] This merited an implied reproof, a special announcement at Bangkok that passengers were under no circumstances to do this! Finally, after we passed over South Vietnam—where there were three big, silent, distant fires—we came down over the vast dim lights of Bangkok. We got out of the plane into tropical heat, a clammy night no worse than Louisville in July. Fascist faces of the passport men, a line of six officials in uniform to stamp a passport once, faces like the officers in Batista's Cuba, and the same pale uniforms. Tired, crafty, venal faces, without compassion, full, in some cases, of self-hate. Men worn out by a dirty system. A conniving one made no move to look at any bag of mine in the customs. He waved me on when I declared fifteen rolls of pan-x film—as if I were a good child. And I was grateful. Why not? He showed sense. I am only in Bangkok for two days this time.

The soldier who was reading the Bible on the plane got out here, too. The nice mother in the white suit, with whom I had a whisky in the Tokyo airport, got off with her baby at Hong Kong—a stopover before Vietnam. There was a list of dangerous places on a blackboard at Tokyo—plague at Saigon and three other Vietnamese airports.

The Temple of the Emerald Buddha, Bangkok

At nearly 1 A.M., Bangkok time, after about twenty-four hours in the plane, I ride through the hot, swamp-smelling night in an "airport limousine," that is more accurately a fast and wildly rattling piece of old bus. There are three others in it: a Chinese and his wife, and a Hindu. They both go to the big fancy Siam Intercontinental. I go to the Oriental, which is thoroughly quiet. The road from the airport could be the road from any airport—from Louisville to Gethsemani[13] in summer. The same smell of hot night and burning garbage, the same Pepsi billboards. But the shops are grated up with accordion grilles, the stucco is falling off everything, and the signs in Thai are to me unintelligible.

❉

Bangkok

This morning, I made a partial purification of the luggage. What will I do with all those books that have to be thrown out? Leave them with Phra Khantipalo, the English bhikkhu at Wat Bovoranives.[14]

I had breakfast on the hotel terrace by the river. A hot wind. Choppy water, and great activity of boats: motorboats waiting to take tourists on a tour of the klong[15] markets, and rowboats as ferries to and fro across the river—one sculled by a strong woman who fought the current bravely and effectively, though I thought she and her passengers would be carried away!

Then about 10 I took a taxi to Wat Bovoranives. We drove through Chinatown with its clutter of shops and wild, dirty streets. Crowds. Motorbikes. Taxis. Buses. Trucks fixed up to look like dragons, glittering with red and chrome. Dirt. Camp. Madness. Enormous nightmare movie ads. And lovely people. Beautiful, gentle people—except those who are learning too

The Temple of the Emerald Buddha, Bangkok

fast from the Americans. A long ride to the wat but we finally get there. I pass through a gate into a quiet maze of shady lanes and alleys, large houses, canals, temples, school buildings. I ask a bhikkhu for directions and arrive at the domicile of Phra Khantipalo. He is extremely thin, bones sticking out in all directions. He has the look of a strict observer. But sensible. ("These people here are very tolerant and uncritical.") Khantipalo is the author of two books on Buddhism. He says he is going to a forest monastery in the northeast part of Siam in four or five days. He will have a quasi-hermit life there, with a good meditation teacher, in the jungle. We talked of satipatthana meditation.[16]

In the evening I met the abbot, Venerable Chao Khun Sasana Sobhana, who was very impressive. He was tired—he had just returned from the cremation of some bhikkhu—but he got talking on the purpose of Theravada. He spoke of sila, samadhi, panna (prajna), mukti, and the awareness of mukti (freedom), with emphasis on following one step after another, ascending by degrees. I enjoyed the conversation—there were occasional translations of difficult parts by Khantipalo—and felt it was fruitful.

The abbot told this story of Buddha and Sariputra.[17] Buddha asked Sariputra: "Do you believe in me?" Sariputra answered: "No." But Buddha commended him for this. He was the favorite disciple because he did *not* believe in Buddha, only respected him as another, but enlightened, man.

What is the "knowledge of freedom?" I asked. "When you are in Bangkok you know that you're there. Before that you only knew about Bangkok. And," he said, "one must ascend all the steps, but then when there are no more steps one must make the leap. Knowledge of freedom is the knowledge, the experience, of this leap."

The abbot's table was piled high with presentation books for temporary bhikkhus who were disrobing and leaving the wat at the end of the rains. A boy student, on his knees, presented hot tea, but behind me. Khantipalo motioned for him to kneel where he could be seen and the tea reached.

The noise of a big motorboat on the river. I am falling asleep. I had better drop this and go to bed. (10:30)

❄

The Thai Buddhist concept of sila, the "control of outgoing exuberance," is basic, somewhat like the Javanese rasa. There is a good pamphlet on the "Forest Wat," the idea of wisdom, beginning with sila. This small book, really only an extended article, "Wisdom Develops Samadhi"[18] by the Venerable Acariya Maha Boowa Nanasampanno, a translation from the Thai published in Bangkok, is a spiritual masterpiece. The author is apparently, or was, one of the masters in the Thai forest wats, abbot of Wat Pa-baru-tard in the jungle of north central Thailand.

Kammatthana: "bases of action," practical application and experiential knowledge, dharma teaching. This controls the "heart with outgoing exuberance." "The heart which does not have dharma as its guardian." Such a heart, when it finds happiness as a result of "outgoing exuberance," is a happiness which plays a part, increases the "outgoing exuberance," and makes the heart "go increasingly in the wrong direction." Samadhi is calm—tranquility of heart. "Outgoing exuberance is the enemy of all beings."

Anapanasati: awarenesss of breathing in and out.

Khanika samadhi: momentary, changing.

Upacara samadhi: "getting close to the object."

Apana samadhi: absorption.

The method should suit one's character. After correct practice one feels "cool, bright and calm."

Inside is "the one who knows"—a function of citta. Preparatory incantations in kammatthana aim at uniting the one who speaks and the one who knows. Attention to breathing: in order to unite breathing and citta: "it becomes apparent that the most subtle breath and the heart (citta) have converged and become one." This leads to "finding that which is wondrous in the heart."

Problem of nivritti (vision) in upacara samadhi. Danger of madness.

✠

October 18 / Bangkok

Mass of St. Luke in a big church. A cathedral? Has it a bishop? It's just around the corner from the hotel. Little girls were singing in choir behind the old high altar while a priest said Mass in the center. Only a few people were present, some Americans or Europeans. A somewhat dilapidated side altar. The altar cards were old, stained with damp. The linens old, too, and the Sacred Heart statue more toneless, dowdy, dusty than many a Buddha. (Many of the Buddhas here seem too golden, too smug, too hollow.)

Yesterday afternoon I was driven out into the country to see Phra Pathom Chedi, one of the oldest and largest stupas. Rice fields. Coronet palms. Blue, shiny buffaloes. Endless lines of buses and trucks traveling like mad. A small wat in the fields. Many of the Buddhas were flaked with small bits of gold leaf stuck on by the faithful. At another tiny country wat, a side Buddha had had his face masked and buried in gold by some benefactor—as though he were being smothered by it. Behind the entrance and around the stupa was a cloister with desks, books, little bhikkhus studying Pali. A master was correcting a bhikkhu who had written something wrong on a blackboard. Khantipalo and I circumambulate the stupa with incense and flowers, he in bare feet and all bony and I sweating with my camera around my neck. The gold-roofed temples against the clouds made me think of pictures of Borobudur.[19] There were men high up on the side of the stupa replacing old tiles and a boy up there pulling out weeds that had grown in between the tiles. Then I wandered interminably around under the trees (mostly frangipani), looking at small, good and bad Buddhas, stupas, reproductions, imitations, a run-down meditation garden confided to the Chinese. Buddhas smothered with gold, one enormous, lying down with chicken wire at his back, a protection against graffiti.

There is an Oedipus-like legend about the first builder of Phra Pathom. He killed his father without knowing it and was told to build a stupa as high as the wild pigeon flies. Phra Pathom was the retreat of King Rama VI, where he retired for the rainy seasons, trained the "Wild Tiger Volunteers," and erected a statue of his favorite dog, with an epitaph.

Phra Pathom is called the "first chedi," the oldest one. The interior parts, inside the present structure, were built in the second century B.C. (about the time of Ashoka[20] in India), and it was restored in 1853. There are old dharma wheels and "Buddha footprints," earlier than any statue and in many ways more handsome.

⌘

"The realizer does not stand outside the reality, but may be said to be at least a part of that reality. So I said that he is a self-manifestation of reality as such. This realization—that one is the self-manifestation of ultimate reality as such—is *his* realization."

> —Professor Masao Abe,[21] on the concept of reality in Zen; Aelred Graham: *Conversations: Christian and Buddhist*, New York, Harcourt, Brace and World, 1968, page 129. See also pages 263 and 265 in Part Two of this volume, "Complementary Reading," for further material from Graham's book.

⌘

"The Self is not attainable by the recitation of *Veda,* nor by an effort of intellectual penetration, nor by many Vedic studies. He whom the Self chooses (selects), he can attain it. The Self makes known to him its intimacy."[22]

—from Ramanuja's commentary on the *Brahma Sutra,* (Merton's translation from the French translation of Olivier Lacombe). See A.-M. Esnoul: *op., cit.,* pages 125–26.

⌘

NOTES: *The Eastward Flight*

[1] Tierce: the service or office for the third of the Roman Catholic canonical hours, usually observed at 9 A.M.

[2] Sister Gerarda: Sister Gerarda Van den Brande, a member of Our Lady of the Redwoods Monastery (see below). She has now returned to her home in Belgium and been dispensed from her vows.

[3] Redwoods: Our Lady of the Redwoods Abbey, a community of Cistercian nuns at Whitethorn, California, where Merton made an extended visit in May of 1968, giving lectures to the sisters and exploring the coastline region with the possibility in mind that a hermitage might be set up for retreat use by Trappist monks. He returned again to the Redwoods, briefly, just before his departure on his Asian journey.

[4] Yakutat: a village at the mouth of Yakutat Bay, about 300 miles east of Anchorage, Alaska, which Merton visited on September 27, 1968. In an earlier journal he wrote of it: ". . . a village of Indians with an FAA station nearby. Bay with small islands. A few fishing boats. Beat-up motorboats, very poor. An old battered green rowboat called *The Jolly Green Giant.* Battered houses. A small Indian girl opens the door of the general store, looks back at us as we pass. Cannery buildings falling down. Old tracks are buried in mud and grass. A dilapidated building was once a roundhouse. . . . After that, all there is is a long straight gravel road pointing in the mist between tall hemlocks out into the nowhere, where more of the same will be extended to a lumber operation. The woods are full of moose & black bear & brown bear & even a special bear found only at Yakutat—the glacier bear (or blue bear). . . . Here there was once a Russian penal colony. It was wiped out by the Thlingit Indians."

At the invitation of Archbishop Joseph T. Ryan, D.D., of Anchorage,

Merton visited Alaska from September 18 to October 2, 1968. While one purpose of his visit was to conduct a workshop for the nuns at the Convent of the Precious Blood, he was also authorized by the Abbot of Gethsemani to explore various parts of Alaska for possible monastic sites or for a hermitage to be affiliated with Gethsemani, which he might himself use part of the year. Thus Archbishop Ryan provided air transportation for him to visit Yakutat, Dillingham, and several other locations.

5 On the airplane, between San Francisco and Hawaii, it appears that Merton was reading *Ramanuja et la mystique vishnouite* by Anne-Marie Esnoul (Paris, Editions du Seuil, 1964) in which (pages 40–42) he found quoted some unpublished French translations by J. Filliozat of devotional hymns written by the 9th-century Tamil poet Periyalvar in collections called the *Tiruppallandu* and the *Tirumoli*. Using the parodistic technique which he had evolved a year or two earlier for his last major poetic work, *The Geography of Lograire*, he composed this and the following poem, which are partly translation of Periyalvar's text and partly his own interjections of images drawn from his immediate experience.

This is the French translation of the extracts given by Filliozat of the Periyalvar hymn on which Merton drew most heavily:

TIRUPPALLANDU

"1. Pour bien construire le pays et la ville, vous dévots qui avez le coeur à chanter 'Adoration à Narayana' venez et clamez 'Nombreuses années!'

"5. Pour Lui, souverain pour l'ensemble des mondes, Hrishikeça, qui enlève et supprime le groupe des Titans, des Ogres et des canailles, vous qui êtes dans le groupe des esclaves, venez! Adorez Ses Pieds! Dites Ses mille noms! Fuyez l'ancien groupe et dites 'Nombreuses années! Nombreux milliers d'années! . . .

"7. Dans le sanctuaire du Fortuné Disque qui resplendit, cercle de lumière rouge brillant dans le feu, nous trouvant marqués de son signe, de génération en génération, nous servons. Au fort dont le disque tournoie pour répandre le sang coulant des mille bras de Bana aux armées de combat magique, nombreuses armées, clame-t-on. . . .

"10. Quel jour?—Ce jour-là même où il a été écrit 'Notre Seigneur, pour Toi, nous sommes esclaves,' nous voilà esclaves et la maison d'esclavage, vois, c'est vivre en gagnant la délivrance! Vers Toi qui, apparaissant au jour glorieux, abattant le rocher dans le fortunée Mathura, as bondi sur les têtes du serpent à chaperon aux cinq têtes, nombreuses années!, clame-t-on."

["4. In order to truly build up the nation and the city, you godly people who have the heart to sing 'Adoration to Narayana,' come and proclaim: 'Many years!']

["5. For the sake of Him, the sovereign of all worlds, Hrishikesa, who carries away and puts down the group of Titans, Ogres and canailles, you who belong to the group of those who are enslaved, Come! Adore His Feet! Proclaim His thousand names! Flee the old group and say: 'Many years! Many thousands of years! . . .]

["7. Within the sanctuary of the Lucky Wheel which shines forth, as a circle of red light, blazing in the fire, finding ourselves marked with His sign, we serve from generation to generation. When the wheel is at the height of its spinning by which it sprinkles with blood flowing from the thousand arms of Bana the armies of magical combat, the many armies, let them shout. . . .]

["10. On what day? On that very day on which it was written 'Our Lord, for you we are slaves,' behold we are slaves and the house of bondage, lo, it is to live in gaining deliverance! To you who, appearing on this glorious day, casting down the rock in the blessed Mathura, have danced on the heads of the five-headed guardian serpent, let them exclaim: 'Many years!' "]

Alain Daniélou in his *Hindu Polytheism* (New York, Pantheon Books, 1964) lists Hrishikesa, Lord of the Senses, as tenth among the twenty-four icons of Vishnu, his symbols being the mace, discus, lotus, and conch. The second poem is based on Periyalvar's "Berceuse pour Krishna" ("Lullaby for Krishna") in the *Tirumoli,* from which Merton takes very few phrases, except for the repetition of the word "talelo." In a private letter, Filliozat defines "talelo" thus: "*Talelo* n'a pas de sens, c'est un refrain de berceuse, pour endormir l'enfant Krishna." ("*Talelo* has no specific meaning, it is the refrain in a lullaby to put the baby Krishna to sleep.") Periyalvar's "Lion de Devaki" (the mother of Krishna) becomes "Lion cub of Yasoda" (or Yashodara, the foster mother of Krishna). Merton seems to have taken some liberty also with "fortunée Mathura," which is more likely the sacred city of Krishna, the abode of wisdom, not a forest. Filliozat identifies Bana as "le nom d'un roi ennemi de Krishna qui l'a tué" ("the name of an enemy king whom Krishna killed").

6 Ad multos annos: Latin, for many years.

7 Tamil: the Tamils are now the predominant branch of the Dravidian race of South India. Many of them also migrated to Ceylon and other countries of Southeast Asia. Their literature is the richest among those of the Dravidian languages.

8 Ramanuja; an 11th-century Tamil religious leader who was instrumental in putting the Vaishnavite school of Hinduism on a solid philosophical basis, a qualified monism based on the *Upanishads* and the *Brahma Sutra* which considered the individual soul an attribute of the supreme soul, but separate from it. His thinking was close to the orthodox Brahmanism of the *Bhagavad-Gita,* but his version of bhakti was more the meditation called for in the *Upanishads* than the concept of universal love.

9 Ganges: the most sacred river of India, which flows from the foothills of the Himalayas eastward to the Bay of Bengal near Calcutta. The river is

personified in the goddess Ganga and worshiped in the annual Dasara festival. Myth has it that Ganga issued from the feet of Vishnu and came to earth by falling on the head of Shiva. There is a special mantra (chanted prayer) invoking Ganga which devotees use when bathing or using water in ceremonies, and it is believed that to bathe in the Ganges on certain holy days or at particular conjunctions of the stars will wash away the most dreadful sins, while, if his ashes or a piece of bone is thrown into the river, a person's soul will be translated to a higher sphere.

10 Vishnu: one of the major triad (Vishnu—Shiva—Brahma) of gods in Hinduism. His devotees are the Vaishnavites.

11 *Siddhartha:* in Sanskrit, the Buddha's actual name was Siddhartha Gautama. Hermann Hesse's novel *Siddhartha,* however, relates the life of one of the Buddha's earliest disciples

12 Kowloon: part of the city of Hong Kong, a peninsula about 3¾ square miles in area, with a population of nearly two million, on the north side of Hong Kong's harbor. Ferries run between the two parts of the city. Kai Tak international airport is in Kowloon. It was the second part of the British Crown Colony to be ceded to Britain by China, in 1860, after the Second Opium (or "Arrow") War of 1856–58. North of Kowloon (Chinese: Chiu-lung) are the New Territories which were leased by Britain from China in 1898 and will revert to China in 1997. Most of the present city of Kowloon was built after World War II, when there was a large influx of refugees from mainland Communist China.

13 Gethsemani: The Abbey of Gethsemani, founded by French Trappist monks in 1848, near Bardstown, Kentucky, is the oldest abbey in the United States. It was Merton's home for twenty-seven years. There are at present about a hundred monks in the community. In all, there are fifteen Trappist-Cistercian monasteries of monks and four of nuns in this country. All belong to the same international order, with a certain autonomy in local administration.

14 Wat Bovoranives: one of the traditional Buddhist temples of Bangkok. Wat (temple) is derived from the Sanskrit "vata" (enclosed space).

15 klong: canal. The chief market of Bangkok is an area of canals running into the Chao Phya River where the shops, which are also the owners' homes, are built on stilts to keep them above the daily tides and yearly floods.

16 satipatthana meditation: Merton took notes on his conversation with Bhikkhu Khantipalo in his small pocket notebook, but so rapidly that the writing is mostly indecipherable. However, Bhikkhu Khantipalo has been

so kind as to write up the points he made in their talk, which is included here as Appendix II, "On Mindfulness."

[17] Sariputra: a wandering, mendicant ascetic of the brahmanical tradition who encountered the Buddha at Rajagaha and became one of his first converts and most important disciples.

[18] "Wisdom Develops Samadhi": while the Ven. Nanasampanno's essay may exist as a separate pamphlet in the Thai language, it appears almost certain that the text which Merton read was the English translation by Bhikkhu Pannavaddho of Wat Pa-barn-tard which appeared in the May 1967 number of the magazine *Visakha Puja,* an annual publication of The Buddhist Association of Thailand, 41 Aditaya Road, Bangkok.

[19] Borobudur: near Jogjakarta in Java, Borobudur, built about 850 A.D. under the dynasty of the Saliendra kings, is said to be the largest Buddhist temple in the world. It was partially destroyed by the Muslims but later restored by the Dutch.

[20] Ashoka: perhaps the greatest of the early emperors of a unified India, who reigned from 264 to 232 B.C. After a period of violent conquest, he became a convert to Buddhism, abandoned warfare, and sent missionaries throughout Southeast Asia to convert the people to Buddhism. His most influential cultural legacy were his edicts, some five thousand words of inscriptions which set forth his rules for religion and ethical conduct. For details on the edicts, see pages 366–67 in the glossary.

[21] Masao Abe: professor at Nara College of Humanities, Nara, Japan. He specializes in Buddhist philosophy and comparative religion, and has twice been a visiting lecturer at Columbia University, New York.

[22] "Le Soi n'est accessible ni par la récitation du Veda, ni par un effort de pénétration intellectuelle, ni par de nombreuses leçons védiques; mais celui que le Soi élit, celui-là peut l'atteindre. Le Soi lui révèle son intimité."

CALCUTTA
October 19–27

October 19 / Calcutta

Last night I had to rush to the Bangkok airport in a taxi to catch my Lufthansa plane. Along the road were kids and kids and kids, thousands, millions of schoolchildren, mostly in neat uniforms. (Bangkok is relatively prosperous, relatively well fed, with lots of cars, trucks, jeeps, and crazy three-wheeled jeep taxis.) Finally my taxi burst out of the traffic onto a highway across the marsh near the airport. Wind. Black clouds. Distant storms. More rushing through the usual idiot process, the stamping of passports and boarding passes. When I had paid the exit tax, I was nearly down to my last baht, with only three or four left to under-over tip the porter who had done noble work getting me through . . . and then an announcement that the Lufthansa plane is late!

I sit in the waiting room, sweating, with all the Germans and Swedes and Indians, the Air France crews and the SAS crews, the pretty Swedish girl, the crippled German lady, the Americans, the children, and outside the glass door, jeeps, airport buses, planes, the distant black storm, lightning, porters milling around, people rushing madly to the wrong gate and returning to the benches, people wandering around with soft drinks in paper cups . . . and I with a paper envelope of Buddhist novitiate instructions and incense presented by the abbot of Wat Bovoranives.

There is TV in the Bangkok airport. The announcements are made by a conventionally pretty Thai girl who makes all languages sound alike—incomprehensible. Her English might be her German, if any, and all of it might be Malayan. Then in between there is a movie, or rather a series of stills, extolling Thai boxing. *FISTS.* "M.S. flight for Kuala Lumpur[1] delayed one hour." *KNEES.* "Passengers on Air France Flight 205 please report for passport check." *FEET.* Still picture of a Thai boxer getting his head kicked off. Picture of American woman tourist screaming as boxer's head is kicked. *EVERY PART OF THE BODY IS USED.* Same American woman tourist seen from a different angle but in the same scream. *EVERY PART OF THE BODY . . .* Picture of a mix-up, maybe someone is getting a knee in the belly. *FISTS.* American lady tourist screams. Pnom-Penh with tourists for Angkor.[2] *FISTS.* Flight now very late. *KNEES.* Air Vietnam lands late and will take off soon. Air Vietnam from Saigon just as if there were no war in the world *EVERY PART OF THE BODY IS USED.* American tourist lady grabs husband's arm with both hands and screams.

When we landed in Calcutta the customs gave two utterly lovely—and haughty—Indian girls in saris a rough time. I got through quite fast though with no rupees yet, and Susan Hyde, a secretary of Peter Dunne,[3] was there to meet me with a garland of flowers: "Welcome to India." V.I.P. treatment. I felt confused, trying to talk sense to Susan about religious affairs. The Indian darkness was full of people and cows. Rough roads on which cars sped toward each other head-on. It takes some time here to discover which side anyone is driving on—he may take either side, right or left. Then into the big, beat-up, hot, teeming, incredible city. People! People! People! Campfires in the streets and squares. Movie posters—those Asian movie posters with the strange, enormous faces of violent or demented Western gods, the enormous gunners, surrounded by impossible writings. They are a crass, camp deification of the more obvious emotions: love, hate, desire, greed, revenge. Why not John Wayne with eight arms? Well, he has enough guns already. Or the Dance of Shiva[4]—with Sinatra?

The situation of the tourist becomes ludicrous and impossible in a place like Calcutta. How does one take pictures of these streets with the faces, the eyes, of such people, and the cows roaming among them on the sidewalks and buzzards by

The Dance of Shiva

the score circling over the main streets in the "best" section? Yet the people are beautiful. But the routine of the beggars is heart-rending. The little girl who suddenly appeared at the window of my taxi, the utterly lovely smile with which she stretched out her hand, and then the extinguishing of the light when she drew it back empty. I had no Indian money yet. She fell away from the taxi as if she were sinking in water and drowning, and I wanted to die. I couldn't get her out of my mind. Yet when you give money to one, a dozen half kill themselves running after your cab. This morning one little kid hung on to the door and ran whining beside the cab in the traffic while the driver turned around and made gestures as if to beat him away. Sure, there is a well-practiced routine, an art, a theatre, but a starkly necessary art of dramatizing one's despair and awful emptiness. Then there was the woman who followed me three blocks sweetly murmuring something like "Daddy, Daddy, I am very poor" until I finally gave her a rupee. OK, a contest, too. But she is very poor. And I have come from the West, a Rich Daddy.

❄

Meditation on the body (satipatthana): "investigating the parts of the body with wisdom." This must be seen and experienced in terms of anicca, dukkha, anatta.

Vipassana: the insight arising out of samadhi.

"The negation of the desires of all beings . . . is the nature of this body," says my bhikkhu, Acariya Maha Boowa Nanasampanno, in a cryptic, condensed explanation of anatta. And so: purification; defilements cannot arise when this "wise investigation" is done. "Wisdom is proclaiming the truth and making the heart listen, and when it is doing this all the time where can the heart go to oppose the truth that comes from wisdom?"

❄

Clearly seeing the "Body City" makes one a lokavidu: "one who knows the worlds." One who has investigated all the realms of existence. So, too, the antitourism of the external city—the true city, the city out of control, whether it be Los Angeles or Calcutta. Whether it be the trace of new cars on superhighways or of old cars on bad highways, or of blood, mucus, fecal matter in the passages of the body. Calcutta, smiling, fecal, detached, tired, inexhaustible, young-old, full of young people who seem old, is the *unmasked* city. It is the subculture of poverty and overpopulation.

Calcutta is shocking because it is all of a sudden a totally different kind of madness, the reverse of that other madness, the mad rationality of affluence and overpopulation. America seems to make sense, and is hung up in its madness, now really exploding. Calcutta has the lucidity of despair, of absolute confusion, of vitality helpless to cope with itself. Yet undefeatable, expanding without and beyond reason but with nowhere to go. An infinite crowd of men and women camping everywhere as if waiting for someone to lead them in an ultimate exodus into reasonableness, into a world that works, yet knowing already beyond contradiction that in the end *nothing* really works, and that life is all anicca, dukkha, anatta, that each self is the denial of the desires of all the others—and yet somehow a sign to others of some inscrutable hope. And the thing that haunts me: Gandhiji led all these people, exemplified the sense they might make out of their life, for a moment, and then, with him, that sense was extinguished again.

⌘

A sign in Calcutta: "Are you worried? Refresh yourself with cigars."

⌘

"Masters of the 7th arm, unless you destroy Mandrake at once, you will be destroyed." (Mandrake the Magician)

Literature on Theravada available from the Buddhist Publication Society, Box 61, Kandy, Ceylon.

✼

October 20

I have been reading the poetry of Milarepa, the great Tibetan yogi, who was born in 1052. "Repa"—"clad in one piece of cotton." (Because of his heat meditation?)[5] He stands at the head of the Kagyudpa tradition. The "whispered transmission,"[6] i.e., esoteric. But he was not a bhikkhu, and his master, Marpa, was a layman.

✼

"In order to perfect any practice, seemingly useless experience must be undergone. Any disciple who has entered any kind of practice must begin with seemingly unnecessary, futile things. But of course these things are a part of the discipline. Without such seemingly trifling things there can be no perfecting of the practice."

—Reverend Kaneko,[7] as quoted in Graham, *op. cit.,* page 155.

"Apart from the daily experience, there is no religious life, so satori is an occurrence of daily life with its joys and sorrows."

"The reason why the lowest can be at once the highest is difficult to say, but it is the ultimate reality of religious experience. And only from that awareness can the religious sense of blessedness—*arigatai* in Japanese—be explained."

—Graham, *op. cit.,* pages 156–57.

✼

Yesterday I visited the Indian Museum, a bewildering big building, now yellow and shabby, with the universal dilapidation of all Calcutta. It has nice things in it if you can find them. And a lot of dull stuff, too. You look for Gupta[8] statues and end in geology or bows and arrows. I found a lot of it tedious, but there were a few sudden joys: Buddha footprints with lovely symbols lightly engraved in them; a room full of musical instruments, string and percussion, of marvelous sophisticated shapes; some Burmese pots, excellent even though 19th-century.

This morning, Sunday, I went to the Jesuit Sacred Heart Church to say the Mass of the XXth Sunday after Pentecost. A bewildered sacristan set me up on a dowdy side altar—no problem!—with a very ancient missal. He filled the water cruet from an old tap at the washbasin, and sure enough I got diarrhea from the bad water. (Later, I took an Entero-vioform pill and stopped it.) A brisk young German Jesuit shook hands with me in the sacristy.

Last night I was invited to dinner at Lois Flanagan's,[9] a pleasant house on Ballygunge Circular Road. Among the guests were P. Lal[10] and his wife. Lal, who is charming and articulate, is working on an English translation of the *Mahabharata*.[11]

I am tired of late hours, like 11:30. Tonight I want to get to bed at 8 or 8:30, hoping I can get away with it and not be hauled out for something. But things seem quiet.

Yesterday, quite by chance, I met Chogyam Trungpa Rimpoche[12] and his secretary, a nice young Englishman whose Tibetan name is Kunga. Today I had lunch with them and talked about going to Bhutan. But the important thing is that we are people who have been waiting to meet for a long time. Chogyam Trungpa is a completely marvelous person. Young, natural, without front or artifice, deep, awake, wise. I am sure we will be seeing a lot more of each other, whether around northern India and Sikkim or in Scotland, where I am now determined to go to see his Tibetan monastery if I can. He is a promising poet. His stuff in Tibetan is probably excellent; in English it is a little flat, but full of substance. He is also a genuine spiritual master. His place in Scotland seems to have become an instant success and I think he has something very good under way. I am certainly interested in it. The newsletter he puts out is good. His own meditations and talks, from what I have seen, are extraordinary. He has the same problems we have with "progressive" monks whose idea of modernization is to go noncontemplative, to be "productive" and academic. These are the types I will evidently find around the Dalai Lama.[13] They showed me a small photo of a lovely shrine on a cliff in Bhutan (Tagtsang) and recommended it as a place for retreat.

Later in the afternoon I piled into a jeep with Trungpa and his secretary, Kunga, and two Australian girls and a driver. The jeep belongs to the Bhutan government. We went roaring off to a market full of things for Divali, the feast of lights, which is tomorrow. Millions of little shapeless statues of Kali, Lakshmi, Parvati, and other beings—soldiers, God knows what, sahibs, foods, sugars, paper garlands, lights, light-holders, incense. Trungpa bought a firecracker from a small, very black, bright-eyed crouching little boy.

I wrote to Dom Flavian,[14] Dom James,[15] Lawrence Ferlinghetti,[16] and the Queen of Bhutan.

Octavio Paz[17] has resigned as Mexican Ambassador to India over the treatment of Mexican students by the police. Jackie Kennedy remarried today on a Greek island.

✺

October 22

I've had the idea of editing a collection of pieces by various Buddhists on meditation, etc., with an introduction of my own. Perhaps two collections, one entirely by Tibetans (I must talk to Chogyam Trungpa about this today) or with representatives from Tibetan Buddhism—from Theravada in Ceylon, Burma, Thailand (Khantipalo). And one from Mahayana in China and Japan. Two very interesting possibilities.

Amiya Chakravarty
and Thomas Merton

Yesterday, I drove with Amiya Chakravarty[18] and his friend, Naresh Guha, to the home of the painter Jamini Roy.[19] Walking barefoot on the cool tiles, through low quiet rooms filled with canvasses of unutterable beauty: simple, formalized little icons with a marvelous sort of folk and Coptic quality, absolutely alive and full of charm, many Christian themes, the most lovely modern treatment of Christian subjects I have ever seen—and also of course Hindu subjects from the *Ramayana*[20] and the *Mahabharata*. Amiya bought a Christ which he will take to the nuns at Redwoods. I wish I could afford to buy a dozen canvasses; they are very cheap, $35 or $40. But money gets away from me like water on all sides and I have to watch it. Some things in the hotel are extremely expensive, others not.

Jamini Roy himself, a warm, saintly old man, saying: "Everyone who comes to my house brings God into it." The warmth and reality of his hand as you shake it or hold it. The luminous handsomeness of his bearded son, who is, I suppose, about my age. Marvelous features. All the faces glowing with humanity and peace. Great religious artists. It was a great experience.

⌘

October 24

A visit to the Narendrapur-Ramakrishna Mission Ashram. College, agricultural school, poultry farm, school for the blind, and

"Christ" by Jamini Roy

orphanage. Ponds, palms, a water tower in a curious style, a monastic building, and guesthouse. Small tomato and cucumber sandwiches, flowers, tea. We drove around in a dark green Scout. Villages. Three big, blue buffaloes lying in a patch of purple, eating the flowers. Communists arguing under a shelter. Bengali inscriptions on every wall; they have an extraordinary visual quality. Large and small cows. Goats, calves, millions of children.

The Temple of Understanding Conference[21] has been well organized considering the problems which developed. It could not be held in Darjeeling,[22] as planned, because of the floods. Instead it has been put on at the Birla Academy in South Calcutta. It is more than half finished now. I spoke yesterday morning, but did not actually follow my prepared text.[23] There were good papers by two rabbis, one from New York and one from Jerusalem, and by Dr. Wei Tat,[24] a Chinese scholar from Taiwan, on the *I Ching*.[25] Also by Sufis, Jains, and others.

The warmth of the Ramakrishna[26] monks, alert and quiet. Especially Swami Lokesvarananda whom I like very much. They invited me back. And I was invited to Israel by Dr. Ezra Spicehandler.[27] And invited tonight to supper at the house of the Birlas,[28] supporters of the Temple of Understanding. In the jeep I had a fine conversation with Judith Hollister,[29] warm, lovely, simple, sincere.

I did not go to a committee meeting today; went back to Narendrapur instead. Much talking yesterday. Tomorrow *Life* magazine is to take our pictures "worshiping" under the banyan tree in the botanical gardens.

Vatsala Amin, the young Jain laywoman from Bombay who presented the Jain message at the Temple of Understanding Conference, is an extremely beautiful and spiritual person. I was very impressed by her talk, and this evening had a long and good conversation with her at the Birla party. We talked about meditation, and her master, Munishri Chitrabhanu,[30] whom I would like to see if I can get to Bombay. And about her desire to live in solitude in the Himalayas, and her project of doing so. Sitting on the floor listening to sitar music was a lovely experience.

Vatsala Amin: great, soft, intelligent, dark eyes. A white sari. Vivacity and seriousness, warmth, spiritual fervor. She meditates on a picture of her guru, preferring the one in which his skull and chin arc shaved. Jain gurus shave once a year. "If he can be so perfect, so can I," she reflects. Today she left for Bombay. I on my part am impressed by her purity and perfection. She gave me a garland, like a lei, made of sandalwood, because I was her special friend. She gave another to Sister Barbara Mitchell[31] from Manhattanville.

A telegram from Tenzin Geshe, the Dalai Lama's secretary. My interview is tentatively arranged for 10 A.M. on November 4th. I am supposed to fly to Delhi at 6 A.M., Monday, October 28th. Probably the best thing would be to go to Dharamsala November 1st or 2nd, by night train and then bus.

❆

October 26

Rain. A cyclone is moving up from South India, threatening once again all the places in North Bengal that were ruined by floods two weeks ago. Tall coconut palms against the stormy sky. Men and women on the balconies of the apartment houses in the cool wind. Cows wandering amid the traffic. We drive with the Birlas to see the schools, the hospital, the very elegant theater they have built. And the Birla Planetarium. They were friends and patrons of Gandhiji.

In the museum at the Birla Academy there are fine Indian and Mogul paintings, folk art of the Calcutta Kalighat school, and Nepalese and Tibetan tankas. In Huston Smith's[32] Tibetan movie the slow dance of a monk in a devil-like mask of fearsome divinity with great red sleeves. The booming, solemn, voice-splitting chant of the monks, each singing a chord by himself.

Yasoda and the infant Krishna.
Calcutta bazaar painting, Kalighat school, c. 1880.

Mass today at Loreto House. I gave a short homily[33] to the Irish nuns in a big, cool academy, quiet, clean, tranquil. After Mass I am surrounded on all sides, praised, questioned, admired, revered—so much so that I can hardly eat breakfast.

At the Temple of Understanding Conference, which ended today, there were two little girls in miniskirts, Schotzy and Pattie, very sweet and naked, touchingly convinced of their own particularity, calling everything so beautiful—except when it was obviously too square—but all Calcutta beautiful, beautiful and the people beautiful. Last night they wandered off with some hippies into a village and smoked pot somewhere and almost got themselves killed and came back laughing about how it was all so beautiful, beautiful.

I had dinner at a Chinese restaurant in Park Street with Wei Tat, who returns to Hong Kong tomorrow.

I miss my dear Miss Vatsala Amin and her dark eyes and white sari and wonder what to do with that sandalwood garland. And for God's sake I hope I can get to the Himalayas and into a quiet cabin somewhere and get back to normal!

⌘

Sankaracharya[34] on the mind and the atman (from *The Crest-Jewel of Discrimination*).

"The Atman dwells within, free from attachment and beyond all action. A man must separate this Atman from every object of experience, as a stalk of grass is separated from its enveloping sheath. Then he must dissolve into the Atman all those appearances which make up the world of name and form. He is indeed a free soul who can remain thus absorbed in the Atman alone. . . .

"The wind collects the clouds, and the wind drives them away again. Mind creates bondage, and mind also removes bondage.

"The mind creates attachment to the body and the things of

this world. Thus it binds a man, as a beast is tied by a rope. But it is also the mind which creates in a man an utter distaste for sense-objects, as if for poison. Thus it frees him from his bondage.

"The mind, therefore, is the cause of man's bondage and also of his liberation. It causes bondage when it is darkened by rajas. It causes liberation when it is freed from rajas and tamas, and made pure. . . .

"Therefore, the seeker after liberation must work carefully to purify the mind. When the mind has been made pure, liberation is as easy to grasp as the fruit which lies in the palm of your hand."[35]

> —Sankaracharya: *The Crest-Jewel of Discrimination, (Viveka-Chudamani)*, translated by Swami Prabhavananda and Christopher Isherwood, Hollywood, Vedanta Press, 1947, pages 67, 71, 72, 73. See also pages 267–70 in Part Two of this volume, "Complementary Reading," for additional passages from *The Crest-Jewel of Discrimination*.

�֍

October 27 / Feast of Christ the King / Calcutta

In ipso omnia constant . . . All is in Him, from Him, for Him, for the Father through Him.

This morning Sister Barbara Mitchell and I went to say Mass in the home of Lois Flanagan. It was quiet and simple. The three little Chinese girls Lois has adopted were there, and Bob Boylan,[36] and a priest from St. Lawrence High School who had brought all the necessary things. The cyclone has not hit here yet. Everyone is now being overwarned. As we drove back to the hotel the air-raid sirens were being tested—for the imaginary war with Pakistan. There is firing at Suez and Tito says there will be a Third World War if the Russians try to take over Yugoslavia, etc., etc. Everyone has long ceased to listen to any of it.

SCIENTIFIC LIFE DIVINE MISSION,[37] A Purely Scientific Nonsectarian All Faiths Fellowship International Movement for the Perfect Development of Body, Mind and Soul . . .
Eminent Supporters of the Views . . .
Eminent Wellwishers . . .

"Creation is the Kingdom of God composed of matters and spirits for a set scientific course to go particular functions to do and gone to reach according to His wishes manifested in the properties of ingredients . . .

"Follow the God-prescribed scientific life . . .

Ingredients of eminent wellwishers . . . changing assemblies . . . with choral voice . . . agreeing . . . wishing well according to ingredients . . . coalitions perfect in all respects . . . With one accord we declare, "Man is a pure scientific being . . ." Carrying on with nebulas, wind, heat, light, and sound. "All are carrying on accordingly! Scientific way of handling the situation is the best." Ashram. "Please communicate only with the headquarters."

How to Make Life Blissful and Worth Diamonds

"To a large majority of people the present state of affairs causes disappointment."

Auspicious Announcement

"The Almighty Father has been at work now for some time and in the near future man's desire for peace and prosperity is going to be fulfilled. You may be surprised to have this news . . .

"*God has declared state of emergency. BE HOLY NOW!*

"All India has become a whorehouse! Do you not love me enough to abandon this dirty habit?"

An Eye Opener for Blind Followers, Devotees and Worshippers[38]

"Religio-political World History Geography and Philosophy being taught by Most Beloved World God Father Shiva like Kalpa (5000 years) ago.

"Look! The science proud European Yadavas will destroy one another in this international atomic war (Mahabharata) like 5000 years ago.

"GREAT BLUNDERS

"By preaching that a human soul is Shiva or that God is omnipresent the preachers have led mankind astray from Me. I get the golden-aged Jiwan Mukt Deity Sovereignty reestablished through Human Brahma by impartation of Godly Knowledge and Yoga to the Iron-Aged People. For further explanation contact Brahma Kumari.

"GOD'S ACTS

"At the confluence of the Iron Age and Golden Age when complete irreligiousness and unrighteousness prevails, I Knowledgeful Shiva, the God-Sermonizer of Gita descend from My Param Dham (Brahmlok) in an old man who comes to be known as Brahma or Adam."

⌘

In 1863 Baha'u'llah[39] announced to the few remaining followers of Bab[40] that He was the chosen Manifestation of God for this age . . . but he was not greeted with enthusiasm by the religious leaders of Islam.

⌘

One of the swamis has flashing eyes, a black beard, rapid speech and sweeping gestures. At times he gives an irresistible impression of Groucho Marx. He has great white teeth and contempt for all competitors. Even his Kleenex is saffron!

⌘

COMPLAIN NOT, BUT CREATE

"Shake off your sloth my sluggard and tunnel your way to truth, make a footpath to fortune, build bridges to business and new highroads to Heaven."

—The Minister of the Silent Spirit (d. 1925)

❈

And amid all this, a pure gem: the little book on King Rama IV Mongkut,[41] Bhikkhu, Abbot of Wat Bovoranives, then King of Thailand (d. 1868). A really beautiful account of a holy life, simple and clear with some Franciscanlike signs and miracles.

"There is nothing in this world which may be clung to blame-lessly, or which a man clinging thereto could be without blame."[42]

—H. M. King Maha Mongkut [Rama IV]

King Rama IV Mongkut

[1] Kuala Lumpur: the capital city of the Federation of Malaysia.

[2] Angkor: hidden in the jungle near Siem Reap in western Cambodia, Angkor was the capital of the Khmer empire from about the 9th to the 15th centuries A.D. The Khmers, ancestors of the present Cambodians, dominated the western part of Indochina from about the 6th century, but were almost constantly at war with the Annamese and the Chams. There was a strong Hindu influence on their culture, but Buddhism also flourished along with Hinduism, and both faiths joined in a cult which deified the reigning monarch. Sculpture and architecture were perfected by the Khmers, and the huge complex of temples and related buildings at Angkor is probably the most remarkable surviving example of religious architecture in Asia. Angkor was overrun by the Thais, and the capital moved to Pnom-Penh in the 15th century. Angkor was abandoned to the jungle and seldom publicized until 1860 by the French naturalist Henri Mouhot. Under the French regime in Indochina, some sixty square miles of the ancient city was reclaimed from the jungle, much of it in a good state of preservation. Angkor Wat, built between 1113 and 1150, is perhaps the best known of the ancient temples, but Baphuon and the Angkor Thom group rank among the finest structures in Asia for the grandeur of their symbolic architectural conception and the perfection of their sculptures, both bas-relief and freestanding. See L. P. Biggs: *The Ancient Khmer Empire*, Philadelphia, American Philosophical Society, 1951; and the sections on Angkor in Heinrich Zimmer: *The Art of Indian Asia*, Bollingen Series, New York, Pantheon Books, 1955; and Louis Frédéric: *The Art of Southeast Asia: Temples and Sculpture*, New York, Abrams, 1965.

[3] Dunne: Finley Peter Dunne, Jr., Executive Director of The Temple of Understanding in Washington, which sponsored the Spiritual Summit Conference in Calcutta in October 1968, at which Merton spoke on "Monastic Experience and East-West Dialogue." See Appendixes III and IV.

[4] Shiva: with Vishnu and Brahma, one of the three deities of the classic Hindu triad of gods. The "Dance of Shiva" is perhaps the best-known iconographic figure in Hindu religious art. Showing the four-armed god dancing in a circle (arch) of flames, it symbolizes the concept of the perpetual dualistic creation-destruction rhythm of the universe. In her *Three Ways of Asian Wisdom* (New York, Simon and Schuster, 1966, page 32), Nancy Wilson Ross writes of "Shiva as King of the Dancers, an embodiment of eternal cosmic energy. The god carries in his upper right hand a drum representing sound as the first element in the unfolding of the universe, while the upper left bears a tongue of flame, the element of the world's final destruction. The gestures of his other hands suggest the eternal rhythmic bal-

ance of life and death. One foot, resting on the demon of 'Forgetfulness' (who holds a cobra), the other raised in dancing pose, denote, says Heinrich Zimmer, 'the continuous circulation of consciousness into and out of the condition of ignorance.' " See also: Ananda Coomaraswamy: *The Dance of Shiva* (New York, Noonday Press, 1957). "The essential significance of Shiva's dance is threefold. First it is the image of his rhythmic play as the source of all movement within the cosmos, which is represented by the arch. Secondly, the purpose of his dance is to release the countless souls of men from the snare of illusion. Thirdly, the place of the dance, Chidambaram, *the Center of the Universe, is within the heart.* In the night of Brahma, Nature is inert and cannot dance till Shiva wills it. He rises from his rapture and dancing sends through inert matter pulsing waves of awakening sound, and lo! matter also dances, appearing as a glory round about him. Dancing, he sustains its manifold phenomena. In the fullness of time, still dancing, he destroys all forms and names by fire and gives new rest. This is poetry; but none the less, science."

5 heat meditation: Marco Pallis (in a private letter) speaks of ascetics who are masters of tummo, "the inward heat," wearing thin cotton cloth even when living near glaciers. See also the chapter "Yoga of the Psychic-Heat" in W. Y. Evans-Wentz: *Tibetan Yoga and Secret Doctrines,* Oxford University Press paperback edition of 1967, pages 171–210.

6 "whispered transmission": ". . . the term 'whispered transmission' refers to that most vital aspect of oral tradition [the handing down of certain elements of doctrine from master to pupil]. Every school of Tibetan Buddhism inherited it in varying degrees of similarity or diversity in form and content." (L. P. Lhalungpa in a private letter) "This tradition is particularly strong in some "Red Hat" sects of the Kagyudpa order. " 'Ka' generally means Buddha's exposition—exoteric & esoteric; 'Gyu,' 'transmission'; 'Pa,' 'upholder.' In a specific case like this both exposition and transmission connote esoteric character, hence the strict rendering being 'the upholder of esoteric transmission. Even this term can be applicable to all other [Tibetan Buddhist] schools in principle." (Lhalungpa) The content of much of the "whispered tradition" may never have been recorded in the sacred books of Tibetan Buddhism such as the *Kangyur* and *Tangyur*. It is difficult to obtain information about these esoteric teachings, but they may concern techniques of meditation, or even descend from the element of magical powers which was brought into Tibetan Buddhism very early on by Tantrists from India. Certainly it is part of the legend of Milarepa that before he became a saint he was considered a wizard, having been encouraged by his mother to learn the arts of black magic to take revenge on relatives in a family quarrel. It is said that, using magic, he was able to cause the collapse of the houses of thirty-seven of his enemies, but that his later remorse for such violent actions led to the penance and austerities which made him a saint, under the guidance of his master in Buddhist training, Marpa.

43

[7] Reverend Kaneko: a priest and scholar associated with the Higashi Hongan-ji temple in Kyoto, Japan, headquarters of the Jodo-Shin-Shu, or (True) Pure Land school of Buddhism, an offshoot of Mahayana Buddhism, originally based on the *Sukhavati-vyuha Sutra* (available in a translation by Max Müller and B. Nanjio in the "Sacred Books of the East" series, Oxford, 1883). In a private letter, Gary Snyder explains the basic Pure Land doctrine thus: "Aeons ago the Bodhisattva Amitabha (in Japanese, Amida) made a vow to create a 'Pure Land' where his believers could be reborn . . . so that it would be easier for them to attain ultimate enlightenment. Although a few remarkable people can become enlightened through study and practice in *this* world, most people don't have the capacity for self-discipline and understanding of an order strong enough to transcend the many problems of this *saha*-world (world of suffering). A 'Pure Land' would be a kind of paradise, but its ultimate purpose would still be total enlightenment—to transcend the 'Pure Land,' too. This present era is the era of Amitabha, who is now a Buddha—one of the five 'Cosmic Buddhas'— and his Pure Land is in the Cosmic West. The name of the land is 'Gold Splendor.' One of Amitabha's vows is, 'If anyone should call my name in a spirit of faith, he will be reborn in my Pure Land.' In Sanskrit, [this invocation is] *'Namah Amitabha Buddhaya'*—'Hail Amitabha Buddha'; in Japanese: *'Namu Amida Butsu,'* or, simplified in rapid speech: *'Nembutsu.'* This is called using 'other power'—not to rely on yourself, or hope that any strength or skill in yourself can help you. To give up all opinions and concerns of yourself. *Then* the grace of Amitabha will fill you and you become freed of 'self.' Sophisticated Buddhist metaphysicians say the Buddha Amitabha is another name for 'Emptiness'—*sunyata.*"

[8] Gupta: a powerful dynasty which was the dominant force in North India from about 320 to 480 A.D., when the Guptas were defeated by the invading White Huns, though there were Gupta kings ruling in eastern India until the early 8th century.

[9] Mrs. Lois Flanagan: Information Center Director of the U.S. Consulate in Calcutta in 1968.

[10] P. Lal: poet, translator, and teacher, P. Lal is Professor of English at St. Xavier's College in Calcutta and was Special Professor of Indian Literature, History, and Religion at Hofstra University in 1962 and again in 1970. As Secretary of the Writers Workshop in Calcutta, he is a leader in the movement to preserve English as one of India's languages for literature. His translations of the *Bhagavad-Gita* and a collection of *Great Sanskrit Plays* have been published in this country by Farrar, Straus & Giroux and New Directions respectively.

[11] *Mahabharata:* one of the two great Sanskrit epics of India (the other being the *Ramayana*), which dates probably from the centuries just preced-

ing the Christian Era. The poem is more than seven times as long as the *Iliad* and the *Odyssey,* and the *Bhagavad-Gita* is one section of it. Its major theme is the story of the struggle between the Pandavas and the Kauravas for control of a kingdom in northern India, but a myriad of minor narratives are woven in, as well as much speculative, social, and ethical material. Although there is a fictitious attribution to Vyasa as the author, the poem is surely anonymous, or rather, the cumulative accretion of the work of many bards in the oral tradition over a considerable period of time.

[12] Chogyam Trungpa Rimpoche: the eleventh Trungpa tulku. The story of his youth and escape from Tibet after the Chinese Communist incursion, "as told to" Esmé Cramer Roberts, *Born in Tibet,* has been published by Harcourt Brace Jovanovich (A Helen and Kurt Wolff Book) in 1968. He is also the author of *Meditation in Action,* available from Shambala Publications, 1409 5th Street, Berkeley, California 94710, and *Mudra,* a selection of poems, obtainable from the Dharmadhatu Meditation Center, 448 Shotwell Street, San Francisco, California 94110, as is *Garuda,* the magazine which he edits. Chogyam Trungpa founded the Samye-Ling Tibetan Center in Dumfrieshire, Scotland, but is now living in this country; in addition to the San Francisco center, he has established one in Barnet, Vermont, called "Tail of the Tiger," and another, Karma Dzong, near Boulder, Colorado.

[13] Dalai Lama: Dalai, from the Mongolian "dalai"—"ocean"; lama, a Tibetan word meaning, literally, "exalted," in actual usage a priest or monk in the religion of Lamaism, which is the form of Buddhism prevailing in Tibet, Mongolia, and parts of China. "The Grand Lama, head or pope of the Lamaist monks. . . ." (Webster's II) The Dalai Lama, presently in exile in India, is now only the spiritual head of the Tibetan Buddhist church, but prior to the Communist Chinese take-over of his country, he was also its temporal ruler, with his seat in the Potala, a great palace in Lhasa. ". . . In 1640 the ruling Mongol prince bestowed temporal and spiritual control of all Tibet upon the fifth grand lama of the [Gelugpa, or 'Yellow Hat'] order, whose title was Ta-lai or Dalai (ocean) Lama. A palace monastery was erected at Lhasa. The Dalai Lama receives divine honors. [He is an incarnation of the bodhisattva Avalokiteshvara (Sanskrit), in Tibetan, Chenrezig, the 'All-Merciful Good Shepherd,' (Pallis), he who '. . . just like Buddha surveys the world in his compassion for all beings . . .' (Thomas)] While in the Sas-kya [Sakyapa] hierarchy son succeeds father, the succession among the celibate Yellow Hats depends upon direct reincarnation. The spirit of the Dalai Lama passes from his body into some infant just born. Tests determine the proper boy, who is carefully trained for his great responsibility. The Tashi or Panchen Lama, the abbot of a powerful monastery, is second to the Dalai Lama." (*The Columbia Encyclopedia,* Second Edition) The present Dalai Lama is Gejong Tenzin Gyatsho, actually born La-mu-tan-chu in 1934 and enthroned as 14th Grand Lama of Tibet in 1940. He went into exile in 1959. His most recent book, *The Opening of the Wisdom-Eye,* which

45

explains the teachings of Tibetan and Lamaist Buddhism, may be obtained from The Theosophical Publishing House, 306 West Geneva Road, Wheaton, Illinois 60187. While he is the head of all the Tibetan orders, and himself a Gelugpa, the Dalai Lama is not the primate of the Gelugpa order; that honor is elective and goes to a learned senior Gelugpa lama, who has the title of Ganden (Gadan) Tri Rimpoche, or "Holder of the throne of the Ganden (Gadan) monastery." The present Gelugpa primate is Ling Rimpoche, the senior tutor of the Dalai Lama.

[14] Dom Flavian: Right Reverend Dom Flavian M. Burns, O.C.S.O., the Abbot of the monastery where Merton lived, Our Lady of Gethsemani, near Bardstown, Kentucky.

[15] Dom James: Right Reverend Dom M. James Fox, O.C.S.O., Abbot of Our Lady of Gethsemani from 1948 to 1968, now living on the monastery grounds as a hermit.

[16] Lawrence Ferlinghetti: the San Francisco poet-novelist-playwright-publisher, proprietor of the famous City Lights Bookshop and editor-publisher of City Lights Books. Merton had stayed with Ferlinghetti in San Francisco prior to the Asian journey. Among Ferlinghetti's best-known books of poetry are: *A Coney Island of the Mind* (1958), *Starting from San Francisco* (1961), *The Secret Meaning of Things* (1968), and *Back Roads to Far Places* (1971).

[17] Octavio Paz: the Mexican poet and philosophic essayist, formerly a member of his country's diplomatic service, and at one time Mexican Ambassador to India. A number of his books have been published in translation in this country, including the volumes of poetry *Sun Stone* (New Directions, 1963), *Selected Poems* (Indiana University Press, 1963), *Configurations* (New Directions, 1971), the essays *The Labyrinth of Solitude* (Grove Press, 1950), and a study of Claude Lévi-Strauss (Cornell University Press, 1970). He delivered the Charles Eliot Norton Lectures at Harvard University in 1971–72, and is now living in Mexico City, where he edits the magazine *Plural*.

[18] Amiya Chakravarty: University Professor in the Department of Philosophy at State University College, New Paltz, New York. A long-time friend, correspondent, and adviser for his reading in Asian religions to whom Merton dedicated his book *Zen and the Birds of Appetite*. Chakravarty's most recent book is *Dynasts & the Post War Age in Poetry*, New York, Octagon Books, 1970, and he earlier edited the *Selected Writings* of Rabindranath Tagore for New American Library, New York, and a *Tagore Reader* for Beacon Press, Boston.

[19] Jamini Roy: (1887–1972) The Roy painting which Merton mentions below (see illustration on page 33) was presented to Our Lady of the Redwoods Abbey by Dr. Chakravarty in the spring of 1972. We are indebted to

Dr. Malcolm Pitt of the Hartford Seminary Foundation, who had seen the same work in Roy's studio, for his notes on the painter's own comment about its conception: "You wonder why the transparent cross? As I read the accounts of the road to Calvary, I could feel in my own body the weight of the cross, the agony of pain in back, shoulder and legs. I fell with Him to the ground, tasted and smelled the dust of the road. I wept with Him. Then slowly it dawned upon me that the physical defeating aspects of this way were deceptive, for his strength, not physical, was more than equal to the journey, and the cross rested lightly on square shoulders and a straight back."

[20] *Ramayana:* an ancient Sanskrit epic, consisting of 24,000 couplets, which recounts the adventures of Rama, a human incarnation of the god Vishnu, his winning of Sita, paragon of womanly virtue, as his wife, her abduction by the demon king of Ceylon, Ravana, her rescue by Rama, aided by the monkey hordes of the god Hanuman, and the final progress of Rama and Sita to heaven. The poem is attributed to Valmiki, but Renou writes that "Valmiki probably gathered together the scattered material of oral tradition and combined it into a semilearned collection." (Louis Renou: *Indian Literature,* New York, Walker and Company, 1964). Dating the composition of the *Ramayana,* and this applies as well to the other great Sanskrit epic, the *Mahabharata,* has proven a difficult problem for scholars; see page 43 of *The Cultural Heritage of India,* Volume IV, edited by Haridas Bhatta charyya, Calcutta, The Ramakrishna Mission Institute of Culture, 1956, for a summary of the points in the matter: parts of the *Ramayana* appear to be older than the *Mahabharata,* and both to date from a period later than the 2nd century B.C.

[21] The Temple of Understanding: an organization with a worldwide membership of religious leaders and concerned laymen established in Washington, D.C., in 1960 "to foster education, communication and understanding among the world religions, and to establish the Temple of Understanding as a center and symbol of this undertaking." One of the most important activities of the group has been a series of "Spiritual Summit Conferences," to the first of which, at Calcutta, in October of 1968, Merton was invited and in which he participated. The second conference was held at Geneva, Switzerland, in 1970, and the third at the Harvard Divinity School, Cambridge, Massachusetts, in October 1971. There is, as yet, no "temple" in the sense of an actual building devoted to worship.

[22] Darjeeling: a famous Himalayan hill station and tourist center (for its views of Kanchenjunga and Mount Everest) north of Calcutta and near to the borders of India with Sikkim and Nepal. The name is from the Tibetan "dorje ling"—"place of thunderbolts."

[23] See Appendixes III and IV (pages 305 and 309) for the texts of Merton's

two talks prepared for the Temple of Understanding Conference in Calcutta. All of the talks given at the conference have been collected and published in the volume *The World Religions Speak,* edited by Finley P. Dunne, Jr., published for the World Academy of Art and Science by Dr. W. Junk N.V. Publishers, The Hague, Holland, and obtainable through The Temple of Understanding, Inc., 1346 Connecticut Avenue N.W., Washington, D.C. 20036.

[24] Dr. Wei Tat: a member of the Yuen Yuen Institute and Vice-President both of the Tao Teh Benevolent Association and of the Dharmalaksana Buddhist Institute in Hong Kong. He is an Academician of the China Academy in Taiwan, where his book *An Exposition of the I-Ching or Book of Changes* was recently published by the Institute of Cultural Studies.

[25] *I Ching:* (Yi-king) "The Book of Changes," one of the Five Classics of Confucianism, thought to have been written by Wen Wang, who lived in the 12th century B.C., but ascribed by other scholars to a much earlier writer, Fuh-hi of the 30th century B.C. It is a book of divination, still much in vogue today with devotees of Oriental thought, based on the eight trigrams and sixty-four hexagrams composed of a whole and broken line, with each possible sextet supported by an enigmatic exigesis which ascribes a meaning to each line. The work was intended to present not only a theory of the phenomena of the physical universe, but of moral and political principles as well. The main text is followed by ten commentaries *(wings),* and it is said to have been one of Confucius' favorite books, which he studied constantly. There are several editions of the *I Ching* in English, the most well-known being James Legge's classic translation (2nd Edition, New York, Dover, 1963) and Cary F. Baynes's rendering of the German text of Richard Wilhelm, with a Foreword by C. G. Jung (Bollingen Series XIX, 3rd Edition, Princeton University, 1967). Also available in paperback are translations by John Blofeld (New York, Dutton, 1965), Ray Van Over (New York, Ace, 1969) and Clae Waltham (New York, New American Library, 1971).

[26] Ramakrishna: Shri Ramakrishna (1836–86) was a Bengali visionary, saint, and teacher who founded the Ramakrishna movement, in which God is worshiped as the Mother of the Universe. Combining the scriptures and disciplines of Hinduism, Christianity, and Islam, Shri Ramakrishna reached the realization of a single God-Consciousness. See *The Gospel of Sri Ramakrishna,* published by the Ramakrishna-Vivekananda Center, 17 East 94, New York City. The world center of the movement is the Ramakrishna Mission at Belur Math, near Calcutta. The teachings of Shri Ramakrishna were popularized in the West by his leading disciple, Swami Vivekananda (1863–1902) who founded the Vedanta Societies of Europe and America.

[27] Dr. Ezra Spicehandler: Professor of Hebrew Literature at the Cincin-

nati School of the Hebrew Union College-Jewish Institute of Religion, and Director of Jewish Studies at the Hebrew Union College Biblical and Archaeological School in Jerusalem.

[28] Birlas: B. K. Birla, one of India's most prominent industrialists, fiinanciers, and philanthropists. He was a dedicated supporter of Gandhi, who was staying in Birla House in Delhi at the time of his assassination.

[29] Judith Hollister: Mrs. Dickerman Hollister of Greenwich, Connecticut, founder in 1960 of the Temple of Understanding, Inc., in Washington, an international organization devoted to better understanding and cooperation among the religions and religious people of the world. She was President of the organization at the time of the 1968 First Spiritual Summit Conference in Calcutta and is now Chairwoman of its board.

[30] Munishri Chitrabhanu: one of the great contemporary leaders of Jainism, the heterodox Hindu religion founded by Mahavira Jnatiputra about the 6th century B.C. Respect for the life of any living thing, even insects, is one of the central tenets of the Jain faith.

[31] Sister Barbara Mitchell, R.S.C.J.: now Financial Aid Officer at Manhattanville College in Purchase, New York.

[32] Huston Smith: Professor of Philosophy at Massachusetts Institute of Technology and author of *The Religions of Man,* New York, 1958, Harper & Row; paperback edition, 1965. His documentary film on Tibetan Buddhism, *Requiem for a Faith,* may be rented from Hartley Productions, Cat Rock Road, Cos Cob, Connecticut 06807. He has also produced a record, *The Music of Tibet: The Tantric Rituals* (AST 4005), which may be obtained from Minute Man Record & Tape Corp., 30 Boylston Street, Cambridge, Massachusetts 02138.

[33] This talk was published in the April 1970 issue of the magazine *Sisters Today,* Volume 41, Number 8, Collegeville, Minnesota.

[34] Sankaracharya: one of the most important Hindu theologians, who lived in India in the 8th century A.D. He wrote commentaries on the *Upanishads* and the *Bhagavad-Gita* and was the founder of the Advaita Vedanta doctrine of nondualism. His best-known work is *The Crest-Jewel of Discrimination (Viveka-Chudamani),* which is available in a number of different translations.

[35] In the holograph notebook, Merton abbreviated the quotations from Sankaracharya into note form; here, and in subsequent quoted passages from *The Crest-Jewel,* they are given in full.

[36] Bob Boylan: Robert J. Boylan, Cultural Affairs Officer with the U.S. Information Service in Calcutta.

[37] This and the following paragraphs appear to be drawn either from billboards or religious cult pamphlets which Merton saw in Calcutta.

[38] See entries in the glossary (page 363) for the meaning of a number of the names and terms in this cult poster which Merton saw and copied down in Calcutta: Shiva, kalpa, Yadavas, *Mahabharata,* Jiwan Mukt (jivanmukta), Brahma, Yoga, Kumari, *Gita (Bhagavad-Gita),* My Param Dham, and Brahmlok.

[39] Baha'u'llah: Mirza Husayn Ali, founder of the Bahai religion. He became leader of the sect in 1863, absorbing what remained of the Babist movement, and took the name "Baha'u'llah," or "the Splendor of God." Bahaism teaches the spiritual unity of all men, is dedicated to universal peace, and contains certain elements of Oriental mysticism.

[40] Bab: Babism was a religious sect founded in Persia in 1844 by Mirza Ali Mohammed ibn-Radhik who took the name Bab-ud-Din ("Gate of Faith"). He taught that revelation was progressive and never final, and proscribed concubinage, polygamy, mendicancy, slavery, and the use of intoxicating drinks or drugs.

[41] King Rama IV Mongkut: (1804–68) King of Siam, a man of great learning and devotion to Buddhism, who spent twenty-seven years of his life as a bhikkhu (monk) and was at one time Abbot of Wat Bovoranives. The book which Merton read about him is *His Majesty King Rama the Fourth Mongkut,* edited by Phra Sasanasobhon, and published in Bangkok in 1968, in commemoration of the hundredth anniversary of the holy monarch's death, by Mahamakuta-Rajavidyalaya, a foundation devoted to the propagation of Buddhism in Thailand. In addition to a brief life of Rama IV by the Supreme Patriarch H.R.H. Prince Pavaresvariyalongkorn and an essay on the king's contribution to Thai historical research by A. B. Griswold, it contains a number of illustrations related to Rama's life and translations of many of the religious chants for the Buddhist liturgy which he composed, translated by Phra Khantipalo.

[42] This quotation is from "The Last Letter of the King [Rama IV] written in Pali on his deathbed, addressed to the Sangha [the Buddhist Monastic Order]." See page 92 of *His Majesty King Rama the Fourth Mongkut.* The entire passage, in the translation of M. R. Seniy Pramoj and M. R. Kukridh Pramoj, reads as follows: "Now by me has been made the resolve to protect the Five Precepts. Attention is practised and developed by me regarding the Five Groups (khanda) [Sanskrit, skandhas; see page 403 of the glossary], the six internal sense-spheres, the six sense-awarenesses, the six sense-contacts,

and the six feeling through the six doors. There is nothing in this world which may be clung to blamelessly, or which a man clinging thereto could be without blame. I train myself in non-clinging thus: 'All conditioned things are impermanent; all dhammas are without selfhood, arising according to conditions; this is not mine, this I am not, this is not my self.' For all kinds of beings death is not to be wondered at because it is the way for all of them." "Maha" in the king's title means "great." His full name was His Majesty Phra Baht Somdech Phra Paramendr Maha Mongkut Phra Chom Klao Chao Yu Hua.

NEW DELHI
October 28–31

October 28 / New Delhi

The flight this morning from Calcutta to New Delhi turned out beautiful. At first it was very stormy and cloudy. Then all of a sudden I looked out and there were the Himalayas—several hundred miles away, but an awesome, great white wall of the highest mountains I have ever seen. I recognized the ones like Annapurna that are behind Pokhara, and could pick out the highest ones in the group, though not individually. Everest and Kanchenjunga were in the distance. Later a big, massive one stood out but I did not know what it was. And the river Ganges. And below, the enormous plain cut up with tiny patches of farms and villages, roads and canals. A lovely pattern. Then the dry plain around Delhi. Rock outcrops. Burnt villages. As soon as I got out of the plane I decided that the air of Delhi was much better than that of Calcutta and that I was happy to be here. Harold Talbott[1] was at the airport and a Birla man also to meet Huston Smith who hopes to show his movie of Tibetan monks to the Dalai Lama. We are to go up by train to Dharamsala next Thursday.

Real India. I haven't seen much of New Delhi yet, except a long avenue leading to a squat, huge, red dome. And the hotel, which is cleaner, newer, less crumbling than the Oberoi in Calcutta.

Soon I will discover what I am going to remember about the hotel in Calcutta. The Grand Hotel Oberoi Karma, with cows on the front doorstep, and turbaned Janissaries, and girl students in saris raising money for flood relief. The endless corridors. The endless salaams. The garden café where they overcharge you in the dark and give you back unrecognizable bills. The beggar with the armstump. The beggar with the humpback. The beggar woman with the baby who ran after me saying "Daddy, Daddy." And men sleeping on the steps of shops. The tall palms, the ugly white courtyard, the kites circling over the tables. Memories of the Raj.[2] Old bathtubs. Old johns of the Raj. The long mirror in which the colonel ruefully sees himself naked, too fat. The red chairs. The incense from Bangkok in the ashtray. The salaams of the elevator men. Long life to the old johns of the Raj!

And the taxis of Calcutta lowing mournfully in the wild streets like walruses or sea cows. And now in New Delhi—more bicycles, motorcycles, trees. A Moslem leaning in the dust toward a tree. The great death house of Humayun.[3] Smoke in the evening. The moon rising in the first quarter over gray domes. There are more guns in the movie posters here. More military bases. More soldiers.

The tomb of Humayun, near Delhi

"Therefore have no fears, have no terror of that deep blue light of dazzling, terrible and awful splendour, since it is the light of the Supreme Way."

> —[Bardo Thödöl][4] See Giuseppe Tucci: *The Theory and Practice of the Mandala*, translated by A. H. Broderick, London, Rider & Company, revised edition, 1969, pages 6–8. See also Part Two of this volume, "Complementary Reading," pages 270–72, for some further notes from Tucci.

❈

October 29

Early morning in New Delhi. A soft rose light, vast gentleness of sky. Many birds. Kites hopping around on the flat roofs of very modern houses. The domes in the smoky distance. The distant throbbing of a drum. I have much to read: Tucci's *The Theory and Practice of the Mandala*, Desjardins'[5] *Message des Tibétains*, the Dalai Lama's pamphlet on Buddhism, essays by Marco Pallis,[6] Trungpa, and things I picked up yesterday from Dr. Lokesh Chandra of the Academy of Indian Culture.

❈

"Man seeks to reconstruct that unity which the predominance of one or other of the features of his character has broken or threatens to demolish."

". . . to help the primeval consciousness, which is fundamentally one, to recover its integrity."

". . . the same desire of achieving liberation of catching that instant, which once lived, redeems the Truth with us."

> —Tucci: *op. cit.*, pages vii–viii

⌘

Maya—avidya—duality develops *within* cosmic consciousness. "A magic liberty" (good!) which causes samsara. The centrifugal force by which original consciousness flies from itself, negates itself by unconsciousness and arbitrary position of images. Shakti: the power creating phantasms. Shakti is *feminine.*[7]

—See Tucci, *op. cit.,* page 13.

Knowledge to which action (and experience) do not conform is not *indifferent.* It is an evil, a disruptive force: because it does not transform. It corrupts. The idea of initiatory knowledge is to unite knowledge, practice, and experience of revulsion and reintegration.

—See Tucci, *op. cit.,* pages 14ff.

⌘

"Over 100 Kuki and Mizo[8] hostiles with arms and ammunition have surrendered to the Manipur[9] police. . . ." (*Times of India*)

⌘

The mandala concept accepts the fact that cosmic processes (maya) express themselves in symbols of masculine and feminine deities, beatific and terrifying. It organizes them in certain schemas, representing the drama of disintegration and reintegration. Correctly read by the initiate, they "will induce the liberating psychological experience."

"First and foremost, a mandala delineates a consecrated superficies and protects it from invasion by disintegrating forces symbolized in demoniacal cycles. . . . It is a map of the cosmos" which rotates round "a central axis, Mount Sumeru," the axis mundi uniting the inferior, underground world, the atmospheric and the celestial. Here is the "palace of the cakravartin,

Mandala of Yamantaka, 18th century

the 'Universal Monarch' of Indian tradition." The initiate identifies himself with this center—his own center is the axis mundi —and is transformed by it.

—Tucci, *op. cit.*, pages 23–25.

"So the mandala is no longer a cosmogram but a psychocosmogram, the scheme of disintegration of the One to the many and of reintegration from the many to the One, to that Absolute Consciousness, entire and luminous, which Yoga causes to shine once more in the depths of our being."

—Tucci, *op. cit.*, pages 21–25.

And yet I have a sense that all this mandala business is, for me, at least, useless. It has considerable interest, but there is no point in my seeking anything there for my own enlightenment. Why complicate what is simple? I am reading on the balcony outside my room. Five green parrots, then eight more fly shrieking over my head.

⌘

Desjardins on the choice of a guru:

"For the 'seeker after Truth' only meetings with very great masters and very great sages can be really interesting. It is better to seek, seek, and seek again a real sage, a truly liberated sage, and spend perhaps no more than a single day with him, than to dissipate one's efforts in encounters and conversations with less representative persons, or persons who are in any case further from true Realisation. It is no longer a matter of talking to Tibetans who have the title lama; it is a matter of meeting masters."[10]

—Arnaud Desjardins, *The Message of the Tibetans,* translated from the French by R. H. Ward and Vega Stewart, London, Stuart & Watkins, 1969, page 29.

"The master's consciousness is enhanced to the point at which it contains the disciple within himself, and is one with the source of the disciple's vital energy. For the master nothing remains to be achieved in any sphere; there is nothing above or beyond what he is. Evolution has reached its end for him. He wants nothing. He rejects nothing."

—Desjardins, *ibid,* page 31.

⌘

Bodhicitta: the seed-thought of illumination. (See Tucci, *op. cit.,* page 15.)

⌘

"He has pity on those who delight in serenity, how much more than upon other people who delight in existence."

—Asanga:[11] Mahayanasutralankara, IX, 13, quoted in Tucci, *op. cit.,* page 17.

⌘

"When knowledge perceives no object, it remains as pure knowledge since, as there is no one perceivable, it perceives nothing."

—Vasubandhu,[12] *Trimsika,* quoted in Tucci, *op. cit.,* page 17.

⌘

Harold Talbott gave me an extraordinarily interesting account of his September audience with the Dalai Lama. He is in a way under close personal care of the Dalai Lama, who is interested in him and in his studies, and has been very kind to him. Harold is impatient for initiation. The Dalai Lama seems to be very wise in his handling of the situation.

I saw some very clean and handsome tankas in Tibet House. There were three rooms full of them. Impressive design, and perfect colors: blue and green from minerals in Lhasa;[13] yellow from minerals of Kham or from Utpal lotus found near Lhasa; red from oxide of mercury; gold from Nepal; blue from lapis lazuli; indigo from the Indian plant nili; black from the soot of pine wood. The brushes are made of pine twigs with goat or rabbit hair inserted. Circles are described with a compass made of split bamboo. Could there be a technical connection between the painters of Russian icons and the tanka painters of Tibet?[14]

The axial, vertical Brahma line of the tanka. The axis of life—Mt. Sumeru—the human backbone. At the summit of the head above the backbone is the hole of Brahma through which one escapes to nirvana. The face of Buddha in tankas is drawn on a full-moon day, colored on a new-moon day.

The need to combine mantra and mudra.

✖

"The artist is a sadhaka. He must ascend, on to the spiritual plane which he intends to paint. He must transform himself into the illustrious beings whom he must adore. 'He who is not God may not adore God.'"

—Dr. Raghu Vira[15]

✖

"*Shoe-lifter Arrested.* New Delhi, Oct. 29—The police today claimed to have arrested a notorious shoe-lifter from Jama Masjid.[16] The alleged accused, Nazir, operated throughout the city, lifting shoes from shrines while devotees were at prayers. Nazir was arrested while striking a deal of stolen fancy shoes and a cycle in the Jama Masjid junk market." *Hindustan Times Correspondent*

October 30 / New Delhi

It would be interesting to see what lamas might think of the visions of the Heavenly City and Temple in *Ezekiel* and the *Apocalypse*.

Early this morning in the hotel a man next door was coughing and vomiting violently. Next he was doing his puja, chanting loudly in Hindi with an occasional cough. It got louder and louder. Maybe a Sikh.

There is nothing of a mandala about the Red Fort, the only sight I have sightseen in Delhi so far. It has a splendid high red wall toward the city and a lower wall with many pleasances toward the meadow where the river Jumna once flowed (now it is further away). There is an interesting high tunnel full of shops and raucous music as one enters. Then the gardens, the porches, the place where there were pools, the place of dancing, the little pearl mosque, most lovely. I obeyed the sign and took no pictures. Refused the importunities of a guide. There were soldiers on motorcycles and an ugly barracks with arched porches, built by the British.

❊

I had a late lunch with Anthony Quainton[17] and his wife from the American Embassy. They are surprisingly young. I learned nothing special about Bhutan. He gave me advice about seeing an Indian official. The meals are too heavy. I wanted to sleep. But it was already past three and time had come to go to tea with Dr. Syed Vahiduddin, one of the speakers at the Temple of Understanding Conference in Calcutta. He is a Moslem and head of the Department of Philosophy at the University of Delhi. A long expensive taxi ride to the other side of Old Delhi, past Raj Ghat, the Gandhi memorial, and some difficulty find-

Tanka of Buddha with worshipers, 18th century

ing his house at 12 Cavalry Line on the university campus. We had a good conversation. He started by talking of the technical problems of Sufism and Hinduism in his courses at the university. Then we discussed the Temple of Understanding Conference. He told me some good Sufi stories, one about a Sufi at a reception where a courtesan has hastily been concealed behind a curtain so as not to give scandal when he arrives. She finally gets tired, comes out and recites a pretty verse to the effect, "I am what I appear to be. I hope you are the same." There was a picture of Rudolf Otto[18] on the table. Vahiduddin had studied at Marburg. He lamented the absence of genuine Sufi masters, though there are some, hidden. And the great number of fakes who are very much in the public eye. He praised a classic Sufi who said that, "To say I am God is not pride, it is perfect modesty." Vahiduddin also said that a religion that ignores or evades the fact of death cannot make sense. (This I myself said in my talk at the Temple of Understanding Conference.)

After my visit Vahiduddin walked out with me to get a taxi. Three men, one with an instrument, another with a bag of cobras, passed us with shrill music and an offer to make the snakes dance for us right there in the dust. No thank you!

About sunset we came to the Ladakh Buddhi Vihara. The taxi drove into the midst of a group of Tibetans playing soccer. It is a school-monastery-residence for Tibetan refugees, with a nice shiny new temple and Buddhas somewhat more convincing than the usual. Nothing is more jejune than a Buddha whose smile is stupid rather than nirvanic.

Tibetans wandered about in the dusk, some looking exactly like Eskimos. Some of the men wore high boots. One carried a rosary. One was wandering about with a big transistor giving out Tibetan music from a local station. One woman was carrying a white baby with blue eyes and red hair.

Lobsang Phuntsok Lhalungpa,[19] a Tibetan layman, runs a radio station which broadcasts a Tibetan program in Delhi, where Harold Talbott is taking Tibetan lessons. He came to the Ladakh Vihara with his wife Deki. We went up to one of

Harold Talbott with Mr. and Mrs. Lobsang Phuntsok Lhalungpa

the cells and talked with Lama Geshe Tenpa Gyaltsan, a teacher who is a Gelugpa monk, and another Nyingmapa monk, a man with a shiny, fresh-shaven head. The latter, I learned, was in fact the Nechung rimpoche, formerly abbot of the great Tibetan monastery of Nechung, and a tulku. Both these monks were impressive people—so different from the Hindu swamis I've seen so far, though these too can be impressive in a different way. The Tibetans seem to have a peculiar intentness, energy, silence, and also humor. Their laughter is wonderful. Lhalungpa translated, but long stretches of talk got lost.

The two laughed when I asked the difference between their orders—Gelugpa and Nyingmapa—and said there was "really no difference." They stressed, perhaps overstressed, their unity. Someone later remarked that it was not unusual to find a Gelugpa and a Nyingmapa getting on so easily as good friends.

We talked about the goal of the monastic life. They emphasized the ideas of discipline and detachment from a life of pleasure and materialism. Nothing too clear was said about meditation, except that it has degrees and must be preceded by study. "Anyone" can do the simpler kind but a master is needed for the "more advanced." Boys begin meditation around fifteen or sixteen. They got into an involved question with Lhalungpa, a "problem" of Gelugpa meditation, which he did not translate.

We agreed on the importance of contact and understanding. They urged me to "help Westerners understand meditation," and the need for a more spiritual life. They laughed when I explained that the contemplative life was not exactly viewed with favor in the West and that monks are often considered useless. There was another lama in the next cell who is related to Lama Deshung Rimpoche at Seattle University who sent me the writings of Gampopa.[20] In the cell there were Tibetan manuscripts wrapped in saffron cloth, bowls of water, an offering of rice in a chalice, and dice for divination.

While we were talking about monastic affairs the King of Gyalrong[21] came in, a quiet, sad man in a gray open-necked shirt. He sat down on the bed and said nothing. After a while, bored by the talk of meditation, he yawned and withdrew.

✾

In the next room of the hotel, having finished his puja my neighbor now talks loudly on the telephone: "Hallo! Hallo! Hallo! I am going to Agra!"

✾

Dr. Lokesh Chandra[22] offered me a mandala, one of his reprints. I picked one, the general pattern of which attracted me as being very lively. On close inspection I find it to be full of copulation, which is all right, but I don't quite know how one meditates on it.[23] It might be a paradoxical way to greater purity.

❈

In his discussion of the symbolism of the mandala, Tucci explains that the Shaivite schools "divide men into three classes: first the common people, those who live a herd-like life, for whom precise laws and prohibitions are suited, since such men do not yet possess a consciousness which can, by itself, govern itself. Then come 'heroes' who have a tendency to emerge from such a night. But their capacity wearies them, They follow their own consciousness and make their own laws, different from and contrary to those of the herd. They are lonely men who swim against the current; courageously they put themselves into contact with God and free themselves from the uniform life of association. Then come the divya, the holy souls, who are fully realized and so beyond the plane of samsara."

—Tucci, *op. cit.,* page 51.

❈

Five breaths pray in me: sun moon
Rain wind and fire
Five seated Buddhas reign in the breaths
Five illusions
One universe:
The white breath, yellow breath,
Green breath, blue breath,
Red fire breath, Amitabha[24]
Knowledge and Desire
And the quiescence
Of Knowledge and Desire.

❈

October 31

Everything I think or do enters into the construction of a mandala. It is the balancing of experience over the void, not the censorship of experience. And no duality of experience—void. Experience is full because it is inexhaustible void. It is not mine. It is "uninterrupted exchange." It is dance. Five mudras. The dancing god embraces and penetrates the Mother. They are one motion, one silence. They are Word. Utterance and return. "Myself." No-self. The self is merely a locus in which the dance of the universe is aware of itself as complete from beginning to end—and returning to the void. Gladly. Praising, giving thanks, with all beings. Christ light—spirit—grace—gift. (Bodhicitta)

✠

"Twofold is the aspect of Divinity, one, subtle, represented by the *mantra* and the other coarse, represented by an image."

—from the *Yamala,* quoted in Tucci, *op. cit.,* page 60.

✠

Air-condition mantra. Tibetan bass of the machines.

✠

For the Tibetans, every conceivable sound is both music and mantra.[25] Great brasses. Trumpets snoring into the earth. They wake the mountain spirits, inviting canyon populations to a solemn rite of life and death. The clear outcry of gyelings, (shawms), the throb of drums, bells and cymbals. The "sonorous icon" with its unending trance of atonal sound repels evil. But a huge mask of evil is pressing down close. The deep sounds renew life, repel the death-grin (i.e., ignorance). The sound is the sound of emptiness. It is profound and clean. We are washed in the millennial silent roar of a rock-eating glacier.

※

Dance is essential for initiates.[26]

The dance of the Supremely Wrathful One, with his long-sleeved retinue and his bride of wrath.

The dance of dorje phurpa, the eternal dagger, which is done in Sikkim[27] by lamas issuing from a long period of retreat.

Padma Sambhava,[28] masked as a stag, smiles, wags his great horns, puts the evil away in a little box.

An oracle with an enormous helmet draped in a score of flags runs in a wild trance along the highest parapet of the temple.

※

I have a view of some of the Delhi embassies from my hotel. Over there, with the tall flagpole and red flag, is the big Chinese Embassy compound. What do they know in there? What do they do? Of what do they accuse one another, and what do they say of those they believe to be in places like this? Or is one of them secretly writing a poem?

※

October 31 / Vigil of All Saints / Delhi

I read the Vespers of All Saints in my hotel room. Tonight I'll go by train to the Himalayas. Monsieur Daridan at the French Embassy gave me the two addresses of Dom Henri Le Saux's[29] hermitages—in the foothills of the Himalayas, one near Madras —but I don't know which one he is at. Probably the Himalaya one is too far from Dharamsala in any case.

69

Today I spent a long time in the Pan American office getting my ticket rewritten. In the end I *don't* go to Katmandu,[30] at least not this time. Maybe I can do it if I come back in January. On returning from Dharamsala, Harold Talbott and I plan to go to Darjeeling and perhaps Sikkim. Then I go to Madras, Ceylon, Singapore, and Bangkok for the meeting. Last night Commissioner and Mrs. George had me to dinner at the Canadian Embassy with Lhalungpa, his wife, Harold Talbott, and Gene Smith.[31] George showed a longish movie he had taken of Tibetan dances at Dalhousie,[32] an extraordinary ceremony presided over by Khamtul Rimpoche. A couple of Tibetan hermits appeared fleetingly in the film—I may perhaps meet them. We compared illustrations from books on Romanesque art with Tibetan mandalas, etc. Gelugpa equals like Cluny![33]

I was invited to another Birla party in Delhi but I did not go. Not much sightseeing either. Only the Red Fort and the big tomb. Some lovely Mogul paintings in the National Museum! Tea with Vahiduddin at the university on Tuesday—lots of good Sufi stories. Supper at the Moti Mahal restaurant where there was unfortunately no Urdu music (only on Saturdays). I am tired of too much food—and too much curry. Back to European food part of the time. The French cooking at the French Embassy was excellent, and two very nice wines. I must say I rather like embassy parties, and Madame Daridan was particularly charming and interesting. We had a good talk sitting in the garden. She likes Shaivism and in a way seems to have some of the grace and maturity that true Shaivism must imply. But I confess I am not very open to Hindu religion, as distinct from philosophy. But I can't judge yet. Will suspend judgment until I get to Madras. I am much more impressed by the Tibetan lamas I have met.

⌘

All official modern religious art is to me forbidding, whether

Christian, or Buddhist, or Hindu or whatever. Only the very unusual means anything to me—Jamini Roy, and then, perhaps, not for any connection with prayer.

✣

NOTES: *New Delhi*

[1] Harold Talbott: an American student of Buddhism, who had become a Catholic in his first year at Harvard (1959) and was confirmed at the Abbey of Gethsemani, where he went to receive Merton's blessing. Later he became a friend and student of the Benedictine theologian Dom Aelred Graham, who, some ten years afterward, urged Merton to look up Talbott in India, where he was then studying under the direction of the Dalai Lama. Talbott arranged Merton's meetings with the Dalai Lama and with a number of other Tibetan lamas in Darjeeling and Dharamsala. They traveled together for several weeks in northern India and spent one week in semiretreat at the bungalow in Dharamsala which the Dalai Lama had provided for Talbott.

[2] Raj: in Hindi, "reign, rule, or kingdom." Used here to refer to the "British Raj," the period of British imperial rule in India.

[3] Humayun: one of the great Mogul emperors of India. He lived from 1508 to 1556, reigning from 1530, making his capital at Delhi. Much of his reign was taken up fighting the Indian Afghans, and he spent fifteen years in exile in Persia, where his son, Akbar the Great, was born. But he defeated the Afghans and re-established Mogul supremacy in northern India the year before his death.

[4] The *Bardo Thödöl,* or *Tibetan Book of the Dead,* describes the assistance of guiding the departed toward a higher rebirth. "Bardo": the period immediately after death. See *The Tibetan Book of the Dead,* or "The After-Death Experiences on the *Bardo* Plane, according to Lama Kazi Dawa-Sandup's English Rendering," compiled and edited by W. Y. Evans-Wentz, Oxford University Press paperback, 1960.

[5] Desjardins: Arnaud Desjardins, author of *Le Message des Tibétains,* English language edition: *The Message of the Tibetans,* translated by R. H. Ward & Vega Stewart, London, Stuart & Watkins, 1969.

[6] Marco Pallis: Marco Pallis was born in Liverpool, England, in 1895 of

Greek parents and was educated at Harrow and Liverpool University. In 1911 he went to British Guiana to study insects, and then to help in a hospital in Epirus during the Balkan War. He joined the British army in World War I, serving in Serbia, Macedonia, and France. Returning to England after the war, he studied music with Arnold Dolmetsch. From his youth, Pallis had been keen on mountaineering, and in 1923 he went to the southern borders of Tibet, where he scaled Riwo Pargyul Peak, 22,500 feet. But soon his main interest became the study of Tibetan art, life, and religion. He revisited the area in 1936, staying in Buddhist monasteries in Sikkim and Ladakh, publishing the account of his experiences in 1939 in the book *Peaks and Lamas* (New York, Knopf, revised edition 1949). He was able to enter Tibet in 1947, where he lived and studied in a mountain town near Shigatse. Back in London in 1951, he became associated with a group of musicians devoted to early music called "The English Consort of Viols." When this group made its second U.S. tour, he was able to visit Merton, with whom he had been corresponding, at Gethsemani. His other book publications are *The Way and the Mountain* (London, Peter Owen, 1960) and a collection of his essays, translated into Italian, *Il Loto e la croce* ("The Lotus and the Cross") (Borla Editore, Turin).

7 Shakti: In a private letter, Marco Pallis has commented on this passage: "Shakti (power) can be of many kinds. The shakti of any divinity is its dynamic aspect, its 'dynamic spouse,' one might say. (Cf. St. Gregory Palamas when he says that 'God creates, not by his essence, but by his Energies.' This gives the sense of shakti.)" (Gregorius Palamas [c. 1296–1359], a Greek mystic and monk of Mt. Athos.)

8 Kuki and Mizo: In the state of Manipur, in the northeast corner of India, adjacent to Burma, some of the hill tribes still carry on intermittent guerrilla resistance to the Indian central government. The Kuki are of Mongoloid origin.

9 Manipur: an independent principality until 1949, Manipur is now an Indian state, with an area of 8,638 square miles, a population of about 780,000, for the most part primitive tribes inhabiting a terrain that is mostly jungle. Its capital is Imphal. It lies in the very northeast corner of India, east of Bangladesh, and bordered on the east by Burma and on the north by the Indian state of Assam.

10 Merton read the Desjardins work in its original French edition and transcribed the quotations in French. The English text quoted here restores some slight ellipses in the notebook version.

11 Asanga: "Asanga is a very interesting and dominating figure in the development of Mahayana philosophy. His three works, *Mahayanasutralankara, Dharma Dharmatavibhanga* and *Madhyanta Vibhaga* are from the

Yogacara point of view and interpret Sunyata on an idealistic basis. . . .
Asanga is an important figure in one other aspect. He seems to be one of the
leaders of the Tantric Buddhism (Vajrayana) if his connection with the
Guhya Samaja Tantra (Tathagata Guhyaka) is accepted." (T.R.V.
Murti, *The Central Philosophy of Buddhism,* second edition, London, Allen & Un-
win, 1960, pages 108–9)

[12] Vasubandhu: brother of Asanga, and disciple of Maitreya, all three
founders of the Yogacara school of Buddhism. Authorities disagree on the
dates of Vasubandhu's life, Thomas placing him in the second half of the
5th century A.D. on the basis of a life of Vasubandhu written by Paramartha
in the 6th century, while Murti prefers the evidence for the life dates 280–
360 A.D. As a young man, Vasubandhu followed the Sarvastivada school,
which he explicated in a work called the *Abhidharmakosa,* but later, after
his conversion by Maitreya to the Yogacara school, his most important work
was the *Trimsika,* or "Thirty Verses." See Thomas: *The History of Buddhist
Thought,* pages 238–40. See also Zimmer: *Philosophies of India,* page 529,
for further information on Vasubandhu and Asanga.

[13] Lhasa: the chief city of Tibet and a sacred Buddhist site because the
Dalai Lamas lived there in the Potala palace. Now occupied by the Chinese.
It is near the Tsangpo (Brahmaputra) River at an altitude of 11,800 feet.

[14] In a private letter, Marco Pallis questions the statement that tanka
pigments were made from lotus or other plants. "The Tibetan painters do
not use vegetable colors; they do not use dyes. Their materials are minerals,
i.e., various earths and also powdered gems. . . , The theory that the Russian
icon painters were at any time influenced by Tibetan painting methods is
most improbable. The Russian technique derived from Byzantium. . . . As
for the Tibetans, they got their technique first from India, but some Chinese
influence *might* have come in rather late, but even this is doubtful."

[15] Dr. Raghu Vira (1902–63), one of the most distinguished Indian
scholars of his generation, founded the International Academy of Indian
Culture in 1935 to promote intercultural studies on the Hindu-Buddhist
traditions of Asia. He was the author of 161 works in Sanskrit, English,
Hindi, Tibetan, Mongolian, Chinese, and Old Javanese, and through his
work on several dictionaries helped to create a modern Hindi scientific
terminology. A leader in the Jan Sangh party, he was a member of the
Parliament of India for twelve years. His son, Dr. Lokesh Chandra, now
heads the Academy of Indian Culture. He has informed us that the quotation Merton attributes to his father is not from one of Dr. Vira's published
books, but from a conversation Merton had with Dr. Chandra in which he
quoted his father from memory.

[16] Jama (sometimes Jami) Masjid: one of the most important Mogul

mosques of Delhi, built of red sandstone and white marble, and architecturally notable for its two tall minarets. Its construction was begun in 1644, in the reign of Shah Jehan, and not completed until 1658, the year in which the emperor was deposed by his son Aurangzeb.

[17] Anthony Quainton: at the time of Merton's visit, Quainton was a specialist in the affairs of the kingdom of Bhutan, which is bounded by Sikkim, Tibet, Assam, and East Pakistan (now Bangladesh), at the American Consulate in Calcutta.

[18] Rudolf Otto: (1869-1937) Professor of Theology at the University of Marburg, Germany; author of *The Idea of the Holy* (Oxford University Press paperback edition, 1958) and other works on religion and mysticism. A copy of Otto's book *Mysticism East and West* was in Merton's personal library at Gethsemani.

[19] Lobsang Phuntsok Lhalungpa: Tibetan scholar, teacher and musicologist who is now living in Vancouver, B.C., Canada. He grew up in Lhasa and was at one time an official of the Tibetan government prior to the Communist Chinese take-over. Later he took refuge in Kalimpong, in the Indian foothills of the Himalayas, then moving to Delhi, where Merton met him and his wife. He contributed the chapter on "Buddhism in Tibet" to *The Path of the Buddha,* edited by Kenneth W. Morgan, and also wrote a paper on Tibetan music, from which Merton quotes, for the International Music Conference, New York, 1968, which was subsequently published in the British magazine *Studies in Comparative Religion.*

[20] Gampopa: (transliterated sometimes as Sgam-po-pa, and also called Dvagpo-lharje Rimpoche), born in 1079 A.D., was a Tibetan medical doctor and, as the favorite disciple of the poet-saint Milarepa, an early and important teacher of the Kagyudpa school of Buddhism. He was the author of the *Dagpoi Thargyen,* translated by Herbert V. Guenther as *The Jewel Ornament of Liberation,* obtainable from Shambala Publications, 1409 5th Street, Berkeley, California 94710. The work is also sometimes called *The Precious Rosary.*

[21] Gyalrong: a small principality between eastern Tibet and China, now taken over by the Communist Chinese. In earlier eras Gyalrong alternated in allegiance to Tibet or China, depending on their relative power at the time.

[22] Dr. Lokesh Chandra: Director of the International Academy of Indian Culture in New Delhi and a Collector of Indian and Tibetan books and artworks.

[23] In a private letter, Marco Pallis points out that maithuna (sexual

union) "is the common symbol of 'non-duality' both in Hinduism and Mahayana Buddhism; e.g., Shiva and Shakti . . . 'wisdom and method' in the Tantras. Cf. the marriage of Christ and His Church." See also Merton's own discussion of prajna and upaya on pages 90 and 271–73.

24 Amitabha: "the Buddha of infinite light." For background on this poem on the Five Buddhas, see Tucci, *op. cit.*, pages 50 and 53. In Japan, Amitabha is Amida, "the Buddha of the Pure Realm," where it is believed that the constant recital of his name is enough to insure salvation.

25 See L. P. Lhalungpa: *Tibetan Music: Sacred and Secular,* New York, International Music Conference, 1968, also published in the English journal *Studies in Comparative Religion,* Bedfont, Middlesex, England, Spring 1969.

26 This paragraph on Tibetan religious dance is based on a conversation with Lobsang P. Lhalungpa. For additional information about Tibetan dance and mystery plays, see Evans-Wentz: *Tibetan Yoga and Secret Doctrines,* pages 282ff.

27 Sikkim: a small, independent Himalayan state lying northeast of India between Nepal and Bhutan. Roughly 2,700 square miles in size, about 85 per cent of its population of 165,000 are Nepalese who displaced the earlier Bhotias and Lepchas. Formerly a British protectorate, Sikkim is now, effectively, governed as a dependency of India. The ruling family is of Tibetan origin, and the present maharajah married an American girl, Hope Cook.

28 Padma Sambhava: known as the "Great Guru," an Indian master of the occult sciences, who was invited to Tibet about 747 A.D. by King Thi-Srong-Detsan and is considered the founder of the Tibetan school of Nyingmapa Buddhism. Under his influence, Indian Tantric works were translated, giving Tibetan Buddhism its Tantric bias, and he founded the first Buddhist monastery in Tibet at Samye. His teaching was largely responsible for the suppression of Tibet's earlier shamanistic religion, Bon-pa. See W. Y. Evans-Wentz: *The Tibetan Book of the Great Liberation,* Oxford University Press, 1954, pages 25–35 in the 1969 paperback edition, for an account of Padma Sambhava's life and the extensive mythology which has grown up about it.

29 Dom Henri Le Saux: known also by his Hindu name of Swami Abhishiktananda; the addresses given in Merton's address book are: Gyansu, Uttarkashi P.O., Uttar Pradesh, and Shanti Vanam, Tannir Polli P.O., via Kuliltalai, Tiruchi District, Madras. A copy of *Ermites du Succidananda* by Henri Le Saux and Jules Monchanin was in Merton's personal library at Gethsemani.

30 Katmandu: the capital city of Nepal.

31 E. Gene Smith: one of the leading Tibetanists among Western scholars, an American who studied at Leiden University in Holland and under Lama Deshung Rimpoche at Seattle University. He is now an officer of the Library of Congress in New Delhi, where, in an effort to preserve the culture of Tibet, he has published a number of volumes of important classic Tibetan texts. He had first corresponded with Merton when he was living in Seattle.

32 Dalhousie: a hill station (resort town) in the foothills of the Himalayas just south of Chamba, one of the Punjabi princely states of the British rule period in India.

33 Cluny: the most famous Benedictine abbey in France, founded in 910 A.D.

THE HIMALAYAS
November 1–25

November 1 / Dharamsala

I came up by train from Delhi to Pathankot[1] with Harold Talbott last night. Then by jeep with a Tibetan driver to Dharamsala.[2] Slept well enough in a wide lower berth. It was my first overnight train trip since I went to Gethsemani to enter the monastery twenty-seven years ago. When light dawned, I looked out on fields, scattered trees, tall reeds and bamboo, brick and mud villages, a road swept by rain in the night and now by a cold wind from the mountains, men wrapped in blankets walking in the wind. Teams of oxen ploughing. Pools by the track filled with tall purple flowering weeds. A white crane starts up out of the green rushes. Long before Pathankot I was seeing the high snow-covered peaks behind Dalhousie.

On our arrival at Pathankot there was a madhouse of noise, bearers balancing several suitcases and packages on their heads and all trying to get through one small exit at once with a hundred passengers. We were met by a jeep from the Dalai Lama's headquarters.

It was a beautiful drive to Dharamsala—mountains, small villages, canyons, shrines, ruined forts, good, well-cared-for forest preserves. Then the climb to Dharamsala itself and the vast view over the plains from the village. It rained when we arrived and thunder talked to itself all over and around the cloud-hidden peaks. We came to the cottage Talbott lives in—everything very primitive.

In the afternoon I got my first real taste of the Himalayas. I climbed a road out of the village up into the mountains, winding through pines, past places where Tibetans live and work, including a small center for publication and a central office. Many Tibetans on the road, and some were at work on a house, singing their building song. Finally I was out alone in the pines, watching the clouds clear from the medium peaks—but not the high snowy ones—and the place was filled with a special majestic kind of mountain silence. At one point the sound of a goatherd's flute drifted up from a pasture below. An unforgettable valley with a river winding at the bottom, a couple of thousand feet below, and the rugged peaks above me, and pines twisted as in Chinese paintings. I got on a little path where I met at least five Tibetans silently praying with rosaries in their hands—and building little piles of stones. An Indian goatherd knocked over one of the piles for no reason. Great silence of the mountain, except for two men with axes higher up in the pines. Gradually the clouds thinned before one of the higher peaks, but it never fully appeared.

On the way down I met a man on the road, a man in European clothes walking with a lama. He introduced himself as Sonam Kazi,[3] the man who translated for Desjardins. He sent the lama on his way, and we went to the Tourist Hotel to drink tea and talk.

⌘

"The milk of the lioness is so precious and so powerful that if you put it in an ordinary cup, the cup breaks." (Tibetan saying)

⌘

November 2 / Dharamsala

Yesterday as I came down the path from the mountain I heard a strange humming behind me. A Tibetan came by quietly droning a monotonous sound, a prolonged "om." It was something that harmonized with the mountain—an ancient syllable he had found long ago in the rocks—or perhaps it had been born with him.

The Tibetan who cooks for us was formerly a monk in

Tibet, who got released from his vows to fight in the resistance against the Chinese.

⌘

The guru is he who "must produce the revulsion of the adept."

—Tucci, *op. cit.*, page 76.

"The aim of all the Tantras is to teach the ways whereby we may set free the divine light which is mysteriously present and shining in each one of us, although it is enveloped in an insidious web of the psyche's weaving."

—Tucci, *op. cit.*, page 78.

Tucci explains that there are four different Tantras to suit four categories of men (and gods).

". . . the *Kriyatantras,* particularly devoted to liturgical complications. It is a homeopathic treatment by which it is sought, gradually, to open the eyes of the officiant and to show him what a complex instrument of psychological revulsion he has at his disposal, provided that he knows how to understand its meaning. The gesture (*mudra*) of the Gods is here a smile.

"The *Caryatantras* are suited for the *rje rigs,* the nobleman, in whom a respect for ceremonial is accompanied by a capacity for spiritual meditation. These Tantras are addressed to persons who may experience the dawn of spiritual anxiety and in whom there may be present the intellectual and spiritual prerequisites for the Return. The gesture here is a look. The *Yogatantras* are addressed to the *rgyal rigs,* of royal family, powerful men, who cannot manage to renounce the goods of this world. For their meditation is offered the *mandala* with a lavish display of Gods, Goddesses and acolytes . . . like the court of a king in his palace. For one must begin by speaking to such men a language which they can understand, if one does not wish to drive them away for ever. What would be the use of renunciation and sacrifice to those who love the joy of living, if they are, to begin with, ignorant of the fact that real beatitude is an overcoming of that which they most desire? The gesture here is an embrace.

"The *Anuttaratantras* are reserved for the creatures who sin most, who do not distinguish good from evil, who lead impure lives. It is on the very fault itself by which they are sullied that is built up slowly the work of redemption. The gesture here is union."

Tucci points out that it would be wrong to imagine that a meditation type should be urged to follow anuttaratantra.

—Tucci, *op. cit.*, pages 79–00.

"The symbolism of the ritual act is clear. A *mandala* . . . is an ideal Bodhgaya, an 'adamantine plane,' that is an incorruptible surface, the representation of the very instant in which is accomplished the revulsion to the other plane, in which one becomes Buddha."

—Tucci, *op. cit.*, page 86.

"One is to attain enlightenment and become a Buddha only for the sake of others; it has therefore been said, 'Bodhicitta is perfect enlightenment (attained) for the sake of others . . .'"

—S. B. Dasgupta: *An Introduction to Tantric Buddhism,* University of Calcutta, 1958, page 8. See pages 280–83 in Part Two of this volume, "Complementary Reading," for additional passages from S. B. Dasgupta.

Mandalas can incorporate non-Buddhist deities and even Christian symbols. "Every shape and form that arises in the soul, every link which, in a mysterious way, joins us to the Universal Life and unites us, maybe without our being aware of it, to Man's most ancient experience, the voices which reach us from the depths of the abyss, all are welcomed with almost affectionate solicitude."

—Tucci, *op. cit.*, page 83.

Sonam Kazi is a Sikkimese who went to Tibet to consult doctors about an illness, then rode all over Tibet and took to meditation, studying under various lamas, including a woman lama in Lhasa. His daughter is supposed to be a reincarnation of this woman. She entranced Aelred Graham[4] by reading comic books while he argued with her father. There is a sweet photo of her in the Desjardins book.

Sonam Kazi is a lay Nyingmapa monk. He has had several good gurus and seems far advanced in meditation. He is of course full of information but also of insight. He thinks I ought to find a Tibetan guru and go in for Nyingmapa Tantrism initiation along the line of "direct realization and dzogchen (final resolution)." At least he asked me if I were willing to risk it and I said why not? The question is finding the right man. I am not exactly dizzy with the idea of looking for a magic master but I would certainly like to learn something by experience and it does seem that the Tibetan Buddhists are the only ones who, at present, have a really large number of people who have attained to extraordinary heights in meditation and contemplation. This does not exclude Zen. But I do feel very much at home with the Tibetans, even though much that appears in books about them seems bizarre if not sinister.

✼

What is the purpose of the mandala? Sonam Kazi said one meditates on the mandala in order to be in control of what goes on within one instead of "being controlled by it." In meditation on the mandala one is able to construct and dissolve the interior configurations at will. One meditates not to "learn" a presumed objective cosmological structure, or a religious doctrine, but to become the Buddha enthroned in one's own center.

✼

Sonam Kazi with his wife and daughter

Elements of the mandala for Tucci: it is man's psychic heritage, to be accepted, not repressed. "It is better, then, to assume possession of them at the first and then by degrees to transfigure them, just as one passes from the outer enclosure of the mandala successively through the others until one reaches the central point, the primordial equipoise regained after the experience of life."

—Tucci, *op. cit.,* page 83.

⌘

I talked to Sonam Kazi about the "child mind," which is recovered *after* experience. Innocence—to experience—to innocence. Milarepa, angry, guilty of revenge, murder and black arts, was purified by his master Marpa, the translator, who several times made him build a house many stones high and then tear it down again. After which he was "no longer the slave of his own psyche but its lord." So too, a Desert Father came to freedom by weaving baskets and then, at the end of each year, burning all the baskets he had woven.[5]

—See Tucci, *op. cit.,* pages 83–84.

⌘

Outside the dirty window I have just opened there is pure morning light on the lower rampart of the Himalayas. Near me are the steep green sinews of a bastion tufted with vegetation. A hut or shrine is visible, outlined on the summit. Beyond, in sunlit, back-lighted mist, the higher pointed peak. Further to the left a still higher snowy peak that was hidden in cloud last evening and is misty now. Song of birds in the bushes. Incessant soft guttural mantras of the crows. Below, in another cottage, an argument of women.

⌘

Sonam Kazi is against the mixing of traditions, even Tibetan ones. Let the Kagyudpa keep to itself. He suggests that if I edit a book of Tibetan texts, let them all be *one* tradition. A fortiori, we should not try to set up a pseudocommunity of people from different traditions, Asian and Western. I agree with this. Brother David Steindl-Rast's[6] idea perplexed me a little—as being first of all too academic. But I had wondered about some different approach: a mere dream. And certainly no good in my own life. Now, since seeing the books the other night in Canada House, I am curious about re-exploring the Romanesque artistic tradition and the 12th-century writers in Christian monasticism in relation to the Eastern traditions . . . i.e., in the light thrown on them by the East.

Sonam Kazi spoke of acting with no desire for gain, even spiritual—whether merit or attainment. A white butterfly appears in the sun, then vanishes again. Another passes in the distance. No gain for them—or for me.

Down in the valley a bird sings, a boy whistles. The white butterfly zigzags across the top left corner of the view.

❊

Man as body—word—spirit. Three ways of handling anger, lust, etc. Hinayana . . . Mahayana . . . Tantric.

❊

Tucci on the liturgy and rites of the mandala:

"The disciple, blindfolded, is led to the eastern gate of the mandala and there receives from the master a short stick of wood (such as is used in India for cleaning the teeth) or a flower which he must throw on to the mandala. The section on to which these fall (which is protected by one of the five Buddhas —or their symbols) will indicate the way that is suited to the disciple."

". . . the initiate should honour this God (in the aspect of jnanasattva) with exoteric and esoteric ritual of various sorts: flowers, incense, lamps, vestments, umbrellas, flags, bells and standards, all of celestial quality." [But a Hinayana master from Burma went to Ceylon and was scandalized to find there monks with umbrellas—this of course was quite different.]

—Tucci, *op. cit.*, pages 90 and 95.

※

The disciple, blindfolded, is led to the east gate of the prepared mandala. Blindfolded, he casts a flower on the mandala. The flower will find his way for him into the palace. Follow your flower!

※

I must ask Sonam Kazi about dreams. Tucci placed under his pillow a blessed leaf given him by the Grand Lama of Sakya. He dreamed of mountains and glaciers. (See Tucci, *op. cit.*, page 92.) A yellow butterfly goes by just over the heads of the small purple flowers outside the windows. Firecrackers explode, perhaps in the yard of the school. Hammering in the village.

Sonam Kazi criticized the facility with which some monks say nirvana and samsara are one, without knowing what they are talking about. Also, though it is true that "there is no karma," this cannot be rightly understood by many, for in fact there is karma, but on another level. He also liked the idea of Trappist silence at meals, at work, everywhere. He said the name Trappist was interesting since in Tibetan "trapa" means "schoolman" or monk. He likes Krishnamurti.[7]

※

The bhikkhus at the conference in Calcutta all had umbrellas.

86

They all sat in a saffron row at the banquet, eating and drinking nothing and saying almost nothing except, "You should have had this affair before noon." They smiled and were content.

※

This cottage has a washroom with two stools. Concrete floor. A hole in the corner leading out. You empty the washbasin on the floor and the water runs out the hole. Through this hole a cobra or krait could easily come. Fortunately the nights are cold. There are banana trees everywhere—the nights are not cold enough to harm them. Two wrenlike birds bicker together in a bush outside the window.

※

Sonam Kazi condemned "world-evasion," which he thinks ruined Buddhism in India. He would be against an eremitism entirely cut off from all contact, at least for me. But in another context he admired the recluses who severed all contacts, seeing only a few people or perhaps none at all, reserving special contacts only for a restricted list. Harold asked whether others would respect this arrangement. Sonam Kazi thought they would. When a hermit goes on full retreat he places a mantra, an image, and a seal on the outside of his cell, and the mantra reads: "All gods, men, and demons keep out of this retreat."

Cocks crow in the valley. The tall illuminated grasses bend in the wind. One white butterfly hovers and settles. Another passes in a hurry. How glad I am not to be in any city.

※

Tucci in explaining the liturgy of the mandala speaks of palin-genesis, "the revulsion which has taken place and by which consciousness that was refracted, lost and dissipated in time and space, has become, once again, one and luminous."

—Tucci, op. cit., page 97.

Whatever may be the value of all the details of mandala meditation—and all the emergences of all the Buddhas from all the diamond wombs—this passage remains exact and important: ". . . the mystic knows that the principle of salvation is within him. He knows also that this principle will remain inert if he does not, with all his strength, *seek it, find it and make it active.* On the way of redemption, to which he has devoted himself, he has need of all his will-power and vigilance in order to put in motion the forces of his own psyche so that it, which keeps him bound, may furnish him, nonetheless with the means of salvation provided that he knows how to penetrate into his psyche and to subdue it."

—Tucci, op. cit., page 110.

⌘

November 3

Quiet after sunrise. In the silent, cool, misty air of morning a sound of someone chanting puja floats up from the village. The report of a gun far down in the valley echoes along the walls of the mountain. Now too they are shooting. Yesterday, near the army post at Palampur, there was machine-gun fire back in the mountains while we sat by the road in the tea plantation talking with Khamtul Rimpoche.

We had some trouble locating Khamtul Rimpoche. We went to the place where he is setting up a new monastery and lay colony, also on a tea plantation near Palampur (he is moving away from Dalhousie), but he wasn't there. A monk served us some tea. We waited a while but Khamtul did not come. Later we met him on the road at a lovely place with many pines and a fine view of the mountains. (Khamtul Rimpoche is the one who was in Commissioner George's film.) He is an impressive, heavily built Tibetan with a brown woolen cap on his head. We sat on the ground amid young tea plants and pines and talked, again with Sonam Kazi translating. Khamtul Rimpoche spoke about the need for a guru and direct experience rather than book knowledge; about the union of study and meditation. We discussed the "direct realization" method, including some curious stuff about working the soul of a dead man out of its body with complete liberation after death—through small holes in the skull or a place where the skin is blown off—weird! And about the need of a guru. "And," he asked, "have you come to write a strange book about us? What are your motives?" After quite a few questions, he said I would be helped by talking to "some of the Tibetan tulkus who are in India" and added that

Khamtul Rimpoche

Gyalwa Karmapa,[8] the important guru who has a monastery in Sikkim, was coming to Delhi on the 15th. Afterward someone said no, it was Calcutta on the 15th. In any case I do hope to meet Karmapa somewhere.

It was a long drive back to Dharamsala. The mountains were lovely in the evening light. We arrived after dark, went to a (rather crumby) restaurant in town for some food, and Harold Talbott bought a paper with a banner headline, LBJ ORDERS COMPLETE BOMBING HALT and WAIT FULL SCALE PEACE TALKS CLEARED—a dramatic announcement. It is long overdue, but I am glad of it, even though it may be only a matter of last minute expediency for the election . . . I hope it can mean peace.

✖

What is important is not liberation from the body but liberation from the mind. We are not entangled in our own body but entangled in our own mind.

✖

Spiritual sterility can be due to the fact that fertilization by the union of prajna and upaya (wisdom and discipline) has not taken place. Wisdom as sperm, discipline as ovum give us the "new creature," the living reintegrated and growing "personality" (in a special spiritual sense: not "individual"). Hence comes new consciousness. "Pollution" is the spilling of the seed without union, without fertilization of discipline, without "return" to the summit of consciousness. A mere spilling out of passion with no realization. "The end of passion is the cause of sorrow, the precipitation of the bodhicitta."

—See Tucci's chapter on "The Mandala in the Human Body," *op. cit.,* pages 108–33.

✖

Bhikkhu Khantipalo in Bangkok has spoken of peaceful co-existence with insects, etc. One tries to catch poisonous ones, tactfully, and throw them out of one's hut. Matchboxes, he said, are good for catching scorpions. In the forest wats, a noisy large lizard sometimes gets in the straw of the roof and disturbs the meditation of the bhikkhu by loud guttural cries.

※

Gandhiji's broken glasses . . . Johnson has stopped the bombing. Two magpies are fighting in a tree.

Are Tantrism, and meditation on the mandala, the evocations of minute visual detail like the Ignatian method[9] in some respects? And as useless for me? A white butterfly goes by in the sun.

One difference is the sixth point above the mandala's five points. The mandala is constructed only to be dissolved. One must see clearly the five points—or there is no sixth, which also includes them all. No six without five. The six make "eternal life." Note that when the body is regarded as a mandala, the five chakras (sex, navel, heart, throat, head) are completed by the sixth "above the head."

For the dissolution of a mandala the dusts and colors are taken in ceremony with the solemn snoring of trumpets and thrown into a mountain stream.

※

The highest of vows, Sonam Kazi said, is that in which there is no longer anything to be accomplished. Nothing is vowed. No one vows it. Tibetans sacrifice their own gods and destroy spirits. They also mock, solemnly and liturgically, the sacrifice itself —a spirit in butter, an image of a god to be burned in a straw temple.

※

Reverend Sirs, I am not here to write a manual of Christian Tantras!

※

I must see John Driver[10] if I get to Wales. He wrote a dissertation at Oxford on Nyingmapa but his professor would not accept it. He is connected with Trungpa Rimpoche and his place in Scotland. The dissertation is apparently brilliant.

※

I met a woman and child walking silently, the woman slowly spinning a prayer wheel—with great reverence and it was not at all absurd or routine—the child with a lovely smile.

※

Harold Talbott says the Dalai Lama has to see a lot of blue-haired ladies in pants—losers. And people looking for a freak religion. And rich people who have nothing better to do than come up here out of curiosity. His Western visitors are not well screened. He has very few real advisers who know anything about the world as it is. The Dalai Lama is still studying under his tutor and also is going on with Tantric studies, and I was told by Tenzin Geshe, his secretary, that he enjoys his new house, where he has quieter quarters, is less disturbed, and has a garden to walk in now, without being followed around by cops.

The Dalai Lama is loved by his people—and they are a beautiful, loving people. They surround his house with love and prayer, they have a new soongkhor for protection along the fence. Probably no leader in the world is so much loved by his followers and means so much to them. He means everything to them. For that reason it would be especially terrible and cruel if any evil should strike him. I pray for his safety and fear for him. May God protect and preserve him.

7 P.M. Tenzin Geshe, the very young secretary of the Dalai Lama, has just left. He came down to tell us of plans for my audience tomorrow at 10 A.M. A young, intelligent, eager guy. He seems to be only in his twenties, and the Dalai Lama himself is only thirty-three. He brought me the first copy of a mimeographed newspaper that is being put out here for Tibetans. There are great problems for the Tibetan refugees like those I saw today in Upper Dharamsala living in many tents under the trees on the steep mountainside, clinging precariously to a world in which they have no place and only waiting to be moved somewhere else—to "camps."

We had walked up, Harold and I, to Upper Dharamsala by the back road to McLeod Ganj, which is where the Dalai Lama lives. It is really the top of the mountain we are on now. Suddenly we were in a Tibetan village with a new, spanking white chorten in the middle of it. There we met Sonam Kazi, who was expecting us to come by bus. We climbed higher to the empty buildings of Swarg Ashram which the Dalai Lama has just vacated to move to his new quarters. A lovely site, but cramped. The buildings are old and ramshackle, and as Sonam said, "the roof leaks like hell." Then further on up to the top—an empty house surrounded by prayer flags.

Tibetans are established all over the mountain in huts, houses, tents, anything. Prayer flags flutter among the trees. Rock mandalas are along all the pathways. OM MANI PADME HUM ("Hail to the jewel in the lotus") is carved on every boulder. It is moving to see so many Tibetans going about silently praying—almost all of them are constantly carrying rosaries. We visited a small monastic community of lamas under the Dalai Lama's private chaplain, the Khempo of Namgyal Tra-Tsang, whom I met. We were ushered into his room where he sat studying Tibetan block-print texts in narrow oblong sheets. He was wearing tinted glasses. The usual rows of little bowls of water. A tanka. Marigolds growing in old tin cans. Artificial flowers in a Coke bottle. A little butter lamp burning. A jar with a plentiful supply of Entero-Vioform tablets. Shelves of Tibetan texts carefully wrapped in bright yellow and orange cloth. A beautiful room—the Coke bottle was not immediately obvious—it did not look like a junk yard, but like a shrine, as a lama's room should. A quiet, scholarly man, eloquent and articulate, with a lot to say.

The Khempo of Namgyal deflected a question of mine about metaphysics—he returned to it later—by saying that the real ground of his Gelugpa study and practice was the knowledge of suffering, and that only when a person was fully convinced of the immensity of suffering and its complete universality and saw the need of deliverance from it, and sought deliverance for *all* beings, could he begin to understand sunyata.

Thus when European authors such as Tucci seem to talk of bodhicitta as an intellectual or metaphysical seed of enlightenment, the khempo showed it clearly to be a right view of suffering and a deep sense of compassion for everything and everyone that suffers. Then he went on to talk of *Prajnaparamita* and the teachings of Nagarjuna[11] as the intellectual basis of his own tradition, and of the need to study these and to practice them, to reduce them to experience. He also—like all the others—stressed the need of a master for progress in meditation. He spoke of Santi Deva and I replied that I liked Santi Deva[12] very much, had reread him this summer. He said the compassion of Santi Deva was so great that his teaching touched the heart very deeply and awakened a spiritual response. When one read the *Prajnaparamita* on suffering and was thoroughly moved, "so that all the hairs of the body stood on end," one was ready for meditation—called to it—and indeed to further study. He was very reserved about mandalas—"I would not even pronounce the name mandala except that you have come from such a great distance"—and insisted on the esoteric secrecy of Tantric disciplines and symbols. This refusal to speak directly of symbols was very interesting.

He insisted on the "ax of true doctrine" which must be

used to cut the root of ignorance—and that one must know how to use the ax, otherwise he harms himself. So a man who is skilled in catching snakes can safely catch them but one who is not skilled gets bitten. Meditation: laying the ax to the root. (The coming of Christ in the desert.)

❀

"It is the tradition of the fortunate seekers never to be content with partial practice."

—Milarepa

Sankaracharya on the ego (from *The Crest-Jewel of Discrimination*).

"When we say: 'This man is that same Devadatta whom I have previously met,' we establish a person's identity by disregarding those attributes superimposed upon him by the circumstances of our former meeting. In just the same way, when we consider the scriptural teaching 'That art Thou,' we must disregard those attributes which have been superimposed upon 'That' and 'Thou. . . .'

"Cease to follow the way of the world, cease to follow the way of the flesh, cease to follow the way of tradition. Get rid of this false identification and know the true Atman. . . .

"Cease to identify yourself with race, clan, name, form and walk of life. These belong to the body, the garment of decay. Abandon, also, the idea that you are the doer of actions or the thinker of thoughts. These belong to the ego, the subtle covering. Realize that you are that Being which is eternal happiness.

"Man's life of bondage to the world of birth and death has many causes. The root of them all is the ego, the first-begotten child of ignorance.

"As long as a man identifies himself with this wicked ego, there can be no possibility of liberation. For liberation is its very opposite.

"Once freed from this eclipsing demon of an ego, man regains his true nature, just as the moon shines forth when freed from the darkness of an eclipse. He becomes pure, infinite, eternally blissful and self-luminous."

—Sankaracharya, *op. cit.,* pages 86, 91, 96.

⌘

I promised Tenzin Geshe I would have people send him information and subscriptions to good magazines. Apparently they are not very well informed here in Dharamsala; they have to depend on *Life, Time, Reader's Digest,* and so on. I said I thought the weekly edition of *Le Monde* was essential and that I would get "Ping" Ferry[13] to put them on the mailing list of the Center for the Study of Democratic Institutions.

An Indian security policeman was here in this room, at this desk, this morning looking at my passport, studying the Indian visa, taking down notes about where I had been and where I intended to go. He got me to write out in block letters the titles of the two books I had written on Zen. And he said, "I suppose we can now expect a book from you on Tibetan Buddhism." I said I thought not.

⌘

When we went on up the mountain from Swarg Ashram I heard a great commotion in the tall trees and looked up to see marvelous gray apes with black faces crashing and swinging through the branches. They were huge, almost as big as people. Six or seven beautiful, funny Hanumans.[14] It would be wonderful to live in a hermitage with apes in the trees around it. They would be fantastic company, better than squirrels, endlessly amusing, seemingly clumsy yet infinitely agile and smart. So much bigger than monkeys, and making much more commotion in the branches. A storm of heavy apes!

※

Yesterday Sonam Kazi, Harold, and I drove to Palampur to meet some lamas at the Tibetan camps there. It was a fine drive on a bad road, with great views of the mountains. We went beyond Palampur to the camp, on a tea plantation, where the Tibetans are newly established, some in tents among the tea gardens, with prayer flags flying, some in the buildings of the village. We had a talk with a Nyingmapa lama, Chhokling Rimpoche, who wanted to know if I believed in reincarnation before answering questions concerning enlightenment. Like everyone else, he spoke of masters, and the need of finding one, and how one finds one—of being drawn to him supernaturally, sometimes with instant recognition. He asked me a koanlike question about the origin of the mind. I could not answer it directly but apparently my nonanswer was "right," and he said I would profit by "meeting some of the tulkus that are in India." Sonam Kazi said, "You have passed the first test," and he seemed pleased.

※

One of the "tulkus that are in India" and whom I met today is a ten-year-old boy, a lively and intelligent kid living up on the mountain here in a rather poor cottage with an older lama, another boy lama, and a Tibetan family with a huge black dog that was all ready to bite a few chunks out of Harold and me. The boy was charming and I took some pictures of him as he was petulantly rolling down his sleeves to be more ceremonious. He went into his cell and sat cross-legged on his seat and received us with poise and formality. I took his picture there too but it was probably too dark to come out. Then we went down

Ten-year-old tulku

to the drama school where a girl was playing a lovely instrument, the name of which I forgot to ask—a string instrument laid out flat and played with two sticks. It had a charming sound—while around the corner was a radio playing popular Indian music—which I find pretty good! Here there was a young Canadian who is teaching the little tulku English and says he does not learn his lessons. "He is intelligent but too lazy to think."

November 4

Today I am to see the Dalai Lama . . . but meanwhile the world goes on, and finance booms (zooms). We have run out of toilet paper and are using Saturday's newspaper. I become absorbed in the news of business—too good to pass over.

MUSTARD OIL SUBDUED ON POOR ENQUIRIES
Groundnut oil eased by Rs.5 to Rs.388 for want of support. Sesame and cottonseed oil also came down by Rs.5 in sympathy. (Happy to report however that later groundnut oils rose again Rs.5 "owing to fall in arrivals from Uttar Pradesh.")

PULSES DEPRESSED, WHEAT LOOKS UP
Pulses, especially dal moong, dal masoor, etc. I like dal. I hate to see it depressed. (Dal = lentils.)

BOMBING HALT IMPARTS FIRMNESS TO SHARES
A smart rally was witnessed on the Bombay stock exchange . . . transactions were mostly squarish and of jobbing in nature [sic]. Reports about the bombing halt order over VietNam [sic] given by President Johnson imparted firmness to the market. . .

❈

A Christ mandala, in St. Paul's "to understand the length and the breadth, the height and the depth. . ."

❈

"The human body is better than a wishing gem."

—Milarepa

❈

The three poisons: craving,
hatred,
ignorance.

⌘

"A virtue for one engaged on any esoteric path is primarily a mode of knowing, or, to be more accurate, a factor dispositive for enlightenment."

—Marco Pallis: "Considerations on Tantric Spirituality" in *The Bulletin of Tibetology,* Volume II, Number 2, August 1965, Namgyal Institute of Tibetology, Gangtok, Sikkim. See also pages 272–74 in Part Two of this volume, "Complementary Reading."

⌘

November 4 / Afternoon

I had my audience with the Dalai Lama this morning in his new quarters. It was a bright, sunny day—blue sky, the mountains absolutely clear. Tenzin Geshe sent a jeep down. We went up the long way round through the army post and past the old deserted Anglican Church of St. John in the Wilderness. Everything at McLeod Ganj is admirably situated, high over the valley, with snow-covered mountains behind, all pine trees, with apes in them, and a vast view over the plains to the south. Our passports were inspected by an Indian official at the gate of the Dalai Lama's place. There were several monks standing around —like monks standing around anywhere—perhaps waiting to go somewhere. A brief wait in a sitting room, all spanking new, a lively, bright Tibetan carpet, bookshelves full of the *Kangyur* and *Tangyur* scriptures presented to the Dalai Lama by Suzuki.[15]

The Dalai Lama is most impressive as a person. He is strong and alert, bigger than I expected (for some reason I thought he would be small). A very solid, energetic, generous, and warm person, very capably trying to handle enormous problems—none of which he mentioned directly. There was not a word of politics. The whole conversation was about religion and philosophy and especially ways of meditation. He said he was glad to see me, had heard a lot about me. I talked mostly of my own personal concerns, my interest in Tibetan mysticism. Some of what he replied was confidential and frank. In general he advised me to get a good base in Madhyamika philosophy (Nagarjuna and other authentic *Indian* sources) and to consult qualified Tibetan scholars, uniting study and practice. Dzogchen was good, he said, provided one had a sufficient grounding in metaphysics—

Thomas Merton with the Dalai Lama

or anyway Madhyamika, which is beyond metaphysics. One gets the impression that he is very sensitive about partial and distorted Western views of Tibetan mysticism and especially about popular myths. He himself offered to give me another audience the day after tomorrow and said he had some questions he wanted to ask me.

The Dalai Lama is also sensitive about the views of other Buddhists concerning Tibetan Buddhism, especially some Theravada Buddhists who accuse Tibetan Buddhism of corruption by non-Buddhist elements.

The Dalai Lama told me that Sonam Kazi knew all about dzogchen and could help me, which of course he already has. It is important, the Dalai Lama said, not to misunderstand the simplicity of dzogchen, or to imagine it is "easy," or that one can evade the difficulties of the ascent by taking this "direct path." He recommended Geshe Sopa of the New Jersey monastery who has been teaching at the University of Wisconsin, and Geshe Ugyen Tseten of Rikon, Switzerland.

❈

Murti on Madhyamika: "Its dialectic is of crucial importance. This dialectic is the consciousness, of the total and interminable conflict in reason and the consequent attempt to resolve the conflict by rising to a higher standpoint."

> —See T. R. V. Murti: *The Central Philosophy of Buddhism,* Study of the Madhyamika System, London, Allen & Unwin, 2nd edition, 1960, page 126. For additional extracts from Murti, see also Part Two of this volume, "Complementary Reading," pages 267, 274–80, 283–84.

❈

In the afternoon I got a little reading done and then had quite a good meditation. Talking with the various rimpoches has certainly been helpful, and above all the Dalai Lama himself. I have great confidence in him as a really charismatic person. The Tibetans are all quite impressive and their solidity does a great deal to counteract the bizarre reports about some of their practices. It is all very good experience.

Thinking about my own life and future, it is still a very open question. I am beginning to appreciate the hermitage at Gethsemani more than I did last summer when things seemed so noisy and crowded. Even here in the mountains there are few places where one does not run into someone. Roads and paths and trails are all full of people. To have real solitude one would have to get very high up and far back!

For solitude, Alaska really seems the very best place. But everyone I have talked to says I must also consider others and keep open to them to some extent. The rimpoches all advise against absolute solitude and stress "compassion." They seem to agree that being in solitude much of the year and coming "out" for a while would be a good solution.

The idea of being in Alaska and then going out to Japan or the U. S. strikes me as a rather good solution. And, in some small way, helping in Alaska itself. On the way back from this trip I think I will need to go to Europe to see Trungpa Rimpoche's place in Scotland and the Tibetan monastery in Switzerland. Also to see Marco Pallis and then John Driver in Wales. I must write to "Donald" Allchin[16] about Wales.

The way in which I have been suddenly brought here constantly surprises me. The few days so far in Dharamsala have all been extremely fruitful in every way: the beauty and quiet of the mountains, my own reading and meditation, encounters with lamas, everything.

In a way it is wonderful to be without letters. No one now knows where to reach me. Undoubtedly there is some mail accumulating for me at the USIS office in Calcutta. But it will be ten days or more before I see any of it. And Brother Patrick[17] is sending on only what is most essential.

Trying to get a better perspective on the earlier part of this year, there is a lot I cannot quite understand. And perhaps do not need to understand. The last months have been demanding and fruitful. I have needed the experience of this journey. Much as the hermitage has meant, I have been needing to get away from Gethsemani and it was long overdue.

This evening the lights in the cottage went dead for a while. I stood out in the moonlight, listening to drums down in the village and looking up at the stars. The same constellations as over the hermitage and the porch opening in about the same direction, southeast toward Aquila and the Dolphin. Aquarius out over the plain, the Swan up above. Cassiopeia over the mountains. . .

❋

November 5

The metaphysician as wounded man. A wounded man is not an agnostic—he just has different questions, arising out of his wound. Recognition of the wound as a substitute for real identity, when one can "think of nothing else."

Buddha rejected the dogmatism of idealism and materialism and substituted a critical dialectic, "long before anything approximating to it was formulated in the West." "Criticism is deliverance of the human mind from all entanglements and passions. It is freedom itself. This is the true Madhyamika standpoint." (Murti, *op. cit.*, page 41.)

Note that Buddha neither said "there is a self" or "there is not a self." But among many Buddhists there appears to be a kind of dogmatism that says "there is not a self" instead of taking the true middle. Also Buddha replied by silence because he considered the *condition of the questioner* and the effect of a dogmatic reply on him. Buddha did not say "there is no self" to prevent the bewilderment of Vacchagotta.[18] "For he would have said: 'Formerly indeed I had a self but now I have not one any more.' "

It was Buddha's aim not to give a "final" speculative answer but *to be free from all theories* and to know, by experience, "the nature of form and how form arises and how form perishes." He wanted "not a third position lying between two extremes but a no-position that supersedes them both." This is the Middle Way. (See Murti, *op. cit.*, pages 45–47.)

❈

Buddhist dialectic and "alienation" might be a good theme for my Bangkok conference. Like Marxism, Buddhism considers that a fundamental egocentrism, "providing for the self" (with possible economic implications in a more modern context) leads to dogmatism about the self—either that it is eternal or that it does not exist at all. A truly critical attitude implies a certain freedom from predetermination by economic and sociological factors. The notion of "I" implies the notion of "mine." I am "my property"—I am constituted by what separates me from "not I"—i.e., by what is mine "and not anybody's else."

As long as "I" assert the "I" dogmatically there is lacking a critical awareness that experiences the "I" dynamically in a continuum of cause and effect—a chain of economic or other causations and coordinated interrelationships.

Hence, the implicit alienation in Samkhya-prakriti exists but has no value except in relation to purusha. It is for purusha. (See Murti, *op. cit.*, pages 61ff.)

❈

November 5

The "mandala awareness" of space. For instance, this mountain, where a provisional Tibetan pattern of dwellings and relationships has been, very sketchily, set up. You get oriented by visiting various rimpoches, each one a reincarnation of a spiritual figure, each one seated in his shrinelike cell, among tankas, flowers, bowls, rugs, lamps, and images. Each rimpoche figures henceforth as one who "is seated" in a particular plane, near or far: the Khempo of Namgyal Tra-Tsang high up on the mountain with his little community. Ratod Rimpoche just up the hill, a quarter of a mile from here, near the official headquarters of the Dalai Lama's administration. The little tulku, who can hardly be imagined as sitting still for very long, higher up, just below the khempo. And the Dalai Lama himself in a sort of center, where he is certainly very "seated" and guarded and fenced in. Thus what was for me on Friday a rugged, nondescript mountain with a lot of miscellaneous dwellings, rocks, woods, farms, flocks, gulfs, falls, and heights, is now spiritually ordered by permanent seated presences, burning with a lamplike continuity and significance, centers of awareness and reminders of dharma. One instinctively sees the mountain as a mandala, slightly askew no doubt, with a central presence and surrounding presences more or less amiable. The rimpoches

Ratod Rimpoche

were all very amiable. The central presence is a fully awake, energetic, alert, nondusty, nondim, nonwhispering Buddha.

Shooting down in the valley: not firecrackers, army rifles. Maneuvers or shooting range. Mock warfare. Outside and below the mandala. I open the window for fresh sunlit air.

A second earthquake: one came about an hour ago—now this one. The first lasted several seconds, shaking the house more violently. This lasted a little longer, long enough for the "when will it stop?" anxiety to surface. But this was less violent. After the silence and rumbling, then the burst of voices, the outcry of birds, the barking of many dogs. And life resumes its quiet course once again. Nothing has fallen. At this moment the elections are perhaps ending, the polls closing in America.

Last night I dreamed that I was, temporarily, back at Gethsemani. I was dressed in a Buddhist monk's habit, but with more black and red and gold, a "Zen habit," in color more Tibetan than Zen. I was going to tell Brother Donald Kane,[19] the cook in the diet kitchen, that I would be there for supper. I met some women in the corridor, visitors and students of Asian religion, to whom I was explaining I was a kind of Zen monk and Gelugpa together, when I woke up. It was 6 A.M. Time to get up.

Other recent dreams, dimly remembered. Strange towns. Towns in the south of France. Working my way along the Riviera. How to get to the "next place"? I forget what the problem is, or if it is solved. Another: I'm in some town and have a small, silvery toy balloon, but it has a dangerous explosive gas in it. I throw it in the air and hope it will float completely away before anything happens. It rises too slowly, departs too slowly— but nothing happens. The dream changes.

❋

Two white butterflies alight on separate flowers. They rise, play together briefly, accidentally, in the air, then depart in different directions.

E. C. Dimock, Jr., on Vaishnava poetry:

Vaishnava (Bengali) poetry originated in the Vaishnava bhakti sects of the 16th and 17th centuries. For the most part they are love poems, of the love between the god Krishna and Radha,[20] most beautiful of the gopis, sung in kirtan ("praise") gatherings with drum and cymbals. But some are hymns to Chaitanya,[21] a 15th-century Bengali Vaishnava saint considered to be an incarnation of Krishna. Krishna has many aspects, but for the Vaishnavas, "Krishna was the lover and beloved, whose foremost characteristic is the giving and receiving of joy, who is approachable only by bhakti, by devotion and selfless dedication."

The sardaya, "the man of sensibility," who is aware of certain associations in Bengali, can appreciate in Vaishnava lyrics their interplay of the erotic and the mystical. The mood of the poems is called madhurya-bhava, a mood of identification in which poet or reader enters into the love-longing of Radha or another of the gopis. One of the formalities is the bhanita, or signature line, usually at the end of the poem, in which the poet identifies himself by name.

—See E. C. Dimock, Jr., and Denise Levertov, in the introduction to *In Praise of Krishna,* Garden City, N.Y., 1967, Anchor Books, pages xvii ff.

⌘

Here are some examples I like from the *In Praise of Krishna* anthology. The translations are by Professor Dimock in collaboration with the poet Denise Levertov.[22]

I would set fire to my house
for him. I would bear
The scorn of the world.

Radha at Krishna's feet. Calcutta bazaar painting, Kalighat school, c. *1830.*

Vrishka, wife of
Nigama Ghosha
(maternal uncle of Krishna)
Krishna fell in love with her.

Krushna

He thinks his sorrow is joy
When I weep, he weeps.

❃

When the sound of your flute reaches my ears
it compels me to leave my home, my friends,
it draws me into the dark towards you.

I no longer count the pain of coming here
Says Govinda-dasa.[23]

❃

His life cuts into my life
 as the stain of the moon's rabbit
 engraves the moon.

❃

Others have many loves, I have
Only you,
dearer to me than life.
You are the kohl on my eyes, the ornaments
on my body,
you, dark moon.

❃

as wing to bird,
water to fish,
life to the living—
so you to me.
But tell me
Madhava,[24] beloved,

who are you?
Who are you really?

Vidyapati[25] *says, they are one another.*[23]

✵

Cruel Kama[26] pierces me with his arrows:
the lightning flashes, the peacocks dance,
frogs and waterbirds, drunk with delight,
call incessantly—and my heart is heavy.
Darkness on earth,
the sky intermittently lit with a sullen glare . . .

Vidyapati says,[23]
How will you pass this night without your lord?

✵

Sankaracharya on brahman, the real samadhi, etc. (from *The Crest-Jewel of Discrimination*).

"The knowledge that we are Brahman is like a fire which altogether consumes the thick forest of ignorance. When a man has realized his oneness with Brahman, how can he harbor any seed of death and rebirth? . . .

"Thus the wise man discriminates between the real and the unreal. His unsealed vision perceives the Real. He knows his own Atman to be pure indivisible consciousness. He is set free from ignorance, misery and the power of distraction. He enters directly into peace. . . .

"Those who echo borrowed teachings are not free from the world. But those who have attained samadhi by merging the external universe, the sense-organs, the mind and the ego in the pure consciousness of the Atman—they alone are free from the world, with its bonds and snares. . . .

"If a man loves Brahman with an exclusive and steadfast devotion, he becomes Brahman. By thinking of nothing but the wasp, the cockroach is changed into a wasp."

—Sankaracharya, *op. cit.*, pages 105–8.

✳

November 6 / Second audience with the Dalai Lama

We drove up earlier, at 8:30, a bright, clear morning. More people and more trucks on the road: army trucks roaring around the corners, ambling buffaloes, students on their way to school, and the Jubilee Bus Company's silver dragons. At the entry to the Dalai Lama's residence there were pilgrims, maybe sadhakas, with marigolds on their hats or in their hair.

Most of the audience was taken up with a discussion of epistemology, then of samadhi. In other words, "the mind." A lot of it, at first, was rather scholastic, starting with sunyata and the empirical existence of things known—the practical empirical existence of things grounded in sunyata—enhanced rather than lessened in a way. I tried to bring in something about sila, freedom, grace, gift, but Tenzin Geshe had some difficulty translating what I meant. Then we discussed various theories of knowledge, Tibetan and Western-Thomist. There is a controversy among Tibetans as to whether in order to know something one must know the *word for it* as well as apprehend the concept.

We got back to the question of meditation and samadhi. I said it was important for monks in the world to be living examples of the freedom and transformation of consciousness which meditation can give. The Dalai Lama then talked about samadhi in the sense of controlled concentration.

He demonstrated the sitting position for meditation which he said was essential. In the Tibetan meditation posture the right hand (discipline) is above the left (wisdom). In Zen it is the other way round. Then we got on to "concentrating on the mind." Other objects of concentration may be an object, an image, a name. But how does one concentrate on the mind itself? There is division: the I who concentrates . . . the mind as object of concentration . . . observing the concentration . . . all three one mind. He was very existential, I think, about the mind as "what is concentrated on."

It was a very lively conversation and I think we all enjoyed it. He certainly seemed to. I like the solidity of the Dalai Lama's ideas. He is a very consecutive thinker and moves from step to step. His ideas of the interior life are built on very solid foundations and on a real awareness of practical problems. He insists on detachment, on an "unworldly life," yet sees it as a way to complete understanding of, and participation in, the problems of life and the world. But renunciation and detachment must come first. Evidently he misses the full monastic life and wishes he had more time to meditate and study himself. At the end he invited us back again Friday to talk about Western monasticism. "And meanwhile think more about the mind," he said as we left him.

⌘

T. R. V. Murti on Tantra:

"Tantra is the unique combination of mantra, ritual, worship and yoga on an absolutistic basis. It is both philosophy and religion, and aims at the transmutation of human personality, by Tantric practices suited to the spiritual temperament and needs of the individual, into the absolute . . . it is sunyata that provided the metaphysical basis for the rise of Tantra. With its phenomenalising aspect, karuna (corresponding to the Hindu conception of sat), the formless absolute (sunya) manifests itself as the concrete world. But the forms neither exhaust nor do they bring down the absolute. It is through these forms again that man ascends and finds his consummation with the universal principle."

—Murti, *op. cit.,* page 109.

With a clear and sensible exposition like the above I am left musing on St. Irenaeus,[27] St. Gregory of Nyssa,[28] the catechesis of St. Cyril of Jerusalem,[29] early Christian liturgy, baptism, and Eucharist as initiation into the Pascha Christi. . .[30] And, of course, the influence of the mystery religions is important here.

⌘

For Marco Pallis, the Buddha icon "touching the earth" means Buddha's reply to Mara,[31] who disputes his right to the "throne" of enlightenment. Sitting on the earth under the bodhi tree, Mara asserts that the earth is "his," as does Satan in the temptation of Christ. Buddha "touched the Earth, mother of all creatures, calling on her to witness that the throne was his by right and the Earth testified that this was so."

Imagine [the Buddha seated on] a lotus on the waters—"existence with its teeming possibilities." (Cf. the baptism of Christ in the liturgy of January 13.) Buddha overcomes samsara, "not by mere denial but by showing forth its true nature." The Buddha's right hand points downward to touch the earth; the other hand supports a begging bowl—symbolizing acceptance of the gift—grace. Pallis says, "In the two gestures displayed by the Buddha-image the whole programme of man's spiritual exigencies is summed up." An *active* attitude toward the world and a *passive* attitude toward heaven. The ignorant man does the opposite: he passively accepts the world and resists grace, gift, and heaven.

—Marco Pallis, "Is There Room for 'Grace' in Buddhism?" in *Studies in Comparative Religion,* August 1968, Pates Manor, Bedfont, Middlesex, England.

⌘

Marco Pallis on grace in Buddhism:

"The word grace corresponds to a whole dimension of spiritual experience; it is unthinkable that this should be absent from one of the great religions of the world."

"The function of grace . . . to condition man's homecoming to the center from start to finish. It is the very attraction of the center itself . . . which provides the incentive to start on the Way and the energy to face and overcome its many and various obstacles. Likewise grace is the welcoming hand into the center when man finds himself at long last on the brink of the great divide where all familiar human landmarks have disappeared."

—Pallis, *op. cit.*, page 5.

✠

Murti on Madhyamika:

Madhyamika does not oppose one thesis with another. It seeks the flaw both in thesis and in antithesis. It investigates the beginningless illusion that holds "views" to be true in so far as they appeal to us and when they appeal to us we argue that they are not "views" but absolute truth. All views are rejected for this reason. "The Madhyamika dialectic, unlike the Hegelian, is purely analytic in character. Criticism is Sunyata—the utter negation of thought as revelatory of the real."

"The death of thought is the birth of Prajna, knowledge devoid of distinction," i.e., intuition of the unconditioned. Absolute reality is not set over against empirical reality. The empirical, liberated from conventional thought forms is identical with the absolute. "Transcendent to thought, the absolute is thoroughly immanent in experience." This is Madhyamika.

Madhyamika is critical of thought, open to experience. It accepts the phenomenalization of the absolute and knows this as twofold.

1) Avidya: through ignorance and defilements.

2) Prajna: "the free conscious assumption of phenomenal forms activated by prajna and karuna."

"The former is the unconscious activity of the ignorant,

and the latter is that of the Enlightened Buddhas and Bodhi-sattvas."

Hence, not escape from the world into idealism, but the transformation of consciousness by a detached and compassionate acceptance of the empirical world in its interrelatedness. *To be part of this interrelatedness.*

—See Murti, op. cit., pages 140–43.

✠

After reading Murti on Madhyamika, a reflection on the unconscious content and inner contradiction of my own drama. There I was riding through Lower Dharamsala, up the mountain, through McLeod Ganj, in the Dalai Lama's jeep, wearing a snow-white Cistercian robe and black scapular. Smiles of all the Tibetans recognizing the jeep. Namaste gestures (palms raised together before the nose), stares of Indians. Am I part of it? Trying to fit into an interrelation, but on my own terms? Trying to find a dogmatic solution to this contradiction? Learning to accept the contradiction? One must, provisionally at least, experience all roles as slightly strange, ridiculous, contrived. Wearing my monastic habit because Marco Pallis strongly urged me to—and it is right, I guess, thoroughly expected. Yet recognizing that it is at odds with my own policy of *not* appearing as a monk, a priest, a cleric, in "the world." The role of "tourist" is less offensive. However, I have the feeling that everybody here knows all about everything and that as an "American lama" I am a joyful and acceptable portent to all the Tibetans. Smiles everywhere. Every Tibetan lights up, even when I am in no jeep, no habit, and only in corduroy pants and turtleneck jersey.

A drum in the village, with an erratic beat; and before, shrill, enthusiastic brass getting nowhere. Cries of children nearer the house. Light of setting sun on the brown mountainside. A long, quiet meditation.

Sankaracharya on the atman, brahman, and maya (from *The Crest-Jewel of Discrimination*).

"Hold fast to the truth that you are the Atman. Give up identifying yourself with the ego, or any of the coverings. Remain completely indifferent to them, as though they were broken jars of clay. . . .

"This entire universe of which we speak and think is nothing but Brahman. Brahman dwells beyond the range of Maya. There is nothing else. Are jars, pots and vessels distinct from the clay of which they are made? Man drinks the wine of Maya, becomes deluded and begins to see things as separate from each other, so that he talks of 'you' and 'I.' "

—Sankaracharya, *op. cit.*, pages 112–14.

❀

November 7

The contemplative life must provide an area, a space of liberty, of silence, in which possibilities are allowed to surface and new choices—beyond routine choice—become manifest. It should create a new experience of time, not as stopgap, stillness, but as "temps vierge"[32]—not a blank to be filled or an untouched space to be conquered and violated, but a space which can enjoy its own potentialities and hopes—and its own presence to itself. One's *own* time. But not dominated by one's own ego and its demands. Hence open to others—*compassionate* time, rooted in the sense of common illusion and in criticism of it.

❀

Marcuse[33] has shown how mass culture tends to be anticulture —to stifle creative work by the sheer volume of what is "produced," or reproduced. In which case, poetry, for example, must start with an awareness of this contradiction and *use* it—as antipoetry[34]—which freely draws on the material of superabundant nonsense at its disposal. One no longer has to parody, it is enough to quote—and feed back quotations into the mass consumption of pseudoculture.

The static created by the feedback of arguments or of cultural declarations—or of "art" into their own system—is enough to show the inner contradictions of the system. So Madhyamika shows the opponent the absurdity of his position "on principles and arguments accepted by him." However, when his supposed values are returned to him in irony, as static, he will not accept the implications. That is *his* problem.

❈

Madhyamika does not propound "another truth." It is content to reduce "the opponent's position to absurdity on principles and consequences which the opponent himself would accept." If he does not in fact accept them in this form the logic of his position demands their acceptance. But then, argument is at an end. The purpose of Madhyamika is not to convince, but to explode the argument itself. Is this sadism? No, it is compassion! It exorcises the devil of dogmatism.

—See Murti, *op. cit.,* pages 145–46.

Quoting from the *Kasyapaparivarta,* Murti points out that "Sunyata is the antidote for all dogmatic views, but him I call the incurable who takes sunyata itself as a theory."

—Murti, *op. cit.,* page 164.

❈

I asked Sonam Kazi about Marxism and monasticism, in view of my Bangkok talk. He said that as long as one is not attached to wealth and power, Communism can do him no harm. Sonam Kazi has often been the official interpreter in important meetings for the Dalai Lama, for instance at a dinner with Nehru and Chou En-lai. He probably knows as much as any one person about the whole Tibetan question, and he is by no means a reactionary about it. He has a definitely broad view, realizes to what extent the Tibetan landlords and abbots were wrong or shortsighted, and discounts stories about the Chinese poisoning lamas at banquets and so on. He was in Tibet in 1957 and spoke to various abbots of the big monasteries, asking what they expected to do. They had no idea, although the Chinese Communists were by that time right on their doorstep. The monasteries were too big and too rich. And too many monks who did not belong there, were intent on holding onto their property until it was taken from them by force. The 13th Dalai Lama had foreseen this many years before and warned them but his warning was not understood.

⌗

I had a fine visit with Chobgye Thicchen Rimpoche, a lama, mystic, and poet of the Sakyapa school, one of the best so far. Sonam says Chobgye Thicchen is very advanced in Tantrism and a great mystic. He even knows how to impart the technique of severing one's soul from the body. He taught this to another lama who was later captured by Communists. The lama, when he was being led off to prison camp, simply severed soul from body—pfft!—and that was the end of it. Liberation!

We talked first about samadhi, beginning with concentration on an object, then going beyond that to meditation without object and without concept. I asked a lot of questions about bodhicitta, Maitreya[35] and karunā. Bodhicitta, Thicchen said, is the most fundamental of these three concepts, which all cen-

Bronze of Maitreya (bodhisattva, the Buddha of the future), 19th century

ter on love and compassion. He spoke of three kinds of bodhi-citta: 1) "kingly"—in which one seeks spiritual power to save oneself and then save others; 2) "that of boatman"—in which one ferries oneself together with others to salvation; 3) "that of shepherd"—in which one goes behind all the others and enters salvation last—and this is the most perfect.

Chobgye Thicchen quoted something from the founder of the Sakyapa school that went more or less like this:

> If you are attached to worldly things you are not a religious man.
> If you are attached to appearances you cannot meditate.

If you are attached to your own soul you cannot have bodhicitta.

If you are attached to doctrines you cannot reach the highest attainment.

He asked me to give an outline of Christian meditation and mysticism, which I did. He seemed very pleased and wrote a poem for me, and I wrote one for him. He also spoke of the need for good interpreters, Sonam Kazi being the best. He told of his experiences with a Polish lady he was instructing: with a good interpreter they went on famously; with a bad one she ended up asking things like, "How many little bowls of water are up there?" and he pointed to the shelf with his water offerings.

On the way down we met the Gadong oracle,[36] an old lama, and a former member of the Tibetan cabinet, an old man with a big brown beard, who had also formed part of a delegation that went to look for and identify the present Dalai Lama as a child.

The Dalai Lama's proper name is Gejong Tenzin Gyatsho.

⌘

Sonam and I were looking at the stars. He said for Tibetans the Dolphin and Eagle go together as "the sling."

⌘

"Know the sufferings although there is nothing to know; relinquish the causes of misery although there is nothing to relinquish; be earnest in cessation although there is nothing to cease; practise the means of cessation though there is nothing to practise."

—The Buddha, as quoted in the Dalai Lama's pamphlet, *An Introduction to Buddhism,* New Delhi, Tibet House, 1965, page 8.

Poem in Tibetan by Chobgye Thiccen Rimpoche

A free translation by Sonam Kazi of the poem by Chobgye Thiccen Rimpoche dedicated to Thomas Merton during his visit in Dharamsala

The flower endeavoring
Of excess good will
Regards him the Sunshine
Making command of many learned.

To that beautiful one
Adored by all the Occident,
This bee wishes all the best
With its heartfelt delight.

⌘

"People who make no mental effort, even if they remain in mountain retreats, are like animals hibernating in their holes, only accumulating causes for a descent into hell."

—Tibetan saying quoted by the Dalai Lama, *op. cit.*, page 15–16.

⌘

"Let us embrace the day which assigns each of us to his dwelling, which on our being rescued from here, and released from the snares of the world, restores us to paradise and the kingdom of heaven. . ."[37]

—St. Cyprian, *De Mortalitate,* Reading V, Second Nocturne, Octave of All Saints (November 8, Autumn Breviary).

⌘

I have to pack early. My last interview with the Dalai Lama will be in the morning, with the jeep coming for me at 8:15. Then right after dinner we leave by jeep for Pathankot to take the evening train for Delhi.

The sky is reddening behind the big spur of mountains to the east. The days here have been good ones. Plenty of time for reading and meditation, and some extraordinary encounters. So far my talks with Buddhists have been open and frank and there has been full communication on a really deep level. We seem to recognize in one another a certain depth of spiritual experience, and it is unquestionable. On this level I find in the Buddhists a deeper attainment and certitude than in Catholic contemplatives. On the other hand, in Catholics, such as the nuns of Loretto Motherhouse[38] and a fortiori the Redwoods, the *desire* is deep and genuine and so too is a certain attainment, even though it is much less articulate.

⌘

Nixon of course has won the presidential election. But Humphrey was closer than I expected. Wallace was nowhere, and I am glad to hear he did *not* take Kentucky (Nixon did). Our new president is depressing. What can one expect of him?

⌘

November 8

My third interview with the Dalai Lama was in some ways the best. He asked a lot of questions about Western monastic life, particularly the vows, the rule of silence, the ascetic way, etc. But what concerned him most was:

1) Did the "vows" have any connection with a spiritual transmission or initiation?

2) Having made vows, did the monks continue to progress along a spiritual way, toward an eventual illumination, and what were the degrees of that progress? And supposing a monk died without having attained to perfect illumination? What ascetic methods were used to help purify the mind of passions?

He was interested in the "mystical life," rather than in external observance.

And some incidental questions: What were the motives for the monks not eating meat? Did they drink alcoholic beverages? Did they have movies? And so on.

I asked him about the question of Marxism and monasticism, which is to be the topic of my Bangkok lecture. He said that from a certain point of view it was impossible for monks and Communists to get along, but that perhaps it should not be entirely impossible *if* Marxism meant *only* the establishment of an equitable economic and social structure. Also there was perhaps some truth in Marx's critique of religion in view of the fact that religious leaders had so consistently been hand in glove with secular power. Still, on the other hand, militant atheism did in fact strive to suppress all forms of religion, good or bad.

Finally, we got into a rather technical discussion of mind, whether as consciousness, prajna or dhyana, and the relation of prajna to sunyata. In the abstract, prajna and sunyata can be considered from a dialectic viewpoint, but not when prajna is seen as realization. The greatest error is to become attached to sunyata as if it were an object, an "absolute truth."

It was a very warm and cordial discussion and at the end I felt we had become very good friends and were somehow quite close to one another. I feel a great respect and fondness for him as a person and believe, too, that there is a real spiritual bond between us. He remarked that I was a "Catholic geshe," which, Harold said, was the highest possible praise from a Gelugpa, like an honorary doctorate![39]

✠

November 11 / Calcutta

Before coming to Calcutta, I spent the week end in Delhi, arriving there before dawn from Pathankot. The afternoon before, a good jeep ride through the Kangra Valley[40] to Pathankot. The mountains were covered with a pile of high clouds, blue under them. Trees. A river. Nurpur and a Mogul castle.[41] Winding roads. Shady villages. Many buses. Flocks of sheep and goats.

In Delhi there were empty streets for the taxi. Wide avenues. Here and there campfires. People living in tents in front of government buildings.

I went to the Imperial Hotel, older, less expensive, and quieter than the Ashoka. A bath and tea and the newspaper; there are student riots in Benares,[42] Rawalpindi,[43] Amritsar,[44] and a dozen other places.

The first thing I did after tea was to go to the 18th-century observatory, Jantar Mantar,[45] with its endless abstract shapes and patterns. In a few minutes I had run out of film. In the afternoon, after too expensive a dinner at the Oberoi Intercontinental, which is shiny and American and depresses me, I drove out into the country with the Lhalungpas to see the Cambodian monk at the Ashoka Vihara. The temple there is an old mosque, small and tranquil. We sat on the floor and talked. The monk spoke of his visit to the U.S., where he had been impressed with Hollywood movies and the RCA building in New York. Then came out again into the sunlight, marigolds, garden, dog, dust, gate, road. Qutb Minar, the tall Moslem tower, rose nearby out of trees and half-ruined domes. The Moslem aspect of Delhi is arresting—but the tombs perplex one. Except the tomb of Sufi Nizamuddin[46]—and the other burial places of poets around it, where poems are sung on the proper anniversary in September. I would have liked to wander quietly among them.

We heard some Urdu singing in the evening at the Moti Mahal Restaurant. We were tearing red chickens with teeth and fingers to the sound of drums and accordion and the civilized gestures, dialogue, complaints, and witticisms of the singers. The singing was accomplished, intelligent, sophisticated, and very human. It belonged to a better civilization; contrast that with the rock music in the Laguna where we stopped first on the way, and the live Muzak at the Oberoi Intercontinental—ap-

palling! The place quickly became crowded. We had to leave so that others could get to the table. Then a wild taxi ride—the Sikh driver nearly killed three people and then got lost, couldn't find our hotel. We found it for him.

⌘

Sunday morning Lobsang Lhalungpa and Deki came and we drove out to a Moslem college, meeting the principal, et al. It seemed to be an alert and sound place. The principal spoke of the Islamic Institute at McGill and other places where he had studied.

There were snake charmers outside the Moslem college, but they had disappeared by the time we left.

After the visit to the Moslem college I said Mass in Holy Family Hospital, not in the chapel, as I at first expected, but in the room of James George, the Canadian High Commissioner, who had had a minor operation the day before. He sat cross-legged on the bed with his wife, their son and daughter on either side. Also there were the Lhalungpas, Kunga, the companion of Trungpa Rimpoche, who is staying at the High Commissioner's, and Harold Talbott, who served the Mass. Afterward we went to the Georges' and had lunch in their garden. Trungpa Rimpoche was there; he is hoping to meet the Karmapa Lama in Delhi.

Sunday morning I finished the notes for my Bangkok talk and sent them off and wrote to Fr. Flavian, asking if I might return through Europe. The cost of many stamps is breaking me! I had borrowed a typewriter from Commissioner George, and today Mrs. George and her son drove us at 5 to the Palam airport in the dark—and there drank coffee, asking questions about reincarnation.

Yesterday I also decided to write a newsletter, mostly about the Dalai Lama, Dharamsala, and all that. I sent it to Brother Patrick for mimeographing.[47] Also sent my films to John Howard Griffin[48] for processing, including a roll on Jantar Mantar—a fascinating place!

Jantar Mantar observatory in Delhi

SONGS OF EXPERIENCE; INDIA, ONE
Poem and Prayer to Golden Expensive Mother Oberoi[49]

O thou Mother Oberoi
Crosseyed goddess of death
Showing your blue tongue
Dancing upon Shiva or someone
With sharks in front gas—
Tanks empty the ambassadors
Coming tonight they
Shine you up
You Intercon—
Tinental Mam—
Moth Mother Kali Con—
Crete Oberoi not yet
Stained with the greygreen
Aftermoss of the monsoons
And a big clean pool
(Shacks out front and kids
In the red flowers and
Goats) a big clean pool I say
With one American
General Motors type
Doing a slow breast—
Stroke in the chlorinated
Indigo water where no
Slate-blue buffalo has ever
Got wet
O thou merciful naked
Jumping millionaire
Rich in skeletons and buffets
You have taken
All our money away
Wearing a precious collar
Of men's heads
(Those blacks love you at night

In a trance of drums
Sitting with red headlights
Between their eyebrows)
With shacks out front
When kids are playing
With dusty asses
In scarlet flowers
While on your immaculate
Carpets all the am–
Bassadors from General Electric
Slowly chase their bluehaired wives
In high-heeled sneakers.

⌘

November 12

Returning to Calcutta, I have a completely new impression: greater respect for this vast, crumby city. There is a kind of nobility in its sordidness: the sheer *quantity* of everything. And in some ways the absence of all that the rich world regards as quality, except in the banks, the Governor's mansion, and the high prices in the Oberoi Grand. First, as we came in from the airport, I saw how many ponds there are along the roads, among the fields, and new, but already shabby, apartments. How many purple flowers in the ponds. How many lotuses. How many long brick walls painted with Communist slogans in Bengali, with powerful decorative effect. And again, all the cows and slate-blue buffaloes, twice as many as in Delhi. Then as we got into town, the sidewalk markets, the rickshaws, the fantastic and dowdy buildings, the tattered posters advertising Bengali movies. On Maniktala Main Road I saw no sign of Bramachari's Ashram,[50] which I am told has moved—no one seems to know where—and I can't find out.

Further and further into town. Buildings. Crowds. Rags. Dirt, laughter, torpor, movement. Calcutta is overwhelming:

the elemental city, with no room left for masks. Only the naked truth of overpopulation, underemployment, hunger, disease, a mixture of great vitality and permanent exhaustion—but an exhaustion in which the vitality renews itself. How does it happen that the skinny men in bare feet trotting with rickshaws don't all drop dead? And maybe many do!

Before, when I was here first, I was too shocked; the trauma made me see the city as a big blur. Now I see detail, contrast, the infinite variety of light and shade. All the colors—though they are drab and obscure, they are colors. This is one of the greatest cities in the world, with a character completely its own, full of contrasts and yet *beyond* contrast. The vast noise of Calcutta seems somehow to be also a silence. There was a spectacular robbery on Sudder Street three weeks ago and it is a city of crime; somehow the crime gets lost in the sheer massive poverty and exhaustion—the innocence of despair. The place gives no impression of wickedness. For the masses of Calcutta, you dimly begin to think, there is no judgment. Only their misery. And instead of being judged, they are a judgment on the rest of the world. Yet curiously nonprophetic . . . nonaccusatory. Passive. Not exactly resentful. Not yet. . .

How long before it explodes? What will the explosion mean?

One imagines an enormous, elemental, thoughtless, confused violence like that of a sweeping storm of rain after a sultry summer day. Will it cleanse anything? Clear the air? Will the city simply go on stifling in its own steam? It breathes, sprawls, broods, sweats, moves, lies down, and gets up again.

⌘

"Exemploque pari furit omnis turba, suoque
Marte cadunt subiti per mutua vulnera fratres"[51]

—Ovid: *Metamorphoses* III, 122–23, quoted by Edward Conze: *Buddhist Thought in India*, London, Allen & Unwin, 1962; Ann Arbor

Paperback, 1967, page 9. See also page 283 in Part Two of this volume, "Complementary Reading," for a further passage quoted from Conze.

Conze deplores the "dragon's brood," . . . the alphabet seed . . . the armed machinery rising out of the earth. It disturbs his meditation. I argue with Harold Talbott that the world is crazy, but he thinks this an extreme opinion.

⌘

November 12 / Darjeeling

This is a much finer place than I expected—a king of places, full of Tibetans, prayer flags, high in mists, wonderful mountains, all hidden as we came up the wretched road along which there have been some seventy very bad landslides. We were held up an hour in Kurseong waiting for the worst stretch to open up again.

But from the plane which we took from Calcutta to Bagdogra, all the high mountains were visible above the clouds: Kanchenjunga nearest, and Everest several hundred miles away, tall with a black side, a stately mountain. And the lovely pointed one next to it. Directly below, it might have been Indiana as well as India. But we went over the Ganges. The ride from Bagdogra was long, through thick woods, then higher and higher into the clouds. Finally we came to the Windamere Hotel, the most pleasant place I have been to in India. We arrived, up a long flight of steps, out of breath, in the dark. Had tea. It is cold.

In the plane I read a good article on Michel Foucault[52]— or fairly good, I did not agree with all the judgments—in *Encounter* and also began one by Raymond Aron[53] on de Gaulle and the Jews. In the morning, before the flight, I had several hours to read in the Oberoi Grand—and then was glad to get out of it!

There was a white-robed, bearded, European Jesuit in the pharmacy at Kurseong. I said nothing. Bought some apple juice. Then some beer further up the road in a clean little Tibetan-run liquor store. I will probably go down again to the scholasticate at Kurseong, but much later. And to St. Joseph's College here also.

✻

November 13 / Darjeeling

The "Windermere"[54] is really named Windamere. And since "the disaster" the town has been short of electric power, so last night in the middle of dinner all the lights went out and we groped our way to the sitting room where there was firelight, then candlelight, then the too bright light of a Coleman lantern. The Windamere is too cenobitic. Everyone gets together and talks, or participates in a kind of common gathering, as do the three silent Englishmen who just drink beer and listen. A German family from East Pakistan are, I guess, the nicest. They have two pretty little children. Then there are the two girls from N'Orleans, one who works for a travel agency and the other for an airline, so they planned themselves a trip which included a stay on a houseboat in Kashmir and of course all the temples of Katmandu. They had shared the same ride with us up the mountain from Bagdogra, which took four hours with the delay at Kurseong.

Will we be able to get into Sikkim? I don't know. There was talk of this last night. The Sikh army major assured us the only way was to drive three hours to Siliguri and then ten hours roundabout to Gangtok.[55] Another said there was a footbridge nearby and if a jeep would meet us at the other side. . . Harold has failed to contact Gangtok by phone and has sent a telegram.

I remained in bed until dawn rather than light a candle. No use trying to read by candlelight, and as I have a slight cold I thought I'd stay under the good blankets. As soon as it was a little light outside the window I got into my clothes and went out, up the hill to the temple on top with all its prayer flags and incense. The children meanwhile were chanting down at the Tibetan school—joyous, lusty chanting that fitted in with the mountains. And there was Kanchenjunga, dim in the dawn and in haze, not colored by the sun but dovelike in its bluegray—a lovely sight but hard to photograph. I went back after breakfast when the light was better. The view of this mountain is incomparable. I need to go back for more.

Seeing the Loreto College next to the hotel, I went to inquire about saying Mass. Mother Damian nearly swooned, then pulled herself together and sent me down to the Loreto Convent. There is no chapel at the college, it's a government school. I said Mass in the big, 19th-century English-type convent-school chapel: a few nuns on one side, a few little girls in uniform, hastily rounded up, on the other. It was about 10:15. Then coffee and talk with the sisters, who are mostly old, all in the regular habit. No experimenting with other clothes here! Two daughters of the Queen of Bhutan are in the convent school here and one of them has information about an interesting back-scratching fire demon that is in Bhutan. I have not met any of the students yet. I'm waiting to hear from the people at the Tibetan Center.

⌘

November 14

A friend took us to the Tibetan Refugee Center today and it seemed, relatively, a happy and busy place. This afternoon, Jimpa,[56] a Tibetan monk who is teaching with the Jesuits, will come to talk about interpreting. Fr. Sherburne,[57] also.

⌘

"The self is not different from the states nor identical with them; there is no self without the states nor is it to be considered nonexistent."

—Nagarjuna, (Cf. Conze, *op. cit.*, page 241; S. B. Dasgupta, *An Introduction to Tantric Buddhism*, pages 14–19; Murti, *op. cit.*, page 137.)

✳

CONVERSATIONS

Madam my action
Thankyo.

I am your Enrico
Don' you remembram?
Thankyo!

Madam it is my turn

(M-m-u-m-rico.)

I am your Traum

Thankyo.

Madam Mein Traum
Ready in a moment.

Thankyo
You are my lifetime Pigeon
I am your dream of flight

Madam: my action
Thankyo
(Sent from Enrico)
Interception by T. Muttons)

A little to one side
(Be my traum)

M-m-m-a-m.
Should we wait?

I am your Enro.

Do you forgat? Is Muttons?

A little to one side

"Not too diplomatic!"

A little to one side
(M'action!)

(To stop is a better mistake.)

"Reflective consciousness is necessarily the consciousness of the false."

"The essence of the Madhyamika attitude . . . consists in not allowing oneself to be entangled in views and theories, but just to observe the nature of things without standpoints."

—Murti, *op. cit.*, page 213.

In Madhyamika, dialectical critique does not clear the way for something else such as Kant's Practical Reason,[58] or the guarantee of God by faith. It is at once freedom and tathata—realization—not of God, in God. Negation and realization become one in the liberation from conceptual "answers about."

—See Murti, *op. cit.*, page 213.

"The Madhyamika method is to deconceptualize the mind and to disburden it of all notions, empirical as well as a priori. The dialectic is not an avenue for the acquisition of information, but a catharsis; it is primarily a path of purification of the intellect."

"It is the abolition of all restrictions which conceptual patterns necessarily impose. It is not nihilism, which is itself a standpoint asserting that nothing is. The dialectic is rejection of all views including the nihilistic."

—Murti, *op. cit.*, page 112.

✠

Our friend's jeep has pleasantly flowered covers over the seat cushions. She met us at the Loreto Convent, out in the sun on the wide terrace after Mass in the cold church. Nuns in black veils and some with shawls and mittens. A diamond jubilarian who sweetly complained that she "couldn't contemplate"; she put her head in the sacristy door to tell me this before Mass. I said Mass in the spacious sanctuary, served by a middle-aged Nepalese called Peter. There were faint answers to the prayers from a few nuns and Indian women. I did not preach. After Mass, breakfast was plentiful. I was surrounded by nuns plying me with questions: Have the Trappists changed their rules? Their Office? Do they have recreation now? Do they have games? Do they speak? Five little girls filed in to look at me to reassure themselves that I could speak. I said I was still able to speak.

Before Mass, I had leafed through a book on Grenoble[59] and the Alps of Dauphiné in the convent parlor—curious to remember how I wanted to go there as a child. Nice mountains but a dull little city. The same points of interest, including the curious "ciborium" in the cathedral which I could never understand. Pictures of the Grande Chartreuse.[60] That place is still able to stir me! La Salette,[61] an ugly church. Maybe after all I shall go there: if I go to those Alps at all it will be because of La Salette.

Tibetan students who waylay you on the road above the Tibetan school and ask your address, inviting you to become their pen pal. I assure them I have more than enough pen pals already. Lusty chanting in the school after dawn when Kanchenjunga is full of light. I walked and said Lauds[62] under the cryptomeria trees on Observatory Hill, and the chanting came up strong and clear from below. A man was doing vigorous exercises by the shelter that overlooks the valley. He had a mean white dog that pissed and scratched in the marigolds and then came over to me with the kind of electric tension and barely audible growl that a dog has when he is not afraid to bite. I continued my promenade in the direction of the hotel. The man was shimmying in the sun.

At the Tibetan Refugee Center there was a young nun with shaved head and a sweet smile who, I learned, went to work in the local carpet factory. She posed for a picture with three others who looked like old men. Also polite, bedraggled monks, in lay clothes, marked with all the signs of a hard frustrated life, working in a carpet factory. One is the dyemaker. He showed me his kettle for boiling green leaves and the weed he used.

Tibetan child, Darjeeling

Little kids in the crèche, some sweetly smiling and making the "namaste" gesture, others crying loudly. Babies hundled up in cribs, one silently lying with its arms in the shape of a cross, staring at the ceiling. In the distance a long line of little children went walking away in the warm sun, guided by teachers.

Women singing at work in the carpet factory. Spinners. Weavers. Dye mixers. In other shops: leatherworkers, carpenters, woodworkers, cooks. One cook was proudly stirring a stew of curry and potatoes in a huge black kettle. I bought a heavy, woolly, shaggy coat, something to wear while reading in the cold hotel. I have it on now. It is good and warm.

In the afternoon I visited with Fr. Stanford[63] at St. Joseph's School in North Point. Noise, kids, tea, wide grassless playgrounds, gardens, hyper-Gothic buildings, a big Victorian courtyard, crests, blazers, scarves, and all sorts of exhortations (sursum corda)[64] to "the boys." Some were neat wide-eyed little kids, including a shy one from Bhutan, the only one I spoke to, and others with mod hairdos and perfect swaggers. Some of them looked like little bastards. Very much the Jesuit School! We got out as fast as we could. A Canadian brother drove me back in a jeep through the cold town, the jeep loaded with students hitchhiking in to the movies.

※

November 15

It is the Feast of the Dedication of the Church of Gethsemani. I said Lauds of the feast on the side of Observatory Hill again, with the Tibetan kids chanting. And men came by, Tibetans, chanting softly to themselves. And a woman with a prayer wheel and a sweet little chant of her own. And an Indian jogging. And an old beggarwoman with no face left, one eye to see with, nose and mouth burned away, chanting, too, her tongue moving inside the hole in the scar tissue that served her for a mouth.

※

Conze comments on the fact that communication between East and West has not so far done much for philosophy. "So far European and particularly British philosophers have reacted by becoming more provincial than ever before."[65]

—Conze: *op. cit.,* page 9.

※

". . . the Madhyamika does not deny the real; he only denies *doctrines* about the real. For him, the real as transcendent to thought can be reached only by the denial of the determinations which systems of philosophy ascribe to it. . . . His denial of the *views* of the real is not denial of the real, and he makes the denial of views—the dialectic itself—the means for realising the real."

—Murti, *op. cit.,* page 218.

⌘

Drove with Fr. Vincent Curmi[66] to the Mim Tea Estate—a marvelous drive. It is one of the places I had heard of indirectly long before coming to India because Gene Smith had spent some time in the little Tibetan gompa near there and the gompa to some extent is supported by the Tea Estate. I hope to make a little retreat at Mim at the beginning of next week, there is a guest cottage there. The drive was marvelous. Past Ghoom, and doubling back into the mountains, one goes down for several miles through jungle and cryptomeria trees on a very steep slope and finally comes out on the plantation, clinging to the slope, with a magnificent view of Kanchenjunga—and of the hills gutted by landslides across the valley. Down in the bottom there is a place where a village was entirely destroyed. A thousand feet below Mim Tea Estate, a man in the valley shot a leopard. Why? Who was it harming? Goats perhaps. Or was it just going to lower and warmer places?

After we had some tea and saw the tea factory (good smell!) we climbed back into the hills to the gompa. A narrow path led among some cottages, then up into the trees and over to another spur. A very small, very poor little building, in a good spot, with a rusty corrugated iron roof. I don't know how they get thirty people into it, except that they are mostly kids. Drugpa Thugsey Rimpoche, the abbot, who was recommended to me by Sonam Kazi, was absent. The others spoke Nepali but did not have much to say. Most of the monks, kids, and students, are Nepalese. I went into the oratory which is dark and poor and not very heavily ornamented. But one got a sense of reality and spiritual power in there. We stopped briefly for tea in the rimpoche's cell. It was very poor, with none of the usual decorations, only a picture of Nehru, an old calendar, etc. Again, a sense that something very real went on here, in spite of the poverty and squalor. There are people who come all the way from France to consult this rimpoche, including doctors.

⌘

November 16

We started out early on a cold morning, about 7:45, in our friend's jeep with Jimpa Rimpoche and a big picturesque Tibetan type as guide to find other rimpoches. Also, Fr. Sherburne and Harold Talbott. I was feeling the cold as we hurried up the road toward Ghoom. I've had a bad throat; it seems to be aggravated by the coal smoke that fills the air. We went looking first for Chatral Rimpoche at his hermitage above Ghoom. Two

Thomas Merton with Chatral Rimpoche

chortens, a small temple, some huts. In the temple there is a statue of Padma Sambhava which is decorated with Deki Lhalungpa's jewels. But I did not see it. Chatral Rimpoche was not there. We were told he was at an ani gompa, a nunnery, down the road, supervising the painting of a fresco in the oratory. So off we went toward Bagdogra and with some difficulty found the tiny nunnery—two or three cottages just down behind the parapet off the road—and there was Chatral, the greatest rimpoche I have met so far and a very impressive person.

Chatral looked like a vigorous old peasant in a Bhutanese jacket tied at the neck with thongs and a red woolen cap on his head. He had a week's growth of beard, bright eyes, a strong voice, and was very articulate, much more communicative than I expected. We had a fine talk and all through it Jimpa, the interpreter, laughed and said several times, "These are hermit questions . . . this is another hermit question." We started talking about dzogchen and Nyingmapa meditation and "direct realization" and soon saw that we agreed very well. We must have talked for two hours or more, covering all sorts of ground, mostly around about the idea of dzogchen, but also taking in some points of Christian doctrine compared with Buddhist: dharmakaya . . . the Risen Christ, suffering, compassion for all creatures, motives for "helping others,"—but all leading back to dzogchen, the ultimate emptiness, the unity of sunyata and karuna, going "beyond the dharmakaya" and "beyond God" to the ultimate perfect emptiness. He said he had meditated in solitude for thirty years or more and had not attained to perfect emptiness and I said I hadn't either.

The unspoken or half-spoken message of the talk was our complete understanding of each other as people who were somehow *on the edge* of great realization and knew it and were trying, somehow or other, to go out and get lost in it—and that it was a grace for us to meet one another. I wish I could see more of Chatral. He burst out and called me a rangjung Sangay (which apparently means a "natural Buddha") and said he had

been named a Sangay dorje.[67] He wrote "rangjung Sangay" for
me in Tibetan and said that when I entered the "great kingdom" and "the palace" then America and all that was in it
would seem like nothing. He told me, seriously, that perhaps
he and I would attain to complete Buddhahood in our next
lives, perhaps even in this life, and the parting note was a kind
of compact that we would both do our best to make it in *this*
life. I was profoundly moved, because he is so obviously a great
man, the true practitioner of dzogchen, the best of the Nyingmapa lamas, marked by complete simplicity and freedom. He
was surprised at getting on so well with a Christian and at one
point laughed and said, "There must be something wrong
here!" If I were going to settle down with a Tibetan guru, I
think Chatral would be the one I'd choose. But I don't know
yet if that is what I'll be able to do—or whether I need to.

Tibetan writing, with transliteration, by Chatral Rimpoche

After that we drove on down to the Sakyapa monastery on
the hillside right by the village of Ghoom. It has a nice, fresh
painted temple. Monks were vigorously chopping wood on the
terrace outside, under the flapping prayer flag, and we sat inside
with the rimpoche whose name I forget—he is a friend of
Jimpa's—a very Chinese-looking man with a long wispy beard.
We talked a bit, though somewhat evasively, of mantras and
mudras, and I told him about LSD. At this he said that realization had to come from discipline and not from pills. (He hadn't

Another rimpoche

heard of psychedelic drugs.) Then we talked of meditation. Once again there was the usual reaction of pleased surprise at learning that meditation existed in the West, and he said, "You in the West have great potentiality for creation, but also for destruction." He gave us all scarves, photos were taken, and we visited the temple, which is quite beautiful inside.

When I got back to Darjeeling I had a very sore throat, so I sat in the sun on the hotel terrace most of the afternoon reading Murti. Then said Office in my room, as the chill of evening crept up the mountain. In the dusk I went out to get some throat lozenges and an inhaler and some brandy, which I have not yet opened. I kept waking up all night but the cold broke and this morning I felt better. I was plied with good American medicines by the Jesuits and their pills seemed fairly effective!

November 17

On being tired of Kanchenjunga. On the mountain being merci-
fully hidden by clouds. On sneaking a look at the mountain anyway before Mass. I walked the length of St. Joseph's College to
sneak a look at the mountain, then turned away back to church.
It was a long Mass, a concelebration with Fr. Curmi, an hour
and ten minutes in Nepali, which meant of course that I just
mumbled along in English during the Canon. But there was
good singing—Nepalese music with drums and small bell-like
cymbals. The women sitting on the pews in front were recollected and devout; the men were at the back. It was very moving. We went afterward to St. Joseph's for breakfast with the
Jesuits. The librarian, an old Belgian with a neat white goatee,
told me, "We have twenty-two of your books in our library."
After we left the Jesuits a cold mist began blowing up out of
the valleys—not comforting for my cold.

On being tired of blue domes. On objecting to pleasure
domes. "Dear Mr. Khan, I take exception to that new dome.
The one in Xanadu."[68] On being tired of icebergs 30,000 feet
high.

The view of Natu-la Pass, where the Chinese stand armed
and ready, from the toilet of room 14 at the Windamere Hotel
Private Limited. View of Tibet from a toilet. Tired of mountains and pleasure domes. On having a cold in the pleasure
domes. Having to use a Vicks inhaler in Xanadu. On being
overcharged by the druggist (chemist) for the Vicks inhaler. On
being given Dristan Nasal Mist by a Jesuit.

By the blue dome of Raj Bhavan,[69] outside the fences of
course, I add my own small contribution of green phlegm to
the gobs of spit on the street. Note the bloody sputum of con-
sumptives and/or betel chewers.

Objection to the blue clouds of soft coal smoke rising from
Darjeeling to aggravate my allergy.

On meeting the Czechs on Mall Road, near the part that is being repaired. Looking down, identifying the Tibetan Refugee Center from high above.

Little Tibetan children carrying bunches of marigolds. An Indian rides on a pony led by a boy. No reins. He holds a baby in his arms. He rides smiling past the mountain which has to be taken for granted. Today is Sunday also at Gethsemani, half around the world from here. No Sunday conference. No conferences for a long time. But I must talk to the Jesuits at St. Joseph's Friday and the Jesuits at Kurseong Sunday—to tell them that all that happens in the American Church is not exactly as presented in *Time*—such is the request.

Several times during the long silent ride in the Land Rover to the Mim Tea Estate today I wondered, "Why am I going there?" But I am glad to be here in this utterly quiet bungalow. The owners are out and won't be back until late. I have already refused dinner and asked for tea only, tea to be sent to the bungalow. A fire is lit in the bungalow grate, and it is good. Hah! It is good. Fog hides the mountains. Fog gets in the sore throat. No matter. Fire and a variety of remedies and a big bed, with covers and fresh sheets turned back, awaits the tired penseur.

"Dear Father Merriton," said the note, "Please make yourself at home the moment you arrive and just ask the bearer for anything you may require." Without my having to ask, the generator went on, the lights began to work, tea was provided in the big comfortable drawing room. I escaped quickly to the bungalow, aside, apart, alone, silent. Fire lit. Books unpacked, including one on Japan by Ruth Benedict[70] and also Anaïs Nin's[71] *Under the Glass Bell,* which I hope to finish. Along with the Buddhist books I have to return to Harold Talbott, who remains in the Windamere where he reads wrapped in a blanket.

✳

November 18 / Mim Tea Estate

I'm glad I came here. All morning alone on the mountainside, in the warm sun, now overclouded. Plenty of time to think. Reassessment of this whole Indian experience in more critical terms. Too much movement. Too much "looking for" something: an answer, a vision, "something other." And this breeds illusion. Illusion that there *is* something else. Differentiation— the old splitting-up process that leads to mindlessness, instead of the mindfulness of seeing all-in-emptiness and not having to break it up against itself. Four legs good; two legs bad.

Hence the annoyance with Kanchenjunga, its big crude blush in the sunrise, outside my bungalow window at 5:45. What do I care for a 28,000-foot post card when I have this bloody cold? All morning Kanchenjunga has been clouded over. Only rarely do you see the peak through the clouds, or one of the other surrounding peaks. Better that way. More modest. Really, Kanchenjunga, you are not to blame for all these Darjeeling hotels. But I think you know what I mean!

I am still not able fully to appreciate what this exposure to Asia has meant. There has been so much—and yet also so little. I have only been here a month! It seems a long time since Bangkok and even since Delhi and Dharamsala. Meeting the Dalai Lama and the various Tibetans, lamas or "enlightened" laymen, has been the most significant thing of all, especially in the way we were able to communicate with one another and share an essentially spiritual experience of "Buddhism" which is also somehow in harmony with Christianity.

On the other hand, though the Jesuits at St. Joseph's have repeatedly dropped hints about the need for contemplative Catholic foundations in India, I do not get any impression of being called to come here and settle down. Certainly not in this "sensitive" border area where there would be constant problems with the government.

If I were to be a hermit in India it would have to mean something other than this comfortable bungalow! Something more like what Dom Le Saux (Swami Abhishiktananda) is doing.

Though I fully appreciate the many advantages of the hermitage at Gethsemani, I still have the feeling that the lack of quiet and the general turbulence there, external and internal, last summer are indications that I ought to move. And so far the best indications seem to point to Alaska or to the area around the Redwoods.

Another question: would this move be *temporary* or *permanent*? I do not think I ought to separate myself completely from Gethsemani, even while maintaining an official residence there, legally only. I suppose I ought eventually to end my days there. I do in many ways miss it. There is no problem of my wanting simply to "leave Gethsemani." It is my monastery and being away has helped me see it in perspective and love it more.[72]

Now suppose some loon comes up to me and says, "Have you found the *real* Asia?" I am at a loss to know what one means by "the real Asia." It is *all* real as far as I can see. Though cer-

Tea plantation in the Himalayas

tainly a lot of it has been corrupted by the West. Neither Victorian Darjeeling nor the Kennedy-era Oberoi can be called *ideal* Asia. I remember Deki Lhalungpa laughing at the phony American minarets in the Taj dining room at the Oberoi. Still, that is Asia too.

Darjeeling is a quaintly fraudulent relic of something incredible. And the Indians, or the Nepalese, Sikkimese, and others around here, are still trying to believe in it, and maintain it. English hats, tweeds, walking sticks, old school ties (St. Joseph's) . . . for the rich ones at least. Shivering in the Windamere over Madhyamika dialectic . . . is that the "real Asia"? I have a definite feeling it is a waste of time—something I didn't need to do. However, if I have discovered I didn't need to do it, it has not been a waste of time.

This deep valley, the Mim Tea Estate, above Darjeeling: it is beautiful and quiet and it is right for Martin Hall, the manager, and his wife, who are in their own way hermits and appreciate my need for a couple of days of silence. Yet it has nothing I could not, essentially, have found at Needle Rock or Bear Harbor[73]—nothing I did not find there last May. Or did I find an illusion of Asia, that needed to be dissolved by experience? *Here?*

What *does* this valley have? Landslides. Hundreds of them. The mountains are terribly gashed, except where the forest is thick. Whole sections of tea plantations were carried away six weeks ago. And it is obviously going to be worse the next time there are really heavy rains. The place is a frightening example of anicca—"impermanence." A good place, therefore, to adjust one's perspectives. I find my mind rebelling against the landslides. I am distracted by reforestation projects and other devices to *deny* them, *forbid* them. I want this all to be *permanent.* A permanent post card for meditation, daydreams. The landslides are ironic and silent comments on the apparent permanence, the "eternal snows" of solid Kanchenjunga. And *political* instability. Over there, only a couple of hundred miles as the crow flies, is the Tibetan border where the Chinese armies are!

The sun is high, at the zenith. Clear soft sound of a temple bell far down in the valley. Voices of children near the cottages above me on the mountainside. The sun is warm. Everything falls into place. Nothing is to be decided; nor is "Asia" to be put in some category or other. There is nothing to be judged. But it must be cold for the lamas, at night, in their high, draughty little gompas!

✽

". . . The roving gaze of the mariner who never attaches himself to what he sees, whose very glance is roving, floating, sailing on, who looks at every person and object with a sense of the enormous space around them, with a sense of the distance one can put between oneself and one's desires, the sense of the enormousness of the world and of the tides and currents that carry us onward."

—Anaïs Nin: "The All-Seeing," in *Under a Glass Bell*, New York, E. P. Dutton, 1948.

✽

As the generator turns off and the lights go out at Mim Tea Estate the bearer brought me two candles and an ancient matchbox marked "Deer and Tiger Safety Matches." A tiger is sneaking up on an unsuspecting stag as it drinks from a pool. On the back it says: Price   6 P

Price   6 P

Price   6 P.

In it there are three ancient matches.

Mrs. Hall, solicitous about my cold, said I must have a fire in the bungalow after lunch because of the cold wind that starts punctually at 11 each morning and brings clouds of icy mist down over the plantation and valley. So I spent the afternoon in the bungalow. I finished Murti on Madhyamika, meditated, sometimes sleepily, and was entirely content. But the bungalow could have been anywhere. It could have been, just as well, my own hermitage at Gethsemani—only much quieter. Mrs. Hall saw to it that the bearer came in with "a proper tea." I only take lunch in the dining room. The rest in the bungalow, and have disconcerted them by wanting only soup for supper.

⌘

November 19 / Mim Tea Estate

Last night I had a curious dream about Kanchenjunga. I was looking at the mountain and it was pure white, absolutely pure, especially the peaks that lie to the west. And I saw the pure beauty of their shape and outline, all in white. And I heard a voice saying—or got the clear idea of: "There is another side to the mountain." I realized that it was turned around and everything was lined up differently; I was seeing it from the Tibetan side. This morning my quarrel with the mountain is

View of Kanchenjunga

ended. Not that it is a big love affair . . . but why get mad at a mountain? It is beautiful, chastely white in the morning sun—and right in view of the bungalow window.

There is another side of Kanchenjunga and of every mountain—the side that has never been photographed and turned into post cards. That is the only side worth seeing.

Out on the mountainside in the warm sun there is the sound of an ax where someone splits wood for fuel at the tea factory. Some children are playing in the same place high up on the edge of the woods. Far below, the lovely blue veil of a woman walking with children along a winding path through a tea garden. Reading the Commemorations of St. Elizabeth[74] in the Office made me want to read her life, study her holiness, her miracles. Will do this when I next have a chance. Thought of Sr. Helen Elizabeth[75] and St. Joseph's Infirmary in Louisville: the time I was there in 1950, already eighteen years ago! How everything has changed—anicca!

Later: I took three more photos of the mountain. An act of reconciliation? No, a camera cannot reconcile one with anything. Nor can it see a real mountain. The camera does not know what it takes: it captures materials with which you reconstruct, not so much what you saw as what you thought you saw. Hence the best photography is aware, mindful, of illusion and uses illusion, permitting and encouraging it—especially unconscious and powerful illusions that are not normally admitted on the scene.

Nonviolent Himalayan bees: after one had lit on me quietly three times without stinging, I let it crawl on my head a while, picking up sweat for some eclectic and gentle honeycomb, or just picking up sweat for no reason. Another crawled on my hand and I studied it. Certainly a bee. I could not determine whether it was stingless, or just well behaved.

⌘

The three doors (they are one door).

1) The door of emptiness. Of no-where. Of no place for a self, which cannot be entered by a self. And therefore is of no use to someone who is going somewhere. Is it a door at all? The door of no-door.

2) The door without sign, without indicator, without information. Not particularized. Hence no one can say of it "This is *it!* This is *the door.*" It is not recognizable as a door. It is not led up to by other things pointing to it: "We are not it, but that is it—the door." No signs saying "Exit." No use looking for indications. Any door with a sign on it, any door that proclaims itself to be a door, is not the door. But do not look for a sign saying "Not-door." Or even "No Exit."

3) The door without wish. The undesired. The unplanned door. The door never expected. Never wanted. Not desirable as door. Not a joke, not a trap door. Not select. Not exclusive. Not for a few. Not for many. Not *for*. Door without aim. Door without end. Does not respond to a key—so do not imagine you have a key. Do not have your hopes on possession of the key.

There is no use asking for it. Yet you must ask. Who? For what? When you have asked for a list of all the doors, this one is not on the list. When you have asked the numbers of all the doors, this one is without a number. Do not be deceived into thinking this door is merely hard to find and difficult to open. When sought it fades. Recedes. Diminishes. Is nothing. There is no threshold. No footing. It is not empty space. It is neither this world nor another. It is not based on anything. Because it has no foundation, it is the end of sorrow. Nothing remains to be done. Therefore there is no threshold, no step, no advance, no recession, no entry, no nonentry. Such is the door that ends all doors; the unbuilt, the impossible, the undestroyed, through which all the fires go when they have "gone out."

Christ said, "I am the door." The nailed door. The cross, they nail the door shut with death. The resurrection: "You see, I am *not* a door." "Why do you look up to heaven?" *Attolite portas principes vestras.*[76] For what? The King of Glory. *Ego sum ostium.*[76] I am the opening, the "shewing," the revelation, the door of light, the Light itself. "I am the Light," and the light is in the world from the beginning. (It seemed to be darkness.)

⌘

Lucernarium.[77] The value of expecting the moment to light up the evening lamps. Here at the Tea Estate the generator goes on at 5 and off at 9. There is a period of about twenty minutes in which it is not easy to read in the bungalow, except right next to the window. But in the meantime a fire has been lighted. It flowers and speaks in the silent room. Prayer of fire! Agni.[78] Worshipful patterns of flame. Each fire is different. Each has its own particular shape. Then suddenly the porch light is on and so I switch on my own light, to write more. To write, among other things, a letter to Brother Patrick, to be mailed in Darjeeling when I return there tomorrow. I haven't heard from J. Laughlin since I got to Asia and he has three books I am wondering about. Apparently the book of poems, *Sensation Time at the Home,*[79] is being considered for publication next and I hear it has passed the censor. I must also send a card to Czeslaw Milosz.[80] During tea I was thinking of the evening in San Francisco with him and his wife and Paul Jacobs[81] and wife and the Ferrys. After dinner at a Chinese restaurant, when the Jacobs had left and "Ping" Ferry had got lost trying to find us after taking Mrs. Jacobs home, we sat for a couple of hours at a sidewalk café drinking wine, while an interminable line of Dixie tourists—Alabama, Tennessee—filed slowly by into a topless joint upstairs.

Kanchenjunga this afternoon. The clouds of the morning parted slightly and the mountain, the massif of attendant peaks, put on a great, slow, silent dorje dance of snow and mist, light and shadow, surface and sinew, sudden cloud towers spiraling up out of icy holes, blue expanses of half-revealed rock, peaks appearing and disappearing with the top of Kanchenjunga remaining the visible and constant president over the whole slow

Another view of Kanchenjunga

show. It went on for hours. Very stately and beautiful. Then toward evening the clouds cleared some more, except for a long apron of mist and shadow below the main peaks. There were a few discreet showings of whorehouse pink but most of it was shape and line and shadow and form. O Tantric Mother Mountain! Yin-yang palace of opposites in unity! Palace of anicca, impermanence and patience, solidity and nonbeing, existence and wisdom. A great *consent* to be and not-be, a compact to delude no one who does not first want to be deluded. The full beauty of the mountain is not seen until you too consent to the impossible paradox: it is and is not. When nothing more needs to be said, the smoke of ideas clears, the mountain is SEEN. Testament of Kanchenjunga. Testament of fatherless old Melchizedek.[82] Testament from before the time of oxen and sacrifice. Testament without Law. NEW Testament. Full circle! The sun sets in the East! The nuns at Loreto kept asking me, "Have you seen the snows?" Could they have been serious?

⌘

Conze says: "By atomizing society, modern civilization has thrown the mutual relations of people into a profound disorder from which it can be rescued only by conscious and sustained effort, and at the same time technical progress and the prestige of science have dimmed the immediate awareness of the spiritual world. Traditional religion saw these things quite differently. There the soul of man was regarded as essentially solitary, the true struggle took place in a condition of withdrawal from society, and the decisive victories were won in solitude, face to face with the deepest forces of reality itself. . . ."

—Conze, *op. cit.,* page 81.

"True love requires contact with the truth, and the truth must be found in solitude. The ability to bear solitude, and to spend long stretches of time alone by oneself in quiet meditation, is therefore one of the more elementary qualifications for those who aspire towards selfless love."

—Conze, *op. cit.,* page 85.

This is the chapter on Buddhist social virtues.[83] Maitri—friendly love—is not exclusive, it is rooted in truth rather than in passionate need. Compassion is proportionate to detachment; otherwise we use others for our own ends under the pretext of "love." Actually, we are dominated by illusion. Love that perpetuates the illusion does no good to others or to ourselves.

Ultimately the illusion has to be destroyed by prajna, which is also one with perfect compassion (karuna).

⌘

My cold is still quite bad but I think that staying indoors with a fire this afternoon has helped it. Whatever may be the answer, or nonanswer, to my question, this is a good retreat and I appreciate the quiet more than I can say. This quiet, with time to read, study, meditate, and *not talk to anyone,* is something essential in my life.

⌘

Darjeeling.

And to dissolve the heaps. Afternoon lumber water filling
can full
Taxi call kids. Sharp cries spread rev motor whisper pony feet
    Hoo! Hoo!
Motor going gone (hill)
Looking back her long hair shining pattern of crosses
    unionjacks
shadows on the walk (Hoo! Hoo! Ponyfeet)
Ponysaddle afternoon all rich god Ganesha[84] fills his waterpot.
All to dissolve the lagers (layers) spreads of sounds—waters,
    boards, planks, plankfall fur, voice near, man holds basket
    of green leaves. Going. Gone.
Sensations neutral low degree burn (sun) warmskin. Hears a
    little
water,
Again fills watercan the poor one—not rich Ganesha, he is gone
    in scarf
and glasses.
All come worship fun in the sun.

And to dissolve the fun. Worker basket empty and gone.
    Ganesha
gone in an
Oxblood muffler though not cold after good hot dinner
All come have fun dissolve values. Tibetan boss explains garden.
Layers of sounds hammer upon the ear spread selves away rich
roaring bark (spurs values) menaces bishop (Distances)
Image yards. Bogus is this freight!
Gate measure stransound gone taxi Water whumps in can and
fills softer, softer, gone of hearing.
Dog is crazy angry barkleap fighting any wires.
Gone basket of foliage
Bangs on an old bucket. *Inutile!*
Motorbike argues with some slops. Taxicry downhill in small
city. Outcry!
Disarms v. chords
Image yards spread wide open
Eye tracks work their way everywhere.
Mountain winds can harm voice.
Sensation neutral low four o'clock tone is general. Must call
a nun on the telephone.
Two bad cheers for the small sun: burning a little
life sunstorm: is not yet overcloudy winter!
Send aid ideas to dissolve heaps—to spread their freight.

※

November 21

Anatomy of nice thought rot. No use isolating consciousness and
then *feeding* it, exacerbating it. The ruse of nourishing the self
with ideas of self-dissolution. The "perfectly safe" consciousness, put on a diet of select thoughts, poisons itself. The ex-
posed consciousness is in less trouble. It relaxes. Is free in fresh
air. Is perhaps a little dirtied—but normal or more normal.

Less garbage. Select garbage, luxury garbage is the worst poison.

Man tortured by telephone (below thin floor.) Cries louder and louder, until he screams high "hellos" that fly beyond Kanchenjunga. Gasps. Despairing cockcrows. Yelps. Hound yells. Pursues a distant fading voice. Over far wires speeds the crazed hound, pleading for help, challenging the victim to turn around and come back. Falls off the wire in despair. Telephone, chair, desk, office, whole hotel, all come crashing to the ground.

⌘

Wrote the card to Milosz this morning, sitting in hot sun. Cards to Sr. Thérèse Lentfoehr,[85] John and Rena Niles,[86] Tom Jerry Smith.[87] Letter to Richard Chi.[88] And one to Nyanaponika Thera.[89]

Mass of the Presentation at Loreto Convent. I hoarsely uttered a homily. Voice gone. Cold still bad. Woke up several times in the night coughing. Double whiskies in the warm drawing room no help. The German Consul from Dacca[90] had better luck with grog; we had a discussion and comparison of the respective value of Indian and German rum. His cold is better. As for me, in the long run I must conclude the Jesuit remedies have failed. As Mother Ludovina said, while I was eating breakfast after Mass, "It must run its course." The old deaf sister inquired whether my week had been consoling or if it had been "the mountain of myrrh?"

My interest in Buddhism has disturbed some of the Catholics, clergy and religious. They wonder what there can be in it. I met the bishop in the dark, Gothic bishop's house last night, Eric Benjamin—he is Nepalese—very nice, a good bishop; alert, straight, concerned about his people and working hard for them, particularly since "the disaster." He hoped I would talk to the nuns, and plans are being made for this on Saturday.

There has been continuous firing all morning of an automatic rifle in the deep valley northeast of here. I looked down toward the sound. Tiny houses clinging to the slope. Further up I discern a quiet, isolated gompa. The shots are from some hidden lair of the army.

I finished Murti at Mim. Also all I intend to read of Conze's *Buddhist Thought in India,* and Dr. Pemba's[91] novel *Idols by the Path.* It is interesting, full of violence, but probably gives a fair idea of Tibet before and after the Chinese takeover. And of Tibetans in this part of India.

✳

"And the ice and the upper radiance of snow are brilliant with timeless immunity from the flux and the warmth of life. Overhead they transcend all life, all the soft, moist fire of the blood. So that a man must needs live under the radiance of his own negation."

—D. H. Lawrence: *Twilight in Italy,* New York,
Viking Compass Books, 1962, page 6.

✳

November 22 / Darjeeling

When you begin each day by describing the look of the same mountain, you are living in the grip of delusion. Today the peak of Kanchenjunga was hidden by massive clouds, but the lower attendant peaks stood out all the more beautiful and noble in their own right. If Kanchenjunga were not there they would all be great mountains on their own. At the end of the line I noticed one that seemed to have had its top cut off, and as I had not noticed anything before I concluded that this beheading had taken place during the night.

When you begin each day by giving small Indian coins to Tibetan beggars with prayer wheels and to the old faceless lady from Lhasa, you are simply entrenching your own position in the wheel of birth and death.

We were admiring the Bhutanese swords and daggers at

Dr. Pemba's house. Fr. Curmi was there, too. The beauty of a great heavy dagger. Mrs. Pemba said she had oiled it a little. I slid it back into its sheath. Pictures of Bhutan. Mrs. Pemba is Bhutanese, a wonderful person with a life and substantiality and strength such as one no longer sees in cities. Her laugh is marvelous; she explodes with delight over little things, and is full of humor. So is Pemba, who is more sophisticated. He is, I think, the first Tibetan M.D.—from Lhasa?—well, he practiced there, having trained at University College Hospital in London. He had a lot of tales about J. B. S. Haldane,[92] whom he admires greatly.

Dr. Pemba admires Chatral Rimpoche, too. He says he is very humble. He laughs about Chatral's unconventional clothes. Chatral puts all the money he gets into building, improving, and ornamenting various gompas on the mountainsides around Ghoom.

Most interesting of all: there have been eight hermits making the three-year retreat at Chatral's place. They have just finished and eight others have started. There is a long waiting list. When we were there the other day one of the monks was laying the foundation for a new hermit cell.

Dr. Pemba was called in to attend to the ruined knee of one of the retreatants. He had gone into the long retreat with a bad knee and it had become progressively worse with a tubercular condition that by then was horrible. Yet he did not want to see a doctor because he feared he would be pulled out and sent to the hospital. He was within a few months of ending his retreat. Dr. Pemba asked him why he withdrew like this instead of going out and helping others, and he replied that everyone had a different thing to do; most people needed to help others, but some needed to seek a very rare attainment which could only be found in solitude. Such attainment was good not only for the monk himself but improved the whole world. Anyway Dr. Pemba fixed him up so he could finish his retreat. The hermits on retreat see no one but their master (who gives them something to meditate on each day) and the brother who brings them food. The life is now a "little easier" in the sense that they are allowed to leave their unheated cells and walk around in a courtyard, but without seeing anyone.

When we left Pemba's there were no lights on the pitch-dark steps and in the streets. A small Bhutanese servant boy lights our way down the long flight of steps to the road. Then we go on in the dark. Past the big old guildhall-type place, now roaring and singing crazily with a movie going on inside. Big dark building afflicted with a disease, possessed by giant voices, amplified gunfire, and the flatulence of electronic symphony. Bam Bam Bam Ro-o-oar! A chest of pent-up Tibetan mountain demons booming in the night? No, nothing so respectable. No real thunders. Only a storm of jail-breaking Anzacs[93] running amok within the secure compass of four walls and a box office.

As we made our way through the dark, past the dimness of the Shangri-La Restaurant, through the emptiness of the big square, Fr. Curmi told of problems in his Nepalese parish: feuds, strains, and now two families ready to war with each other over a knocked-up teen-age girl.

⌘

November 24 / The 24th Sunday after Pentecost

On Friday I said the Mass of St. Cecilia[94] in the bishop's chapel. And yesterday the Mass of Our Lady, with the new Eucharistic prayer IV, in Latin, which is very fine. A quiet chapel with a Burma-teak altar. But this morning there was no one around, the bishop's house was locked up and I couldn't get in. I leave at 11:30 for Kurseong and may be able to say Mass at the Jesuit scholasticate there.

Under the entry porch at the bishop's house there are many flowers in pots and on stands. And two sets of red buffalo horns. The motorcycle is absent. The door is locked and though I press the white bell button five, six times, I never hear anything ring. I walk around to the back. The back door is locked. I start up the hill, soon meeting a young man who salutes me as if he knows me. Perhaps one of the seminarians I spoke to the other day. I ask him about somewhere to say Mass, but he doesn't seem to understand. I decide not to go down to the Loreto Convent, their chapel being also a parish church and indeed a cathedral, and arrangements made for Sunday Masses. Don't interfere. Wait till Kurseong.

Yesterday, a visit to Karlu Rimpoche at his hermit center at Sonada. He is a small, thin man with a strange concavity at the temples as if his skull had been pressed in by huge thumbs. Soft-spoken like all of them, he kept fingering his rosary, and patiently answered my many questions on the hermit retreat.

At first he was evasive about it and talked of Mahayana in general until he was apparently satisfied and said I had the "true Mahayana spirit." Then he went on in more detail. There are sixteen hermits, fifteen men and one woman, now in the three-year retreat at his place. They are not admitted to the retreat until after their fundamental monastic formation. They are examined by him on their capacity to undertake the retreat, and each case is decided on its own merits.

Karlu Rimpoche

The three-year period is divided into various stages: first, one with a great deal of active praying, with many genuflections and prostrations and mantras counted in lakhs[95] on the rosary. Then prayers and prostrations before the Buddha image must be accompanied by meditation. They are in addition to the ordinary daily puja of the monks. The puja is done in private. The hermits do nothing in common. They see only their guru, the cook who dishes out their food, and the doctor, if they are ill. They use a Tibetan doctor for small things, a "modern" doctor for serious complaints.

During this active prayer there is much attention to taking refuge in the Buddha, the dharma, and the Sangha. Renouncing all sin. Meditation on hell and death. An offering of unbloody sacrifice, a round silver dish (I saw one) full of barley and rice, representing the world and all good things in it, offered in praise and thanks. Emphasis on *compassion* and unselfishness. The hermit's retreat is not for his own salvation but for that of all sentient beings. Much contemplation of guardian deities, the nice ones and the terrible.

This initial period goes on for four months and is followed by another of proximate preparation for an initiation, after which the hermit spends about two years, the remainder of his retreat, in the higher dzogchen contemplation. The translation was not clear, but I think Karlu said that in this period there was more emphasis on contemplation of "terrifying deities." Jimpa Rimpoche, my translator, had by now become sensitive about the "terrifying deities" and tended to giggle when they were mentioned; so some things got lost in his translation.

The hermit's day begins about 2 or 3 A.M. He gets some tea about 5, a meal about 11. All go to collect their food, it is not brought secretly to their cells. At this time they see each other but don't talk probably. They can walk outside the cells. Is firewood provided?

Khempo Karlu Rimpoche invited me to come and make this hermit retreat at his place or, failing that, to write to him with my questions. That was very kind of him. With my reaction to this climate at its best and with the noise of the Indian radio in a cottage across the road from the hermitage, I guess it's still Alaska or California or Kentucky for me.

Karlu Rimpoche gave me three pictures of deities, printed in black and white outline, colored by him, quite touching.

⌘

Harold Talbott and I briefly discussed the possibility of getting Sonam Kazi or someone to set up a good Tibetan meditation center in America, perhaps in New Mexico, in some indirect connection with Christ in the Desert.[96] Harold left this morning for Bagdogra, Calcutta, Delhi, and Dharamsala. He has been extremely helpful and generous; he paid my bill at the Windamere and shared all kinds of time, ideas, information, and help.

My cold is not yet cured. Because of it I'll be glad to get out of Darjeeling. The weather has been "perfect" these last days, but has not helped. It's one of the most stubborn colds I have ever had. I reflect that where I really caught it was Calcutta, and it was the same cold that landed Peter Dunne in the hospital after the Temple of Understanding Conference. I still have it, with a headache. I do not especially look forward to Kurseong where I am to talk to the Jesuit scholastics. I spoke at St. Joseph's, North Point, to the fathers and brothers, and at Loreto Convent to the communities of Loreto and Bethany. There were more Indians and Nepalese among the latter. I was consoled by the intent faces of the Nepalese who seemed to respond even more than all the others to what I tried to say about prayer. But they all responded and I got the impression of a great hunger for encouragement and instruction about the life of prayer and meditation. At St. Joseph's I talked about dialogue with Buddhists and many seemed interested, but I wonder if it was worthwhile, or if they were interested for the right reasons—hard to say.

After the Loreto talk I came back in the lightless streets.

But there was some light from Victoria Hospital and some light from the new moon. Two women were screaming abuse at each other in the dark, in one of the "apartments." And two men on the road above listening with interest.

Harold and I had a farewell party, sitting in my room.

⌘

Have I failed in my solemn tourist duty of perpetual motion by not going to Kalimpong? Or even to the old Ghoom monastery, a "sight"? Not even getting out to take a photo of the shiny little new one just by the road to Darjeeling? To go to Kalimpong would take most of the day, now that the bridge is out, and one would have to spend the night there.

To go to Sikkim, I find, one needs a permit from Delhi—I was going to be smart and get one here in Darjeeling—and again it takes hours by roundabout roads to get there since "the disaster."

No answer from the Queen of Bhutan. ("Well you know," said our friend, "she has her family problems.")

No special interest, after all, in Katmandu. Literally everybody here seems to be either coming from Katmandu or going there. All the hippies at the Calcutta meeting were keyed up about it. The Mim Tea Estate, a couple of miles from the Nepal border, full of Nepalese, run by a Nepalese, seemed to me to be good enough as far as Nepal is concerned, at least this time. Maybe later in January?

My mind turns to Ceylon, Thailand, Indonesia. I want to see something else. I have seen the mountains and the gompas.

Out there this morning the Natu-la Pass stood out clear in the distance, and I have seen the road winding up to it out of Gangtok, in Sikkim. Hundreds of little children were running through the dirty main street of Ghoom. Women were taking advantage of the sun to wash their hair. Sitting in the sun combing one another's hair. Or delousing the children.

Have I failed in my solemn duty as tourist by not taking a

photo of a woman of Ghoom, sitting by the roadside, delousing the head of her eight-year-old son?

In Calcutta there has been a Marxist riot led by Maoist students. They burned McNamara[97] in effigy and set fire to buses. Tomorrow I will be there.

Kanchenjunga has been hidden for three days. I will probably not see it again.

※

Kurseong

True, Kanchenjunga was hidden as we drove out from Darjeeling. The lower peaks were visible but the higher peak itself was lost in a great snowcloud. Some of the flanks were visible in a dim room of shadow and snow. I looked back as we swung into Ghoom, and that was the end of it.

Outside the window of a Jesuit scripture scholar's cell, which has been loaned to me for the night, there is a brilliant and somber fiery sunset amid low blue clouds. The scholasticate here at Kurseong is high up on the mountain and looks far out over the Ganges plain. The school has an excellent library. I wanted to dip into Fr. De Smet's thesis on the theological ideas in Sankaracharya, but did not get a chance. I read a few songs of Tukaram, the greatest Marathi poet, and some Sufis; there was no time for more.

Tukaram lived in Maharashtra (the region around Bombay) from 1598 to 1650—within two years of being an exact contemporary of Descartes.[98] He was ordained by Chaitanya in a dream and began teaching. He was ordered by some brahmins to throw his books in the river. He did so and went into a seventeen-day fast and meditation, after which the river returned his books to him.[99]

Said Mass in a private oratory during the afternoon of Sunday—better than Darjeeling.

⌘

Sankirtana is the Indian term for singing the names and exploits of the Lord in the company of the saints. "To join the Lord in his sports (*lilas*)."

⌘

In his preface to a book by the Abbé Monchanin, a Frenchman who became a hermit on the banks of the sacred river Cauvery in South India, Pierre Emmanuel writes of vocation: "What is a vocation? A call and a response. This definition does not say everything: to conceive the call of God as an expressed order to carry out a task certainly is not always false, but it is only true after a long interior struggle in which it becomes obvious that no such constraint is apparent. It also happens that the order comes to maturity along with the one who must carry it out and that it becomes in some way this very being, who has now arrived at full maturity. Finally, the process of maturing can be a mysterious way of dying, provided that with death the task begins . . . there has to be a dizzying choice, a definitive dehiscence [rupture] by which the certitude he has gained of being called is torn asunder. That which—as one says, and the word is rightly used here—*consecrates* a vocation and raises it to the height of the sacrifice which it becomes is a breaking with the apparent order of being, with its formal full development or its visible efficacy."[100]

—Pierre Emmanuel: "La Loi d'exode," preface to *De l'esthétique à la mystique* by Jules Monchanin, Paris, Casterman, 1967, pages 7–8.

⌘

November 25

I wanted to copy a few more lines from Pierre Emmanuel in

the Kurseong scholasticate but some people came in to see me and I was occupied until 8:15, when I went down to the front door to get in the jeep and go down to the main road. There I was eventually picked up by the Mount Everest Taxis' car 291, which was full—only room for one man in the front seat—and moreover the driver was determined to get to Bagdogra without using gas. He coasted most of the way down the hill with the motor off, and in the end conked out fifty yards from the gate to the airport. We walked in. There are about two hours left until plane time (flight 224 to Calcutta). I sit in the relatively cool restaurant. Fans are going slowly. Army types are shouting in Bengali—or is it Hindi?

A last sight of Kanchenjunga, bright and clear in the morning sun, appearing over the hills of Ghoom as I came out into the corridor with my bags. Good view from the front of the monastery. A surprise.

Kurseong has a big, cold, solid, Belgian-type Jesuit scholasticate. One gets the impression of a well-ordered and "fervent" community in the old style, a typically good Jesuit house in the familiar tradition. I talked about prayer and Job arguing with God, basically from notes I'd used in Alaska and California with quite a few added notions about a possible *Indian* contribution to a renewal of the Catholic theology of prayer. I also spoke of bhakti sacrifice, the contemplation of the Trinity and the *theological* idea of the Person. Many liked it, though some of the faculty may have misunderstood it, and a few of the questions were critical. The best of the Indian group, especially Fr. Cherian Curiyikad,[101] the scripture man, and quite a few scholastics seemed much in favor. On the whole it was a good response.

I was in the room of Fr. Volkaert, another scripture scholar, whose Revised Standard Version of the Bible I borrowed for use in my lecture. I had a couple of talks with Fr. Louis Schillebeeckx, S.J., the brother of Fr. Edward Schillebeeckx, O.P.[102] He has notes on prayer and on the Holy Spirit from the days when he was Magister Spiritus, and they are quite good. He is a contemplative. In his last words to me he urged me to see his brother in Nijmegen. It was a concelebration in English in a renovated chapel. "Om" was inscribed over the lectern.

✽

Calcutta—"A-a-a-a-chya!"

It is a city I love. Flying out today was beautiful. I don't mean the bizarre, macabre beauty of the disintegrating slums, the old fallen splendor, but the subtle beauty of all the suburban ponds and groves, with men solemnly bathing in the early morning and white cranes standing lovely and still amid the lotuses and flying up in twos and threes against the fresh green of the coconut palms. Yet the city, too, its crumbling walls alive with Bengali inscriptions and palimpsests of old movie posters. And the occasional English spires, 18-century domes . . . I do not tire of Calcutta. But perhaps it was only because I was there only a few hours; I stayed overnight in Bob Boylan's apartment and read all the mail that had piled up for me. There was one from Dom Leclercq[103] who is now in Delhi, at the Oberoi Intercontinental. He is going on to Tokyo. I wired him from the Calcutta airport. And contact prints had come from John Griffin of the photos I had taken at Dharamsala. The one of the Dalai Lama is especially good, also the one of Khamtul Rimpoche, and the little tulku in his cell was very visible. Mother Myriam Dardenne[104] of the Redwoods writes that the commission of bishops to take care of contemplatives has been set up. Fr. Flavian says "Come home if you get sick." (This written before he received my request to prolong the trip!) Fr. Eudes Bamberger[105] is going to Rome. Fr. Chrysogonus Waddell[106] is out on some commission. Naomi Burton[107] is going ahead with the publication of *My Argument with the Gestapo* at Doubleday. She wants a preface by W. H. Auden or Robert Lowell, the poets. The *Time-Life* Bible[108] with my piece in it is coming out after all, so I will have some money. Dan Walsh[109] has sent a big check for my travel fund. Most generous! Bob Lax[110] says Emmett Williams[111] wants some of my stuff for an anthology of concrete poetry. My talk at Bangkok is to be on December 10th; address: c/o Mission Etrangère le Pacis, 254 Silom Road.

I had a long wait in the airport talking to a man from Melbourne who had been to Rishikesh[112]—and was disappointed—and who had been looking for lamas in Darjeeling. He had met a couple I did not know. He knows the Mouni Sadhu[113]-Arthur Osborne[114] set in Melbourne.

❉

NOTES: *The Himalayas*

[1] Pathankot: a rail junction and town in northern India named for the rajas of Pathan, who frequently rebelled against the Delhi emperors of the Mogul period.

[2] Dharamsala: a hill station below the Himalayas at the head of the Kangra Valley, where the Dalai Lama now has his residence in exile.

[3] Sonam T. Kazi: born into one of Sikkim's leading feudal families, he lived in Tibet for many years prior to the Chinese take-over. As a young man he attended the Scottish Mission College in Kalimpong and St. Stephen's College in Delhi, but his most extended study was under several of the Nyingmapa Buddhist masters in Tibet, from whom he received advanced meditational and spiritual instruction qualifying him to become himself a teacher of Tantric Buddhism. For ten years he served as official interpreter for the Dalai Lama and also interpreted for many Indian government officials, including Prime Minister Nehru. He helped prepare exhibitions of Tibetan art at Tibet House in Delhi and worked with French television on films of Tibetan life and religious practices. He is also the editor of the Ngagyur Nyingmay Sungrab Series of editions of classic Tantric Buddhist texts which seek to preserve the ancient culture of Tibet. Sonam Kazi is now in this country, having recently founded the Longchen Nyingthig Buddhist Society in New York and the Zogchen Pema Choling Meditation Centre in Philadelphia.

[4] Dom Aelred Graham: born in Liverpool, England, in 1907, studied theology at Oxford, and joined the Monastic Community at Ampleforth, Yorkshire, in 1930, where he was Professor of Dogmatic Theology from 1937

to 1951. Later he became Prior of the Benedictine Community and head-master of Portsmouth Priory School in Rhode Island. A leader of the ecumenical movement, he has traveled widely throughout the world, but now lives in retirement at Ampleforth Abbey. The most recent of his many books is *The End of Religion: Autobiographical Explorations,* published by Harcourt Brace Jovanovich in New York. *Conversations: Christian and Buddhist,* the book from which Merton quotes, and which he took to Asia, appeared with the same publisher in 1968. Although it is not listed in the catalog of Merton's Asian books at Gethsemani, it is probable that he had studied Dom Aelred's *Zen Catholicism* ("An inquiry into the religious encounter of East and West, with the suggestion that the two may meet at the spirit's center"), first published in 1963 and now available as a Harvest paperbook.

[5] The Desert Father was Abba Paul. See Cassian's *Institutes,* Book X, "De Spiritu Acediae," Chapter XXIV. See also Merton's own book, *The Wisdom of the Desert, Sayings from the Desert Fathers of the Fourth Century,* translations and introduction, New York, 1961, New Directions.

[6] Brother David Steindl-Rast, O.S.B., a Benedictine monk of Mt. Saviour Monastery, Pine City, New York, whom Merton met at a meeting of contemplatives at Our Lady of the Redwoods Abbey in Whitethorn, California, in the spring of 1968. In the same year, Brother David organized a Center for Spiritual Studies, in which Buddhists, Hindus, Jews, and Christians participated.

[7] Krishnamurti: Jiddu Krishnamurti, "philosopher of the inner self," was born into a brahmin family in South India in 1895. He came to England in 1911 and was privately educated there, first publishing several books of poetry. In 1929 he repudiated all organized religions and ideology, saying "I maintain that truth is a pathless land, and you cannot approach it by any path whatsoever, by any religion, by any sect. . . ." For many years he has lectured all over the world, and each summer there is a six-week gathering of his disciples and others at Saanen, Switzerland. His many books are published in this country by Harper & Row, New York, and information about his appearances may be obtained from the Krishnamurti Foundation of America, P.O. Box 216, Ojai, California 93023.

[8] Gyalwa Karmapa; or, as Merton later refers to him, the Karmapa Lama: a lama so called because he is the current incarnation of the head of the Karma branch of the Kagyudpa (Kargyud-pa) sect of Tibetan Buddhism. "The *Kargyud-pa* Order is divided into the *Dug-pa-kargyud* and the *Karma-kargyud* sects. . . . The *Karmapa* were founded in the twelfth century by Dusum Khyenpa. They are subdivided into the Black Hats—and it was with them that the idea of a system of successive reincarnation originated, which was later to be put into effect with the Dalai Lamas and so many other dignitaries and abbots—and, since the fourteenth century, into Red Hats. The

head of the *Karma-kargyud,* Gyalwa Karmapa, is himself a *tulku,* successor to the great Karmapas whose influence has ailways predominated in Tibet, and whose spiritual importance was almost comparable to the Dalai Lama's. The present Karmapa has taken refuge in the monastery at Rumtek, near Gangtok in Sikkim." (Arnaud Desjardins: *The Message of the Tibetans,* translated from the French by R. H. Ward and Vega Stewart, London, Stuart & Watkins, 1969, page 55.) There are two photographs of Gyalwa Karmapa in the Desjardins book. Some, though not all, of the Kagyudpa monks are known as the "entombed ones," because they become hermits in hillside caves, sometimes for long periods, or even for life, leaving only a hole in the cave entrance through which they are supplied with food and water.

[9] Ignatian method: the reference is to the *Spiritual Exercises* of Saint Ignatius of Loyola (1491–1556), founder of the Jesuit Order (Society of Jesus) in the Roman Catholic Church. "The one idea of St. Ignatius' life was the imitation of Christ. This is most clearly expressed in his *Spiritual Exercises,* written first in rough, plain Spanish and translated by the author himself into Latin. It is a series of religious reflections, examinations of conscience, prayers and the like grouped into four 'weeks,' according to a traditional series of four steps to the perfect life of mystical union with God." (*The Columbia Encyclopedia,* Second Edition) As a young man, in 1939, after his conversion to Catholicism but before joining the Trappists at Gethsemani, while he was still living in Greenwich Village in New York, Merton studied the *Spiritual Exercises,* attempting to teach himself and to put into daily practice the Ignatian methods of meditation. The experience is recounted in some detail in *The Seven Storey Mountain.* See pages 268–70 of the original Harcourt Brace edition, or pages 262–64 of the Signet paperback reprint.

[10] John Driver: an Englishman who went to India in 1956 to study the Nyingmapa school of Tantric Buddhism. Later he was associated with Chogyam Trungpa Rimpoche's Samye-Ling Tibetan Center in Scotland, though he is now living in London working with computers.

[11] Nagarjuna: a South Indian who lived probably in the 2nd or 3rd century A.D., was converted to Buddhism and became one of the founders of the Madhyamika, or "Middle Path" sect of Buddhism. Christmas Humphreys, in his *Buddhism* (London, Penguin, 1951, page 54), calls Nagarjuna "perhaps the greatest Buddhist philosopher . . . [who] attempted to reconcile the doctrines of realism and nihilism, the vehicle of his teaching being the veritable library of works known as the Prajna-Paramita." (Not to be confused with Nagarjuna-pada, a Tantric Buddhist scholar of the 7th century A.D., who wrote the *Pancakrama.*)

[12] Santi Deva: 691–743 A.D., the son of a king who renounced his inheri-

tance to become a Buddhist monk. After Nagarjuna, he was probably the most important philosopher of the Madhyamika school of Mahayana Buddhism. Murti states that Santi Deva's two principal works, the *Siksasamuccaya* and the *Bodhicaryavatara*, "are our chief sources for the Madhyamika path of Spiritual realisation."

[13] "Ping" Ferry: Wilbur H. Ferry, formerly Vice-President of the Center for the Study of Democratic Institutions (successor to the Fund for the Republic) in Santa Barbara, California, and now a free-lance writer, lecturer, and consultant to foundations. He was one of Merton's most devoted friends during the later years at Gethsemani and visited there frequently. When Merton came to California in 1968, he stayed with the Ferrys in Santa Barbara, and Ferry and his wife then drove him along the California coastline.

[14] Hanuman: "In Hindu mythology, a monkey god, the son of the wind and a monkey nymph. In the *Ramayana* he leads the monkey hosts that assist [Rama] the hero." (*Webster's II*)

[15] Suzuki: Daisetz Teitaro Suzuki (1870–1966), one of the great "intercultural" scholars of our time who, in his many books and his lectures at various universities here and in Japan, interpreted Zen Buddhism to the West and Christianity to the East. Merton came to New York to meet Suzuki when he was at Columbia in 1964, and they corresponded frequently before and after. Merton's book *Zen and the Birds of Appetite* (1968) includes an essay "D. T. Suzuki: the Man and His Work" and also their joint dialogue "Wisdom in Emptiness," which explores the congruencies of Christian mysticism and Zen. Some of Dr. Suzuki's most important books were: *Essays in Zen Buddhism, A Manual of Zen Buddhism, An Introduction to Zen Buddhism,* with a foreword by C. G. Jung, and *Mysticism, Christian and Buddhist.*

[16] "Donald" Allchin: the Rev. Arthur Macdonald Allchin. Educated at Westminster School and Christ Church, Oxford. Studied Eastern Orthodoxy in Greece in 1955–56. He was ordained in the Church of England in 1956, and from 1960 was living and teaching in Oxford. He is at present Warden of the Convent of the Incarnation in Oxford. He made three visits to Merton at Gethsemani and was Visiting Lecturer at the General Theological Seminary in New York in 1967–68. Allchin has written books and articles on the monastic life, Christian unity, and the frontier between theology and poetry (English and Welsh). He is the editor of *Sobornost,* an Anglo-Orthodox ecumenical periodical.

[17] Brother Patrick: Brother Patrick Hart was born in Green Bay, Wisconsin, educated at the University of Notre Dame, and taught in secondary schools before joining the community of Gethsemani in 1951. He was sec-

retary to the former Abbot, Dom James Fox, from 1957 to 1966, then spent two years at the Trappist headquarters in Rome. Returning to Gethsemani in 1968, he became secretary to Merton and also editor of *Monastic Exchange,* a Trappist journal of private opinion. He is now Registrar and Secretary of the Abbey of Gethsemani. He contributed the foreword and postscript to this volume.

[18] Vaccha(gotta): a wandering ascetic who recognized the uniqueness of the Buddha and whose discussions with him, as recorded in several of the earliest texts, present some of the most important points of the Buddha's doctrine.

[19] Brother Donald Kane: cook for the infirm refectory at Gethsemani; by doctor's orders, Merton was on a special protein diet, including meat, for the last fifteen years of his life.

[20] Radha: in the mythology of the earthly incarnation of the Hindu god Krishna, Radha, leader of the gopis, cowherdesses of Vrindavana, was Krishna's favorite love. As such, over the centuries she, and their relationship, became the subject of countless songs, poetry, and paintings. As these mythic stories found their way to a higher religious level in Hinduism, the gopis became enthralled devotees of the god, and Radha herself to be regarded as the shakti, or divine female principle, in the cult of Krishna worship. See Renou: *The Nature of Hinduism,* pages 46–47; E. C. Dimock, Jr.: *In Praise of Khrishna,* pages viiff.

[21] Chaitanya: (1485–1533) a Hindu saint of the Vaishnava sect who wrote many commentaries and dialogues. Dimock tells us that he is also called Gaura, "the Golden One," and that some Vaishnavites "reverence [him] as an incarnation of Krishna, some as Krishna himself, and some as Radha and Krishna in one body, in the most intimate possible embrace." (*In Praise of Krishna,* page xi.)

[22] Denise Levertov, born in England in 1923, but now an American, married to the writer and antiwar activist Mitchell Goodman. Her recent books of poetry include *The Sorrow Dance, Relearning the Alphabet, To Stay Alive,* and *Footprints,* all published by New Directions. The passages of Vaishnava poetry quoted are, in the order printed, from pages 22, 21, 17, 16, 15, and 61 of *In Praise of Krishna.*

[23] Bhanita, or signature lines.

[24] Madhava: as used here in the Bengali Vaishnavite lyric, Madhava is an epithet for the Hindu god Krishna, but, earlier, Madhava is "Lord of Knowledge," third of the twenty-four icons of Vishnu.

25 Vidyapati: a 15th-century Vaishnavite poet and Sanskrit scholar who was court poet to the kings of Mithila, an area west of present-day Bengal.

26 Kama: desire, passion, physical love; hence, the god of love, though Daniélou writes of Kama as the "lord of lust," who was burned to ashes by a glance from Shiva's third, or frontal eye, "the eye of fire." (Alain Daniélou: *Hindu Polytheism*, New York, Pantheon Books, Bollingen Series LXXIII, 1964, pages 214 and 218.)

27 St. Irenaeus: born in Smyrna and bishop of Lyons, France, in the 2nd century; one of the most distinguished theologians of the ante-Nicene Church, his chief work being *Against the Heresies*, or "Refutation and Overthrow of Gnosis, falsely so called." He was martyred in the persecution of Septimus Severus in 202.

28 St. Gregory of Nyssa: (*c*. 331–*c*. 396) one of the four great fathers of the Eastern (Greek) Church, a notable orator and author of numerous theological treatises.

29 St. Cyril of Jerusalem: (*c*. 315–386) bishop of Jerusalem and an ardent supporter of the Nicene Creed, best known for his catechesis (oral instruction), twenty-three addresses which he delivered about 348 to the catechumens (those receiving rudimentary instruction in the doctrines of Christianity) of his diocese.

30 Pascha Christi: the Passover, hence the Easter season.

31 Mara: the tempter, a spirit of evil, who tried to divert the Buddha from his meditation on the path to truth. Cf. the Hindu Kama, and Satan tempting Jesus in the wilderness.

32 "temps vierge": French, literally, "virginal time." Cf. in Merton's *Conjectures of a Guilty Bystander* (page 117 of the original Doubleday edition) his use of the phrase "point vierge" to describe "the first chirps of the waking birds" at dawn near the monastery in Kentucky. "They begin to speak to Him, not with fluent song, but with an awakening question that is their dawn state, their state at the '*point vierge*.' Their condition asks if it is time for them to 'be.' He answers 'yes.' Then, they one by one wake up, and become birds."

33 Marcuse: Herbert Marcuse, born in Berlin in 1898, now a naturalized American, and emeritus Professor of Philosophy at the University of California, San Diego, in La Jolla. His books include: *Reason and Revolution* (1941; revised edition, Boston, Beacon Press, 1960), *Eros and Civilization* (Beacon Press, 1955; Vintage paperback, 1962), *Soviet Marxism* (New York,

Columbia University Press, 1958; Vintage paperback, 1961), *One-Dimensional Man* (Beacon Press, 1964), *Negations* (Beacon Press, 1969), and *Counterrevolution and Revolt* (Beacon Press, 1972).

[34] antipoetry: Even before he met the Chilean poet Nicanor Parra, author of *Poems & Antipoems,* who visited with him at Gethsemani Monastery in the spring of 1966, Merton had begun to think about and experiment with his own kind of "antipoetry," as evidenced by some of the poems in *Emblems of a Season of Fury,* which appeared in 1963. This vein in his work was further developed in *Cables to the Ace* (1968) and the posthumous *Geography of Lograire.*

[35] Maitreya: in addition to the founder of Yogacara, this name, which comes from the Sanskrit word for "friendly," is used to denote the bodhisattva who is expected to appear as another Buddha 5,000 years after the death of Gautama, the first Buddha.

[36] Gadong oracle: before the Chinese take-over of Tibet and his flight to India, this lama had been the medium for a spirit in a temple at Gadong, a small town west of Lhasa, and was frequently consulted by the leaders of the lamaistic government of Tibet.

[37] "Amplectamur diem qui assignat singulos domicilio suo, qui nos istinc ereptos, et laqueis saecularibus exsolutos, paradiso restituit et regno caelesti . . ."

[38] Loretto Motherhouse: the Motherhouse of the Sisters of Loretto, located in Nerinx, Kentucky, a few miles away from the Abbey of Gethsemani. (Not to be confused with the Loreto Colleges and Convents in Darjeeling and Calcutta which Merton visited.) The American order (spelled with two *t*'s) is distinct from the order in Europe and Asia, which takes its name from the pilgrimage town of Loreto in central Italy, where, according to legend, the house of the Virgin Mary was brought through the air by angels at the end of the 13th century.

[39] In a private letter of November 9, 1968, to Dom Flavian Burns at Gethsemani, Merton wrote: "The talks with the Dalai Lama were very fine. He did a lot of off the record talking, very open and sincere, a very impressive person, deeply concerned about the contemplative life, and also very learned. I have seldom met anyone with whom I clicked so well, and I feel that we have become good friends. He asked me a lot of questions about Western monasticism, and they all had to do with 'attainment' or, in other words, whether or not the monks were reaching the higher degrees of the mystical life, and what we did to help them make it. He talked a lot about Tibetan methods of samadhi (concentration, lower degree of contemplation in which one is working for one pointedness) and said he

had several monks working at a scientific experiment over two years in this practice and that they had attained unusual clarity of mind. This is just elementary stuff for them. We also discussed some of the more technical stuff and he gave me some very good suggestions, so that I am going to study the philosophical groundwork which underlies both Tibetan meditation and Zen. This is Madhyamika philosophy, which is not speculative and abstract but very concrete and fits in with the kind of sweeping purification from conceptual thought which is essential for that kind of meditation. . . .

"These days in the Himalayas have been great, and I am looking forward to seeing the highest mountains and other monasteries. I am glad to have started here and glad I will see the Zen people only later, as I think that will be a step beyond what is here. The Tibetan thing is very complex and deep, and they have certainly attained to something extraordinary. At the same time, they seem very respectful of our own contemplative tradition in the terms in which I presented it to them, and one of them told me, after I had given an outline of our mysticism, that we had everything they had and even were parallel to some of their esoteric traditions (which are usually kept very secret). At the same time, Tibetan mysticism is just beginning to be known in the West, and inevitably there is going to be a lot of popularization which will be quite misleading and irresponsible. I'll send you a little book of the Dalai Lama's which I think you'll enjoy. He is really a great person. You'd like him. . . ."

⁴⁰ Kangra Valley: a place of pilgrimage for devout Hindus who visit the shrines at Jawala Mukhi, Kangra, and Baijnath, where religious festivals called mclas are held. The valley has also given its name to the Kangra school of miniature painting which flourished here under the patronage of the Pahari rajahs in the 18th and early 19th centuries. See Benjamin Rowland· *The Art and Architecture of India,* Baltimore, Penguin Books, 1953, pages 204–6.

⁴¹ The castle which Merton saw was probably the 16th-century Shahpur Kandi Fort, near the town of Nurpur, which the rajahs of Pathan used as a base in their battles with the Mogul emperors of Delhi.

⁴² Benares (Banaras): a city on the Ganges River in north-central India, which is a center for the worship of Shiva and could well be called the capital of Hinduism, since millions of people from all parts of the country try to make, at least once in their lifetimes, a pilgrimage to Benares to bathe at dawn in the sacred waters of the Ganges. A Chinese, Hsuan Chang, who came to Benares in the 7th century A.D. told of its having thirty Buddhist monasteries and one hundred Hindu temples, but these ancient structures were destroyed by the Moslem rulers in the 12th century, so that the present holy places are of more recent date. Along the banks of the river are burning ghats for the cremation of the dead, whose ashes are

scattered on the water, a sacred ritual intended to assist reincarnation at a better level of karma in the next life.

[43] Rawalpindi: a city in the northern part of West Pakistan, not far from the border of Kashmir, which was the capital of Pakistan until the new capital of Islamabad was built nearby.

[44] Amritsar: a city about 300 miles northwest of Delhi, near the border of West Pakistan, which, with its Golden Temple, is the center of the Sikh religion.

[45] Jantar Mantar: a Hindu observatory in New Delhi, built during the Mogul rule by Maharaja Jai Singh II of Jaipur, who also built similar structures in Ujjain, Jaipur, and Benares. It has not been restored, but one can see the immense equatorial sundial, or gnomon, which the Raja called the "Prince of Dials," and near it two circular buildings made with niches in their walls so that the ascension and declension of the stars could be marked on them.

[46] Sufi Nizamuddin: (or Nizam-ud-din Aulia) a Sufi poet and saint who plotted against the Moslem king Tughlaq Shah and was executed in 1324 A.D. Sufism originated in Persia and came into India with the Moslem invasions, beginning in the 12th century. The Sufis allied themselves with the Moslem rulers, helping to convert many Hindus to Islam. Sufi influence is seen in the name of the Qutb Minar, since in Sufi mystical doctrine "Qutb" (literally, "axis") was a mysterious personage who stood at the head of the Sufi hierarchy of saints.

[47] See Appendix VI, page 320, for the text of this "November Circular Letter to Friends."

[48] John Howard Griffin: John Howard Griffin of Fort Worth, Texas, was one of Merton's closest friends and has since been chosen by the Trustees of the Merton Legacy Trust to write the authorized biography, which is being published by Houghton Mifflin. It was Griffin, who first met Merton in 1962 and made frequent visits to Gethsemani in later years, who provided him with a camera and taught him how to use it. The story of their friendship is told in *A Hidden Wholeness: The Visual World of Thomas Merton,* a book of Griffin photographic portraits of and text on Merton, together with photographs and drawings by Merton himself (Houghton Mifflin, 1970). Griffin's best-known book is *Black Like Me,* the account of a white man's penetration of the Deep South with his skin stained dark so that he might pass for black, but he has also written two novels, *The Devil Rides Outside* (1952) and *Nuni* (1956), and many stories and essays, which are represented in *The John Howard Griffin Reader,* edited by Bradford Daniel (Houghton Mifflin, 1968). Griffin was born in Dallas, Texas, spent much of his life in

France, was a member of the French Resistance, and for many years was blind as a result of wounds sustained in the Pacific in World War II. While sightless, he had the opportunity to study theology with the Catholic philosopher Jacques Maritain, and it was during this period that he wrote his two novels. He is an authority on Gregorian chant and also lectures on aesthetics, race relations, and history.

[49] Oberoi: name of the owner of a chain of modern hotels in India.

[50] Bramachari's Ashram: M.B. Bramachari, a monk from Calcutta, a follower of the "messiah" Jagad-Bondhu, whom Merton's Columbia classmate Seymour Freedgood had befriended when Bramachari came to the U.S.A. in the early 1930s. See Merton: *The Seven Storey Mountain,* Part Two, Chapter III. In the archives of the Merton Studies Center at Bellarmine College in Louisville, Kentucky, there is a four-page carbon typescript entitled "Dr. M.B. Bramachari: A Personal Tribute," apparently written for a festschrift volume in honor of Bramachari's sixtieth birthday, probably published in India. It is dated October 1964. Ashram: a hermitage where holy men live.

[51] "The same madness raged through them all, and those who had been brothers an hour before perished by wounds they gave each other." (From the story of Cadmus)

[52] Michel Foucault: French psychologist and professor at the Collège de France. Two of his books have been published in translation in this country by Pantheon Books, New York: *Madness and Civilization, A History of Insanity in the Age of Reason* (1965) and *The Order of Things, An Archaeology of the Human Sciences* (1971).

[53] Raymond Aron: Raymond Claude Ferdinand Aron, born in Paris in 1905, one of France's most distinguished university professors and influential political journalists. He edited the magazine *La France Libre* from London during World War II. Half a dozen of his books have been published here in translation, the most recent being *Marxism and the Existentialists,* New York, Harper & Row, 1970.

[54] "Windermere": Merton is playing here on Windermere, largest of the lakes in the Lake District of England, where Wordsworth spent nearly sixty years of his life and which so many other notable English poets celebrated in their poetry.

[55] Gangtok: the capital of Sikkim.

[56] Jimpa Rimpoche: Lama Nawang Jimpa Rimpoche, a Gelugpa (Yellow Hat) monk, educated and ordained in Lhasa, now exiled to India and

a teacher of the Tibetan boys at St. Joseph's College in North Point. He acted as interpreter for Merton in many of his meetings with Tibetan holy men in the Darjeeling area.

[57] Fr. Sherburne: Fr. Richard Sherburne, S.J., is preparing a doctoral dissertation on an 11th-century Indian source of later Gelugpa (Yellow Hat) meditational practice at Seattle University. When he met Merton in Darjeeling, he was studying Sanskrit and Tibetan in preparation for his work in Buddhist studies.

[58] Kant's Practical Reason: Immanuel Kant (1724–1804), the German philosopher, his *Kritik der praktischen Vernunft* ("Critique of Practical Reason") was published in 1788.

[59] Grenoble: the principal city of the southeastern part of France, situated in the foothills of the French Alps.

[60] Grande Chartreuse: the first Carthusian monastery, founded in 1084 by St. Bruno in the mountains near Grenoble.

[61] La Salette: La Salette-Fallavaux, a pilgrimage site in France, south of Grenoble. The Church of Our Lady of La Salette stands on the spot where it is said the Virgin Mary appeared in a vision to two children in 1846.

[62] Lauds: ". . . from Latin . . . *laus* praise . . . a religious service that constitutes the second or with matins the first of the canonical hours and that is usually sung at dawn in [Roman Catholic] monastic houses. . . ." (Webster's III)

[63] Fr. Stanford: Fr. Maurice Stanford, S.J., a Canadian who has been an educator for some twenty years in the Darjeeling district. At the time of Merton's visit he was headmaster of St. Joseph's College in North Point, where he now serves as professor of English.

[64] sursum corda: "Lift up your hearts," a versicle in the Roman rite.

[65] See Conze's review of Koestler's *The Lotus and the Robot* in *Hibbert Journal*, Vol. LIX, 1961, pages 178-81.

[66] Fr. Vincent Curmi, S.J.: A French-Canadian Jesuit, pastor of Our Lady of Snows Church near North Point, who has made a Nepali-language liturgy for his parishioners.

[67] Sangay dorje: "Sangay" is a Tibetan name for a Buddha. "Dorje" is the Tibetan equivalent of the Sanskrit "vajra"—"adamantine" or "dia-

mond," hence, "pure and indestructible." Thus, the term is an honorific accorded only to the most saintly or learned lamas.

68 Xanadu: "In Xanadu did Kubla Khan
    A stately pleasure-dome decree:
    Where Alph, the sacred river, ran
    Through caverns measureless to man
    Down to a sunless sea."
        —Coleridge: "Kubla Khan"

69 Raj Bhavan: Government House; probably the former hot-weather residence of a British governor.

70 Ruth Benedict: American anthropologist (1887–1948) who first specialized in the study of the Indians of the American West, but then broadened her interests to general world cultural configurations. Her most influential books were: *Patterns of Culture* (1934), *Race, Science and Politics* (1940), and her book on the Japanese, *The Chrysanthemum and the Sword* (1946).

71 Anaïs Nin: born in Paris in 1903, and now an American citizen, she published her first three books in Paris: *D. H. Lawrence: An Unprofessional Study, House of Incest,* and *Winter of Artifice.* Coming to this country, and at first unable to find a publisher, she printed *Under a Glass Bell* herself on a hand press. But fame and success came with the publication of her *Diaries,* of which four volumes have now appeared, all edited by Gunther Stuhlmann and published by Harcourt Brace Jovanovich.

72 In his private letter of November 9, 1968, to Dom Flavian Burns at Gethsemani, Merton had written. "After the [Bangkok] meeting, then Indonesia as planned and so on through to Japan. After Japan, I believe it is necessary to make a change of plans. I was going to fly back to San Francisco via Hawaii in April or so, but the Dalai Lama suggested that I speak to some people in Europe, including a Tibetan who is setting up a monastery in Switzerland, and also this abbot friend of mine has a meditation center in Scotland. I ought also to see Marco Pallis, who is one of the great experts on Tibetan Buddhism and another expert in Wales. I can fly from Tokyo over the N. Pole to Europe and take in Switzerland and Scotland, avoiding Cistercian monasteries as much as possible and keeping out of sight, coming back to the U.S. about the end of May. Please let me know if this is ok with you, and I can plan accordingly.

"I assume when I get back to the U.S. you would want me to come back to Gethsemani, and we could plan any future steps from there. I am still keen on the idea of trying something in Alaska, and I am certain of full support from the bishop there. But naturally this would have to be planned carefully with you, and in the light of whatever may come up between now and then. I often think of the hermitage at Gethsemani and of the many graces it has meant to me: but I still think that I ought to be elsewhere, though always as a member of my monastic family there. I am certainly willing to go slow and be patient about it. But let's be thinking about it and praying to know God's will."

73 Needle Rock and Bear Harbor: places on the California coast north of San Francisco which Merton explored when he was visiting Our Lady of the Redwoods Abbey.

74 Commemorations of St. Elizabeth: a short prayer at the end of the Roman Catholic Divine Office for November 19 commemorating St. Elizabeth of Hungary (1207–31). The daughter of King Andrew II of Hungary, and the wife of Louis IV, Landgrave of Thuringia, she devoted her life to charity, nursing persons sick with loathsome diseases, and penances of the greatest severity. Four years after her death she was canonized by Pope Gregory IX because of the miracles reported to have taken place at her tomb.

75 Sr. Helen Elizabeth, S.C.N.; supervisor of the first floor (east) of St. Joseph's Infirmary in Louisville, where Merton was hospitalized in the 1950s.

76 *"Attolite portas principes vestras"*: Latin, "Lift up your heads, O gates." (Psalm 23[24]:9) *"Ego sum ostium"*: Latin, "I am the door." (John 10:7)

77 Lucernarium: Latin, "the time when the lamps are lighted." (Lewis and Short: *Latin Dictionary*)

78 Agni: "Sanskrit *Agni,* the god of fire. . . . The most important of the [Hindu] Vedic gods. Primarily the god of the altar fire, he yet represents a trinity in which to earthly fire are joined the lightning and the sun. As the altar fire, consuming the sacrifice, he is the mediator between the gods and men among whom he dwells. He is represented as red, with two faces and a forked tongue. . . ." (Webster's II)

79 *Sensation Time at the Home:* this small collection of Merton's last shorter poems will be included in his *Collected Poems,* to be published by New Directions.

80 Czeslaw Milosz: poet and Professor of Slavic Languages and Literatures at the University of California in Berkeley since 1960. Born in Lithuania in 1911, he had three anti-Nazi books published clandestinely in Nazi-occupied Poland, later served five years in the Polish diplomatic service, defected and lived ten years in Paris. The story of his conversion

from Communism is told in his most famous book, *The Captive Mind,* New York, Vintage Books, 1953. His *Postwar Polish Poetry* appeared with Doubleday in 1965 and his *Selected Poems* with Penguin in 1968.

[81] Paul Jacobs: author, lecturer, and TV speaker who lives in San Francisco. He calls himself a "radical journalist" and prefers to write on social and political issues. He spent some years as a labor union organizer, and later was a consultant to the Peace Corps, the War on Poverty Program under Sargent Shriver, and to the Fund for the Republic. His books include *The State of the Union, Between the Rock and the Hard Place,* and *The New Radicals.*

[82] Melchizedek: a pre-Aaronic and pre-Levitical priest-king to whom Abraham paid tithes. (Genesis 14:18)

[83] Actually, the chapter (chapter 6) in Conze's *Buddhist Thought in India* is entitled "The Cultivation of the Social Emotions." The discussion of maitri ("friendliness") begins near the top of page 82 in the Ann Arbor paperback edition.

[84] Ganesha: ". . . the [Hindu] god of wisdom or prudence and the remover of obstacles. He is represented as a short, fat yellow or red man with a large belly and an elephant's head." (Webster's II) He is also known as Ganapati, the "Lord of Categories" ("Gana"—"category," or one of the fundamental elements of existence). In the *Shiva Purana* there is a characteristically Indian myth of how Ganesha got his elephant head. Alain Daniélou transcribes it thus: ". . . once Shiva's consort, the Lady-of-the-Mountain (Parvati), was disturbed by her lord, who entered the house while she was bathing. Worried not to have a servant of her own to guard her door, she rubbed her body, and from some scurf she gathered a being was born whom she called her son and used as a guard. His name was Ganapati. When the boy attempted to prevent Shiva from entering the house, the god sent his squires against him and in the battle Ganapati's head was cut off. On seeing Parvati's sorrow over this deed, Shiva severed the head of the first living being that came his way and joined it to the child's body. This happened to be the head of an elephant." (Daniélou: *Hindu Polytheism,* page 292.) As if to heighten the comic aspect, in Hindu iconography Ganesha's "vehicle" is a mouse.

[85] Sr. Thérèse Lentfoehr: Sr. M. Thérèse Lentfoehr is a member of the congregation of the Sisters of the Divine Savior and Associate Professor of English at The College of Racine in Wisconsin. In 1939, when he was living in Greenwich Village, Merton wrote to Sr. Thérèse about a poem of hers which he had read in a magazine, and this was the beginning of a friendship which continued till his death. It was Merton's custom to send her copies of almost everything he wrote, usually in manuscript form, as well as drafts

and worksheets, so that her collection of Mertoniana is perhaps the most extensive which has been assembled. She typed for him over 700 pages of the "Orientation Notes," for his lectures to the novices at Gethsemani, and also the final text of his book *The Sign of Jonas*. Her last visit to Merton at Gethsemani while he was living was in November 1967, when Merton read to her parts of *The Geography of Lograire,* the long poem which he was then composing. Sr. Thérèse is now preparing a book about Merton's poetry.

[86] John and Rena Niles: John Jacob Niles, singer of ballads and folk songs, composed the music for twenty-two poems by Merton, known as the *Niles-Merton Song Cycle*. He and his wife, Rena, make their home in Lexington, Kentucky, and were friends of Merton.

[87] Tom Jerry Smith: Dr. T. J. Smith, M.D., an allergy specialist in Louisville, Kentucky, who had treated Merton while he was at Gethsemani.

[88] Richard Chi: Dr. Richard S.Y. Chi, B.Sc., M.A., Ph.D. (Cambridge), D. Phil. (Oxford), now Professor of East Asian Languages and Literature at Indiana University. Dr. Chi, who, as a young man, spent a year in a Peking monastery studying under the great Zen master Cheng Kung, carried on an extensive correspondence with Merton, advising him on his reading in Zen and other Asian religions, and visited him twice at Gethsemani. Merton wrote an introduction for Dr. Chi's still unpublished translation of *The Ch'an of Shen Hui,* a classic 8th-century Zen text. In the letter here referred to, Merton asked Dr. Chi for the names of Ch'an and Zen scholars whom he might look up when he got to Taiwan and Japan.

[89] Nyanaponika Thera: the German Buddhist bhikkhu whom Merton was later to visit in Ceylon. (See pages 216–18) Author of *The Heart of Buddhist Meditation,* London, Rider & Company, 1962; paperback edition, 1969. Merton also had copies of Nyanaponika Thera's pamphlets *The Power of Mindfulness,* "An Inquiry into the Scope of Bare Attention and the Principal Sources of its Strength," The Wheel Publication No. 121/122, Kandy, Ceylon, Buddhist Publication Society, 1968; and *Anatta and Nibbana,* "Egolessness and Deliverance," The Wheel Publication No. 11, Kandy, Ceylon, Buddhist Publication Society, 1959.

[90] Dacca: a city of some 800,000 inhabitants about 200 miles northeast of Calcutta. In the 17th century it was the Mogul capital of Bengal, after partition that of East Pakistan, and now of the new Bengali country of Bangladesh.

[91] Dr. Pemba: Dr. T.Y. Pemba. (See pages 161–63)

[92] J.B.S. Haldane: the British biologist (1892–1964). Among his principal books, available in this country, are: *Science and Human Life* (1933), *Marxist Philosophy and the Sciences* (1939), *Science Advances* (1948), and *Causes of Evolution* (1966).

[93] Anzacs: acronym for Australian and New Zealand Army Corps; the colloquial name for the soldiers from these countries who served in World War I.

[94] St. Cecilia: a noble Roman lady, converted to Christianity, who was martyred around 178 A.D. in Sicily in the reign of Marcus Aurelius. Legend has it that she praised God by instrumental as well as vocal music, and she has become the patron saint of music and of the blind. Her story inspired notable paintings by Raphael and Rubens, and in literature Chaucer's "Seconde Nonnes Tale" and Dryden's "Song for St. Cecilia's Day," which was set to music by Handel.

[95] lakhs: in Hindi (and in Indian English), the number 100,000 is called a "lakh."

[96] Christ in the Desert: the Benedictine Monastery of Christ in the Desert at Chama Canyon, Abiquiu, New Mexico. Merton visited there in May and again in September, 1968.

[97] McNamara: Robert S. McNamara, Secretary of Defense in the U.S. Government, 1961–68 and now president of the International Bank for Reconstruction and Development (the "World Bank").

[98] Descartes: René Descartes (1596–1650), the French philosopher, scientist, and mathematician, perhaps best known for the key phrase of his epistemology: "Cogito ergo sum"—"I think, therefore I am." He believed that the physical world was mechanistic, that rationalization and logic should replace experience as the basis of philosophy, and that the methods of mathematics could be extended to all human knowledge. His two most important works were the *Discourse on Method* (1637) and the *Principles of Philosophy* (1644).

[99] See Toukaram: *Psaumes du pèlerin,* translated and edited by G.-A. Deleury, UNESCO, "Connaissance de l'orient" Series, Paris, Gallimard, 1956, pages 13 and 17–18. Louis Renou, in his *Indian Literature,* gives Tukaram's life dates as 1607–49, and says that he represents the culmination of the bhakti influence in western India.

[100] "Qu'est-ce qu'une vocation? Un appel, et une réponse. Cette définition ne nous tient pas quitte: concevoir l'appel de Dieu comme l'ordre

exprès d'accomplir une tâche, certes ce n'est pas toujours faux, mais ce n'est vrai qu'après une longue élaboration intérieure où il arrive que rien de tel ne soit perçu. Il arrive aussi que l'ordre mûrisse avec l'être qui devra l'accomplir: qu'il soit en quelque sorte cet être même, parvenu à maturité. Enfin, mûrir peut être une mystérieuse façon de mourir, pour qu'avec la mort commence la tâche. . . . il faut qu'il y ait un choix vertigineux, une déhiscence définitive par quoi se déchire la certitude qu'il a conquise d'être appelé. Ce qui—comme on dit, et le mot ici est juste—*consacre* une vocation et l'élève à la hauteur du sacrifice qu'elle devient, c'est une rupture avec l'ordre apparent de l'être, avec sa maturité formelle ou son efficacité visible."

101 Fr. Cherian: Fr. Cherian M. Curiyikad, an Indian Jesuit from Kerala State who was teaching scripture and Hebrew at St. Mary's College, Kurseong, at the time of Merton's visit there. He is now at the Vidya Jyoti Institute of Religious Studies in Delhi.

102 Fr. Louis Schillebeeckx, S.J.: third-year instructor at the Jesuit Scholasticate of St. Joseph at Kurseong, where he has also taught at St. Mary's College. "Magister Spiritus"—spiritual director of students. (His brother, Fr. Edward Schillebeeckx, O P., entered the Flemish Province of the Dominican Order in 1935. He served as theological expert for the Dutch bishops at the Second Vatican Council. He has written prolifically on theological subjects, and many of his books are available in English translation, among them, *Christ, the Sacrament of the Encounter with God,* New York, Sheed and Ward, 1963, and, more recently, *Revelation and Theology,* 2 volumes, Sheed and Ward, 1967–68, and *Celibacy,* Sheed and Ward, 1968.)

103 Dom Leclercq: Dom Jean Leclercq, O.S.B., a Benedictine monk of Clervaux Abbey in Luxembourg. He wrote the introduction for one of Merton's posthumous books, *Contemplation in a World of Action,* New York, Doubleday, 1971, and has also published here *Love of Learning and the Desire for God,* New York, Fordham University Press. He is the author of a nine-volume critical edition of the works of St. Bernard.

104 Mother Myriam: Myriam Dardenne, Abbess of the Cistercian Abbey O.L. of Nazareth, Brecht, Belgium, came to the United States with several Belgian sisters of the same house to begin a new, rather small Cistercian Monastery at Whitethorn, California, Our Lady of the Redwoods, of which she is Mother Abbess. She writes: "Our community? Ten persons at the present time. Our orientation is Cistercian. Our style of life simple, open, searching. We pray, we work, we live." Merton visited Our Lady of the Redwoods twice, once in May of 1968, and again, in the fall, just before his flight to Asia.

105 Fr. Eudes Bamberger: Fr. John Eudes Bamberger, O.C.S.O., for many years a monk and doctor-psychiatrist at Gethsemani, later Secretary Gen-

eral of the Cistercians, and, in 1971, elected Abbot of the Cistercian monastery at Genesee, New York.

[106] Fr. Chrysogonus Waddell: a monk of Gethsemani; a liturgist and musicologist.

[107] Naomi Burton: Naomi Burton Stone was born and educated in England. She came to this country in 1939 and met Merton in 1940 when he brought his first novel to the literary agency, Curtis Brown Ltd., where she worked. Greatly admiring his writing (they were both in their twenties) she tried to sell this and a later novel but without success. It was the beginning of a friendship and business relationship that lasted until his death. In 1947 Merton sent her, from Gethsemani Monastery, which he had entered in 1941, his autobiographical *Seven Storey Mountain,* and she handled the arrangements for the publication of this and all his books until 1959, when she resigned as head of the Book Department, Curtis Brown, and joined Doubleday as a Senior Editor. Since then she has acted as editor for *Conjectures of a Guilty Bystander* and the novel *My Argument with the Gestapo,* and, since Merton's death, as editor for the Merton Legacy Trust, of which she is one of the trustees. Merton established this trust prior to his death to manage his literary properties for the benefit of the Abbey of Gethsemani; the other two trustees are Mrs. Frank E. O'Callaghan III of Louisville and James Laughlin of New Directions, a friend of Merton's since 1944, when, at the suggestion of Mark Van Doren, who had been one of Merton's professors at Columbia, New Directions published Merton's first volume of poetry, *Thirty Poems.*

[108] The *Time-Life* Bible did not materialize, but Merton's contribution to it, a long essay, has been published as a book by The Liturgical Press, Collegeville, Minnesota, under the title *Opening the Bible.* Merton's piece was intended to be a bridge between the Old and New Testaments in the projected series.

[109] Dan Walsh: Father Daniel C. Walsh. As Visiting Professor of Medieval Philosophy at Columbia University, he taught courses taken by Merton in the philosophies of St. Thomas Aquinas, Duns Scotus, and William of Ockham, as well as privately tutoring him in the reading of the original Greek text of the *Metaphysics* of Aristotle. (See Merton's *The Seven Storey Mountain,* pages 215ff. and 253ff. in the Signet paperback edition.) Later, for a period of about ten years, Fr. Walsh lived and taught at Gethsemani, while also teaching courses at Loretto College in Nerinx, and at Bellarmine College in Louisville, Kentucky.

[110] Bob Lax: Robert Lax, a fellow student of Merton's at Columbia University and one of his closest friends, with whom he corresponded over the years. (See Merton's *The Seven Storey Mountain* for the story of the early

years of their friendship.) A poet of distinction (*The Circus of the Sun, Oedipus, Thought, New Poems,* and other books, all published by Emil Antonucci at his Journeyman Press, 86–46 Fort Hamilton Parkway, Brooklyn, New York 11209), Lax now makes his home on the Greek Island of Kalymnos.

111 Emmett Williams: one of the leading figures in the international concrete poetry movement; editor of *An Anthology of Concrete Poetry,* New York, Something Else Press, 1967.

112 Rishikesh: a Hindu holy place of pilgrimage on the upper reaches of the river Ganges.

113 Mouni Sadhu, who died in 1972, lived for many years in Australia, but he came from a German family, long resident in Poland, and his native language was German. He took the name "Mouni Sadhu" when he became a disciple of Sri Ramana Maharshi, the contemporary South Indian sage and teacher of Advaita Vedanta, and joined Maharshi's ashram at Tiruvannamali. As a young man in Europe, he had belonged to an order of Rosicrucian Hermetists and published work on the tarot and on theurgy. Two of Mouni Sadhu's books, *Meditation* and *In Days of Great Peace,* were in Merton's personal library of Orientalia at Gethsemani. *In Days of Great Peace* (London, Allen & Unwin, 1957) carries the subtitle "The Highest Yoga as Lived" and is a diary (with flashbacks) concerned chiefly with the teachings of Maharshi, especially the technique of Jnana-Yoga (vichara) through which the transcendental spiritual state of samadhi may be achieved. In Australia, Mouni Sadhu established a group of Ramana Maharshi devotees, but the survival of some of his early interest in occultism led to its separation from the main body of the Maharshi cult. (In Sanskrit, "mouni" means "silent"; "sadhu," "ascetic or holy man.")

114 Arthur Osborne: an English student of Hinduism and Vedanta, who died in 1971. He was a disciple of Sri Ramana Maharshi and spent the last twenty years of his life at Maharshi's ashram in South India, where he edited the ashram journal, *The Mountain Path.* His books include: *Buddhism and Christianity in the Light of Hinduism, Ramana Maharshi and the Path of Self-Knowledge, The Collected Works of Ramana Maharshi, Teachings of Bhagavan Sri Ramana Maharshi in His Own Words,* and *The Incredible Sai Baba.*

MADRAS
November 26–28

November 26 / Madras

Flying into Madras is lovely. The city is all self-evident, spread out along the ocean with its vast beach, its harbor, its rivers, its broad avenues. Then the plane swings inland over the hot fields, neat, cultivated, green flat land. Many coconut palms. Many huts made of palm-leaf matting. Poor as they are, they weather much better than the somewhat pretentious "modern style" houses that are shiny and bright for a month and go black or gray-green in the first monsoon.

Madras is a bright and leisurely city. The people are less desperate than the Bengalis. It is more truly India than Delhi or Calcutta (whatever "truly India" might be—as if I were capable of knowing and defining it!).

Coming in, I spotted St. Thomas Mount[1]—again bright, neat, self-evident. I have not yet seen the cathedral, which is probably confusing rather than evident.

✻

"The discovery of a violently active star, the hottest known and apparently newly created, was reported by Leicester University scientists. The star is considered an important find for X-ray astronomy. . . ."

"A snake weighing over two maunds[2] and twenty-five feet long and two feet in diameter was caught by two villagers in the Buatnagar District of Nepal on Sunday. . . ."

"When the train was passing through a jungle area . . . he removed a hose pipe and brought the train to a halt. His accomplices hiding in the jungle came out and looted forty bags of peas. The guard and other crew were made to keep silent, being threatened with dire consequences. . . ."

"Ho Dons in front of us, my father on our trail behind us: what can you do now, tailless one?" (Tarzan)[3]

"Butar—listen! If I untie you will you guide this Ben-ko while I battle your enemies on the gryf?"

Butar: "I will guide." (Tarzan)

—*The Indian Express,* Madras

⌘

November 27 / Madras

There is cholera in North Madras. And in many places in South India attacks are made on police stations or houses of merchants by gangs of Naxalites[4] presumably Maoist Communists. Brutal killings in any case. Yet nothing can change the loveliness of this city of which I saw something last evening with Dr. Raghavan.[5] He came over from the university, where

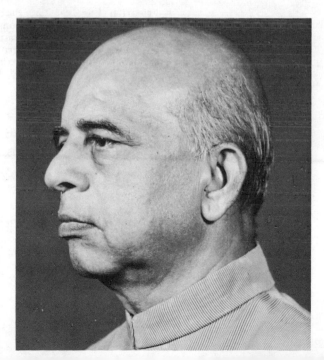

Dr. V. Raghavan

a Gandhi seminar is in progress. We had some tea and then drove around in the dusk. And then the dark of nightfall.

Today there is rain outside; it is one of the monsoon seasons here.

⌘

"Many hundreds and thousands of years ago, during an epoch, not yet definitely determined, of that period of the earth's history which geologists call the Tertiary period, most likely toward the end of it, a specially highly-developed race of anthropoid apes lived somewhere in the tropical zone—probably on a great continent that has now sunk to the bottom of the Indian Ocean. Darwin has given us an approximate description of these ancestors of ours. They were completely covered with hair, they had beards and pointed ears, and they lived in bands in the trees."

"Perfectly white cats with blue eyes are always, or almost always, deaf."

—Friedrich Engels: "The Part Played by Labour in the Transition from Ape to Man," in *Dialectics of Nature,* translated by Clemens Dutt, New York, International Publishers, 1940, pages 279 and 282.

⌘

Some important dates in history of the East India Company:[6]

1639 Fort St. George, which became Madras.

1659 Fort William, a "factory," to become the city of Calcutta.

1661 The British acquire Bombay from Portugal.

1686 The Company is at war with Aurangzeb,[7] the Mogul emperor.

⌘

We drove past Fort St. George in the shadows, with a large garden around it. Stairways and walls and windows and a steeple. The old East India Company headquarters. University of Madras—a long line of spanking new buildings on the sea front. Dr. Raghavan pointed out his office. The old law college is fantastic, a Saracenic Coney Island, but dignified.

The beach is the finest thing in Madras. There was a new moon and a strong, steady breeze off the water; people sitting in small scattered groups, cooling off in the dark. Hulls of fishing boats ("country boats") pulled up on the sand. A very wide beach. Dr. Raghavan and I watched the surf roll in and looked at the stars. He told me the names of some of the constellations in Sanskrit. The moon prevented our seeing the Southern Cross clearly.

Then we went to San Thomé. Smaller than I expected, the cathedral is in an entirely Christian quarter. Its architecture is standard 19th-century Gothic, spacious, full of the old-style statues, and over the chancel arch the words "Thomas, one of the twelve, called Didymus." I find the inscription strangely touching. I kneel for a while looking up to the shadows of the sanctuary where all is still as it was before the Council. Then we depart. An Indian Christian beggarwoman displays a dramatically spread-eagled sleeping baby on her lap. I give her a few picc. But Dr. Raghavan stands no nonsense from other beggars and is particularly severe with the ones in the Shaivite temple in Mylapore, not far from San Thomé. It is called Kapaleeswara, the temple of Shiva, whose goddess consort took the form of the peacock to worship him. Extraordinary life and seeming confusion of the temple, full of people milling around barefoot (I too) in the sand, children playing and yelling, dozens of shrines with different devotions going on—especially one with waving camphor torches for Ganesha, who has a prominent well-lighted booth facing the entry. Less going on at the Shiva lingam[8] which stands alone, half draped, black, heavy, tumescent. Other shrines and porches and halls. A group of women doing a puja of their own. And a group of

Vedic scholars chanting the *Vedas* strongly in another place. Over it all the chant of ancient *Devaram* hymns in Tamil comes over a public address system. We trace the music to its source and find an affable temple singer, a friend of Dr. Raghavan's, seated in a small cell before a microphone, accompanied by an acolyte with cymbals. Handsomeness of the Tamil chant. Then other shrines, and two dowdy peacocks in a big enclosure with iron railings. Finally out the back to the dark broad tank full of lotuses. This was my first real exposure to South Indian Hinduism. Very alive—especially the many young pilgrims dressed in black, as a sign of their vow to go to Sabarimalai, a holy place sacred to Ayyappan[9] in the jungles of Kerala.[10]

Mass this morning at St. Thomas Mount. I drove out there in pounding rain, the monsoon is running late here, and the car climbed the hill by a back way. Otherwise you go up a long flight of steps. I entered the little church and found the high altar prepared. It was delightful, a perfect hermitage, with a few Indian women and a couple of Italians—a priest and layman visiting their relative, the pastor. I said the Mass of St. Thomas, looking at the ancient gray carved stone that was found on the site. The altar is a sort of folk-art baroque, with a folk-type icon of the saint in a quasi-Franciscan tunic, being pierced by a spear. Then another folk-art-type Virgin and Child, garlanded by the faithful, ascribed to St. Luke, naturally, but obviously 17th- or 18th-century. The old pulpit was charming, too. A very lovely little church, so quiet, so isolated, so simple, so fresh. It stands on an abrupt hill overlooking an army camp and the airport. One of the nicest things I have found in India or anywhere. I felt my pilgrimage to it was a great grace. Next door there is a crèche for abandoned children, run by some Franciscan sisters. I saw the little dark-eyed babies, drank some lemonade, signed the visitors' book and escaped before the sisters could read it. More rain, and we drove on to Mahabalipuram.[11]

⌘

I got Lawrence's *Twilight in Italy* in Darjeeling and now, here in Madras, a little way down Mount Road, a thin volume of his *Selected Poems* (edited by J. Reeves).[12] I'm curious to read again after so many years his "Virgin Youth" when today I have seen the Shiva lingam at Mahabalipuram, standing black and alone at the edge of the ocean, washed by spray of great waves breaking on the rocks.

> He stands like a lighthouse, night churns
> Round his base, his dark light rolls
> Into darkness, and darkly returns.
>
> Is he calling, the lone one? Is his deep
> Silence full of summons?

There is no "problem," however, in the black lingam. It is washed by the sea, and the sea is woman: it is no void, no question. No English anguish about Mahabalipuram. How right the "lighthouse" stanza of Lawrence is, though, for this lingam on the rocky point! Night and sea are the same: so they are transferable. Lawrence's experience is convincing though his poetry is usually bad. Does rasa apply here? Not really. Something else perhaps. Too much mother, too many wrong words. I mean now in some of the other poems. ("But when I draw the scanty cloak of silence over my eyes. . . .")[12] Beautiful things in his prose, such as the two monks walking in a yard above Lago Maggiore, reminding me somehow of Kurseong. I forget where I read this—maybe while waiting in the room at Darjeeling, waiting to leave that Sunday morning.

Much more sophisticated than Lawrence is a love song of Vidyapati in which Radha complains that Krishna is a "country boy" and rough, and does not know the art of love. Yet she hears her ankle bells buzzing like bees.

This morning two Indian nuns gave away the secret of how to get to St. Thomas Mount. I had looked in vain in the phone book. Quite by chance I ran into them in the corridor by my room just as I was getting ready to leave. They were setting up a table of linens and purses to sell. They said they were of the same order as those at the Mount and one fished out a little address book with the phone number. When I came back late in the afternoon, they were tired and smiling, getting their things together. I asked if they had a good day and they said yes.

⌘

November 28 / Madras

The trip to Mahabalipuram was fine. Especially the South Indian landscape under monsoon clouds. Dark green foliage, bright green paddy, thousands of tall palms, sheets of bright water, blue mountains in the south with fine shapes. I asked the Catholic driver if those were the mountains where Ramana Maharshi[13] had been. He said yes and smiled. Then the sea, and the little thatched huts of the fishing villages. In a way all this was more charming than anything I had seen in India—more peaceful, more relaxed, better kept. Here one finally got some sense of what rural India might once have been.

Mahabalipuram is the remains of a culture such as I have not seen before. A complex of shrines carved out of, or built into, a great ancient rock formation—not cliffs but low rambling outcrops and boulders, smoothed and shaped by millions of years. Caves, porches, figures, steps, markings, lines of holes, gods and goddesses—but spread around without too much profusion.

⌘

I remember the black cat on the roof at Darjeeling, with two crazy little kittens playing and sliding on the green corrugated iron, and grabbing at her, tackling her while she stared at me fixedly, her tail slightly twitching. Cat on the kitchen roof, amid the coal smoke from the hotel chimney. The mountains and the deep valley and the big blue flowers, the view from the toilet window of room 14!

Bob Lax wants me to come to Greece. I still don't know if I can get to Europe at all. I looked today at the JAL, Air France, and Lufthansa schedules. Probably better *not* to try a direct flight—not that there is one really. But, say, via Moscow? (JAL and then what?). Or come back through India. Bombay-Athens, Delhi-Athens, all reasonable. But not in May! Better perhaps Tokyo-Anchorage-Amsterdam. Then Switzerland-Athens, and then back to England for Wales, and Scotland. What about the letter from the man at Orval[14] about the old Grandmontine[15] priory that is falling into ruins? . . . (At Puy near Chevier in the Indre.)

❋

"Seven Pagodas," Mahabalipuram

High relief at "Seven Pagodas," Mahabalipuram

On personal Isvara, the only means of realization of atman.

". . . Steadfast devotion to a personal isvara who is but the highest expression of the Absolute, the crystallization of the formless. The personal isvara, in the fullest measure of his grace, reveals his highest nature which lies far beyond all predications and form, to that devotee who has merged his entire being in the Lord."

(Source not yet identified—Ed.)

High relief at "Seven Pagodas," Mahabalipuram

A sense of silence and of space, at Mahabalipuram, of un-predictable views, of the palms and nearby sea. I would have liked to wander a long time among the rocks, but the kids selling post cards and trying to act as guides were a nuisance, so I moved on. To the beach, which is also admirable. Bright blue of the Bay of Bengal. A cool wind coming in strongly off the sea. The shore temple, smaller than I expected, very weather-beaten, but a real gem. It is especially interesting when seen in relation to the rest of the complex. And in relation to San-kara, a contemporary of this shrine, who lived at Kanchee-puram, which I did not see.

※

Dr. Raghavan has had quite a bit to say about his guru, Sankara-charya of Kanchi,[16] whom I have not met—he is traveling in the villages. I forgot I had read about him in Koestler's (bad) book *The Lotus and the Robot*.[17] Rereading an excerpt—I find Sankaracharya saying: "Adaptations have no place in the stand-ards of spiritual discipline."

Against shortening or changing the ancient rituals. No concessions to be made. One who cannot fulfil his obligations can somehow substitute by regret and repentance, but the obli-gations are not to be slackened. Koestler was bothered by this "unyielding attitude." Sankaracharya's views, he thought, "bore no relation to contemporaneity."

※

In the discourses of Sankaracharya of Kanchi (Raghavan gave me a book of them) I find great emphasis for instance on the *oral* tradition of the *Vedas* and the *exact* chanting of the Vedic texts—and the discipline of learning how to do so. His belief in the importance and efficacy of this. Also, his belief in strict ascetic and religious practice. "To the extent that we make sacrifices in performing acts which we sincerely believe to be good, to that extent will our soul, or atman, get elevated. Even acts done in ignorance, but with faith, will produce spiritual reward. The moment we begin to question why a particular religious practice should be observed . . . we are beginning to lose faith, or bhakti.

"When we perform with faith the prescribed karmas and anushthanas and dedicate them to God, as taught by the Vedas, we attain jnana which clears the way for God-realisation."

"If sannyasins are to take up a profession . . . they could not become brahmanishtas, persons with their minds fixed in the Paramatman which is their only avocation according to the Sastras [Shastras]."

Sannyasins, he adds, should not be grouped in associations (sangha). "Forming an association pulls down the sannyasins to the level of worldly men."

—Sankaracharya of Kanchi: *Madras Discourses,*
1957–60, pages 21–28.

Sankaracharya of Kanchi interpreted the Adam and Eve story as a degradation of a Hindu philosophical idea. Atman (Adam) and Jiva (Eve). Jiva eats the fruit of the tree while Atman looks on.[18] (Some interesting possibilities here: cf. my dialogue with Suzuki.[19] Koestler dismisses the whole thing.)

Sankaracharya of Kanchi on the difference between hallucinations and mystic experience: hallucinations are temporary and due to lack of control. "They are caused by the wishes and fears of the ego. The mystic's mind is a blank, his experience is shapeless and without object."

By Hindu tradition, the bramachari or student begs food for himself and his guru. This gives time for study, instead of work, and it instills into him "a sense of vinaya (discipline) without which no vidya (knowledge) can be received and can fructify in the mind.

Aardra darsanam: a puja to be performed at the conjunction of the full moon and the star Aardra in December-January. One bathes the images of Shiva in milk and sandal-paste in honor of Shiva and his dance, for everything that happens is his divine play.

❊

A conversation last evening with Dr. Raghavan on rasa and Indian aesthetics. He spoke of the importance of suggestion to convey aesthetic implications which transcend ordinary speech. Poetry is not ordinary speech, nor is poetic experience ordinary experience. It is closer to religious experience. Rasa is above all santa: contemplative peace. We discussed the difference between aesthetic experience and religious experience: the aesthetic lasts only as long as the object is present. Religious knowledge does not require the presence of "an object." Once one has known brahman one's life is permanently transformed from within. I spoke of William Blake and his fourfold vision.

I visited the National Gallery and Government Museum this morning. Nice paintings of the Rajput, Mogul, and Kangra schools.[20] What is the relation of painting to modes of music? Excellent bronzes. Some nice folk art. Musical instruments again—I seek them out especially. Such lovely shapes! A vina, sitars, temple drums, an arrangement of eighteen porcelain cups to be filled to different levels with water and lightly played with a stick of bamboo. Among the modern paintings—mostly Indian and third-rate—I spotted one which I thought was a very good imitation of Dufy. The card said Duffy. The signature said Dufy. There was also a not very good Gauguin. And a couple of standard Jamini Roys.

❊

Surendranath Dasgupta on idealism:

The *Ahirbudhnya Samhita* is a post-*Upanishadic* work from the Vaishnava school of thought which deals with time and Isvara.

204

"Time is regarded as the element that combines the prakriti with the purushas." It is the instrument through which the spontaneous thought of Isvara acts. The power of God is not *physical* or mechanical; it is self-manifestation in thought movement that separates thought and object (mind substance) passing entirely into actuality without obstruction. It is creativity emerging in self-diremption from pure stillness, not as event but as pure consciousness. This self-diremption with power and object is *time* and all that is measured by time. The brahman perceived he would be many and thus he became many, in time. "Time is identified with the thought movement of God and is regarded as the first category of its inner movement, which is responsible not only for the creation of the cosmos but also of the colony of individual selves." It is without external cause.

Individuals are pure insofar as they are "in God" but involved in moral struggle insofar as they are "outside him," cut off by extraneous limits, but they must purify themselves of separative root tendencies. *Not, however, from matter.* Matter and spirit are two necessary poles in the dialectic.

—Surendranath Dasgupta: *Indian Idealism,*
Cambridge University Press, second edition,
1962, pages 61–80. See also pages 286–87 in
Part Two of this volume, "Complementary
Reading."

NOTES: *Madras*

[1] St. Thomas Mount: a hill eight miles west of Madras proper, site of the Church of Our Lady of Expectation, built in 1547; known to the Indians as Faranghi Mahal ("The Hill of the Franks"), it was mentioned by Marco Polo as early as the 13th century. Legend has it that the Apostle Thomas came to India to convert the Indians to Christianity and that he was martyred on this hill. However, his tomb is claimed for the Cathedral of San Thomé in the Mylapore district of Madras. There is also a fort of San Thomé, built by the Portuguese in 1504, captured by the French in 1672, then taken from them by the Dutch two years later, and finally occupied by the British in 1749.

2 maunds: the maund is a greatly varying measure of weight in India, in Madras about 25 lbs., in Bombay 28, and in Bengal 82.

3 Tarzan: "Hero of a series of stories of adventure by Edgar Rice Burroughs. He is a white man of prodigious strength and chivalrous instincts. reared by African apes." (Webster's II) Now a comic-strip character.

4 Naxalites: while some of the Naxalites may be "Maoist Communists," as someone evidently characterized them to Merton, it does not appear certain that all of them are Communist-organized. Writing in *The Nation*, New York, Volume 214, Number 5, January 31, 1972, in an article entitled "Punjab, Bengal and the Green Revolution," Richard Critchfield described the Naxalites thus: "In both the Eastern and Western halves of Bengal during the past five years there has been a steady growth of movements by dispossessed peasants who lack bullocks, money, land or hope, to seize land by force. These Naxalite gangs, named after the village where the land-grab movement began, roam about, killing, looting and condemning landlords by 'people's courts' on the old Chinese pattern. Until recently, they defined a 'landlord' as a peasant with more than 5 acres. Now the standard is down to 3 acres."

5 Dr. Raghavan: Dr. V. Raghavan, Professor-emeritus of Sanskrit at the University of Madras; one of the world's most eminent Sanskritists, he is the author of many scholarly books and journal papers, but perhaps the most useful for the general public is his *The Indian Heritage, An Anthology of Sanskrit Literature*, published in 1956 by the Indian Institute of Culture in Bangalore as part of the UNESCO Collection of Representative Works.

6 East India Company: "a company organized in England for trade in India and first chartered by Elizabeth (Dec. 31, 1600). . . . It continued essentially a trading company till about 1765, when it was given territorial sovereignty of India, jointly with the crown. . . . The Company was deprived of its governing powers in 1858, and it was dissolved in 1873. . . . Similar companies were chartered by other European nations: the Dutch East India Company from 1602 to 1798, the French from 1664 to 1769, the Danish from 1729 to 1801." (Webster's II)

7 Aurangzeb: (1618–1707) one of the sons of Shah Jehan, he became Mogul emperor of North India, with his capital at Delhi, by defeating his brothers and imprisoning his father, reigning from 1658 to 1707. A scholarly, self-righteous man, he was strongly devoted to the religion of Islam and suppressed Hinduism aggressively. A great warrior, he extended his empire as far south as the Deccan (the great plateau in the center of the peninsula which includes the modern states of Mysore and Hyderabad), but his successors were unable to hold so much territory, and the empire soon began to collapse.

8 lingam: "the symbol of Shiva in the form of a phallus, indicating his divine creative function." (Ross) Usually made of stone, several feet high, enshrined in the inner vault of a Hindu temple where worshipers bring offerings.

9 Ayyappan: ". . . a well-known [Hindu] deity. The name is Tamil and Malayalam. In Sanskrit the deity is called Shasta and Arya. It is from the latter name that the Tamil-Malayalam name Ayyappan is derived. There are several shrines to Ayyappan all over Kerala; and although not so numerous, there are several shrines to him in the Tamil country also. He is considered to be the son of Hari and Hara, that is Shiva and Vishnu, born on the occasion when the latter, namely Vishnu, took a female form with the name Mohini. The Ayyappan cult is very popular and has received a fresh impetus now. Every year several thousands of people take a vow, grow a beard, observe strict austerities and go across forests and hills to his most sacred place called Sabarimalai, a hill in Travancore. This is the holy place in the jungles of Kerala referred to by Merton." (Dr. V. Raghavan in a private letter)

10 Kerala: the state of modern India which occupies the southwesternmost part of the peninsula, embracing the former princely states of Cochin and Travancore. In 1957, it became the first state in India to elect a Communist government.

11 Mahabalipuram: sometimes called the "Seven Pagodas," this site is on the seashore 37 miles south of Madras. It was built by the Pallava kings (600–750 A.D.) and consists of a series of pagodalike temples stretching out into the sea, a number of raths (monolithic rocks carved in bas-relief), and a group of mandapams (cave temples).

12 It appears that Merton was reading two different selections of the poetry of Lawrence, probably the Penguin paperback as well as the Selected Poems, edited by James Reeves, published by Heinemann of London. The poem "Virgin Youth" is not included in the Reeves selection, but it does include "End of Another Home Holiday," from which Merton quotes the line "But when I draw the scanty cloak of silence over my eyes . . ." In the definitive American edition, The Complete Poems of D. H. Lawrence, edited by Vivian de Sola Pinto and F. Warren Roberts, 2 volumes, New York, Viking Press, 1964, "Virgin Youth" will be found on pages 38–40 and "End of Another Home Holiday" on pages 62–64.

13 Bhagavan Sri Ramana Maharshi: (1879–1950) one of the great Hindu saints and teachers of modern times in India, accorded by popular devotion the title of "Bhagavan," one of the supreme sages who are recognized as being "one with God." Following a mystical experience of transformation at the age of seventeen, he set up an ashram at the sacred hill of Arunachala, where to the end of his life and attracting thousands of disci-

ples, he taught a form of Advaita Vedanta (nonduality) through the discipline of self-examination. See Mouni Sadhu: *In Days of Great Peace,* London, Allen & Unwin, 1953; Arthur Osborne: *Ramana Maharshi and the Path of Self-Knowledge,* London, Rider, 1914, and New York, Samuel Weiser (paperback), 1970; Arthur Osborne, editor, *The Collected Works of Ramana Maharshi,* London, Rider, 19—; Arthur Osborne: *Teachings of Bhagavan Sri Ramana Maharshi in His Own Words,* London, Rider, 1962. Merton had studied the work of Maharshi at Gethsemani. (Dr. Raghavan has confirmed that the driver who thought the saint had lived in the mountains near Madras was mistaken. Arunachala is near Tiruvannamali, which is in Madras State, but a good hundred miles southwest of the city of Madras and about fifty miles inland from the sea.) In a private letter, Marco Pallis makes the interesting point that Ramana Maharshi "did not at any time become the disciple of a known guru; he is one who 'perfected his sadhana [spiritual training] in a previous life.' " Merton's notes on his reading of Maharshi are in Notebook 68 in the collection of his papers at the Thomas Merton Studies Center, Bellarmine-Ursuline College in Louisville, Kentucky.

[14] Orval: an abbey in Belgium, founded originally about 1070 by the Benedictines and re-established by the Cistercians in 1926.

[15] Grandmontine: the Grandmontines were an eremitical order founded by Stephen of Thiers in 1076 at Muret, near Limoges, France, and later resettled in Grandmont, from which the name of the order was derived.

[16] Sankaracharya of Kanchi: His Holiness Sri Chandrasekharendra Sarasvati Swamigal, Kanchi Kamakoti Mutt, founded by Sankara Bhagavatpada. Merton had taken down from Dr. Raghavan the full title and address of Raghavan's guru. In a private letter, Dr. Raghavan explains as follows: " 'Sri Chandrasekharendra Sarasvati' in his personal name as Pontiff. The word 'Swamigal' refers to his holy aspect and is a Sanskrit-cum-Tamil expression. Kanchi is a place forty miles from the city of Madras where he has his headquarters. 'Kamakoti' is the name of his Mutt [muth, math— monastery]. It was founded by Adi Sankara [Sankaracharya] the great [8th-century] Advaita philosopher. 'Bhagavatpada' means the most reverend one; it is a title of Adi Sankara and all those monks and Pontiffs who occupy the different Mutts founded by him."

[17] Arthur Koestler: *The Lotus and the Robot,* Macmillan, New York, 1961, pages 54–63.

[18] Atman: the self, overself or supreme self. *Vide* the *Rigvedic Hymn;* I, 164, 20, and the *Upanishads,* Mandaka, III, 1.1. (Dr. V. Raghavan in a private letter)

208

[19] "Wisdom in Emptiness," a dialogue by D. T. Suzuki and Merton, in Merton: *Zen and the Birds of Appetite,* New York, New Directions, 1968, pages 99–138.

[20] For a concise but authoritative exposition on the Rajput, Mogul, and Kangra schools of Indian painting see "Some Notes on the Art of Painting," pages 383–87, and the preceding illustrative plates, in Volume I of Heinrich Zimmer: *The Art of Indian Asia,* Bollingen Series XXXIX, New York, Pantheon Books, 1955, For more detailed discussion of these schools, see Stuart C. Welch: *The Art of Mughal India,* New York, Asia House Gallery, 1963, and Stuart C. Welch & Milo C. Beach: *Gods, Thrones, and Peacocks,* New York, Asia House Gallery, 1965, both distributed by New York Graphic Society, Greenwich, Connecticut.

CEYLON
November 29–December 6

November 29 / Colombo

The follies of tourism. *Time* and tourism! The dissolution of one's touristic duty into incredibly long blank areas of time. Waiting in strange airports. Or in airline offices. Or in free buses from airports to hotels. The flight to Colombo[1] was barely two hours, perhaps less. (I forgot to look.) But there were more than two hours of waiting before we started and we were almost an hour in the airport bus at Colombo. Some Poles had visa problems and eventually could not come with us. Yet it was cool in the Air Ceylon office in Madras, next to the hotel with the sea wind blowing in everywhere, and the faces at the airport were good, the chairs comfortable. I read large chunks of Lawrence's *Twilight in Italy* and found it boring, especially the bit about the amateur dramatics. It's not a good book, barely interesting, though occasionally he'll have an intuition that makes sense—such as, self and not-self. The "selfless" world of the machine. A good angle. Are we really heading for a kind of technological corruption of Buddhism? A secular nirvana?

The flight to Ceylon: flying smokes of hot, steamy, monsoon cloud and the flat gray-green coast of South India full of rain-ponds and lagoons. Then India veered off blackly to the west, the sun went down, and presently the lights of Jaffna[2] were under us. There are many flat islands along the Ceylon coast. Coming down into Colombo was lovely. We sailed in low over the harbor full of lighted ships.

⌘

"On the West the City of Columbo, so-called from a Tree the natives call Amba[3] (which bears the mango fruit) growing in

that place; but this never bare fruit but onely leaves, which in
their Language is Cola, and thence they call the Tree Colambo,
which the Christians in honor of Columbus turned to Columbo."

—Robert Knox: *Historical Relation of Zeilon*,
London, 1681; reissued, Colombo, 1958.

�֍

Driving into any Asian city at night is like driving into, say
Flushing, Long Island—except for the coconut palms. Colombo,
evidently, is cleaner and better ordered than any of the others
I have seen so far: Bangkok, Delhi, Calcutta. (Madras is not
bad.) Neat houses, open to the night air, with people sitting
peacefully talking inside. Good shops. Gardens. Flowers in the
dark. Flowers in lighted shops. Piles of fruit. As usual I am in
Hotel Karma. My karma. Nineteen Twenties, British Raj-
karma. The faded cream splendor of the Galle Face Hotel.
Everywhere I run into it: the big empty rooms, carpeted stairs,
slowly turning fans, mahogany floors, where once the Cantabs[4]
walked grandly in black tie (at night) or blazer and flannels
(afternoon). And the music, too—now American—but still the
same songs (names I forget) they played in the Thirties. Mean-
ingless songs that still disturb some dark residue of sentiment
somewhere in me, enough to embarrass me, but not much.

I ordered arrack[5] in the Mascarella Room but the waiter
told me, in horror, they could not carry it. "A wild crowd would
come. There would be no respect for the hotel." My idea of the
magic powers of arrack was thus confirmed. I drank some local
rum, with profound sentiments of "respect for the hotel." As
for the Mascarella Room, it could be any room in any college
town, any bar and grill off any campus or in an Omaha hotel.
The same dim lights, same tables, same people, same dancing.
A local band, but straight American music, competent, brisk,
and entirely devoid of rasa. I went quickly to bed, after a few
minutes of quiet watching the moonlit sea, and discovered I

213

was directly over the night club and the muffled noise of the band reached up through the pillow. I went right to sleep anyway.

※

On the shore. A hot night. Warm, rubbery waves shining under the moon. It is just after the first quarter; Poya day[6] was the day before. A new strange feeling out there—westward nothing until Africa. And out there—to the south, nothing til Antarctica. Wow! I was shocked to see Orion hanging almost upside down in the north. I still could not pick out the Southern Cross with assurance but think I saw some of it in the mist and moonlight in the south.

It is evening and again I have not done my duty as a sightseer. I went out onto Galle Face Green this morning (earlier two men were vigorously shadowboxing there), walked along the shore to "The Fort," that is to downtown Colombo, and found the place charming. I went to check my Singapore flight at Air Ceylon, then walked about the streets looking at the big old English buildings—banks, shipping offices, government offices, etc. A couple of shiny new buildings are there, too. But the clock-tower lighthouse right in the middle of town gives the place a curiously *West* Indian flavor for some reason. Big gardens around what I take to be the governor general's mansion. Everywhere there are police and military, very aggressive, with sharp fixed bayonets or machine guns even. Ed Rice[7] told me something of this but I had forgotten. There is a Post Office strike and I suppose they are there to prevent rioting, looking vicious and humorless as such types usually do. It's their business.

※

The King of Kandy, wrote Knox, has a palace like a labyrinth called "The Woodstock Bower," "with many turnings and wind-ings and doors, he himself having contrived all these Buildings and the manner of them. . . . By means of these contrivances it is not easie to know in what part or place his Person is, neither doth he care they should. He has strong Watches day and night about his Court. . . . At night they all have their set places within the Court where they cannot one come to the speeche of the other. . . . There are also elephants which are appointed all night to stand and watch, lest there should be any Tumult; which if there should, could presently trample down a multitude."

—Knox, *op. cit.*

⌘

I went into the old Anglican Church on the harbor front and prayed a little. It has a certain charm, built in Dutch times. Afterward I read some of the memorial tablets, curiously touching in their "eloquence," or in the simple visual quality of their lettering, especially the older ones in the back. Then I went into the Taprobane Hotel and got a bottle of Ceylonese beer which turned out to be fairly good, better than Indian. I bought Elias Canetti's[8] *Auto-da-Fé* at the Taprobane bookstand, anticipating future hours in airports.

There is little that is Oriental here—or little that I have seen that is so. I have not been to any Buddhist temples, but tried a couple of times, vainly, to contact Walpola Rahula[9] at the Buddhist University. I went to the USIS office at Bob Boylan's suggestion and ended up having lunch with the director, Victor Stier,[10] at his house. Some talk with his child about the relative merits of various funnies. But the wife is the one who has seen Buz Sawyer in the international edition of the *Herald-Tribune*. Buz has been out of jail for some time. The Mexican mine problem is settled. A new adventure has begun. I am glad to hear of this evident progress.

I went back to the Taprobane in the evening only to find it hot, messy, full of drunks, and with an accordionist wander-

ing among the tables playing "Danny Boy" and "Annie Laurie."
A disaster. However, upstairs in the Harbor Room I got a (bad)
dinner with a good view of the docks and lighted ships, so that
I began to consider the idea of returning to India, if I return,
by boat from Djakarta. Back at my own home, the Galle Face,
I thought the Mascarella Room, though pretty awful, was a bit
better and more decent than the Taprobane, at least the musical
part of it! But here too the Ceylonese girl singer calls herself
"Heather."

✳

November 30 / Kandy

Last night I did manage to contact Walpola Rahula by phone
and plan to see him when I get back to Colombo on Tuesday.
Today I took the early train to Kandy. Got here about 10:30.
The trains in Ceylon are extraordinarily cheap. I paid only 6/55
for the three-hour journey, second class, and had a compartment
("For Clergy Only") all to myself, though expecting a bunch of
bhikkhus to move in on me at any station.[11] Six rupees are what
a taxi might easily charge you just to get to the station. Actually,
the taxi in Colombo was three, and the one in Kandy two. The
latter was pure robbery; no distance at all from the hotel to the
station. The views from the train were sometimes quite impressive: coconuts, rice, tea, bananas, bamboo, and mountains covered with jungle.

Now I find myself looking out the hotel window at an in-
explicable English village church up against what might, but
for a couple of coconut palms, be a Surrey hillside. But the
breeze is cool and a letter was awaiting me from the German
bhikkhu, Nyanaponika Thera. After dinner I went to him in
his hermitage in the jungle. It is a very solid little house near a
rest house for convalescing monks. One cave-dwelling monk was
there convalescing; he looked seedy and harassed. But we went

Nyanaponika Thera with younger bhikkhu in front of hermitage near Kandy

to see another cave hermit and his cave was reasonably tidy and comfortable, after having been suitably humanized by generations of hermits. It seemed perfectly dry. The front had been blocked off with a brick wall and a door. It was an attractive cave with slanting ceiling and floor, a ledge to sleep on, one to eat on, and a place for a small, simple shrine. It was roomy and I must say attractive. The tenant was a young German bhikkhu who recently completed his training at the same South Ceylon island monastery in a lake near Galle as Nyanaponika Thera. He is only temporarily there, occupying the place of another hermit who is on a trip to India.

Nyanaponika Thera is old now, in his sixties or perhaps seventies. Originally a German Jew, he became a Buddhist years ago. Now he lives as a hermit in the cottage once occupied by his master, also a German and now dead. He writes and is charged with a great deal of editorial work for the local Buddhist publishing outfit, which does some quite good things. He went to Europe last year and saw the Tibetans in Switzerland. (Rikon is near Winterthur which is near Zurich. Tössthal is the name of the locality.) His hermitage is in full jungle, in a reservation, but the jungle is right at the edge of Kandy so he is really not far from town. But it is very wild and quiet. We walked out on the brow of a hill where the jungle has been cleared a bit and there is a fine view of the peaks to the southwest and northwest. I hope my camera caught some of the enchanted beauty of this landscape! Ceylon is incomparable!

After that I saw a little temple, Gangaramaya, on the edge of the same jungle, but down below. There is a great Buddha carved out of a huge rock rising out of the earth, and a small temple built around it. Fascinating Ceylonese folk-type paintings on the walls and ceiling. And the Buddha figure, behind glass, still quite impressive, much more so than modern ones. This one must be about two hundred years old.

Later I visited Bishop Nanayakkara in the cathedral compound; built by Sylvestrines,[12] it was originally a monastery. The cathedral is fairly handsome in its 18th-century colonial sort of way. Bishop Nanayakkara is very progressive and we talked long about my idea of Buddhist dialogue and of a meditation monastery that would be open to Buddhism. He drove me up to the top of the hill looking down on Kandy—it is lighted up after nightfall—and continued to talk about the Church today and the problems of Christians. I think he sees the situation clearly—or in any event we agree.

Anything going to or coming from the King of Kandy is held sacred, says Knox, and the people move aside out of the way not only of the white flowers that he likes, when they are being brought to him, but also his dirty linens when they are taken to the lake to be laundered. "And when they are carried to washing, which is daily, all, even the greatest, rise up, as they come by, which is known by being carried on a hand heaved upwards, covered with a painted cloth."

—Knox, *op. cit.*

✣

December 1

It is hardly like any December or Advent[13] I have ever known! A clear, hot sky. Flowering trees. A hot day coming. I woke at the sound of many crows fighting in the air. Then the booming drum at the Temple of Buddha's Tooth.[14] Now, the traffic of buses and a cool breeze sways the curtains. The jungle is very near, it comes right to the top of the city and is visible a bare hundred yards from this window. Yet I am on a very noisy corner as far as traffic is concerned!

✣

December 2 / Kandy

Yesterday much of my time was spent with the bishop, visiting the monastery of the Sylvestrines, a quiet place on a hillside amid tall palms, with pleasant cloister and chapel. There I met the retired bishop of Kandy, a jovial and deaf Italian with a long gray beard, Bishop Regno. He said he judged from my *Seven Storey Mountain* that I had been one of the "first hippies." "Oh! Oh! Oh!" he said with upraised hands, "All the whisky! All the cigarettes!" I reminded him that hippies had no interest in whisky and that they smoked pot, not cigarettes, but I don't think this penetrated the wall of deafness. In spite of which he urged me, since the world was going utterly mad, to write on the authority of the Pope. Then I saw the seminary, a large, roomy, shady place, where all the twelve dioceses of Ceylon send their candidates for training. A big Romanesque German-style church. When I came back in the evening for dinner and a talk to the seminarians, the Alma Redemptoris[15] was sung rather faintly in Latin and Gregorian[16] and I could not feel this was any more out of place than, say, English hymns!

The bishop then took me out to a village called Ibbagamuwa where there is an Anglican ashram on a coconut estate. It is the ashram of Brother Johan Devananda, a nice young Anglican priest. The official name of the place is Devasarana. Even the Ceylonese, as we approached the sign, had to read it out slowly the first time, syllable by syllable. The buildings are all very simple; in fact, they are nothing but the watchhouses, chicken runs, etc., that were there before. The chapel is in an open chicken house with a concrete floor. One sits on mats. The altar is a low table. The bronze lamps are Ceylonese. The Anglican bishop of Kurunegala was on retreat at the ashram and we spoke to him briefly. The atmosphere of the place is quiet, open, filled with concern for liturgical experiment and ecumenism, i.e., adaptation to a Buddhist type of spirituality. It is certainly "poor" and simple, a good example of what a monastic experiment in Asia should look like. There are no postulants at present, but an Anglican priest in the United States is waiting "enthusiastically" to come here. There were some postulants but they left. A few lay volunteers are helping and one of them brought us fresh green coconuts, of which we drank the sweet liquid before driving away.

A village on the way back: a movie house and a temple standing side by side at the foot of a huge rock, on top of which a steel frame shows the outline of a Buddha figure. Apparently a giant statue is to be poured in concrete. I thought at first it must be an electric sign! I saw one elephant working with logs by the road on the way out, two on the way back. On the whole one sees fewer than I expected. (I saw none in India.) I hear they are slowly dying out.

A hot afternoon. I walked alone, glad to be alone, to the Kandy museum, a little up the road past the Temple of the Tooth. There are curious and delightful small things in the museum: ivories, lacquers, paintings, textiles, swords, bronzes, vessels, medical texts on strips of bark. The red-black-gold style of Kandyan painting I find very pleasing and the painted "ceremonial boards" are diverting. All essentially folk art, the paintings at least. The lacquers and ivories are very sophisticated. Fine carved ivory combs. There is a great sense of design in everything. Lovely lacquer boxes. Three especially fine lacquer jars from the Maldive Islands [17] The rest local. After that I walked a little by the lake in the cool breeze, thinking of my Advent sermon to be preached in the cathedral where I said the most crowded evening Mass.

⌘

December 3 / Kandy

Heavy rain. A longer and louder drum continues in the Temple of the Tooth. It is pre-Poya day. My bags are packed and I am ready to leave, not sure whether or not the railroad is on strike, but everyone says it is not. (Ceylon was threatened with an almost general strike; the postal strike nearly turned into a bigger one, involving utilities, transportation and other public services. But now everyone says it is being settled.) Yesterday was spent entirely on a long trip to Dambulla [18] and Polonnaruwa [19] —the most impressive things I have seen in Asia, and doubtless I would have liked Anuradhapura [20] even better, but it was too far. I drove 186 miles in a car provided by the bishop. (The hired car rate of a rupee a mile would have been for me exorbitant.) On and off, since I have been here, there have been suggestions and queries about the possibility of a contemplative Christian monastery, a small foundation from Gethsemani or a hermitage. It needs some thought. I hope to write to Fr. Flavian about it. There is much to be said for the idea. Also, should I come back, after Indonesia? The only thing is that I don't want to get caught in endless talks and visits to novitiates and seminaries.

⌘

KANDY EXPRESS

Inward parcels
Outward parcels
(Chamber of Horrors?)
Lordly blue ponds.
Men standing in river pouring water over
themselves from beat-up pails.
Coconuts, bananas, everywhere.
A Baur & Co Manure Works (Kelaniya)
Grand Land Auction
Little boy in yellow suit too big hat walks
tracks with brother
Schoolgirls walk tracks
Everybody walks tracks.

"Trespassers on the Railway will be prosecuted!"

2nd class on Kandy Express much more comfortable than plane
—entire compartment to myself—plenty of room, air, see everything etc.

Enderamulla

Tall girl in green—lovely walks on tracks.
Bhikkhu with umbrella walks tracks.

Please refrain from
Traveling on footboards
Keeping carriage doors open
They are dangerous practices

Ragama
Man selling papers chants like sutras
"Never drink cold water lest the souls in it be injured."
                    (*Digha Nikaya*)

Little boy in tall grass near tracks waves
back delightedly when I wave.

Straw i.e. palm-mat flags scarecrows (or scaredemons?) in paddy.

Train speeds gladly amid paddy and
coconut—saying "Mahinda, Mahindi, Mahinda!"[21]

Buffaloes swimming, great muzzles
yawning up out of the green-brown water.

Great train monster   Buddhabuddha!
Sawing everything down to tea's smallest leaf.

High blue mountains begin to show
their heads in distance.

Magelegoda. Buddha shrine on station platform.

"The people, pleased with one another and happy dancing
their children in their hands, dwelt with open doors!"

A white crane standing in sunny water
briefly shakes herself.
Another flies low over green paddy and alights.

Now the creeks are faster—begin to have rapids.
Hills. Irrigation tanks.

Ambepussa—slopes, tunnels, jungle.
Steep black rocks.

A lovely swift-flowing river with large sandbanks.
Jungle covered hills.

More coconut and paddy—bamboo and banana
Yellow robed bhikkhu walking away in coolgreen shadow

Far ahead—a big stone block of mountain
standing as monolithic as a fat lingam.
Polgahawela. (new station being built—obviously
                with endless delays)
Rambukkana.
A new side to the same mountain—it is two.
An interesting and massive shape.

White stupa in the midst of rice fields.
An enchanted dirt road winds (empty) into the hills.
Train slowly climbs.
Spear pointed peaks to the north.
Peaks everywhere—
Sweet cool smell of vegetation.
Tunnels.
Rock cluttered mountainsides.
Now we look down a hundred or two hundred feet
to paddy in the valley below.
Rock pools shaded by immense green leaves.
Longer and longer tunnels.
Deeper and deeper valleys.
Lovely pattern of terraced paddy
Waterfalls. White thatched houses far below.
Looking back—lingam from other side.

We have climbed the flank of it.
Ranges of peaks behind us. Deep valleys.
Two small boys with bundles on their heads
stand on path and watch train.
Black cliffs shine with water.
Small houses buried in masses of red flowers.
Kadugannawa.
Three pigeons sit motionless on the tile roof.
Men setting out rice seedlings.
First tea factory I've seen yet (about 1000 feet)
Others follow.
Man and dog walk quickly through paddy,
Fresh paddy set out in shallow water.
full of cloud reflections.
Women washing clothes in all the creeks.
We go faster—going down   the streams are with us,
rushing down the watershed to Kandy
(It is 10.30)
Tea set out everywhere in the shade of coconuts.
Women in a stream cover their breasts as train passes.

Graceful girl looks up at train, turns away, throws a bar of red
soap in the grass, takes bucket and stands in stream, pours water
suddenly over her head once—then moves out and does it again
and again rapidly, vigorously. Her wet shift clings to her body.
She is very beautiful— in her gestures. Little boy comes to
stream with a tiny puppy and a string. Ties one end of string to
puppy's neck, tethers him safely on the bank, goes to wash.

Girl is beautifully cool and wet.
Boy flings clods of earth at tethered cow.
Woman scrubs another woman's back.
Bathers and launderers everywhere.

Peradeniya Junction. Kandy soon.

New white houses
Shady gardens
Red earth
We come to Kandy.

University in valley
Stupa on mountainside
Temple on a ridge
Radio tower on the top.

On August 3, 1858, Sir Henry Ward cut the first sod for the
railway line from Colombo to Kandy and forever ended a long
drawn out discussion which had gone on for about 40 years
about a proposed railway connection to the hills.

Picks up spade, ends controversy

I now ride in car number 6700 (2nd class)
Amid the wet shadows of massive plantations
and cocoa trees.

Do not block corridors.
Proceed from talk to action.
"I am afraid, I am afraid of silence,"
Said the Vicar General,
"I was afraid of those Trappists."
Dark night of the soul:
"I too am disgusted:
But how avoid illusion?"

What if the mind becomes one-pointed
And the "one point" is then removed?

Return journey—heavy rains—a line of red oil barrels—a crow
flies down onto the rainy station platform—dances awkwardly

along the edge, investigates a very wet sheet of newspaper. He tries to pick it up. It falls apart. He flies up again into the rain.

At the place where the girls were bathing the river is now red and swollen with up-country storms. Rain falls—no human being is to be seen.

The mountains are all buried in rain-mist. The valleys are full of it. The shadows of palms rise up in it near at hand, then vanish in the clatter of a black cut full of ferns and cobras.

Sanghamitta Poya. Full moon Poya day of Unduwap[22] (Dec 4) marks anniversary of establishment of bhikkhuism in Ceylon at Anuradhapura, by Arhat Theri Sanghamitta. 245 B.C.

Rattling down the mountain the Kandy Express sings
Tsongkapa, Tsongkapa, Tsongkapa . . .
Praise of Yellow Hats.
Mirigama East.
Pink orchids among coconuts.
Veyangoda.

That which grew slowly toward me Friday
Flies rapidly away from me Tuesday.
I have seen that buffalo before
I have seen that boy before.

No man twice crosses the same river.

I have seen that felled coconut trunk before.

We rush blindly
In a runaway train
Through the great estates
Headlong to the sea.

That same sea which Queen Victoria
By a miracle of steam
Changed into sodawater.

✠

Promotion of the essentials of religion is possible in many ways.[23] "The root is this: guarding one's speech, so that neither praising one's own sect nor blaming other sects should take place . . . or that it should be moderate. Other sects ought to be duly honored in every case."

"If one is acting thus, he is both promoting his own sect and benefiting other sects. . . ."

"Therefore concord alone is meritorious, that they should both hear and obey each other's morals. . . ."

—*12th Rock Edict of Ashoka*

"Here no living being must be killed or sacrificed
And no festival meeting must be held
For King Devanampriya Pryadarsin saw much evil in festival
    meetings. . . ."

—*1st Rock Edict of Ashoka*

✠

December 4 / Colombo

Today I fly to Singapore and the long day of sitting around has begun. I moved out of room 208, in the Galle Face, at 11:15 to pay my bill and wait for the Air Ceylon bus, promised at 11:45. At 11:55 a pretty Air Ceylon hostess tells me the bus will be at 12:30. So I open up the bag again . . .

    Outside on Galle Face Green the kites rise and dip in the strong sea wind—wild and happy Asian kites—two like big black dishevelled and long-legged birds that flap and jump in the wind. Others with long spotted tails twist in the air like freckled dragons or serpents. Others have unidentifiable shapes. Asia is a kite-loving continent; there were wrecks of small Tibetan boys' kites on all the roofs and wires of Darjeeling.

⌘

BUZ SAWYER

(A whole new scene in The Paris *Herald-Tribune* of December 2)

Mr. Sawyer, here's Mr. Price, US Treasury Department.
Yes I'm interested in the kind of plants and flowers grown on the Butterfly Ranch.
Now here's an aerial survey. Did you get a good look at the flowers in the center?
No I landed on the side.
Or these tall plants growing at the upper end?
No, why, are you a botanist?
Confidentially, he's from the Bureau of Narcotics.

Do you understand? "Tall plants"?
Mr. Tallplants are you growing narcotics on your rancho?
No I landed only yesterday on the butterfly.
But confidentially: take a look at this flower. What do you sniff?
Yes, it is growing immense at the upper end!
There must be something growing here Mr. Rancho!
I agree: and I give you full control of the department.
None too soon. There are criminals everywhere;
Fortunately there are also folks like ourselves.
Viva Mister Sawyer!

(After his visit with Hunter Rockwell, Rex Morgan returns home to find Keith already there.)

⌘

De Gaulle's gold flows back . . . New clashes along the Jordan River . . . New fears grip Italy . . . Scientist probes riddle of night lights and babies (major breakthrough in improving the reliability of the rhythm method of birth control).

"Dr. Duvan said the idea of night lights came to him during research on the effects of moonlight . . . on the breeding habits of certain marine animals, chickens and rats. Sea urchins apparently had their sexual cycles 'entrained' by the cycles of the moon, he said. Thus at full moon the ovaries of sea urchins are unusually large in size."

Smiling boy died from poison.

Week-long *Koran* reading contest will be telecast from the Herdeka Stadium, Kuala Lumpur.

"A soldier who pleaded guilty to causing hurt to ten children by rashly discharging his shotgun was told by a magistrate today, 'This is a rash action on your part . . .' The incident occurred when Private Ho Ngen, of the crow eradication team, was on his rounds in L. Sorong 3, Geylang . . ."

✳

I remember the Moslems' sunset gun going off in Kandy and shaking the bishop's house. And the evening I returned from Polonnaruwa the gun went off as I stepped out of the car and a thousand crows flew up into the rain by the Temple of the Tooth.

Polonnaruwa was such an experience that I could not write hastily of it and cannot write now, or not at all adequately. Perhaps I have spoiled it by trying to talk of it at a dinner party, or to casual acquaintances. Yet when I spoke about it to Walpola Rahula at the Buddhist University I think the idea got across and he said, "Those who carved those statues were not ordinary men."

✳

I visited Polonnaruwa on Monday. Today is Thursday. Heavy rain in Kandy, and on all the valleys and paddy land and jungle and teak and rubber as we go down to the eastern plains. ("We" is the bishop's driver and the vicar general of the Kandy diocese, a Ceylonese Sylvestrine with a Dutch name.) By Dambulla the rain has almost stopped. The nobility and formality of an ancient, moustachioed guide who presents himself under a bo tree. We start up the long sweep of black rock, the vicar general lagging behind, complaining that he dislikes "paganism," telling me I will get much better photos somewhere else, and saying they are all out to cheat me. ("They" being especially the bhikkhus.) Over to the east the black rock of Sigiriya stands up in the distant rain. We do not go there. What I want to see is Polonnaruwa. The high round rock of Dambulla is also quiet, sacred. The landscape is good: miles of scrub, distant "tanks" (artificial lakes dating back to the Middle Ages), distant mountains, abrupt, blue, heads hidden in rain clouds.

At the cave vihara of Dambulla, an undistinguished cloisterlike porch fronts the line of caves. The caves are dark. The dirt of the cave floors under bare feet is not quite damp, not quite dry. Dark. The old man has two small candles. He holds them up. I discover that I am right up against an enormous reclining Buddha, somewhere around the knee. Curious effect of big gold Buddha lying down in the dark. I glimpse a few frescoes but those in this first cave are not so exciting. Later, some good ones, but hard to see. The guide is not interested in the frescoes, which are good, only in the rank of Buddhas, which are not good. Lines of stone and sandalwood Buddhas sit and guard the frescoes. The Buddhas in the frescoes are lovely. Frescoes all over the walls and roof of the cave. Scenes. Histories. Myths. Monsters. "Cutting, cutting," says the guide, who consents to show a scene he regards as worthwhile: now sinners being chopped up in hell, now Tamils being chopped up in war. And suddenly I recognize an intent, gold-faced, mad-eyed, black-bearded Ceylonese king I had previously met on a post

card. It is a wood sculpture, painted. Some nice primitive fish were swimming on the ceiling, following a line of water in the rock.

Polonnaruwa with its vast area under trees. Fences. Few people. No beggars. A dirt road. Lost. Then we find Gal Vihara and the other monastic complex stupas. Cells. Distant mountains, like Yucatan.

The path dips down to Gal Vihara: a wide, quiet, hollow, surrounded with trees. A low outcrop of rock, with a cave cut into it, and beside the cave a big seated Buddha on the left, a reclining Buddha on the right, and Ananda,[24] I guess, standing by the head of the reclining Buddha. In the cave, another seated Buddha. The vicar general, shying away from "paganism," hangs back and sits under a tree reading the guidebook. I am able to approach the Buddhas barefoot and undisturbed, my feet in wet grass, wet sand. Then the silence of the extraordinary faces. The great smiles. Huge and yet subtle. Filled with every possibility, questioning nothing, knowing everything, rejecting nothing, the peace not of emotional resignation but of Madhyamika, of sunyata, that has seen through every question without trying to discredit anyone or anything—*without refutation*—without establishing some other argument. For the doctrinaire, the mind that needs well-established positions, such peace, such silence, can be frightening. I was knocked over with a rush of relief and thankfulness at the *obvious* clarity of the figures, the clarity and fluidity of shape and line, the design of the monumental bodies composed into the rock shape and landscape, figure, rock and tree. And the sweep of bare rock sloping away on the other side of the hollow, where you can go back and see different aspects of the figures.

Looking at these figures I was suddenly, almost forcibly, jerked clean out of the habitual, half-tied vision of things, and an inner clearness, clarity, as if exploding from the rocks them-

Figures at Polonnaruwa, Ceylon

Seated Buddha, Polonnaruwa, Ceylon

selves, became evident and obvious. The queer *evidence* of the reclining figure, the smile, the sad smile of Ananda standing with arms folded (much more "imperative" than Da Vinci's Mona Lisa because completely simple and straightforward). The thing about all this is that there is no puzzle, no problem, and really no "mystery." All problems are resolved and everything is clear, simply because what matters is clear. The rock, all matter, all life, is charged with dharmakaya . . . everything is emptiness and everything is compassion. I don't know when in my life I have ever had such a sense of beauty and spiritual validity running together in one aesthetic illumination. Surely, with Mahabalipuram and Polonnaruwa my Asian pilgrimage

Reclining Buddha, Polonnaruwa, Ceylon

has come clear and purified itself. I mean, I know and have seen what I was obscurely looking for. I don't know what else remains but I have now seen and have pierced through the surface and have got beyond the shadow and the disguise. This is Asia in its purity, not covered over with garbage, Asian or European or American, and it is clear, pure, complete. It says everything; it needs nothing. And because it needs nothing it can afford to be silent, unnoticed, undiscovered. It does not need to be discovered. It is we, Asians included, who need to discover it.

The whole thing is very much a Zen garden, a span of bareness and openness and evidence, and the great figures, motionless, yet with the lines in full movement, waves of vesture and bodily form, a beautiful and holy vision. The rest of the "city," the old palace complex, I had no time for. We just drove around the roads and saw the ruined shapes, and started on the long drive home to Kandy.

⌘

December 5 / Singapore

Lee Beng Tjie, professor of philosophy at the University of Singapore, met me at the plane with his wife. He drove me to the hotel, The Raffles, and then out to Mount Faber, where we had a view of the lights of the city and the harbor in rain. Today I said Mass in the dining room of his flat and we went to an excellent Chinese lunch at a hotel in Chinatown, the Majestic. They called for me again in the evening and we went to a place up Beach Road where they provide you with the fixings, and with a hibachi-type of stove. You put this on the table, pick out your own fragments of hard-to-identify meats with chopsticks, and drop them in the boiling water. You hope that when you fish them out again they will be more or less done. I must admit that as an experience this was highly instructive, but as a dinner it turned out to be somewhat less than impressive. The Chinese families sitting around us seemed to be busy with the enjoyment. I admit that I have much to learn before I can profitably enter into it!

Beng Tjie says that he has a hard time getting Chuang Tzu and Lao Tzu[25] through to Asian students. The ones here have been formed by English linguistic analysis to some extent. He thought what I have done in "War and the Crisis of Language"[26] was the sort of thing that Wittgenstein[27] was really getting at—but I am not so sure.

✳

SULTAN LEADS RAIDS ON SEA-MINE "PIRATES."

"The Sultan of Perak[28] led a police party on a raid yesterday that dealt a crippling blow to the million-dollar syndicates engaged in illegal mining of tin off the Duidings Coast." The whole story is good funnypaper stuff: even floating pumping stations, "palongs" (fishing boats) "converted at an average cost of $35,000 . . . boats seized . . . men "detained." Huts burnt! Hurray for the Sultan of Perak! He is thwarting rich evildoers!

Two more Bonn[29] officials commit suicide. France threatened by crisis, strikes, etc.

✳

December 6 / Singapore

I am now preparing to leave Singapore, the city of transistors, tape recorders, cameras, perfumes, silk shirts, fine liquors . . . carrying away only a stock of 35 mm. Plus X film. I am glad I came here. It is an interesting, "worldly" town, very different from India, a new Asian city, the cosmopolitan kind, "worldly" too in a Chinese sense. Singapore has a Chinese kind of practicality and reality along with the big Western buildings which, as it happens, are clean and well-kept. The place is not run down, and hence Calcutta is not a *necessary* pattern for all Asia!

And these evidences are needed in order to give a complete picture of Asia. Out in the suburbs by the university, it is like Santa Barbara or Sacramento.

I saw the other side of Colombo going out to the Katunayake airport. There were many screwy Catholic statues exhibited in public but sometimes under glass, so that the Catholic saints come a little closer to Ganesha and Hindu camp after all. Suddenly there is a point where religion becomes laughable. Then you decide that you are nevertheless religious . . .

My next stop will be the Bangkok meeting to which I do not especially look forward. Then Indonesia, a whole new journey begins there. And I am still not sure where it will take me or what I can or should plan on. Certainly I am sick of hotels and planes. But the journey is only begun. Some of the places I really wanted to see from the beginning have not yet been touched.

✳

"Most men will not swim before they are able to."

> —Novalis,[30] quoted with approval by Hesse's Steppenwolf.[31]

For Nagarjuna, all things are self-contradictory. The root of the Steppenwolf sickness is . . . Steppenwolf's conviction that he is *uniquely* self-contradictory, and that his self-contradiction is resolved into a duality of wolf and man, self-love and self-hate. But this duality arises from ignorance of the fact that all "things" are self-contradictory in their very claim to privacy. The Steppenwolf, however, creates a double illusion by the price he places on private individuality as capable of special and unique relationships.

✳

"They had run out of seashells and were using faded photographs, soiled fans, time-tables, playing cards, broken toys, imitation jewelery, junk that memory had made precious, far more precious than anything the sea might yield."

—Nathanael West:[32] *Miss Lonelyhearts,* page 26 of the New Directions paperback edition of *Miss Lonelyhearts & The Day of the Locust.*

✖

NOTES: *Ceylon*

[1] Colombo: the capital and main port city of Ceylon, with about half a million inhabitants. In 1565 the Portuguese built a fort at Colombo and made it an important base for their trading operations in the East. Later, it was taken over by the Dutch, and then by the British who held it until Ceylonese independence in 1948.

[2] Jaffna: a city of over 60,000 inhabitants, most of them Tamils, at the very northernmost tip of Ceylon. Held in the 17th century both by the Dutch and the Portuguese, it is now the capital of the northern province of Ceylon.

[3] amba: Webster does not currently list a tree with this name, but it might have been Knox's phonetic rendering of the Tamil word "man-kay" for the mango tree. In Bengali, the word "am" or "amra" is used for the mango tree and also for its fruit.

[4] Cantabs: short for Cantabrigian, i.e., a student of Cambridge University in England; from the Latin name for Cambridge, Cantabrigia.

[5] arrack: "Arabic *'araq* sweet juice, liquor: an alcoholic beverage from the Far East or Near East; especially: a liquor of high alcoholic content resembling rum in taste and distilled in the Far East from the fermented juice of the coconut palm or from a fermented mash of rice and molasses." (Webster's III)

[6] Poya day: "In Ceylon the weekly holiday is no longer Sunday but Poya day, the day of the moon's quarter phase. The day preceding Poya day is a half-day, like Saturday, and all business offices and Government departments are closed on this day also." (Jones: *Golden Guide to South & East Asia*)

[7] Ed Rice: Edward Rice, a free-lance photographer and writer who was one of Merton's friends at Columbia University. (See Merton: *The Seven Storey Mountain,* pages 280ff. in the Signet paperback edition.) In 1970, Rice published a book of his photographs and reminiscences of Merton entitled *The Man in the Sycamore Tree,* New York, Doubleday & Company.

[8] Elias Canetti: born in 1905 in Bulgaria, the son of Sephardic Spanish parents. He took a Ph.D. at the University of Vienna, after earlier study in Frankfurt and Zurich, and has lived in England since 1939. His novel *Auto-da-Fé* won the French Prix International.

[9] Walpola Rahula: Rev. Dr. Walpola Rahula, a Buddhist monk and professor at Buddhist University, Colombo, Ceylon. A leading authority on early Buddhist scriptures of various schools, and especially the Sanskrit "Tradition" (Agamas) and the Pali "Canonic Corpus" (Nikayas), he spent nearly a decade in the 1950s as visiting lecturer at the Sorbonne in Paris, working on a study of Asanga, one of the most important philosophers of the Mahayana sect. His books include *History of Buddhism in Ceylon, The Heritage of the Bhikshu,* and *What the Buddha Taught,* New York, a Grove Press Evergreen paperback, 1962.

[10] Victor Stier: Merton had had a letter of introduction to Stier from their mutual friend W. H. Ferry. Stier has now been transferred to the U.S. Embassy in Helsinki, Finland.

[11] "Kandy Express," the impromptu poem which Merton drafted in his pocket notebook during the train journeys to and from Kandy will be found on pages 222–28.

[12] Sylvestrines: ". . . a [Roman Catholic] monastic order founded by St. Sylvester Gozzoloni, in 1231. They follow the Benedictine Rule in its primitive austerity. . . . an associated order of nuns." (Webster's II)

[13] Advent: ". . . from Latin . . . *advenire* to come to: the period beginning four Sundays before Christmas and observed by many Christians as a season of prayer and fasting . . ." (Webster's III)

[14] Temple of Buddha's Tooth: "the 'sacred tooth' is said to have been brought to Ceylon in the reign of Sri Meghavanna, 304–332 A.D. . . . in charge of a Princess of Kalinga, who concealed it in the folds of her hair. It was taken by the Pandyans about 1283 A.D., and again carried to India, but was recovered by Parakrama Bahu III. Later on the relic was at Kotta, but in 1560 was discovered by the Portuguese at Jaffna, taken to Goa by Don Constantine de Braganza, and burned by the Archbishop in the presence of the Viceroy and his court. The Buddhists insist that the real tooth was hidden and is the one now at Kandy. This is a piece of discolored

ivory, two inches long and less than an inch in diameter, resembling the tooth of a crocodile rather than that of a man. . . . It is taken in procession in the month of August for a week. Some sixty elephants take part, and there is a Kandyan dance in gold robes." (Murray's *Handbook for Ceylon*)

15 Alma [Mater] Redemptoris: Latin, literally, "Loving Mother of the Redeemer"; an early Gregorian antiphon in honor of the Blessed Virgin for the Advent season which was sung at the end of Vespers, the sixth and next to the last of the canonical hours.

16 Gregorian: Gregorian chant: "one of the monodic and rhythmically free ritual melodies in one of the eight ecclesiastical modes comprising the liturgical chant of the Roman Catholic Church: *plainsong*." (Webster's III) "Plain song is as old as the Christian Church itself and was for many centuries the only church music. Byzantine plain song, which was the basis for the music of the Eastern Church, had its roots in the music of the Near East, but there was mutual influence to some degree between Eastern and Western church music. The various chants of the Western Church all seem to be derived from similar sources, principally Hebrew and Greek music . . . Gregorian chant, which is the norm throughout the Western Church . . . underwent much development in the early centuries of the Christian era, but its greatest period of development and codification was in the 7th century, when [Pope] Gregory I founded or reorganized the Schola Cantorum and may have compiled the Roman antiphonary. . . ." (*The Columbia Encyclopedia,* Second Edition)

17 Maldive Islands: a group of 2,000 small islands in the Indian Ocean about 400 miles southwest of Ceylon, originally a British Protectorate and dependency of Ceylon, but since 1968 a republic. Most of the inhabitants are Malays, but with a Dravidian (South Indian) and Arab admixture.

18 Dambulla: one of the most important archaeological sites in Ceylon, about 45 miles north of Kandy, Dambulla is an enormous black rock in which are five cave-temples with magnificent carvings. They were built about the 1st century B.C., and the motifs of the sculpture show the influence both of Hinduism and Buddhism. One of the recumbent stone figures of the Buddha is 47 feet long.

19 Polonnaruwa: an ancient ruined city in central Ceylon. It became a royal residence for the Sinhalese in the 3rd century A.D., and was the capital of the Sinhalese kings from the 8th to the 12th centuries. The ruins of palaces and temples, both Hindu and Buddhist, still survive, and three colossal figures of Buddha carved out of huge stones. The greatest Sinhalese king, Prakrama Bahu, was crowned here in 1153, and his reign is known as the "golden age of Lanka." Lanka was the ancient Indian name

of Ceylon, and, in the *Ramayana,* it was Ravana, the mythical demon king of Lanka, who abducted Sita, wife of the hero, Rama. Ceylon was called Taprobane by the Romans, and Serendib by the Arab traders who dominated the Indian Ocean before the coming of the European sea merchants.

²⁰ Anuradhapura: " 'the buried city of Ceylon,' famous for its ancient and extremely interesting ruins—the relics of a civilisation that existed more than 2000 years ago, when the city was the capital of a succession of ancient kings." (Murray's *Handbook for Ceylon*)

²¹ Mahinda (Pali) Mahendra (Sanskrit): probably the son, though perhaps the brother of Ashoka, king of Magadha and emperor of India, who brought Buddhism to Ceylon about 250 B.C. He was assisted in the task of conversion by his sister, the princess-nun Sanghamitta, who, according to legend, planted at Anuradhapura a cutting from the Buddha's bo tree. It is said that he had memorized, for the texts had not yet been written down, many of the basic Pali texts of Buddhism, such as the three *Pitakas,* which he translated into Sinhalese. These, in turn, were handed down by oral tradition until they were recorded in writing about 80 B.C. Despite frequent invasions of Ceylon in later history by Tamils from South India, who attempted to suppress Buddhism and restore Hinduism, Buddhism of the Hinayana, or Theravada, school remains to this day the predominant religion of Ceylon. See Heinrich Zimmer: *The Philosophies of India,* page 498.

²² Unduwap: a month in the Ceylonese calendar.

²³ These two quotations from the edicts of the Indian emperor Ashoka are from page 38 of Merton's pocket notebook, a left-hand page facing one of the right-hand pages on which he drafted the poem "Kandy Express" on his train ride from Colombo to Kandy. However, the firmness of the handwriting indicates that they were not written during the trip on the train. There are a number of published translations of the *Edicts* in English (B. M. Barua, D. R. Bhandarkar, E. Hultsch, R. Mookerji, G. S. Murti & A. N. K. Aiyangar, N. A. Nikam & R. McKeon, R. Sarma, A. Sen, D. C. Sircar, Vincent A. Smith, A. C. Woolmer, et al.), but it has not yet been possible to determine which version Merton was reading. One might assume that he had picked up a pamphlet guide to the Ceylonese archaeological sites and was quoting from that, except that there are no monuments of the Ashokan edicts in Ceylon, though many legends about Ashoka are to be found in old Ceylonese chronicles such as the *Dipavamsa.* Pending exact identification of the source, we give the full text of the first and twelfth edicts, from which Merton has excerpted, in the version of Vincent A. Smith (*The Edicts of Asoka,* edited in English, with an introduction and commentary, by Vincent A. Smith, M.A., London, Essex House Press, 1909).

"Rock Edict I.
"The Sacredness of Life.
" 'This pious edict has been written by command of His Sacred and Gracious Majesty the King. [Devanampriya Pryadarsin]
" 'Here (in the capital) [Pataliputra] no animal may be slaughtered for sacrifice, nor may holiday-feasts be held, because His Sacred and Gracious Majesty the King sees manifold evil in holiday-feasts, although holiday-feasts in certain places are meritorious in the sight of His Sacred and Gracious Majesty the King.
" 'Formerly, in the Kitchen of His Sacred and Gracious Majesty the King from day to day many hundred thousands of creatures were slaughtered for savoury meats. But now, when this pious edict is being written, there are slaughtered (daily) for savoury meats only three living creatures, to wit, two peacocks and one antelope—the antelope, however, not invariably. Even these three living creatures in future shall not be slaughtered.' " (pages 6-7)

"Rock Edict XII.
"Toleration.
" 'His Sacred and Gracious Majesty the King does reverence to men of all sects, whether ascetics or householders, by gifts and various forms of reverence.
" 'His Sacred Majesty, however, cares not so much for gifts or external reverence as that there should be a growth of the essence of the matter in all sects. The growth of the essence of the matter assumes various forms, but the root of it is restraint of speech, to wit, a man must not do reverence to his own sect or disparage that of another man without reason. Depreciation should be for specific reasons only, because the sects of other people all deserve reverence for one reason or another.
" 'By thus acting, a man exalts his own sect, and at the same time does service to the sects of other people. By acting contrariwise, a man hurts his own sect, and does disservice to the sects of other people. For he who does reverence to his own sect while disparaging the sects of others wholly from attachment to his own, with intent to enhance the splendour of his own sect, in reality by such conduct inflicts the severest injury on his own sect. Concord, therefore, is meritorious, to wit, hearkening and hearkening willingly to the Law of Piety as accepted by other people. For this is the desire of His Sacred Majesty that all sects should hear much teaching and hold sound doctrine.
" 'Wherefore, the adherents of all sects, whatever they may be, must be informed that His Sacred Majesty cares not so much for gifts or external reverence as that there should be growth in the essence of the matter and respect for all sects.
" 'For this very purpose are employed the Censors of the Law of Piety, the Censors of the Women, the (?) Inspectors, and other official bodies. And this is the fruit thereof—the growth of one's own sect, and the enhancement of the splendour of the Law of Piety.' " (pages 17–18)

In the edicts, Ashoka only twice uses his own name. Instead, he refers to himself as Devanamprya Pryadarsin, literally, in Prakrit, "Devanamprya" —"beloved of the gods"; and "Pryadarsin"—"one who sees to the good of others," which Smith renders as "His Sacred and Gracious Majesty." These terms, which are also found applied to Ashoka's ancestors in the Maurya dynasty, are either "coronation names" or honorific epithets. For further background on Ashoka see page 366 in the glossary.

[24] Ananda: the Buddha's favorite disciple. He was a cousin of the Buddha's and his personal attendant for the last twenty-five years of his life. Ananda is credited with having persuaded the Buddha to permit the admission of women into his order.

[25] Chuang Tzu and Lao Tzu: "Chuang Tzu, who wrote in the fourth and third centuries, B.C., is in many respects the greatest and most spiritual of the Chinese philosophers. He is also the chief authentic spokesman for Taoism, its founder Lao Tzu being legendary and known to us largely through Chuang Tzu's writings. D. T. Suzuki, the most articulate modern exponent of Zen Buddhism, sees in Chuang Tzu without exception the greatest of all Asian philosophers and the ancestor of Zen. Indeed, it was because of Chuang Tzu and othe other Taoist sages that Indian Buddhism was transformed, in China, into the completely original and unique vehicle which we call by its Japanese name of Zen. Chuang Tzu abounds in wit, paradox, satire, and shattering insight into the true ground of being." (Merton's own text for the jacket copy of his selection of "interpretations" in English, *The Way of Chuang Tzu,* New York, New Directions, 1965)

[26] See *Thomas Merton on Peace,* with a foreword by Gordon C. Zahn, New York, McCall Publishing Company, 1971, pages 234–47.

[27] Wittgenstein: Ludwig Josef Johann Wittgenstein (1889–1951), the Austrian-born philosopher whose *Tractatus Logico-Philosophicus* was one of the most influential works in philosophy of the present century. After World War I he became a professor at Cambridge, later he lived as a hermit in Norway, and at his death he was a lecturer at Oxford. Toward the end of his life he changed some of his basic doctrines, which were then circulated only as lecture notes, and it is probably these final works, more religious in their orientation, to which Merton is here referring. Among his books available in English translation are: *Tractatus Logico-Philosophicus, Lectures & Conversations on Aesthetics, Psychology & Religious Beliefs, On Certainty, Remarks on the Foundations of Mathematics,* and *Notebooks.*

[28] Perak: one of the sultanates of the former British Protectorate of Federated Malay States which are now independent as Malaysia.

29 Bonn: a city on the Rhine River and capital of West Germany since World War II.

30 Novalis: pseudonym of Georg Friedrich Philipp von Hardenberg (1772–1801), one of the leading writers of German Romanticism, best known for his poems, *Hymns to the Night,* and his poetic novel *Henry von Ofterdingen.*

31 Hermann Hesse: *Steppenwolf,* page 17 of the Bantam paperback edition, New York, 1969.

32 Nathanael West: (1903–40) American novelist, author of *The Dream Life of Balso Snell, Miss Lonelyhearts, A Cool Million,* and *The Day of the Locust.* For his biography, see Jay Martin: *Nathanael West, The Art of His Life,* New York, Farrar, Straus & Giroux, 1970.

BANGKOK
December 7–8

December 7 / Bangkok

I find that I was secretly enraged and humiliated by the fact of having overweight luggage yesterday. Today, first thing after getting up and saying Office, I went all through my baggage, ruthlessly separating out things to be somehow disposed of. For instance, all cold-country clothes can go into the zipper bag which perhaps I can get the abbot from Hong Kong to take there. Which means, however, I won't be able to go back to Sikkim, Bhutan, or Nepal. Stupid books I bought can be discarded here or somewhere. I make a desperate plan to finish several books here in Bangkok. But of course with the conference this will be impossible. I sent contact prints to John Griffin with a few marked for enlargement. Took nine rolls of Pan X to the Borneo Studio on Silom Road, hoping they will not be ruined.[1] Better finally burn up that incense. Threw some useless pills in the toilet. But I find it hard to make any firm plan that *positively* excludes a return to India, South India that is, in January.

After arranging my flight for Djakarta on the evening of the 15th, I went dutifully to the palace and the Temple of the Emerald Buddha. I didn't see the palace—it wasn't open to the public today—but went through the temple. I saw some of the paintings but was distracted by a Thai soldier who had four U. S. quarters and wanted to change them for 20 baht. But 20 was all I had. The temple itself was impressive in a dark, ornate, spacious way and the small, precious, green Buddha enshrined high up in a lighted niche was somehow moving. The buildings and sculptures of the temple compound I thought precious and

The Temple of the Emerald Buddha, Bangkok

bizarre rather than beautiful. They are saved by a kind of proportion which is very evident as soon as you get away from them a little. The guardian deities are not frightening, only grotesque. I kept remembering a picture of one of them on a calendar in the infirm refectory at Gethsemani sometime back in 1965.

The palace temple, however, has a basic dignity, a kind of splendor that is genuine, not gross. A bit decadent, perhaps, but I hesitate to say it. There are of course Disneyland tendencies in all these Thai wats, and I suppose at times they go over the line. For instance, in another wat I passed near the palace, the "guardian deities" on two doors were British 19th-century soldiers with white uniforms, helmets, and rifles. All this makes the Tiger Balm Gardens in Singapore (which I missed) more understandable. As for the frescoes: yes, they were good too, in their way, yet so close to a comic strip. (This is not meant to imply a judgment, good or bad.) After all I think the murals are perhaps the best thing in the whole temple. Well, Hanuman has a prominent place in all this. He is at once a monkey, god, and a successful fighter. And I think this says much that illumines the whole comic-book, and pre-comic-book, tradition.

One of the villains of the temple is a "bad yak" called Non-katal. Here a "yak" is not a Tibetan animal but an inhabitant of Ceylon. "Nonkatal behaves carelessly with a girl in heaven . . . he is commanded to become a buffalo."

"Rama,[2] the hero, arrives at the palace of the king and sees the second queen on the throne alone. She tells Rama that the king wants him to become a hermit for a period of fourteen years and after that time he is to return and take the throne as king of Ayodhya. Rama is pleased to do as the king's will commands. . . . The chief officer has set up a farewell parade for Rama. . . . The king's heart grows sad and troubled by what he has done to Rama, and, as if he can stand no more, dies suddenly in the night."

Caption of a picture in which the yaks are trying to force Hanuman into a huge black cauldron: "The Yaks try very hard

Thai guardian figure

to slay Hanuman by putting him in the mash. Hanuman turns and slays the Yaks instead."

✼

"The human merry-go-round sees many changes: the illusion that cost India the efforts of thousands of years to unmask is the same illusion that the West has labored just as hard to maintain and strengthen."

—Hermann Hesse: Steppenwolf, page 69 in the
Bantam paperback edition, New York, 1969.

✼

December 8 / Bangkok

A Dutch abbot who is staying with an attaché of the Dutch Legation came around to the hotel yesterday and we went to Silom Road again, to find Dom Leclercq and others who had arrived. Most of the delegates were arriving today and I will go to the Red Cross place where we are supposed to stay and where the meeting is to be held. It is 30 kilometers out of Bangkok. The Dutch abbot was trying to talk me into participating in a TV interview but I am not sure it is such a good idea, for various reasons. And first of all I find the idea very distasteful. The suggestion that it would be "good for the Church" strikes me as fatuous as far as my own participation is concerned. It would be much "better for the Church" if I refrained.

It is good to have a second time round with these cities. Calcutta, Delhi, and now Bangkok. It now seems quite a different city. I did not recognize the road in from the airport, and the city which had seemed, before, somewhat squalid, now appears to be, as it is, in many ways affluent and splendid. What has happened, of course, is that the experience of places like Calcutta and Pathankot has changed everything and given a better perspective in which to view Bangkok. The shops are full of good things. There is a lot to eat. Lots of fruits, rice, bottles, medicines, shirts, shoes, machinery, and meat (for non-Buddhists). And the stores near the Oriental Hotel are really splendid. So too is the Oriental itself. I have a fine split-level dwelling high over the river, and you enter it through an open veranda on the other side, looking out over the city.

I went to Silom Road, walked into the French Foreign Missions place and found it deserted. I wandered around in the rooms looking at the titles of books on the shelves: Scott's[3] *Marmion*, André Maurois,[4] along with Edward Schillebeeckx, a set of Huysmans,[5] I forget what else . . . lots of magazines from, *Etudes* to *Paris-Match*. Finally Fr. Leduc[6] appeared, and presently—he told me to wait—the superior, P. Verdier,[7] came in with Abbot de Floris,[8] who is running the meeting, and Fr. Gordan.[9] They said there was mail for me; it turned out to be a letter from Winifred Karp, the young girl who stayed with the nuns at the Redwoods, forwarded from Calcutta. I have a hunch some of my mail will be getting lost in this shift.

The flight over Malaysia: dark-blue land, islands fringed with fine sand, aquamarine sea. Lots of clouds. It was a Japan Air Lines plane. They made me weigh my hand luggage, which put me overweight for the economy class allowance, so instead of just paying more for nothing I paid the difference for a first-class ticket, thus covering it with the bigger baggage allowance. And had a very comfortable ride, overeating, drinking two free, and strong, Bloody Marys, and talking to a diplomatic courier for the State Department, who by now is getting ready to fly on to Karachi in Pakistan on the night Pan Am plane.

This evening I took a walk through Bangkok, down past the Post Office and into Chinatown. A Chinese Buddhist temple was all lit up and having some kind of fair, preparing a stage for a show, food for a banquet, and booths were selling all kinds of trinkets, lights, and incense. I went in and wandered around. There were hundreds of kids playing. Older people happy and fairly busy preparing whatever it was. Perhaps something to do with the king, whose birthday was yesterday. The city is full of flags, signs saying "Long live our noble King" and huge pictures of Phumiphol Aduldet himself, now as a Thai general and now as a bhikkhu in the lotus posture.

⌘

Last night I had a good Hungarian dinner at Nick's No. 1 (where however I seem to have been grossly shortchanged) and went on to see an Italian movie about some criminals in Milan, a quasi-documentary. It was not bad, very well filmed, and worth seeing.

⌘

Today is the Feast of the Immaculate Conception. In a little while I leave the hotel. I'm going to say Mass at St. Louis Church, have lunch at the Apostolic Delegation, and then on to the Red Cross place this afternoon.

NOTES: *Bangkok*

[1] After Merton's death, John Howard Griffin wrote to the Borneo Studio and obtained the rolls of film. See *A Hidden Wholeness, The Visual World of Thomas Merton,* photographs by Thomas Merton and John Howard Griffin, text by John Howard Griffin, Boston, Houghton Mifflin, 1970.

[2] Rama: the hero of the Indian epic, the *Ramayana;* also believed to be and worshiped as one of the avatars of Vishnu and an incarnation of the sun. In the course of history, through trade, conquests, and migrations, the mythology of Hinduism was carried eastward to Thailand and other lands as far as Indonesia.

[3] Scott: Sir Walter Scott (1771–1832), the Scottish novelist and poet.

[4] André Maurois: (1885–1967) the French man of letters famous for his biographies of Byron, Shelley, Dickens, Chateaubriand, and many others. He also wrote histories of France and of the United States.

[5] Huysmans: Joris Karl Huysmans (1848–1907), the French man of letters

best known for his novels *A Rebours* ("Against the Grain") and *Là-bas* ("Down There").

6 Fr. Leduc: a priest of the French Foreign Missions Society of Paris, bursar of the organization at the time of the Bangkok meeting, but now Superior of the Society's residence in Bangkok.

7 P. Verdier: Fr. Verdier, a Belgian priest, is the Superior of a small recently organized monastic community in Bangkok.

8 Abbot de Floris: Abbot Marie de Floris, O.S.B., Secretary General of A.I.M. (Aide à l'Implantation Monastique) of Vanves, France, the organization which sponsored the Bangkok conference which Merton attended.

9 Fr. Gordan: Fr. Paul Gordan is a monk of the Benedictine Abbey of Beuron in Germany. Since 1967, he has served as Secretary General of the Benedictine Confederation at the International College of St. Anselm in Rome.

POSTSCRIPT

On the day of his last entry in the *Asian Journal,* December 8, 1968, only two days before his death in a small cottage room in Bangkok, Thailand, Thomas Merton wrote me what was to be his last letter, which concluded: "I think of you all on this Feast Day and with Christmas approaching I feel homesick for Gethsemani. But I hope to be at least in a monastery—Rawa Seneng (in Indonesia). Also I look forward to being at our monastery at Hong Kong, and may be seeing our three volunteers there (or is it two?).[1] No more for the moment. Best love to all. Louie."

He wrote these lines in his room at the Oriental Hotel in Bangkok, just a few minutes before leaving for the Red Cross place on the outskirts of the city. By Christmas he was, after all, back at Gethsemani, lying buried alongside the Abbey church overlooking the woodland knobs that had become so familiar to him during his twenty-seven years of monastic life in Kentucky.

At about 10 o'clock on the morning of December 10th, we received an incredible cable from the American Embassy in Bangkok. It said little more than that Father Thomas Merton had died. But how? And where? These agonizing questions remained unanswered. The Abbot called me into his office at once, where I stayed for the next two hours, which seemed to us an eternity. Two hours of waiting and consoling one another and hoping against hope that it was all a terrible mistake. While

[1] Two monks from Gethsemani were helping out at the Lantao Island monastery.

we desperately tried to telephone the American Embassy in Bangkok, and the State Department in Washington, for further clarification, the American Embassy in Bangkok was trying to reach us by phone. About noon the call finally got through to us, and the news was confirmed.

We learned that death was caused by accidental electrocution at about 2 P.M. (Bangkok time) on December 10th. He had delivered a paper entitled "Marxism and Monastic Perspectives" at 10 o'clock that morning.[2] It was received with great enthusiasm by the members of the conference, and all of them were looking forward to a discussion of the paper, with questions and answers, in the evening. A group of the participants had lunch with Father Merton, after which they went to their respective rooms. He had told one of his companions that he felt rather tired, and that he was looking forward to the siesta.

Having read the medical and police reports, as well as several eyewitness accounts that were sent to us from Bangkok, I have attempted to reconstruct the circumstances of his death as follows: Thomas Merton returned to his cottage about 1:30 and proceeded to take a shower before retiring for a rest. While barefoot on the terrazzo floor, he apparently had reached for the large standing fan (either to turn it on or pull it closer to the bed) when he received the full 220 volts of direct current. (This is normal voltage for Bangkok.) He collapsed, and the large fan tumbled over on top of him. When he was discovered about an hour later by two of the monks who shared his cabin, the fan, still running, lay across his body. They could not get into the room at first because the door was bolted from the inside. One of them ran for help, and two of the abbots came immediately. They broke through the upper panel of the door, opened it, and entered. One of the abbots tried to remove the fan at once from the body, but though he wore shoes, he also received a severe electrical shock. Fortunately, someone rushed over to the outlet and pulled the cord from the socket. Later examination

2 See Appendix VII.

revealed defective wiring in the fan. A Korean prioress, who was a distinguished medical doctor, came immediately. After examining the body, she pronounced him dead by electric shock.[3]

Almost a week later, after an attempt to have an autopsy performed, which proved unsuccessful due to international red tape, his body was flown back to California (ironically, by U.S. Air Force jet plane from Vietnam). From there it was transferred to commercial plane in Oakland, and then on to Louisville, where the body was met by the Abbot and a group of the monks with the local undertaker. The casket was opened at the funeral parlor in New Haven, where several of the monks identified the body. The casket was then sealed, never to be opened again.

The body arrived at the Abbey early in the afternoon of December 17th. Services in the church began almost immediately with the chanting of the funeral liturgy by the monks and the many friends who came to pay their last respects to our Father Louis and the world's Thomas Merton. At dusk under a light snowfall, his body was laid to rest in the monastic cemetery beneath a solitary cedar tree. A simple white cross marks his grave, no different from the rest of the monks who have been buried there during the past 120 years. May he rest in peace.

BROTHER PATRICK HART

3 See Appendix VIII, "Letter to Abbot Flavian Burns" from six Trappist delagates attending the Bangkok Conference.

THE ASIAN JOURNAL
OF THOMAS MERTON

Part Two

Complementary Reading

A Moslem commentator on the *Koran,* Abu Ishaq al-Zajjaj[1] (died 922 A.D.), says some Christians, "unable to bear the conduct of their kings, fled to caves and cells and instituted this form of life" [the monastic life], which then became obligatory, just as a vow to fast would be obligatory. However he reproves monastic life insofar as it substitutes human institutions for divine providence, according to his interpretation.

Another, Antaki:[2] "True rahbaniyah" consists not in talk but in action in silence. Compare St. John of the Cross.

❊

In Graham's *Conversations,* Morimoto Roshi[3] says of the Zen monk's vow to save all beings: "At the beginning it just exists as a saying. But when it comes to his own wish, he has to live with it. It's his training now."

—Aelred Graham, *Conversations: Christian and Buddhist,* New York, Harcourt, Brace and World, 1968, page 45.

❊

Mysticism. "This experiential knowledge, this introspective method, by definition aims at the reality itself, the depths of man, the intention under the intonation—the smile under the mask—it searches beneath outward behavior of the person for a grace which is wholly divine. It is consequently based on the appreciation of each one's degree of sincerity, it examines each conscience 'by transparency'. . . ."[4]

—Louis Massignon: *Essai sur les origines du lexique technique de la mystique musulmane,* Paris, J. Vein, 1954, page 138.

"Then . . . Jesus, Son of Mary: and we gave him the Gospel, and we planted in the hearts of those who follow him the seeds of meekness (ra'fah), compassion (rahmah), and of monastic life (rahbaniyah). They are the ones who instituted it (monastic life). We only prescribed it to them to make them desire (i.e., as an aid to desire) to conform to God's good pleasure, but now it turns out that they have not followed the method required for this rule of life: to those who have remained faithful to it we have given their reward, but many among them have been sinners."

> —*Koran,* LVII, 27 ("Monastic Life of Christians," based on translation in Massignon, *op. cit.,* page 148).

The Moslem interpretations of this: that Allah did not prescribe the monastic life but some disciples of Jesus invented it, with its obligations, and once they accepted its obligations they were bound to them in His sight. The moral being: how much more will He require others to keep what He has prescribed.

> —See Massignon, *op. cit.,* pages 148–49.

✳

The "noble lie" in Plato's *Republic?* Cornford calls it a simple mistranslation of the phrase γενναῖον τι ʼεν ψευδομένοις, ψεῦδος is "fiction" or "myth." γενναῖον is "on a grand scale." The "noble lie" is the myth-dream by which in fact every society lives, only some are "nobler" and more credible than others. Maybe the "noble lie" is really the credible and workable myth. The trouble is that such myths cannot be consciously fabricated.

> —See F.M. Cornford: "The Marxist View of Ancient Philosophy" in *The Unwritten Philosophy,* Cambridge University Press, 1950, pages 132–33.

"I realized that what I was doing was all the unnecessary work."

—Morimoto Roshi, in Graham, *op cit.*, page 48.

✼

"If we would really understand what a philosopher says we must keep a wakeful eye on what he does *not* say, because both he and his opponents take it for granted."

—F. M. Cornford, *op. cit.*

✼

Gary Snyder says that Zen and Tibetan Buddhism are "closer than any other schools in Buddhism," but their methods are in reverse of each other. Zen goes directly to the ground of consciousness and then comes up, exploring other realms of mind, having seen the ground first. Tibetan Buddhism goes down gradually, until the ground of consciousness is reached and then "comes up swiftly."

—See Gary Snyder,[5] in Graham, *op. cit.*, page 65.

✼

"Whoever hath lived in accordance with the law of discipline, in gentleness and purity, will, having transcended deaths and births, put an end to his sorrow."

—from the *Udanavarga,* one of the Tibetan, Pali canonical scriptures, as translated by W.W. Rockhill, and quoted in W.Y. Evans-Wentz: *Tibetan Yoga and Secret Doctrines,* second edition, Oxford University Press, 1958, page 22.

✼

Anne-Marie Esnoul on Ramanuja's concept of God (Vishnu).[6]

"The Lord, the first of these entities, is Vishnu, whom also Ramanuja quite frequently designates with the name borrowed from the Upanishads: Brahman. But this identity of appellation must not lead us into error; although the term is in the neuter, it does not represent the homogeneous Absolute without qualifications of the intellectualist glosses. God is All without limit, but He remains a Person, simultaneously immanent and transcendent. This Supreme Person is the object of adoration, the ineffable Subject, the Sole Principle which unifies all multiplicity. As opposed to the Brahman of Sankara, which was defined only negatively and declared to be void of all qualification, Ramanuja's Absolute has all the qualities to an infinite degree. . . .

". . . for Ramanuja the Lord does not express Himself by a duality of modes, but under the form of a duality of nature. . . . He is therefore at once change and immutability. Creation presents itself to Him as a world limited, which only He can know exhaustively. The *Purushottama* (the Supreme Person) is actual at all times. . . .

"His Supreme Form . . . remains inaccessible to the limited understanding of the faithful. It dwells in the *Vaikuntha,* Vishnu's Paradise, adorned with all the traditional attributes: conch, disc, mace, sword, bow, lotus. . . ."

—A.-M. Esnoul: *Ramanuja et la mystique vish-nouite,* Paris, Editions du Seuil, 1964, pages 115–16.

"In fact, what most dominates Ramanuja's thought is the emphasis put on personality—whether the Supreme Person or the human person is concerned. In this, he further prolongs the teachings of the *Gita.*"

—A.-M. Esnoul: *op. cit.,* page 122.

✠

Notes from "Wisdom Develops Samadhi" by the Venerable Acariya Maha Boowa Nanasampanno.

This is the Buddha's original discourse on the "Foundations of Mindfulness."

Rupa dhamma: the body and its parts
Nama dhamma: the mind or heart
Vedana: feelings, good and bad
Sanna: memory of names, sounds, objects
Samskara: thought construction, e.g. of the future based on the past
Vijnana: awareness of sense impression at the moment of impact[7]

". . . they come from the heart, they may be known in the heart, and if the heart is not careful they are the deceivers of the heart—so they are also the things which can hide or obscure the truth."

—Translated from the Thai by Bhikkhu Pannavaddho in *Visakha Puja,* annual publication of The Buddhist Association of Thailand, 41 Aditaya Road, Bangkok, 1967.

⌘

Avijja (avidya): the opposite not of *knowledge* but of *insight.*

—See T. R. V. Murti: *The Central Philosophy of Buddhism,* London, Allen & Unwin, 2nd edition, 1960, page 238ff.

⌘

Sankaracharya on the attainment of liberation (from *The Crest-Jewel of Discrimination*).

"A man should be intelligent and learned, with great powers of comprehension, and able to overcome doubts by the exercise of his reason. One who has these qualifications is fitted for knowledge of the Atman.

"He alone may be considered qualified to seek Brahman who has discrimination, whose mind is turned away from all enjoyments, who possesses tranquility and the kindred virtues, and who feels a longing for liberation.

"In this connection, the sages have spoken of four qualifications for attainment. When these are present, devotion to the Reality will become complete. When they are absent, it will fail.

"First is mentioned discrimination between the eternal and the non-eternal. Next comes renunciation of the enjoyment of the fruits of action, here and hereafter. Then come the six treasures of virtue, beginning with tranquility. And last, certainly, is the longing for liberation.

"Brahman is real; the universe is unreal. A firm conviction that this is so is called *discrimination* between the eternal and the non-eternal.

"*Renunciation* is the giving-up of all the pleasures of the eyes, the ears, and the other senses, the giving-up of all objects of transitory enjoyment, the giving-up of the desire for a physical body as well as for the highest kind of spirit-body of a god.

"To detach the mind from all objective things by continually seeing their imperfection, and to direct it steadily toward Brahman, its goal—this is called *tranquility*.

"To detach both kinds of sense-organs—those of perception and those of action—from objective things, and to withdraw them to rest in their respective centers—this is called *self-control*. True *mental poise*, consists in not letting the mind react to external stimuli.

"To endure all kinds of afflictions without rebellion, complaint or lament—this is called *forbearance*.

"A firm conviction, based upon intellectual understanding, that the teachings of the scriptures and of one's master are true —this is called by the sages the *faith* which leads to realization of the Reality.

"To concentrate the intellect repeatedly upon the pure Brahman and to keep it fixed there always—this is called *self-*

surrender. This does not mean soothing the mind, like a baby, with idle thoughts.

"*Longing for liberation* is the will to be free from the fetters forged by ignorance—beginning with the ego-sense and so on, down to the physical body itself—through the realization of one's true nature.

"Even though this longing for liberation may be present in a slight or moderate degree, it will grow intense through the grace of the teacher, and through the practice of renunciation and of virtues such as tranquility, etc.: And it will bear fruit.

"When renunciation and the longing for liberation are present to an intense degree within a man, then the practice of tranquility and the other virtues will bear fruit and lead to the goal.

"Where renunciation and longing for liberation are weak, tranquility and the other virtues are a mere appearance, like the mirage in the desert.

"Among all means of liberation, devotion is supreme. To seek earnestly to know one's real nature—this is said to be *devotion.*"

—Sankaracharya: *The Crest-Jewel of Discrimination (Viveka Chudamani)*, translated by Swami Prabhavananda and Christopher Isherwood, Hollywood, Vedanta Press, 1947, pages 42–44.

Sankaracharya on the atman (from *The Crest-Jewel of Discrimination*).

"Now I shall tell you the nature of the Atman. If you realize it, you will be freed from the bonds of ignorance, and attain liberation.

"There is a self-existent Reality, which is the basis of our consciousness of ego. That Reality is the witness of the three states of our consciousness, and is distinct from the five bodily coverings.

"That Reality is the knower in all states of consciousness—waking, dreaming, and dreamless sleep. It is aware of the presence or absence of the mind and its functions. It is the Atman.

"That Reality sees everything by its own light. No one sees it. It gives intelligence to the mind and the intellect, but no one gives it light.

"That Reality pervades the universe, but no one penetrates it. It alone shines. The universe shines with its reflected light.

"Because of its presence, the body, senses, mind and intellect apply themselves to their respective functions, as though obeying its command.

"Its nature is eternal consciousness. It knows all things, from the sense of ego to the body itself. It is the knower of pleasures and pain and of the sense-objects. It knows everything objectively—just as a man knows the objective existence of a jar.

"This is the Atman, the Supreme Being, the ancient. It never ceases to experience infinite joy. It is always the same. It is consciousness itself. The organs and vital energies function under its command.

"Here, within this body, in the pure mind, in the secret chamber of intelligence, in the infinite universe within the heart, the Atman shines in its captivating splendour, like a noonday sun. By its light, the universe is revealed. . . .

"The Atman is distinct from Maya, the primal cause, and from her effect, the universe. The nature of the Atman is pure consciousness. The Atman reveals this entire universe of mind and matter. It cannot be defined. In and through the various states of consciousness—the waking, the dreaming and the sleeping—it maintains our unbroken awareness of identity. It manifests itself as the witness of the intelligence."

—Sankaracharya, *op. cit.,* pages 62–64.

✠

Some further notes from Tucci's *The Theory and Practice of the Mandala.*

Mandala mysticism—to structure the mandala and then re-absorb it—the effect described (romantically?) by Tucci:

"The images that the mystic sees come forth from the centre of his own heart, pervade space and then reabsorb themselves in him. They deify him and almost burn him with their lightning flashes. They are not inert and insignificant images. They calm the stormy sea of the subconscious and they illuminate his darkness. The soul's discord is extinguished and on to its agitation there dawns a steady and serene light." (pages 105–6)

This may be followed by a further revulsion from the whole mandala plane, an instantaneous annihilation and loss (ascent) in the absolute, "a revulsion of plane that occurs suddenly and immediately from the centre of the *mandala* when it has been reached." (page 106)

"[The mystic] does not deny the body but he uses it as a necessary instrument of salvation. 'The essence of all things is in our bodies, when thou shalt know thy own body, thy own foundation is firm.' (*Amritaratnavali*)" (pages 110–11)

" 'Without the body Man can obtain no result.' (*Rudrayamala Tantra*, I, v., 160)" (page 111)

" '. . . that same thought by which fools are bound to *samsara* may become, for ascetics, a means through which they arrive at the condition of Buddha' (*Pancakrama*, page 37, v. II)" (page 119)

> —Giuseppe Tucci: *The Theory and Practice of the Mandala,* translated by A. H. Broderick, London, Rider & Company, revised edition, 1969.

✄

Further notes on Tantric terms:

Or is it the other way round: prajna—feminine, upaya—masculine? Tucci may have got it wrong?

Dorje—the scepter. Tilbu—the bell. See Pallis article. In Hindu Tantrism, Shiva is passive. Shakti is dynamic and creative. In Buddhism, the male element is upaya—dynamic; the female is prajna—receptive.

" '. . . Three sorts of men are known, the inborn eternal man (*sahaja*), the uncreated man, and the body of the *karma* man.'

"Such transference is brought about by considering man as enjoyment and woman as beatitude. The relation between the two is not *kama*, physical love, but *priti* or *prema* which is the spiritual sublimation of love. This is brought about by substituting (*aropa*) for the psychophysical entity of the ordinary individual, his essential divine nature (*svarupa*).

" 'If a man worship this *svarupa*, then he attains to his human reality. If this substitution does not take place, then a man falls into hell.' (*Sivasamhita*, 68)."

—Tucci, *op. cit.*, page 128.

✵

Tummo—heat-yoga.
Pho-va—spirit transference.[8]

✵

Sadhaka—"he who causes experiences to be realized."

✵

Marco Pallis outlines three approaches to Tantrism:
1) Scholarly.
2) Traditional: theoria . . . combination of prajna-upaya: "appropriate means of concentration."
3) "A generalized Tantric sense whereby it is possible to recognize the existence, in places where the name of Tantra has been unknown, of evidence in favor of the spiritual methods in question."

—Marco Pallis: "Considerations on Tantric

Spirituality" in *The Bulletin of Tibetology,* Volume II, Number 2, August 1965, Namgyal Institute of Tibetology, Gangtok, Sikkim.

✻

N.B. Critique of Jungian approach to religious experience.
Hans Jacob: *Western Psychology and Hindu Sadhana.* Allen and Unwin.
Titus Burckhardt: "Cosmology and Modern Science," *Tomorrow,* Summer-Autumn 1964, Winter 1965, London.

✻

Pallis on prajna-upaya: "Wisdom is essentially a state or quality of being—upaya, method—carries dynamic implications since it is thanks to a deploying of the right means with their accompanying effort, that prajna is able to be reached in the heart of the *Sadhaka.*"

—Pallis, *op. cit.,* page 21.

✻

The upaya par excellence is compassion. The "skillful means."

✻

"By using skilled methods arising out of loving conduct
Brilliant gurus gave to the fortunate ones the eye
For seeing all the Sacred Scriptures and the best way
To achieve deliverance. . ."

—Versification by Merton of a comment on Milarepa by L.P. Lhalungpa, quoted in Pallis's "Considerations on Tantric Spirituality."

✻

273

The Way—in an age of impurity?

1) "The world is always the world even when times seem fair; so also Bodhi is Bodhi even in an accursed hour. Therefore I myself, be I even left as sole follower of the Way in a world grown hopelessly inattentive, shall continue to pursue the Way and not look back."

2) Can Tibetan upayas be transplanted to the West? Theoretically perhaps. In practice, "less complex spiritual instruments would seem to lend themselves best to so critical a situation."

V.g., [Shaivite] japa, [Sufi] dhikr, [Zen] nembutsu, Jesus prayer.[9]

Methods "which require long periods free from interruption for their normal accomplishment remain relatively unadaptable."

3) Focus on "Tantric sense" or "spirit."

Oriented to transformation of consciousness—emergence of bodhi mind so that it "takes command."

Alchemy of spirit—i.e., nothing destroyed—all put to good use.

"Lead is gold fallen sick."

—See Pallis, *op. cit.,* pages 24ff.

✳

T. R. V. Murti on Madhyamika:

Madhyamika is the dialectical resolution of the atma and anatma systems.

"Buddha resolves the conflict by an intuitive perception of the Real as non-dual (advaya); the Madhyamika does it by turning Reason against itself, through the dialectic."

Madhyamika refuses to characterize the absolute.

Vijnanavada identifies the absolute with consciousness.

Madhyamika is a critical and dialectical reaction against speculative systems which claim to give answers—what is reality? This credits them all as subjective and illusory.

Buddhism itself was not only a revolt against Vedic ritualization but also against the substance—metaphysics of the *Upanishads* as realized in discovering atman (substance) as true reality and bliss.

To accept a permanent substantial self is for Buddhism the root of all attachment, or avidya.

—Murti, *op. cit.*, pages 9ff.

※

Murti on reincarnation:

If there is no atman in Buddhism, what is it then that is "reincarnated"?

"There is no element which migrates from this world to the other; but there is recognition (realisation) of the fruition of karma, as there is continuity of causes and conditions. It is not as it were that one, dropping out from this world, is born into another but there is continuity of causes and conditions." (from *Madhyamika Karika Vritti,* quoted by Murti)

What is emphasized is not the individual soul but continuity through causal connection. But "who" is it that recognizes events in past existences? Surely this theory implies a continuity of "mind." What is mind? Memory is the consciousness that *"I* have experienced it before." But *I* is the ultimate illusion for Buddhism.

Interpretation of experience depends on interpretation of the real. But if interpretation itself is illusory? Who is it that interprets? How does one work out a systematic interpretation of reality on the basis that the interpreter is illusory? The answer of Buddha was silence—in the face of all attempts to conceive and formulate a speculative interpretation of reality. The dialectic of Madhyamika is the systematic form of the Buddha's silence.

—See Murti, op. cit., pages 33–35.

✳

"To hold that the world is eternal or to hold that it is not, or to agree to any other of the propositions you adduce, Vaccha, is the jungle of theorising, the wilderness of theorising, the tangle of theorising, the bondage and the shackles of theorising, attended by ill, distress, perturbation and fever; it conduces not to detachment, passionlessness, tranquility, peace, to knowledge and wisdom of Nirvana. This is the danger I perceive in these views which makes me discard them all."

—Buddha, in the Majjhima Nikaya, quoted by
Murti, op. cit., page 47.

✳

"When do we know rupa as rupa, a theory as theory? Not when we are using it implicitly, putting all our trust in it, enamoured of its externals, but only when we realise its shortcomings."

—Murti, op. cit., page 46.

✳

Murti on Abhidharma:

Abhidharma was a metaphysical system developed in the Theravada and Sarvastivada (North Indian) schools of Buddhism, while the Vaibhasika system, which Nagarjuna, founder of Madhyamika, opposed, was expounded by Vasubandhu. The question of the influence of Abhidharma on the other schools is disputed, though they have similarities.

"The Vaibhasika system is a radical pluralism erected on

the denial of Substance (soul) and the acceptance of discrete momentary entities. Dharma is the central conception in this, as it is in the other systems of Buddhism."

Abhidharma implies universal impermanence and is anti-atman. "The real is the efficient. . . . It is the seed as *changed* that produces the effect . . . at no two moments is a thing identical. . . ." (Sprouting)

For Abhidharma, a thing does not continue to exist as permanent until destroyed by something more permanent. Things contain in themselves their own destruction. "But if a thing is not capable of destruction by itself, no amount of external influence can effect it, much less reduce it to nothing." Only because the pitcher is destroyable does the blow of a stick destroy it.

—See Murti, *op. cit.*, pages 66–71.

❖

Existence is flux. There is no duration. There is no substantial unity. There are no universals, except as thought constructs—vikalpa. Cf. Hume.[10]

Avidya is the tendency to believe in permanent, universality, and identity. But "the series" has empirical validity, as with frames in a movie.

But there are vatsiputriyas, heretics, who, in reaction to the above, hold to the doctrine of pudgalatman, the individual self.

—Murti, *op. cit.*, pages 74 & 81.

❖

"The rejection of theories (ditthi) is itself the *means* by which Buddha is led to the non-conceptual knowledge of the absolute, and not vice versa."

—Murti, *op. cit.*, page 49.

❖

Murti on the development of Madhyamika:

"The Madhyamika [Middle Way] system seems to have been perfected at one stroke by the genius of its founder—Nagarjuna. There have not been many important changes in its philosophy since that time. In a system that is all dialectic, criticism, progress cannot be measured in terms of doctrinal accretion or modification. The Madhyamika system performs the high office of philosophy in taking stock of itself from time to time. A close study of the system reveals to us the stresses and strains to which philosophy was subject in India down the ages.

"The Madhyamika system has had a continuous history of development from the time of its formulation by Nagarjuna (A.D. 150) to the total disappearance of Buddhism from India (11th Cent.). We have a succession of brilliant teachers practically in every period. It is possible to distinguish three or four main schools or rather stages in the course of its development. The first is the stage of systematic formulation by Nagarjuna and his immediate disciple—Arya Deva.[11] In the next stage there is the splitting up of the Madhyamika into two schools— the Prasangika and the Svatantrika, represented by Buddhapalita[12] and Bhavaviveka[13] respectively. In the third period Candrakirti[14] (early 7th Cent.) re-affirms the Prasangika (reductio ad absurdum) as the norm of the Madhyamika; the rigour and vitality of the system is in no small measure due to him. Santi Deva (691–743), though coming a generation or two later, may also be taken as falling within this period. These two account for the high level attained by the Madhyamika system. The fourth and last stage is a syncretism of the Yogacara and the Madhyamika—the chief representatives of which are Santaraksita[15] and Kamalasila.[16] It is they who culturally conquered Tibet and made it a land of Buddhism. The Madhyamika remains to this day the official philosophy of the Tibetan Church."

—Murti, *op. cit.*, page 87.

". . . the proof that all things are sunya is itself sunya, within

278

appearance. Bhavaviveka further clarifies his position by stating that sunyata does not mean the assertion of the non-existence of things, but only the denial of the dogmatic assertion of existence."

—Murti, *op. cit.*, page 97, quoting from the *Karatalaratna,* pages 49–51.

"The Idealism of the Yogacara (Vijnanavada) school has to be understood as a significant modification of the Madhyamika sunyata on a constructive basis. The formula now is: That which appears is real but not the manner of its appearance; *that which is devoid is real,* while that *of* which it is devoid is unreal. . . . 'All is real' or 'All is nothing' are both incorrect forms of sunyata. The rope is inherently devoid of the 'snake'-appearance, which is foreign to it; but it is not devoid of its own intrinsic nature as rope. With this logic, the Vijnanavadins contend that the reality of vijnana (consciousness) must be accepted as it cannot be denied at all, while the duality of subject and object with which it is apparently infected must be considered non-existent; sunyata applies to this unreal aspect. The real is identified with vijnana.

"The Vijnanavadin maintains two contentions; vijnana is *real,* not apparent; vijnana *alone* is real, not the object. The first is against the Madhyamika, for whom both the knowing consciousness and the object known are relative to each other, and are therefore nothing in themselves, i.e., unreal. The second is against the realist (like the Abhidharmika) who uncritically accepts the object as real on a par with vijnana. Both are extreme positions, and the Vijnanavada steers a middle course between them."

—Murti: *op. cit.,* pages 104–5.

". . . [the Vijnanavadins] give substance to the sunya by identifying it with Pure Consciousness (vijnapti-matrata) that is devoid of duality (dvaya-sunyata). They consider themselves the true Madhyamika—adopting the middle course between the extremes of Nihilism and Realism. . . .

"The founder of the Yogacara school is Maitreya(natha) (A.D. 270–350) whose historicity is now generally accepted. But he is represented solely by his illustrious disciple Asanga (*c.* 350) and his brother Vasubandhu."

—Murti: *op. cit.,* page 107.

The *Lankavatara Sutra* contains Yogacara teachings.

❊

S. B. Dasgupta on bodhicitta:

Dasgupta quotes from the *Gandavyuha Sutra:* "O son of a noble family, the attitude characterized as being bent on enlightenment (bodhicitta) is the seed of all the virtues of the Buddhas; it is like a field, because in it grow all the bright virtues of the world; it is like the earth, because all the world takes refuge in it; it is like water, because it washes away all the impurities due to self-centered passions (klesa); it is like the wind, because it is present everywhere in the world; it is like the fire, because it burns all the remaining undergrowth [of] wrong views; etc."

—Translated by Dr. H.V. Guenther, *Stepping Stones,* Vol. I, No. 8, as quoted by Shashi Bhushan Dasgupta: *An Introduction to Tantric Buddhism,* second edition, University of Calcutta, 1958, footnote to pages 8–9.

". . . Bodhicitta comprises in it two elements, *viz.,* enlightenment of the nature of essencelessness (*sunyata*) and universal compassion (*karuna*). This definition of Bodhicitta as the perfect commingling of *sunyata* and *karuna* had far-reaching effects in the transformation of the Mahayanic ideas into the Tantric ideas. After the production of Bodhicitta the adept becomes a Bodhisattva and proceeds on in an upward march through ten different stages which are called the *bodhisattva-bhumis* (i.e., the stages of the Bodhisattva). The first of these is the stage of *Pramudita* or the stage of delight or joy. Here the Bodhisattva rises from the cold, self-sufficing and nihilistic conception of *Nirvana* to a higher spiritual contemplation. The second is styled as the *Vimala* or the stage free from all defilement. The third is the *Prabhakari* or that which brightens; in this stage the Bodhisattva attains a clear insight—an intellectual light about the nature of the dharmas. The fourth stage is the *Arcismati* or 'full of flames,'—these flames are the flames of Bodhi which burn to ashes all the passions and ignorance. At this stage the Bodhisattva practices thirty-seven virtues called *bodhipaksikas* which mature the *bodhi* to perfection. The next is the *Sudurjaya* stage or the stage which is almost invincible. This is a stage from which no evil passion or temptation can move the Bodhisattva. The sixth stage is called the *Abhimukhi,* where the Bodhisattva is almost face to face with *prajna* or the highest knowledge. The seventh is the *Durangama* which literally means 'going far away.' In this stage the Bodhisattva attains the knowledge of the expedience which will help him in the attainment of salvation. Though he himself abides here by the principles of void and non-duality and desirelessness, yet his compassion for beings keeps him engaged in the activities for the well-being of all the creatures. The eighth is the stage of *Acala,* which means 'immovable.' The next is the *Sadhumati* or the 'good will'; when the Bodhisattva reaches such a stage all the sentient beings are benefited by his attainment of the highest perfect knowledge. The tenth or the last is the stage of *dharma-megha* (literally 'the clouds of dharma'), where the Bodhisattva attains perfect knowledge, great compassion, love and sympathy for all the sentient beings. When this last stage of *Dharma-megha* is reached, the aspirer becomes a perfect Bodhisattva or a Buddha."

—S.B. Dasgupta, *op. cit.,* pages 9 and 10.

⌘

Dasgupta on Madhyamika:

"The *Sunyata*-doctrine of Nagarjuna may seem incompatible with the doctrine of *nirvana*. If everything be void and there be neither origination nor destruction, then by the destruction or arrest of what should we attain *nirvana?* The reply of Nagarjuna is that *nirvana* is not something which is to be attained through the destruction or arrest of anything whatsoever; it is but the complete cessation of all mental constructions. . . . *Nirvana* is no Ens [being], neither non-Ens [non-being], it is like a knot entwined by the empty space (*akasa*) and untied again by that same empty space."

—S.B. Dasgupta, *op. cit.*, page 18.

✣

Asvaghosha (2nd century A.D.) on tathata ("suchness," "thatness"):

"As soon as you understand that when the totality of existence is spoken of, or thought of, there is neither that which speaks, nor that which is spoken of, there is neither that which thinks nor that which is thought of; then you conform to suchness; and when your subjectivity is thus completely obliterated, it is said to have the insight."

—Asvaghosha:[17] *Discourse on the Awakening of Faith in the Mahayana (Mahayanashraddhotpada),* as translated from the Chinese version by D.T. Suzuki, Chicago, 1900, and quoted by S.B. Dasgupta, *op. cit.*, page 20.

". . . but in the absolute nature things are neither ens nor non-ens; this absolute nature can only be somehow indicated as the 'thatness' (*tathata*) of things, and this 'thatness' of things is nothing but pure consciousness. . . . it is the involution of the *Alaya-vijnana* through the eradication of the two veils (of passion and ignorance); that is the immutable element which is beyond the reach of all mentation;—it is all-good, permanent, perfect bliss—or the form of liberation—it is the substance itself."

—S. B. Dasgupta, *op. cit.,* pages 28–29.

❋

Dasgupta on pure consciousness (*vijnapti-matrata*):

"These instructions of the Lord were ultimately intended for making the disciples realise the non-entity of the self (*pudgala-nairatmya*) [absence of notion of ego] and the non-entity also of things *(dharma-nairatmya)*[absence of notion of things]."

—S.B. Dasgupta, *op. cit.,* page 26.

❋

"As contrary to the ways of the whole world is this dharma demonstrated,—it teaches you not to seize upon dharmas, but the world is wont to grasp at anything."

—*Perfection of Wisdom in 8,000 Lines,* XV, 305.[18]
Quoted in Conze, *op. cit.,* page 7.

❋

Murti on the concept of freedom:

"We are attracted to things as we invest them in our imagination, with this or that quality. This is a subjective affair; it is not real. Freedom is the total cessation of imagination (sarvakalpana-ksayo hi nirvanam). Summing up the essence of spiritual discipline Arya Deva characterizes it as a 'Take away all.' Desisting from vice, freeing oneself from the substance-view and lastly giving up all (standpoints) are the stages of this process."

—Murti, *op. cit.,* page 256.

Person? "Buddha—which the Bodhisattva eventually becomes —is a person—the Highest Person. In Buddha, we have the conception of a person without any trace of the ego. There is activity without attachment. There is nothing which the Bodhisattva cannot sacrifice for the good of others. He dedicates his present and future lives unreservedly in the service of all beings."

—Murti, *op. cit.*, pages 263–64.

✳

Spiritual (bodhi) discipline means "bringing about *a change in oneself* not in the environment. Changing the external world to suit one's desires is the way of worldly men; that is like carpeting the whole earth to avoid being hurt by thorns."

—Murti, *op. cit.*, page 267.

✳

"Upaya is bondage when unassociated with prajna, and even prajna is also bondage when unassociated with upaya: both of them again become liberation when one is associated with the other." [S. B. Dasgupta, *Introduction to Tantric Buddhism*, page 93.] Compare the relation of *caritas* and *sapientia* in Augustinian[19] mysticism—*veritas caritatis: caritas veritatis.*[20] And in St. Bernard,[21] and others. The union of prajna and upaya in bodhicitta is "the door," the "way out," insofar as it is prajna-sunyata, but "no escape" (no exit) insofar as by compassion (karuna) it elects not to escape, and remains identified with all suffering existents.

"Supportless is Prajna, and supportless is the great compassion; they should be united like the union of the sky with the sky. In that stage there is no thinker—no thought—nothing to be thought of; there all seeing of sights, hearing of sounds—muttering, laughing—enjoyment—doing of all deeds—all become yoga for a man."

—S.B. Dasgupta, *op. cit.,* page 94.

⌘

G. B. Mohan on rasa:

Rasa has had many meanings: water, milk, soma-juice, later the flavor of soma, "blessedness," "taste," "essence." Rasa is so called because it is relished. Then, with further abstraction, some sages began to say "rasa is brahman." "Raso vai sah." ("He is the essence."—*Taittiriya Upanishad,* II, 7)

Rasa is not only the *poet's* creative experience, but also the *reader's* experience in re-creating, fusing various intellectual and emotional elements.

Rasa is compassion (karuna) and creative imagination (pratibha)—art versus thanatos.

"It is evident that this rasa of the poet, which is a contemplative creative experience and not a personal emotion, is the root of the creative process."

Conflict between different rasas is objectified in poetry. And there is need for aucitya (propriety) to get the right one. Rasa as the total of qualities in the poem.

Dhvani (suggestion) is the means by which poetry arouses rasa.

"Beauty in poetry consists in the predominance of the suggested tertiary meaning over the primary referential and the secondary contextual meanings."

"Rasadhavani (the suggestion of rasa, or the suggested rasa) is the soul of poetry." Santa (serenity) is thought by some to be the one basic rasa, linked with a realization of identity.

Pratibha, or "poetic sensibility," becomes "mirror-like" by exercise, i.e. the combination of (enriched fund of) experience and training of sensitive response of susceptibility, the capacity for identification and openness to subtle suggestion.

—G.B. Mohan: *The Response to Poetry*, New Delhi, 1968, People's Publishing House, pages 9–25.

This observation of Mohan's also serves, analogically, for anti-poetry. The antipoet "suggests" a tertiary meaning which is *not* "creative" and "original" but a deliberate ironic feedback of cliché, a further referential meaning, alluding, by its tone, banality, etc., to a *customary and abused context,* that of an impoverished and routine sensibility, and of the "mass-mind," the stereotyped creation of quantitative preordained response by "mass-culture."

⌘

Surendranath Dasgupta on bhutatathata:

"Nirvana is merely the cessation of the seeming phenomenal flow. It cannot, therefore, be designated either as positive or as negative, for these conceptions only belong to phenomena. In this state there is nothing which is known, and even the knowledge of the phenomena having ceased to appear is not found. Even the Buddha himself is a phenomenon, a mirage or a dream, and so are all his teachings."

Bhutatathata: "thatness," reality, "has no attribute and it can only be somehow pointed out in silence as the mere 'that.' Since you understand that when the totality of existence is spoken or thought of, there is neither that which speaks nor that which is spoken of, there is neither that which thinks nor that which is thought of, you have the stage of 'thatness.' . . . It is negative in the same sense that it is beyond all thàt is conditional, and it is positive in the sense that it holds all within it. It cannot be comprehended by any kind of particularisation or distinction."

The truth is that which subjectively does not exist by it-self, that the negation (sunyata) is also void (sunya) in its nature, that neither that which is negation nor that which negates is an independent entity. It is the pure soul that manifests itself as eternal, permanent, immortal, which completely holds all things within it. On that account it cannot be called affirmation; and there is no trace of affirmation in it because it is neither the product of the creative function of thought nor the sub-conscious memory as the integrated past history of experiences, and the only way of grasping this truth—the thatness—is by transcending all conceptual creation. . . . It is by the touch of ignorance that the truth [bhutatathata] comes in the phenomenal form of existence.

> —Surendranath Dasgupta: *Indian Idealism*, Cambridge University Press, second edition, 1962, pages 78–84.

❊

Dharma: from the root *dhr*, "to hold" or "to support."

"Dharma is that which holds, supports and sustains life. It is the essential law of life; it is the law of a person's essential character. It is also virtue, not the virtue prescribed in manuals of ethics, but virtue in conformity with the essential law of one's own personality. The supreme function of poetry is to make us aware of this dharma which is the sanction of all moral values."

> —Mohan, *op. cit.*, page 131.

❊

"No moral life is possible without an insight into the complexities of concrete human situations. The individual yearns to enrich his self by assimilating the meaningful experiences of others. Spiritual enlightenment is dependent on our capacity to embrace the varied experiences of humanity. By recreating another's experience in our self and by thus strengthening our imagination poetry provides us with an insight into the complexities of our moral existence."

—Mohan, *op. cit.,* pages 133–34.

⌘

"The concept of rasa . . . dissolves the end-means conflict. Aestheticism which fails to integrate art with life and crude moralism which reduces poetry to sermons perpetuate the end-means conflict. Aesthetic experience is both an end in itself and a means for a fuller realization of human values. . . . By pointing out unsuspected affinities between apparently dissimilar things, by establishing meaningful relations between apparently unrelated phenomena, poetry extends the range of our awareness."

—Mohan, *op. cit.,* page 144.

⌘

NOTES: *Complementary Reading*

1 Zajjaj: Abu Ishaq al-Zajjaj. Merton's information about Zajjaj, and the quotation, are from Louis Massignon: *Essai sur les origines du lexique technique de la mystique musulmane,* Paris, J. Vein, 1954, page 150.

2 Antaki: Ahmad ibn Asim al-Antaki, died about 835 A.D. See Massignon, *op. cit.,* page 153.

3 Morimoto Roshi: "Roshi"—Japanese for "Zen Master." (See under *roshi* in glossary, page 396) Morimoto Shonen was born in 1888. He studied Western philosophy in college and later taught at one of the Japanese universities. He lived for seventeen years in a Jodo sect (Pure Land Buddhism) temple, caring for his ailing mother. He became a Buddhist monk at the age of forty-five and studied under Otsu Roshi of Shokoku-ji ("ji"—Japanese for temple or monastery) in Kyoto. He is a dharma-heir of Otsu Roshi. For a number of years Morimoto Roshi has been master of the Nagaoka Zen-juku, a privately endowed boarding school for the study of Zen and the classics, on the outskirts of Kyoto. In addition to some twenty-

five regular students, several Zen monks have been his disciples, and his monthly lectures are attended by a wide range of people. (Based on a private letter from Gary Snyder)

4 *La mystique.* "Cette science expérimentale, cette méthode introspective vise, par définition, la réalité même, le fond de l'homme, intention sous l'intonation,—le sourire sous le masque,—elle cherche, sous le geste de la personne, une grâce toute divine. Elle est fondée, par conséquent, sur l'appréciation du degré de sincérité de chacun, elle examine chaque conscience 'par transparence. . . .' "

5Gary Snyder: American poet, student of Oriental religions and the culture of the American Indian, and a leader in the ecological conservation movement, was born in San Francisco in 1930. He grew up in the Pacific Northwest and was graduated from Reed College, Portland, in anthropology and literature, in 1951. He did Chinese and Japanese studies at the University of California, Berkeley, from 1953 to 1956. Later he went to sea as crew on merchant vessels and worked in the woods, chiefly mountaineering and backpacking. From 1956 to 1968 he lived mostly in Japan, studying Zen Buddhism at the Daitoku-ji monastery, and made a trip through India. Of his work with Zen in Japan, Snyder writes: "I studied briefly with Isshu Miura Roshi [whose *The Zen Koan* is a Harcourt Brace Jovanovich paperbook] and then for a number of years with Sesso Oda Roshi, the Abbot of Daitoku-ji and Master of the monastery. I was working during part of this period as an assistant to Mrs. Ruth Sasaki, in her temple Ryosen-an, a branch temple of Daitoku-ji, on various translations and publications. . . . I met Morimoto Roshi through my first friend in Japan, the Zen monk Gisen Asai, Morimoto's leading disciple who will be his dharma-heir. . . . The only true conversations I've ever had with a Zen Master were with Morimoto Roshi, whom I now somewhat consider my teacher, since Oda Roshi died." Snyder now lives, with his wife, Masa Uehara, and their two sons, in a small commune, which he himself designed and built, in the foothills of the California Sierras. With the help of Gisen Asai, he hopes to develop it into a sister-center of Morimoto's school near Kyoto, the Nagaoka Zen-juku, where they will teach a "hopeful fusion of Zen, modern science & the archaic skills & mysteries of the wilderness." Snyder's most recent books are the collections of poetry *The Back Country* (1968) and *Regarding Wave* (1970), and *Earth House Hold,* essays and journal sections (1969), all published by New Directions. For some years he has been working on a book on Zen, to be entitled *Practice.*

6 Anne-Marie Esnoul on Ramanuja's concept of God (Vishnu):

"Le Seigneur, première de ces entités, est Vishnu, que Ramanuja désigne d'ailleurs assez souvent du nom emprunté aux Upanishad: le Brahman. Mais l'identité d'appellation ne doit pas nous induire en erreur; bien que le terme soit au neutre, il ne représente pas l'Absolu homogène et sans qualifications des gloses intellectualistes. Dieu est Tout, sans limite, mais il demeure une Personne, à la fois immanente et transcendante. Cette Personne Suprême est objet d'adoration, Sujet ineffable, principe Un qui unifie toute multiplicité. Contrairement au Brahman de Çankara, qui ne se définissait que négativement et que l'on déclarait vide de toute qualification, l'Absolu de Ramanuja possède toutes les qualités à un degré infini. . . .

". . . pour Ramanuja, le Seigneur ne s'exprime pas par une dualité de modes mais sous la forme d'une dualité de nature. . . . Il est donc à la fois changement et immutabilité. La création se présente à Lui comme un monde borné que Lui seul peut connâitre de façon exhaustive. Le *Purushottama* (Personne Suprême) est à tout moment actuel . . .

"Sa Forme Suprême . . . reste inaccessible à la compréhension limitée des fidèles. Elle réside dan le *Vaikuntha*, paradis de Vishnu, revêtue de tous les attributs traditionnels: conque, disque, massue, épée, arc, lotus . . ." (A.-M. Esnoul: *op. cit.*, pages 115–16.)

"En fait, la grande dominante de la pensée de Ramanuja est l'accent mis sur la personnalité . . . , qu'il s'agisse de la Personne Suprême ou de la personne humaine. En cela, il prolonge encore l'enseignement de la Gita . . ." (A. M. Esnoul; *op. cit.*, page 122)

7 At another point in the journal, but without attribution of source, Merton defines these terms with slightly different phrasing: rupa—"physical being"; vedana—"sensatory feelings"; samjna—"discriminating perception"; samskara—"ground of karma experience giving future orientation"; vijnana—"personal consciousness, center of responsibility." In his *Buddhism,* page 94, Christmas Humphreys defines a number of these terms (though in slightly different transliteration) under the heading "The Nature of Self." ("Samjna" is the Sanskrit version of the Pali "sanna.")

8 "The Tibetan of the text for these . . . occult doctrines is as follows: (1) *Gtum-mo* (pronounced *Tum-mo*) meaning 'Psychic (or Vital or Secret) Heat (or Warmth),' which is the necessary driving force for the devotee seeking spiritual development, and the means for the solitary hermit, in the very severe cold of the snowy ranges of Tibet, to be comfortable without fire . . . (6) *Pho-va* (pronounced *Pho-wa*), "Transference [of the consciousness], as in yoga.'" (W.Y. Evans-Wentz: "The Path of Knowledge: the *Yoga* of the Six Doctrines," in *Tibetan Yoga and Secret Doctrines,* London, Oxford University Press, 1935, page 172n)

9 "Japa . . . Jesus prayer": Merton's source for this line seems clearly to have been Marco Pallis's essay, "Discovering the Interior Life" in *Studies in Comparative Religion,* Bedfont, Middlesex, England, Volume 2, Number 2, Spring 1968, pages 90–93, though the same themes may also have

been dealt with by Pallis in another essay, "Considerations on Tantric "Spirituality," which is cited on pages 272–74, from which other themes in this passage of Merton's notes and quotations are drawn. "Jesus prayer" —Merton is probably referring to the chanting of ~~Russian monks~~ in the 18th and 19th centuries.

10 Hume: David Hume (1711–76), the Scottish philosopher and historian, renowned for his skepticism. ". . . He could see no more reason for hypothesizing a substantial soul or mind than for accepting a substantial material world. A complete nominalist in his handling of ideas of material objects, he carried the method into the discussion of mind and found nothing there except a series of sensations. Causal relations are only apparent from the customary conjunction of two sensations. . . ." (*The Columbia Encyclopedia*, Second Edition)

11 Arya Deva: "the chief pupil and worthy successor of Nagarjuna. The Madhyamika system owes much of its popularity and stability to him. He lived near the turning point of the 2nd and 3rd centuries."(Murti, *op. cit.*, page 92)

12 Buddhapalita: the French scholar N. Peri places Buddhapalita as living in the first half of the 5th century A.D.

13 Bhavaviveka: dated by Murti as a younger contemporary of Buddhapalita. His works include *Karatalaratna* ("The Jewel in Hand"), *Tarkajvala, Madhyamartha Sangraha,* and *Nikayayabedha Vibhanga.* He is also sometimes known as Bhavya.

14 Candrakirti: a prolific commentator on earlier Madhyamika works whose texts include *Prasannapada, Madhyamika Karika Vritti,* and *Madhyamakavatara.* Murti deals at length with the fine points of his teachings.

15 Santaraksita: (705–62 A.D.) one of the philosophers who encouraged the spread of Buddhism in Tibet. His *Madhyamihalankara Karika* "laid the foundation of another school of the Madhyamikas which denies the Empirical Reality of the External world, acknowledges the introspective perception, but on the other hand does not consider consciousness to have an Ultimate Reality . . ." (Murti, *op. cit.*, page 103) He also wrote the *Tattvasangraha.*

16 Kamalasila: (713–63 A.D.) a disciple of Santaraksita's who was also instrumental in bringing Buddhism to Tibet. He wrote a commentary on his master's work called *Panjika,* and also wrote extensively on Tantra and on *Prajnaparamita.* Together, the teachings of Santaraksita and Kamalasila "represent a syncretism of the Madhyamika with the Yogacara." (Murti, *op. cit.*, page 102)

[17] Asvaghosha: a 2nd-century Mahayana Buddhist poet and religious commentator who wrote in Sanskrit. For details about his works, see page 367 in the glossary.

[18] Professor Conze is here quoting from his own translation of the *Ashtasahasrika Prajnaparamita Sutra,* first published by the Asiatic Society of Calcutta in 1958 and reprinted in 1973 by the Four Seasons Foundation (Bolinas, California).

[19] Augustinian: St. Augustine (354–430), bishop of Hippo and author of the *Confessions.*

[20] *caritas:* Latin, "charity"; *sapientia,* Latin, "wisdom"; *veritas caritatis* —"the truth of charity"; *caritas veritatis*—"the charity of truth." Fr. Daniel C. Walsh, Merton's teacher and friend, writes of "Veritas-caritatis: caritas-veritatis": "An expression which might be described as a cryptic and summary description of Augustinian mysticism in the Middle Ages and modern world. The foundation for it is, of course, in the *Confessions* of St. Augustine. The Cistercian mystics emphasize the former, where love is given priority over the truth of knowledge, whereas the School of St. Victor, the Victorines, give priority to truth and consequently emphasize the intellectual aspect of love. Both are to be distinguished from scholastic mysticism of a Thomistic variety, where both these aspects are treated as formally distinct. (Cf. Etienne Gilson: *History of Christian Philosophy.*)"

[21] St. Bernard: (1090–1153) abbot of Clairvaux, one of the most illustrious preachers and monks of the Middle Ages. It was he who was largely responsible for the extraordinary growth of the Cistercian order in the 12th century.

APPENDIXES

APPENDIX I

September 1968 Circular Letter to Friends

Abbey of Gethsemani, Ky. 40073

Dear Friends:

As you know, I have been cutting down more and more on letters and now my contacts will be almost completely severed. I will not even receive most of the mail addressed to me. You may already know by rumor the reason for this, and I'd better make the whole thing clear. Otherwise gossip may completely distort the real picture—as has happened before.

I have been asked to attend two meetings in Asia, one of them a meeting of the abbots of Catholic monastic orders in that area, the other an interfaith meeting with representatives of Asian religions. I will also be spending some time in at least two Asian monasteries of our order, to help out there, and will doubtless be invited to others. Considering the crucial importance of the time, the need for monastic renewal, the isolation and helplessness of our Asian monasteries, their constant appeals for help, I feel it a duty to respond. And I hope this will also enable me to get in contact with Buddhist monasticism and see something of it firsthand. The length of my stay in Asia is indeterminate. Needless to say, this is not anything unusual in the monastic life. I ask your prayers for the success of this undertaking: and of course, please do not believe anything that rumor may add to this simple scenario.

I am certainly grateful to those who have contributed something toward paying my way, and especially to those who have helped me in making contacts. Outstanding among them has been Dom Aelred Graham, O.S.B., who last year visited many religious centers in Asia and has been most generous and helpful in sharing with me the fruits of his experience.

By the time you receive this letter I hope to be on my way. It is understandable that I cannot undertake to answer any requests about writing articles, prefaces, or to give out statements on this or that. It will be impossible for me to think of keeping in touch with political issues, still less to comment on them or to sign various petitions, protests, etc. Even though the need for them may be even greater: but will they by now have lost any usefulness? Has the signing of protests become a pointless exercise? In any case, anything I do on this trip will be absolutely nonpolitical. I have no intention of going anywhere near Vietnam.

I have no special plans for immediate new writing, though perhaps this trip will be very significant in that regard. However, I am leaving more than one manuscript with Doubleday and New Directions, and I trust they will appear in print in due course.

Once again, let me say I appreciate the loyalty of so many old friends and the interest of the new ones. I shall continue to feel bound to all of you in the silence of prayer. Our real journey in life is interior: it is a matter of growth, deepening, and of an ever greater surrender to the creative action of love and grace in our hearts. Never was it more necessary for us to respond to that action. I pray that we may all do so. God bless you. With all affection in Christ.

THOMAS MERTON

APPENDIX II

On Mindfulness

by Bhikkhu Khantipalo

All meditation in Buddhism is based on a discourse given twice in varying forms, with its parts and aspects many times repeated by the Buddha. This discourse, or sutta, is called the Satipatthana Sutta: The Discourse on the Establishing of Mindfulness. Whatever methods of meditation are practiced by Buddhists, all of them have satipatthana as their fundamental source.

What is mindfulness? And how is it established? Mindfulness is the awareness of what one is doing while one is doing it, and of nothing else. That is, while walking, instead of the usual distracted state of memories, hopes and fears, and so on, a jumble of thoughts and fantasies which have nothing whatever to do with walking, one confines attention to consciousness of bodily movements of the legs and such eye and ear consciousness as is necessary The meditator concentrating on these bare essentials thereby clears out of his mind a lot of junk. Clearly this is useful to the ordinary living of life as well, for the person who allows his mind to be overgrown by a jungle of irrelevant thoughts is a careless person, and his personal confusion may bring about the harm, or even death, both of himself and others.

A story famous in another Buddhist tradition illustrates

very well the difference between the mind of the ordinary untrained person and the serene heart of the master disciplined by long practice and at last gone beyond the need for self-discipline by penetration inward to the Truth. This is a Zen story I quote from memory, for Zen Buddhism is based no less than our Buddhism in Thailand upon the Establishment of Mindfulness. A certain Zen master was approached by a disciple who asked about the essentials of dhamma, probably expecting to receive a lengthy exposition of subtle Buddhist philosophy or perhaps something marvelous and mysterious. He got neither. The Zen master only said, "When hungry I eat; when tired I sleep." The disappointed disciple asked then: "But this is what ordinary people do! How do you differ?" To which the Zen master replied: "When they eat most people think a thousand thoughts; when they sleep they dream a thousand dreams."

What this means is that most people are not very mindful, since they allow their minds to wander as they will with very little restraint, whereas one who has finished the job, reached Enlightenment by cutting out of his heart the defilements, has no wandering mind, no delusions, no fantasies, but brilliant awarenes of *NOW* all the time.

Satipatthana is the basis of everything from the very beginning of Buddhist training. Unless a person has mindfulness present, opportunities to cultivate oneself and benefit others in the way of dhamma are lost. Without general mindfulness one cannot be generous, kindly, or compassionate, nor can one practice the various codes of precepts for the layman, such as the five basic moral precepts. And then, any sort of meditation without mindfulness present will either degenerate into the usual state of distracted thoughts, or else drift toward drowsiness and then sleep.

All of the Buddhist training is contained under: Moral Conduct, Meditation, and Wisdom. Just as the first two are impossible without some mindfulness, so the last cannot be developed without very strong mindfulness; for in Buddhism the higher one wishes to go, the more mindfulness must be developed. And if one wishes for the penetration of the dhamma-truth that all the constituent parts of mind and body which are conventionally called "me" and "mine" are not-me and not-mine, and that there is no owner behind these transient phenomena—the Truth of Anatta, or Not-Self—then one's level of supreme wisdom must be supported by mindfulness for this to occur. There is no chance of fathoming the complexities of oneself, mind and body, without the aid of mindfulness.

Although at the beginning of any Buddhist meditation there is the concept "I am meditating" or "I am being mindful," if the right path is followed, then this sense of "I-ness" and "mine-ness" becomes less marked, or rather its bases in mind and body become less identified with "myself," until this concept dissolves away completely and not-self (or not-soul, as anatta may also be translated) is seen with penetrative wisdom.

When non-self has been seen in this way, then the Three Roots of Evil—Greed, Aversion, and Delusion—are cut off, so that they cannot grow again and can never afterward sway the heart toward evil. Greed here means the tendency toward all sorts of desires, gross and subtle, from the slightest liking to the coarsest lust, all kinds of attachment, all tendencies to make "me" and "mine," whether the objects are physical or mental, sentient or nonsentient. The Evil Root of Aversion is the opposite of all this and can be seen when the various kinds of greed and desire cannot be satisfied. The range is similar to mere dislike round to revenge and fury, and the objects vary in the same way. Whenever either of these Evil Roots are operating (and they cannot operate simultaneously, though they may alternate), there is also present the Evil Root of Delusion. Only when delusion is present in the heart is it possible for people to be greedy or averse. Only deluded people would harm themselves (what to speak of others) by expressing their greed and aversion in mind, speech, and body. Delusion is dullness, stupidity, boredom, not understanding and not making any effort to understand. These Three Roots of Evil are present in every unenlightened person, and out of their combinations are born all the range of defilements: lust, attachment, jealousy, pride, malice . . . which dirty the unenlightened heart from time to time and cause evil action (papakamma) to be made in speech and body, resulting in troubles for both the doer and for many others.

The Three Evil Roots can be cut off only by the wisdom called supermundane, which is sharp and penetrating and has been compared to a sword. You may see in Mahayana paintings that the bodhisattva Manjusri, the personification of Supermundane Wisdom, wields in one hand a flaming sword for cutting off the defilements, while in the other he has a book, the treatise on the Perfection of Wisdom.

Supermundane Wisdom, in cutting off the Evil Roots, leaves one nothing to grasp at, for "being," as we think ourselves, is founded upon these Roots. When these Evil Roots are eradicated, then the concept of "self," which arises due to attachment to body, feeling, memory, thoughts, and consciousness—all that is found in a person—vanishes, becoming as unreal as a flower in the sky. The enlightened person, with the fires of craving extinguished, attains nirvana even in this life, seeing things as they really are with a heart grown great in Wisdom, Purity, and Compassion. He no longer grasps at theories and speculations, and he has no faith left, he has something much better—Wisdom, for he is One who Knows.

So meditation, by way of calm and by way of insight and their combination, is the progressive unwrapping of grasping from an illusory self. The further one goes along this path, the less selfish one becomes and the more full of loving-kindness and compassion. The less selfish also means the more contented, though this does not mean contentment with evils and does not preclude such action as is necessary to set them right. The bhikkhu-life, which depends on others for livelihood, is the condition where contentment can be most highly developed, while of course lay meditators with their more numerous responsibilities cannot cultivate it so highly.

Now we come to the second question: How is mindfulness

established? For this, there are a number of exercises under four main headings: mindfulness of body, mindfulness of feeling, mindfulness of mental state, and mindfulness of mental concomitants.

For instance, under the heading of "mindfulness of the body," there are such exercises as mindfulness of breathing in and out, clear awareness of the four postures of the body (walking, standing, sitting, and lying down) and of its actions (such as bending the limbs, dressing, eating, talking, keeping silent, defecation, and urination), mindfulness of the messy bits and pieces of which this body is composed, perception of the body in various states of decay (thinking, "as that is, so this will be"), and the analytic reflection of the body as made up of the four great "elements." All these exercises have the purpose of unwrapping grasping at the body as "me" or "mine" by way of first calming the mind and then developing insight. But these exercises are not all suitable for everyone. For instance, those with strong greed and lust should work upon the repulsiveness of the body's contents or reflect upon the decay of their body toward one of the stages of this seen in a corpse. On the other hand, one of distracted temperament should use mindfulness of breathing to concentrate his mind, and one of intelligent temper take up the analysis of the elements. This is where a teacher is needed: to instruct a meditator which aspect should be his own work, for it is difficult to judge oneself.

Suppose that a teacher gives the subject the discrimination of the four elements—earth, water, fire, and air. What is earth? This is hardness, solidity, and can be seen in such parts of one's body as the bones, sinews, muscles, and other organs. This "earth" should be thoroughly identified with the other "earth" outside oneself—all sorts of hardness, such as earth, rock, trees, concrete, and so on—having the purpose to see that all earth is just earth-element, whether interior or exterior, and not "me" or mine," and so gaining dispassion for the body. In the same way, water-element is all liquidity inside or out; fire-element is all temperature, heat and cold, whether bodily or otherwise; and air-element is likewise found inside or outside—but all should be seen as just elements without ownership.

Then there are further exercises in satipatthana: the thirty-two parts of the body, for instance. This meditation is given to all novices and monks when they are ordained. During their ordination they repeat after their teacher (in the Pali language) "Head hair, body hair, nails, teeth, skin; skin, teeth, nails, body hair, head hair." These are the first five parts of the thirty-two and actually all that we can see of the body. Usually thought of as desirable when young and in good health, some reflections on these will soon uncover facts which lead to calm and dispassion of the mind toward the body: as when these parts are not washed, cleaned, and titivated regularly, they soon become unattractive to oneself and others. These five only add up to beauty in oneself or in others when they are not closely inspected.

They can also be meditated on as dead, for all the outsides and the ends of these five parts are dead, so that what gives rise to pride in our own beauty or lust for that of others is already dead!

Or one may select especially repulsive parts of the body from among the thirty-two, such as the five above, or "bones," or "bones, blood, and guts," and attend only to them, at first by repetition, and later by experiencing them.

But whatever one takes from among these parts, the aim is to reach insight, so that these very things are seen with interior sight and revealed in their repulsiveness, from which estrangement is born, and then dispassion, and so to the knowledge: "This is not mine, this am I not, this is not my self." Then there is no more grasping at them, no reliance upon them for what they are not, and so no dukkha—mental or physical trouble, because they are seen as they really are.

These exercises are methods, they are medicines for helping to rid the mind of the three great diseases—greed, aversion, and delusion. They are not dogmatic statements about the body but ways to be used by those who are interested to find out what the body really is. Most people do not view the body as it really is, and do not wish to. They consider either that bodies are desirable, impelled by craving born of the Evil Root of Greed, or if they turn to some repressive ethic to control their desires, then the tendency is to swing to the other extreme and hate the body, making it the scapegoat for one's troubles. In either case these come from the mind, not the body. It is seldom that people find the Middle Way between extremes.

Then of course there is fear regarding the body—the fear of death; for many people seem to have the idea that their bodies will live forever. For overcoming the fear of death and for putting down sensual attachment to the body, there is viewing the body as a corpse. In the commentaries there is frequent reference to seeking out corpses and gazing at them as a way of establishing detachment. But while this may have been done in ancient India, where after death bodies were often thrown away to rot in secluded fields or woods, it is not very practicable now. Nor is this particularly recommended by teachers today, who say that one's own body should be viewed as a corpse in some stage of decay. With strong meditation this can be done, but such interior visions need the close guidance of a teacher.

Perhaps the most widely practiced way of working on the establishment of mindfulness (while seated) is mindfulness of breathing. This is the awarenes of natural breathing; it is not the setting up of any artificial pattern. And it is a very convenient subject for meditation because it is always present and does not have to be sought elsewhere. When one concentrates upon the breath, usually at the tip of the nose, the breath becomes finer. With coarseness of breath goes excitement, both physical and mental, but when the breathing becomes fine, the mind also is refined and steady. Breathing and one's mindfulness of it becomes so fine with strong concentration that another person seeing such a meditator would say that breath had stopped. When the breathing process stops and the mind has gone down into the heart, there is the attainment of a jhana (or absorbed contemplation), in which there is no awareness through the five senses (eye, ear, etc.) but only mindfulness through "the mind-door." When the mind (or mind-heart, as the Pali "citta" covers both intellectual and emotional aspects) has become so strong and concentrated, it should then be turned to the cultivation of insight, such as seeing clearly in mind and body the three characteristics of all existence in any state: impermanence, dukkha (unsatisfactoriness), and not-self.

It is not enough to use a meditation subject just to develop calm, concentration, and spiritual happiness. One must, in Buddhist teachings, use this strong and temporarily pure mind to penetrate or look within what one calls "self."

There are many kammatthana, or subjects for (meditative) work, according to the character of the meditator and his needs, and only a few have been mentioned here: mindfulness of feelings (pleasant, painful, and neither-painful-nor-pleasant); mindfulness of mental states (for instance, with or without greed, aversion, delusion); and mindfulness of mental concomitants, the most subtle of these exercises. Indeed, even mindfulness of the body has been but briefly outlined.[1]

---

[1] For further information, two books are recommended: *The Heart of Buddhist Meditation,* by Nyanaponika Thera (London, Rider & Co., 1969); and *The Path of Purification"* (Visuddhimagga, translated from Pali) by Nyanamoli Thera (Colombo, Semage and Co.). Both books are obtainable from the Buddhist Publication Society, Kandy, Ceylon.

APPENDIX III

Thomas Merton's View of Monasticism

(Informal talk delivered at Calcutta, October 1968)

First, let me struggle with the contradiction that I have to live with, in appearing before you in what I really consider to be a disguise, because I never, never wear this (a clerical collar). What I ordinarily wear is blue jeans and an open shirt; which brings me to the question that people have been asking to a great extent: Whom do you represent? What religion do you represent? And that, too, is a rather difficult question to answer. I came with the notion of perhaps saying something for monks and to monks of all religions because I am supposed to be a monk. . . I may not look like one.

In speaking for monks I am really speaking for a very strange kind of person, a marginal person, because the monk in the modern world is no longer an established person with an established place in society. We realize very keenly in America today that the monk is essentially outside of all establishments. He does not belong to an establishment. He is a marginal person who withdraws deliberately to the margin of society with a view to deepening fundamental human experience. Consequently, as one of these strange people, I speak to you as a representative of all marginal persons who have done this kind of thing deliberately.

Thus I find myself representing perhaps hippies among

you, poets, people of this kind who are seeking in all sorts of ways and have absolutely no established status whatever. So I ask you to do me just this one favor of considering me not as a figure representing any institution, but as a statusless person, an insignificant person who comes to you asking your charity and patience while I say one or two things that have nothing to do with my (prepared) paper. If you are interested in the paper, it is there for you to read. I do not think it is a terribly good paper. I think there are a lot of other things you could be better employed in doing.

Are monks and hippies and poets relevant? No, we are deliberately irrelevant. We live with an ingrained irrelevance which is proper to every human being. The marginal man accepts the basic irrelevance of the human condition, an irrelevance which is manifested above all by the fact of death. The marginal person, the monk, the displaced person, the prisoner, all these people live in the presence of death, which calls into question the meaning of life. He struggles with the fact of death in himself, trying to seek something deeper than death; because there is something deeper than death, and the office of the monk or the marginal person, the meditative person or the poet is to go beyond death even in this life, to go beyond the dichotomy of life and death and to be, therefore, a witness to life.

This requires, of course, faith, but as soon as you say faith in terms of this monastic and marginal existence you run into another problem. Faith means doubt. Faith is not the suppression of doubt. It is the overcoming of doubt, and you overcome doubt by going through it. The man of faith who has never experienced doubt is not a man of faith. Consequently, the monk is one who has to struggle in the depths of his being with the presence of doubt, and to go through what some religions call the Great Doubt, to break through beyond doubt into a certitude which is very, very deep because it is not his own personal certitude, it is the certitude of God Himself, in us. The only ultimate reality is God. God lives and dwells in us.

We are not justified by any action of our own, but we are called by the voice of God, by the voice of that ultimate being, to pierce through the irrelevance of our life, while accepting and admitting that our life is totally irrelevant, in order to find relevance in Him. And this relevance in Him is not something we can grasp or possess. It is something that can only be received as a gift. Consequently, the kind of life that I represent is a life that is openness to gift; gift from God and gift from others.

It is not that we go out into the world with a capacity to love others greatly. This too we know in ourselves, that our capacity for love is limited. And it has to be completed with the capacity to be loved, to accept love from others, to want to be loved by others, to admit our loneliness and to live with our loneliness because everybody is lonely. This is then another basis for the kind of experience that I am talking about, which is a new approach, a different approach to the external experience of the monk. The monk in his solitude and in his meditation seeks this dimension of life.

But we do have to admit also the value of traditional monastic ways. In the West there is now going on a great upheaval in monasticism, and much that is of undying value is being thrown away irresponsibly, foolishly, in favor of things that are superficial and showy, that have no ultimate value. I do not know how the situation is in the East, but I will say as a brother from the West to Eastern monks, be a little careful. The time is coming when you may face the same situation and your fidelity to your ancient traditions will stand you in good stead. Do not be afraid of that fidelity. I know I need not warn you of this.

Behind, then, all that I have said is the idea that significant contacts are certainly possible and easy on the level of experience, not necessarily institutional monasticism, but among people who are seeking. The basic condition for this is that each be faithful to his own search.

And so I stand among you as one who offers a small message of hope, that first, there are always people who dare to seek on the margin of society, who are not dependent on social acceptance, not dependent on social routine, and prefer a kind of free-floating existence under a state of risk. And among these people, if they are faithful to their own calling, to their own vocation, and to their own message from God, communication on the deepest level is possible.

And the deepest level of communication is not communication, but communion. It is wordless. It is beyond words, and it is beyond speech, and it is beyond concept. Not that we discover a new unity. We discover an older unity. My dear brothers, we are already one. But we imagine that we are not. And what we have to recover is our original unity. What we have to be is what we are.

APPENDIX IV

Monastic Experience and East-West Dialogue

(Notes for a paper to have been delivered at Calcutta, October 1968)

by Thomas Merton

1. In all the great world religions there are a few individuals and communities who dedicate themselves in a special way to living out the full consequences and implications of what they believe. This dedication may take a variety of forms, some temporary, some permanent; some active and some intellectual; some ascetic, contemplative and mystical. In this paper the term "monastic" is applied in a broad way to those forms of special contemplative dedication which include:

(a) A certain distance or detachment from the "ordinary" and "secular" concerns of worldly life; a monastic solitude, whether partial or total, temporary or permanent.

(b) A preoccupation with the radical inner depth of one's religious and philosophical beliefs, the inner and experimental "ground" of those beliefs, and their outstanding spiritual implications.

(c) A special concern with inner transformation, a deepening of consciousness toward an eventual breakthrough and discovery of a transcendent dimension of life beyond that of the ordinary empirical self and of ethical and pious observance.

This monastic "work" or "discipline" is not merely an individual affair. It is at once personal and communal. Its orientation is in a certain sense suprapersonal. It goes beyond a merely psychological fulfillment on the empirical level, and it goes beyond the limits of communicable cultural ideals (of one's own national, racial, etc., background). It attains to a certain universality and wholeness which have never yet been adequately described—and probably cannot be described—in terms of psychology. Transcending the limits that separate subject from object and self from not-self, this development achieves a wholeness which is described in various ways by the different religions; a self-realization of atman, of Void, of life in Christ, of fana and baqa (annihilation and reintegration according to Sufism), etc.

This is not necessarily a matter of personal charismata (special divine illuminations or prophetic tasks), but it is usually expected to follow from discipline and initiation into a "traditional religious *way*," that is to say a special mode of life and of consciousness which meets certain unwritten, indeed inexpressible, conditions. The special formation required to meet these conditions is imparted by experienced persons, or judged by a community that has shared something of the traditional consciousness we may call mystical, contemplative, enlightened, or spiritually transformed.

2. At this point—a parenthesis on the problems of language. There are great difficulties inherent in words like "mystical." Lack of agreement on their meaning, etc. Without deciding all these problems here, what matters is to clarify the distinction between the "monastic" type of dedication, the "monastic" quest for a higher type of consciousness, from "active" types of dedication oriented to "good works" like education, care of the sick, etc. Jesuits are not monks (though in fact they include today scholars who have a more sympathetic

understanding of monastic questions and problems than many monks have). Missionaries are generally not monks. Confusions on this point are nevertheless present in the Western Church, especially now, when the very notion of the "contemplative life" is under attack even in the (Catholic) monastic milieu. Having referred in a general way to these problems, one might emphasize two points:

(a) Even in the highly active "West" there is nevertheless a monastic tradition which is primarily contemplative, and this tradition is being renewed even in the Protestant milieu which was originally hostile to it.

(b) There is a real possibility of contact on a deep level between this contemplative and monastic tradition in the West and the various contemplative traditions in the East— including the Islamic Sufis, the mystical lay-contemplative societies in Indonesia, etc., as well as the better-known monastic groups in Hinduism and Buddhism.

3. A word on Orthodox as distinguished from Catholic (Western) mysticism. The emphasis on contemplation in Greece and Russia. The Hesychast tradition. Mt. Athos. Problems of Orthodox monasticism today.

Though Catholic monasticism is less frankly contemplative, it is in a better position for dialogue with Asia at the moment because of the climate of openness following Vatican II. Christian monasticism has a tradition of adaptation and comprehension with regard to Greek philosophy, and many Catholics realize that this could also apply very well to Hindu and Buddhist philosophies, disciplines, experiences. An articulate minority exists. It is ready for free and productive communication. Encouragement has been offered by the Vatican Council.

4. To return to our main theme, we can easily see the special value of dialogue and exchange among those in the various religions who seek to penetrate the ultimate ground of their beliefs by a transformation of the religious consciousness.

We can see the point of sharing in those disciplines which claim to prepare a way for "mystical" self-transcendence (with due reservations in the use of the term "mystical").

Without asserting that there is complete unity of all religions at the "top," the transcendent or mystical level—that they all start from different dogmatic positions to "meet" at this summit—it is certainly true to say that even where there are irreconcilable differences in doctrine and in formulated belief, there may still be great similarities and analogies in the realm of religious experience. There is nothing new in the observation that holy men like St. Francis and Shri Ramakrishna (to mention only two) have attained to a level of spiritual fulfillment which is at once universally recognizable and relevant to anyone interested in the religious dimension of existence. Cultural and doctrinal differences must remain, but they do not invalidate a very real quality of existential likeness.

5. The purpose of this paper is primarily to make clear that, on this existential level of experience and of spiritual maturity, it is possible to achieve real and significant contacts and perhaps much more besides. We will consider in a moment what this "much more" may be. For the present, one thing above all needs to be emphasized. Such dialogue in depth, at the very ground of monastic and of human experience, is not just a matter of academic interest. It is not just something for which foundation money could be obtained. That is probably true, but this paper is not considering that particular aspect of it. This is not just a matter of "research" and of academic conferences, workshops, study groups, or even of new institutional structuring—producing results that may be fed into the general accumulation of new facts about man, society, culture, and religion.

I speak as a Western monk who is pre-eminently concerned with his own monastic calling and dedication. I have left my monastery to come here not just as a research scholar or even as an author (which I also happen to be). I come as a pilgrim who is anxious to obtain not just information, not just "facts" about other monastic traditions, but to drink from ancient sources of monastic vision and experience. I seek not only to learn more (quantitatively) about religion and about monastic life, but to become a better and more enlightened monk (qualitatively) myself.

I am convinced that communication in depth, across the lines that have hitherto divided religious and monastic traditions, is now not only possible and desirable, but most important for the destinies of Twentieth-Century Man.

I do not mean that we ought to expect visible results of earth-shaking importance, or that any publicity at all is desirable. On the contrary, I am convinced that this exchange must take place under the true monastic conditions of quiet, tranquility, sobriety, leisureliness, reverence, meditation, and cloistered peace. I am convinced that what one might call typically "Asian" conditions of nonhurrying and of patient waiting must prevail over the Western passion for immediate visible results. For this reason I think it is above all important for Westerners like myself to learn what little they can from Asia, *in* Asia. I think we must seek not merely to make superficial reports *about* the Asian traditions, but to live and share those traditions, as far as we can, by living them in their traditional milieu.

I need not add that I think we have now reached a stage of (long overdue) religious maturity at which it may be possible for someone to remain perfectly faithful to a Christian and Western monastic commitment, and yet to learn in depth from, say, a Buddhist or Hindu discipline and experience. I believe that some of us need to do this in order to improve the quality of our own monastic life and even to help in the task of monastic renewal which has been undertaken within the Western Church.

6. At this point—a parenthesis on the problems of "monastic renewal"—state of confusion resulting from a collapse of formal structures that were no longer properly understood—exterior and formal ritualism, etc., or external observance for its own sake—a traditionalism that was emptied of its truly

living traditional content, repudiation of genuine tradition, discipline, contemplation—trivializing the monastic life. This has resulted in a true monastic crisis in the West. It is entirely possible that many hitherto flourishing monastic institutions, which preserved a genuine living continuity with the Middle Ages, may soon cease to exist. Both good and bad in this. Will Asian monasticism sooner or later face the same kind of crisis? Source of the problem: obsession with "relevance" to the new generation—but the problem is only half understood. In reality, the secular quasi-monastic movement of the hippies in America shows that the contemplative dimensions of life (which some monks and clergy are actively repudiating) is definitely relevant to modern youth.

7. In order not to prolong this paper overmuch, let us confine ourselves to two particularly important topics: that of "communication" between monastic traditions, and that of the more obvious "wrong directions" we must avoid. Necessarily, both topics will have to be treated more briefly than we might desire.

8. The question of "communication" is now no longer fraught with too great difficulties. The publication of classical Asian texts and of studies on them, especially in English and in German, has led to the formation of what one might call an intertraditional vocabulary. We are well on our way to a workable interreligious lexicon of key words—mostly rooted in Sanskrit—which will permit intelligent discussion of all kinds of religious experience in all the religious traditions. This is in fact already being done to some extent, and one of the results of it is that psychologists and psychoanalysts, as well as anthropologists and students of comparative religion, are now able to talk a kind of lingua franca of religious experience. I think this "language," though sometimes pedantic, seems to be fairly reliable, and it is now at the disposition of theologians, philosophers, and plain monks like myself.

This is a first step only, but it is an important step—which will often have to be completed by the services of an interpreter. He in his turn will be more helpful if he knows the "common language," and is interested in the common pursuit of inner enlightenment. Incontestably, however, this kind of communication cannot get far unless it is carried on among people who share some degree of the same enlightenment.

Is it too optimistic to expect the monks themselves to make this contribution? I hope not. And here we come to the "something more" that I referred to above. True communication on the deepest level is more than a simple sharing of ideas, of conceptual knowledge, or formulated truth. The kind of communication that is necessary on this deep level must also be "communion" beyond the level of words, a communion in authentic experience which is shared not only on a "preverbal" level but also on a "postverbal" level.

The "preverbal" level is that of the unspoken and indefinable "preparation," "the predisposition" of mind and heart, necessary for all "monastic" experience whatever. This demands among other things a "freedom from automatisms and routines," and candid liberation from external social dictates, from conventions, limitations, and mechanisms which restrict understanding and inhibit experience of the new, the unexpected. Monastic training must not form men in a rigid mold, but liberate them from habitual and routine mechanisms. The monk who is to communicate on the level that interests us here must be not merely a punctilious observer of external traditions, but a living example of traditional and interior realization. He must be wide open to life and to new experience because he has fully utilized his own tradition and gone beyond it. This will permit him to meet a discipline of another, apparently remote and alien tradition, and find a common ground of verbal understanding with him. The "postverbal" level will then, at least ideally, be that on which they both meet beyond their own words and their own understanding in the silence of an ultimate experience which might conceivably not have occurred if they had not met and spoken . . .

This I would call "communion." I think it is something

that the deepest ground of our being cries out for, and it is something for which a lifetime of striving would not be enough.

9. The wrong ways that are to be avoided ought to be fairly evident.

First of all, this striving for intermonastic communion should not become just another way of adding to the interminable empty talk, the endlessly fruitless and trivial discussion of everything under the sun, the inexhaustible chatter with which modern man tries to convince himself that he is in touch with his fellow man and with reality. This contemplative dialogue must be reserved for those who have been seriously disciplined by years of silence and by a long habit of meditation. I would add that it must be reserved for those who have entered with full seriousness into their own monastic tradition and are in authentic contact with the past of their own religious community—besides being open to the tradition and to the heritage of experience belonging to other communities.

Second, there can be no question of a facile syncretism, a mishmash of semireligious verbiage and pieties, a devotionalism that admits everything and therefore takes nothing with full seriousness.

Third, there must be a scrupulous respect for important differences, and where one no longer understands or agrees, this must be kept clear—without useless debate. There are differences that are not debatable, and it is a useless, silly temptation to try to argue them out. Let them be left intact until a moment of greater understanding.

Fourth, attention must be concentrated on what is really essential to the monastic quest: this, I think, is to be sought in the area of true self-transcendence and enlightenment. It is to be sought in the transformation of consciousness in its ultimate ground, as well as in the highest and most authentic devotional love of the bhakti type—but not in the acquisition of extraordinary powers, in miraculous activities, in a special charismata, visions, levitation, etc. These must be seen as phenomena of a different order.

Fifth, questions of institutional structure, monastic rule, traditional forms of cult and observance must be seen as relatively secondary and are not to become the central focus of attention. They are to be understood in their relation to enlightenment itself. However, they are to be given the full respect due to them, and the interests of dialogue and communication should not be allowed to subvert structures that may remain very important helps to interior development.

10. It is time to conclude. The point to be stressed is the importance of serious communication, and indeed of "communion," among contemplatives of different traditions, disciplines, and religions. This can contribute much to the development of man at this crucial point of his history. Indeed, we find ourselves in a crisis, a moment of crucial choice. We are in grave danger of losing a spiritual heritage that has been painfully accumulated by thousands of generations of saints and contemplatives. It is the peculiar office of the monk in the modern world to keep alive the contemplative experience and to keep the way open for modern technological man to recover the integrity of his own inner depths.

Above all, it is important that this element of depth and integrity—this element of inner transcendent freedom be kept intact as we grow toward the full maturity of universal man. We are witnessing the growth of a truly universal consciousness in the modern world. This universal consciousness may be a consciousness of transcendent freedom and vision, or it may simply be a vast blur of mechanized triviality and ethical cliché.

The difference is, I think, important enough to be of concern to all religions, as well as to humanistic philosophies with no religion at all.

APPENDIX V

Special Closing Prayer

(Offered at the First Spiritual Summit Conference in Calcutta by Father Thomas Merton)

I will ask you to stand and all join hands in a little while. But first, we realize that we are going to have to create a new language of prayer. And this new language of prayer has to come out of something which transcends all our traditions, and comes out of the immediacy of love. We have to part now, aware of the love that unites us, the love that unites us in spite of real differences, real emotional friction. . . The things that are on the surface are nothing, what is deep is the Real. We are creatures of love. Let us therefore join hands, as we did before, and I will try to say something that comes out of the depths of our hearts. I ask you to concentrate on the love that is in you, that is in us all. I have no idea what I am going to say. I am going to be silent a minute, and then I will say something. . .

Oh God, we are one with You. You have made us one with You. You have taught us that if we are open to one another, You dwell in us. Help us to preserve this openness and to fight for it with all our hearts. Help us to realize that there can be no understanding where there is mutual rejection. Oh God, in accepting one another wholeheartedly, fully, completely, we accept You, and we thank You, and we adore You, and we love

You with our whole being, because our being is in Your being, our spirit is rooted in Your spirit. Fill us then with love, and let us be bound together with love as we go our diverse ways, united in this one spirit which makes You present in the world, and which makes You witness to the ultimate reality that is love. Love has overcome. Love is victorious. Amen.

APPENDIX VI

November Circular Letter to Friends

November 9, 1968
New Delhi, India

Dear Friends:

This newsletter is not a reply to mail because I have not been getting mail on this Asian trip and have not had time to write letters either. As you probably know, I have received permission to be absent from my monastery for several months, chiefly because I was invited to attend a meeting of Asian Catholic abbots in Bangkok and give a talk there. Since this gave me an opportunity to be in Asia, I have been permitted to extend the trip a little in order to learn something about Asian monasticism, particularly Buddhist. I will also be visiting our Cistercian monasteries in Indonesia, Hong Kong, and Japan, and giving some talks there. Apart from that, the trip is not concerned with talking but with learning and with making contact with important people in the Buddhist monastic field. I am especially interested in Tibetan Buddhism and in Japanese (possibly Chinese) Zen. (Maybe there are still some Chinese Ch'an [Zen] centers in Taiwan.) I hope to see John Wu in Taiwan.

I am writing this in New Delhi, the capital of India, an impressive city which I like very much. My first contact with India was at Calcutta, which, no matter how prepared you may be, is always a shock. The poverty and misery are overwhelming there—and even more so in rural India. Some towns are indescribable. This morning I went to put a small coin into the hands of a beggar and saw he was a leper whose fingers had been eaten away. . . It's like that. People sleep in the streets—some have never had a house to live in. People die in the streets. In Calcutta you walk out the front door of your hotel on the "best" street in the city and find a cow sleeping on the sidewalk. I rather like the cows wandering around. They make the Asian traffic more interesting.

Bangkok was the worst place for traffic I ever saw; no lights, you just step on the gas and race five hundred other cars to the crossing. The main rule of Asian driving seems to be: never use the brake, just lean on the horn. It is wildly exciting. Especially in the Himalayas, where you whiz around corners at dizzy heights and speeds and meet these huge buses coming the other way painted to look like dragons. Usually the road is just about one lane wide anyway, but somehow one manages. I am still alive.

I don't want to waste time and paper in gossip. The main point of this letter is to tell you something about my contacts with Tibetan mysticism and my meeting with the Dalai Lama in his new headquarters, high on a mountain at Dharamsala, which is an overnight train trip from Delhi, up in the Himalayas. (The Himalayas are the most beautiful mountains I have ever seen. There is something peculiar about the light there, a blue and a clarity you see nowhere else.) I spent eight days at Dharamsala making a kind of retreat, reading and meditating and meeting Tibetan masters. I had three long interviews with the Dalai Lama and spoke also with many others.

The Dalai Lama is the religious head of the Tibetan Buddhists and also in some ways their temporal leader. As you know, he had to escape from Tibet in 1959 when the Chinese Communists took over his country. There are many Tibetan refugees living in tents in the mountains, and many also forming colonies on tea plantations. I have seen some monastic communities on these plantations. The Dalai Lama is much loved by his people, and they are the most prayerful people I have seen. Some of them seem to be praying constantly, and I don't mean monks, lay people. Some always have rosaries in their hands (counting out Buddhist mantras), and I have seen some with prayer wheels. It is customary in the West to laugh at prayer wheels, but the people I have seen using them looked pretty recollected to me. They were obviously deep in prayer and very devout.

The Dalai Lama is thirty-three years old, a very alert and energetic person. He is simple and outgoing and spoke with great openness and frankness. He is in no sense what you would expect of a political emigré, and the things he said about Communism seemed to me fair and objective. His real interests are monastic and mystical. He is a religious leader and scholar, and also a man who has obviously received a remarkable monastic formation. We spoke almost entirely about the life of meditation, about samadhi (concentration), which is the first stage of meditative discipline and where one systematically clarifies and recollects his mind. The Tibetans have a very acute, subtle, and scientific knowledge of "the mind" and are still experimenting with meditation. We also talked of higher forms of prayer, of Tibetan mysticism (most of which is esoteric and kept strictly secret), especially comparing Tibetan mysticism with Zen. In either case the highest mysticism is in some ways quite "simple" —but always and everywhere the Dalai Lama kept insisting on the fact that one could not attain anything in the spiritual life without total dedication, continued effort, experienced guidance, real discipline, and the combination of wisdom and method (which is stressed by Tibetan mysticism). He was very interested in our Western monasticism and the questions he asked about the Cistercian life were interesting. He wanted to know about the vows, and whether the vows meant that one became committed to a "high attainment" in the mystical life. He wanted to know if one's vows constituted an initiation into a mystical tradition and experience under a qualified master, or were they just "equivalent to an oath"—a kind of agreement to stick around. When I explained the vows, then he still wanted to know what kind of attainment the monks might achieve and if there were possibilities of a deep mystical life in our monasteries. I said well, that is what they are supposed to be for, but many monks seem to be interested in something else. . . . I would note, however, that some of the monks around the Dalai Lama complain of the same things our monks do: lack of time, too much work, inability to devote enough time to meditation, etc. I don't suppose the Dalai Lama has much time on his hands, but in the long talks we had on meditation I could see that he has certainly gone very thoroughly and deeply into it and is a man of high "attainment." I have also met many other Tibetans who are impressive in this way, including Tibetan lay people who are very far advanced in a special type of Tibetan contemplation which is like Zen and is called dzogchen.

At this point in the letter I was interrupted, and went out to meet a Cambodian Buddhist monk who has been running a small monastery in India for years. He is of the Theravada (Southern or Hinayana) tradition, different from the Tibetan. Here too the emphasis is on disciplining the mind and knowing it inside out. But the methods are simpler than the Tibetan ones and go less far. He told me that the best monks in the Theravada tradition are in Burma and Thailand. In fact I did see a monastery in Bangkok and met a very interesting English Buddhist monk [Phra Khantipalo] who has a great reputation for scholarship and fervor among the Thais. He was just about to withdraw to one of the "forest wats" or small eremitical meditation monasteries in the northern jungles of Thailand where the best masters are found. These are almost completely unknown to Westerners.

One of the most interesting people I have met is a young Tibetan abbot who, since escaping from Tibet, has been trained at Oxford and has started a small monastery in Scotland. He is very successful there, apparently, and is a talented man. He has written a book called *Born in Tibet* about his experiences in escaping. I recommend it. (His name is Chogyam Trungpa Rimpoche.)

I have also had some contact with the Sufi tradition (Moslem), which has penetrated India in the Delhi area (which used to be capital of the Mogul empire and is still quite Moslem.) I met an expert on Sufism who told me of the meetings at which the Sufis of this area use singing to induce contemplation, but I have not been to any of them. I do hope to hear some singing of this type in Urdu at a local restaurant where it is featured on week ends. The food here by the way is wild, it is a positive menace. For the most part I try to stick to Chinese food rather than Indian, which is (for me at least) lethal.

In summary: I can say that so far my contacts with Asian monks have been very fruitful and rewarding. We seem to understand one another very well indeed. I have been dealing with Buddhists mostly, and I find that the Tibetans above all are very alive and also generally well trained. They are wonderful people. Many of the monasteries, both Thai and Tibetan, seem to have a life of the same kind as was lived, for instance, at Cluny in the Middle Ages: scholarly, well trained, with much liturgy and ritual. But they are also specialists in meditation and contemplation. This is what appeals to me most. It is invaluable to have direct contact with people who have really put in a lifetime of hard work in training their minds and liberating themselves from passion and illusion. I do not say they are all saints, but certainly they are men of unusual quality and depth, very warm and wonderful people. Talking with them is a real pleasure. For instance, the other day one of the lamas, at the end of our meeting, composed a poem for me in Tibetan, so I composed one for him (in English), and we parted on this note of traditional Asian monastic courtesy. There is much more I could write about: the rich art, music, etc. But it would get too involved.

I hope you will understand why I cannot answer my mail these days. I am entirely occupied with these monastic encounters and with the study and prayer that are required to make them fruitful. I hope you will pray for me and for all those I will be meeting. I am sure the blessing of God will be upon these meetings, and I hope much mutual benefit will come from them. I also hope I can bring back to my monastery something of the Asian wisdom with which I am fortunate to be in contact—but it is something very hard to put into words.

I wish you all the peace and joy in the Lord and an increase of faith: for in my contacts with these new friends I also feel consolation in my own faith in Christ and His indwelling presence. I hope and believe He may be present in the hearts of all of us.

With my very best regards always, cordially yours in the Lord Jesus, and in His Spirit.

THOMAS MERTON

APPENDIX VII

Marxism and Monastic Perspectives

by Father Louis, O.C.S.O. (Thomas Merton)

(Talk delivered at Bangkok on December 10, 1968)

After the very complete and authoritative lecture by Father Amyot,[1] which you have just heard, I must apologize for giving you what will inevitably be a rather impressionistic treatment of something I do not know very much about, because I cannot possibly pretend to be an authority on Marxism. My purpose is perhaps to share with you the kind of thing a monk goes through in his, shall we say, identity crisis. (The term was used by Dom Leclercq yesterday and has been widely used in certain circles, anyway.) The monk, I mean, who questions himself in the presence of the Marxist—who has certain answers and certain views of the world that are not necessarily quite those of the monk—trying to find where he stands, what his position is, how he identifies himself in a world of revolution. And in speaking of this, I hope I will be able to give you at least a minimum of information about the kind of thought we stand

---

[1] Father Jacques Amyot, S.J., born in Canada, teaches at Chulalongkorn University in Bangkok. The subject of his lecture, which immediately preceded Merton's, was "The Monastery in the Human and Social Context of the Theravada Buddhist Countries of Southeast Asia."

up against, and against the light of which we try to identify ourselves.

This lecture might have been entitled "Marxist Theory and Monastic Theoria," because I am concerned much more with the thought, and indeed with a kind of mystique, of Marxism than with orthodox Marxist thinking and, still less, actual Marxist political techniques and tactics. I would say, too, that what I am going to be talking about will be much more Western than Asian. I am not talking about Asian Marxist thought because I do not know much about it. The Western Marxist thought against whose background I shall be speaking is Neo-Marxist and strictly Western; it is the kind of thought that underlies the riots and rebellions in the universities of the West. Specifically my background is the work of Herbert Marcuse, who is a very influential thinker in Neo-Marxist student circles. And I would add, quite bluntly and brutally, that I regard him as a kind of monastic thinker. So if you wanted to be completely irresponsible, you could say this is a lecture on the monastic implications of Marcuse at the present moment.

This is *not* a talk addressed to the needs of those brethren here present who have been in a totally different and much more existential contact with Marxism, namely, those who have had to flee for their lives from Communist countries. This is not the problem I am talking about, the problem of life and death, when for bare survival one simply has to get away from an enemy who seeks to destroy or completely convert one. I don't see that there is much that can be said about this, except indirectly. You save your life by saving your life; you do what you can. Perhaps something I say may have an implication for the possibility of survival in a completely totalized society of the future, something that might very well take place. But, as I said, I am thinking much more in terms of the kind of Marxist thought that influences the youth of the West and will possibly influence some of the youth of Asia—and that will, I think, be influential with the kind of people we could really be in vital contact with in the East, that is to say, the intellectuals.

So I am addressing myself to the monk who is potentially open to contact with the intellectual, the university student, the university professor, the people who are thinking along lines that are going to change both Western and Eastern society and create the world of the future, in which inevitably we are going to have to make our adaptation.

An alternative to a strictly anti-Communist and negative attitude toward Marxism is, of course, the attitude of dialogue. I will not speak at great length about Western dialogue between Catholics and Marxists except to say that it exists. I shall breathe with respect the name of Roger Garaudy,[2] the French Marxist who is notably in contact with Catholic thinkers. I would just make one remark about Garaudy and his attitude toward monasticism. The significant fact is that one of the points Garaudy sees to be interesting in Christianity, something that really strikes him as important, is the existence of somebody like St. Teresa of Avila.

Now, I think this is something we ought to keep in mind. This is something that concerns us deeply as people for whom the contemplative life is so important that we have dedicated ourselves to it completely and definitively. We will be relevant in the world of Marxism in proportion not as we are pseudo-Marxists or semi-Marxist monks, or something like that, but in proportion as we are simply monks—simply what we are. I think that that takes care of the point of relevance for the moment. I shall return to it afterward.

At the head of my notes, which I am not necessarily following, there is an allusion to a remark that I heard in California before coming to Asia. I was at a meeting to which many revolutionary university leaders from France, Italy, Germany, the Low Countries had been invited. This meeting took place in

---

[2] Roger Garaudy (1913–) was, until his expulsion from the Communist party in 1969, a member of the French Politbureau. A professor at the University of Poitiers, and the director of the Center for Marxist Studies and Research, his published works explore humanism, ethics, existentialism, and the problem of freedom from a Marxist point of view. Paperback editions of two of his books are available in English: *Crisis in Communism* (New York, Grove Press, 1972) and *Marxism in the Twentieth Century* (New York, Scribner's, 1971).

Santa Barbara, California, at the Center for the Study of Democratic Institutions, and the purpose of it was to give these young people a forum in which to express their views and to state what they were trying to do. In a lull between lectures I was speaking informally with some of these students, and I introduced myself as a monk. One of the French revolutionary student leaders immediately said: "We are monks also."

This seemed to me to be a very interesting and important statement, and it had all kinds of interesting implications. One of the implications, for me, was a sort of undertone of suggestion that perhaps he was saying: "We are the true monks. You are not the true monks; we are the true monks." I am willing to accept that kind of challenge from people who are dedicated in this particular way.

What does such a statement, such a suggestion, mean? What was he alluding to when he said that the revolutionary student is the "true monk," and the monk in his monastery is not a true monk? I think it gets around to one of the things that is most essential to the monastic vocation, which we have to some extent neglected.

The monk is essentially someone who takes up a critical attitude toward the world and its structures, just as these students identify themselves essentially as people who have taken up a critical attitude toward the contemporary world and its structures. But the criticism is undoubtedly quite different. However, the student seemed to be alluding to the fact that if one is to call himself in some way or other a monk, he must have in some way or other reached some kind of critical conclusion about the validity of certain claims made by secular society and its structures with regard to the end of man's existence. In other words, the monk is somebody who says, in one way or another, that the claims of the world are fraudulent.

Now this, of course, is a dreadful thing to say—and especially now that it is being said on TV! But nevertheless there is something essentially valid in this kind of claim.

I think we should say that there has to be a dialectic between world refusal and world acceptance. The world refusal of the monk is something that also looks toward an acceptance of a world that is open to change. In other words, the world refusal of the monk is in view of his desire for change. This puts the monk on the same plane with the Marxist, because the Marxist directs a dialectical critique of social structures toward the end of revolutionary change. The difference between the monk and the Marxist is fundamental insofar as the Marxist view of change is oriented to the change of substructures, economic substructures, and the monk is seeking to change man's consciousness. Permit me, then, to spell this out a little for the information of those who have not been meditating on Marxism recently, and who have not really done much homework on Marxism, which I think would be important for monks.

Remember that in Marxist thought you have the priority of matter. Marxist materialism is a doctrine that insists that everything is grounded in matter, and that the explanation and the understanding of things amount to an understanding of processes that take their origin in matter and in material elements, so to speak. I could quote to you the famous statement of Feuerbach: *Mann ist was er isst,* which means "Man is what he eats."[3]

In other words, the basic approach to reality that the Marxist takes is that if you want to understand man's predicament in the world, you have to understand the economic processes by which he makes his living. And if you fail to understand these processes, no matter how good your explanations and answers may be, they are wide of the mark. Because, ignoring this basic economic subculture, they build something that has no validity, on a different approach, which ignores this economic starting point and becomes what they call a mystification. In these terms, therefore, for Marxism, you have three

[3] Ludwig Andreas Feuerbach (1804–72), a German materialist philosopher, who held that the religious impulse is a natural product of man's yearnings. His book *The Essence of Religion,* from which Merton quoted somewhat incorrectly, is available from Harper & Row, New York, as a Harper Torchbook; the exact wording, found on page xiv, reads, *Der mensch ist was er isst.*

great sorts of mystification: religion, philosophy, and politics. Religion, philosophy, and politics ignore the economic basis of man's being, and so forth, and therefore they are wide of the mark.

Now, I was speaking to a Marxist professor about this thesis the other day in Singapore, and I asked him what he thought about it. He said: "Well, you must be careful to note that Marxist thought is not essentially and militantly antireligious—that is to say, in Marx himself. Marx simply discarded religion as an honest and sincere attempt to answer certain fundamental questions, which had been attempted in the past but had not fully answered the question. It had been a good attempt but was now no longer valid." So the Marxist view of religion, according to this man, was not really that it was something to be militantly put down, but that it was something that would disappear by itself as soon as man began to mature. This, of course, is tied in with the familiar cliché we hear these days about the maturity of man.

Teilhard de Chardin[4] steps into the picture at this particular point and meets Marxism halfway by his scientific approach to man, and he is very well accepted by Marxist thought. Teilhard is the one Christian thinker today who is widely read in Marxist countries, and precisely because he moves in the direction of an interpretation that takes matter into account as basic. All right, I don't want to go any farther on that. This is just enough to give you some idea of what Marxism says; and of course it is very insufficient.

Traditional monasticism faces the same problem of man

[4] Father Pierre Teilhard de Chardin, S. J. (1881–1955) was a French priest known, before his death, primarily for his work as a paleontologist and geologist. He was forbidden during his lifetime to publish his philosophical and religious speculations, a fusion of evolutionary and Christian principles within a mystical framework. From the mid-1920s onward, he traveled widely in the East, principally in China, pursuing his scientific investigations. He returned to France in 1949 and moved to New York two years later. After his death, Teilhard's most important religious work, *Phenomenon of Man* (available from Harper & Row, New York, as a Torchbook paperback) was finally published. In less than a decade, it was translated into eight languages and in this country alone sold more than 75,000 copies; there are now close to two dozen of his books available in English.

and his happiness, what his life is for—and approaches it from a different angle. When I say "traditional monasticism," I mean Buddhist monasticism as well as Christian. Buddhist and Christian monasticism start from the problem inside man himself. Instead of dealing with the external structures of society, they start with man's own consciousness. Both Christianity and Buddhism agree that the root of man's problems is that his consciousness is all fouled up and he does not apprehend reality as it fully and really is; that the moment he looks at something, he begins to interpret it in ways that are prejudiced and predetermined to fit a certain wrong picture of the world, in which he exists as an individual ego in the center of things. This is called by Buddhism avidya, or ignorance. From this basic ignorance, which is our experience of ourselves as absolutely autonomous individual egos—from this basic wrong experience of ourselves comes all the rest. This is the source of all our problems.

Christianity says almost exactly the same things in terms of the myth of original sin. I say "myth of original sin," not trying to discredit the idea of original sin, but using "myth" with all the force of the word that has been given to it by scholars like Jung, and people of the Jungian school, and those psychologists and patristic scholars who meet, for example, at the Eranos meetings annually in Switzerland,[5] where they understand the vital importance and dynamism of myth as a psychological factor in man's adaptation to reality. So our myth of original sin, as explained for example by St. Bernard, comes very close indeed to the Buddhist concept of avidya, of this fundamental ignorance. Consequently, Christianity and Bud-

[5] Eranos meetings have been held annually late in August since 1933 at the home of Frau Olga Froebe-Kapteyn, in a hall built for this purpose on the grounds of her residence at the northern end of Lago Maggiore. With the idea that her estate should become the site of a perennial round table of ideas, a meeting place of East and West, the late Professor Rudolf Otto of the University of Marburg suggested the Greek word *eranos* (meaning a meal to which each contributes his share) as a name evoking the convivial spirit of unsystematic interchange and the classical prototype of all such discussions, the Platonic symposium.

dhism look primarily to a transformation of man's consciousness —a transformation, and a liberation of the truth imprisoned in man by ignorance and error.

Christianity and Buddhism alike, then, seek to bring about a transformation of man's consciousness. And instead of starting with matter itself and then moving up to a new structure, in which man will automatically develop a new consciousness, the traditional religions begin with the consciousness of the individual, seek to transform and liberate the truth in each person, with the idea that it will then communicate itself to others. Of course, the man par excellence to whom this task is deputed is the monk. And the Christian monk and the Buddhist monk—in their sort of ideal setting and the ideal way of looking at them—fulfill this role in society.

The monk is a man who has attained, or is about to attain, or seeks to attain, full realization. He dwells in the center of society as one who has attained realization—he knows the score. Not that he has acquired unusual or esoteric information, but he has come to experience the ground of his own being in such a way that he knows the secret of liberation and can somehow or other communicate this to others.

Now, in patristic doctrine and in the teaching of the monastic fathers, you find this very strongly stressed. You find, for example, the Cistercians of the 12th century speaking of a kind of monastic therapy. Adam of Perseigne[6] has the idea that you come to the monastery, first, to be cured. The period of monastic formation is a period of cure, of convalescence. When one makes one's profession, one has passed through convalescence and is ready to begin to be educated in a new way—the education of the "new man." The whole purpose of the monastic life is to teach men to live by love. The simple

[6] Adam of Perseigne, son of a serf, was born c. 1145 in Normandy and educated in one of the cathedral cities of Champagne, either Rheims or Sens. He was ordained to the diocesan clergy and was chaplain to the Countess of Champagne. Later, he took monastic vows, transferred to the Benedictines, and finally to the Cistercians. In 1188, he was made Abbot of Perseigne, from which his name is derived.

formula, which was so popular in the West, was the Augustinian formula of the translation of *cupiditas* into *caritas,* of self-centered love into an outgoing, other-centered love. In the process of this change the individual ego was seen to be illusory and dissolved itself, and in place of this self-centered ego came the Christian person, who was no longer just the individual but was Christ dwelling in each one. So in each one of us the Christian person is that which is fully open to all other persons, because ultimately all other persons are Christ.

Now, I don't want to get into this deeply mysterious and mystical doctrine here. I have to keep on the subject of Marxism. But I would just point out that in Marx himself you can see something of this same desire to evolve from *cupiditas* to *caritas,* when you see the idea of Communism—which is a progress from capitalist greed (in their terms) to Communist dedication, according to Marxist formula in which Communism consists in a society where each gives according to his capacity and each receives according to his needs. Now, if you will reflect for two seconds on that definition, you will find that it is the definition of a monastic community. That is precisely what monastic community life has always attempted to realize, and it is my personal opinion that monastic community life is really the only place in which this can be realized. It cannot be done in Communism. It *can* be done in a monastery. (I am subject to correction on this particular point. This is just a personal idiosynscrasy of mine, perhaps, but that is what I believe.)

We come now to the ideas of Marcuse. I am not going to develop him at great length. I would simply recommend quite strongly that you make yourselves acquainted, in one way or other, with Marcuse's very important book, *One Dimensional Man.* This book is much more important for the West than it is for the East, but I still think it has considerable importance even in the East, because Marcuse's theory is that all highly organized technological societies, as we have them now, all so-called managerial societies, as found both in the United

States and in the Soviet Union, end up by being equally totalitarian in one way or another.

Marcuse's thesis is that the society of the United States of America is just as totalitarian as the society of Russia, the only difference being that the totalitarianism in the United States is benign and benevolent and smooth and sweet, whereas that in Russia is a little bit tougher. (I am not preaching this; I am just giving you the stuff. This is what the man says, although I must admit that I agree with it to some extent.) Marcuse and the students who are revolting in the universities contend that, in fact, significant choices can no longer be made in the kind of organized society you have either under capitalism or under Soviet socialism. The choices that are really important have all been made before you get around to trying it yourself. The choices that are left to us are insignificant choices, like the choice between which toothpaste I will use, which airline I will take, or what time I will go from Bangkok to Hong Kong, or what time I will go from Bangkok to San Francisco—whether I will go Tuesday or Wednesday, or whether I'll go this week or next week. But these, as far as Marcuse is concerned, are not significant choices.

I will not elaborate on this, but there is something to be said for Marcuse's statement. It has also been made, incidentally, by Erich Fromm, whom you ought to know, in works like *Escape from Freedom, The Sane Society,* and the like, which are now quite dated but nevertheless still have validity.

Erich Fromm is an American psychoanalyst living in Mexico who has gone deeply into the idea of alienation in modern society. The idea of alienation is basically Marxist, and what it means is that man living under certain economic conditions is no longer in possession of the fruits of his life. His life is not his. It is lived according to conditions determined by somebody else. I would say that on this particular point, which is very important indeed in the early Marx, you have a basically Christian idea. Christianity is against alienation. Christianity revolts against an alienated life. The whole *New Testament* is, in fact

—and can be read by a Marxist-oriented mind as—a protest against religious alienation. St. Paul is without doubt one of the greatest attackers of religious alienation. Alienation is the theme of the *Epistle to the Romans* and the *Epistle to the Galatians,* and it is something worth knowing about.

In the monastic life, it is extremely important that we take account of this concept because, in fact, we have to face with sorrow the bitter truth that the life of many monks and many dedicated women, and many other dedicated people, is a life of total alienation in the sense that it is a legal surrender of things that perhaps they should not have surrendered, and a failure to fulfill potentialities that the monastery should allow them to fulfill. Now, this is an enormous problem, but on this point we have to come together with the Marxists and admit there is something to be done about it.

I will pass on now to something that might be more interesting to you—some conversations I had with Tibetan monks who had gone through the experience of being thrown out of their country, driven out of their country, by Communism. First of all, I spoke of this to the Dalai Lama, and I asked his ideas on this whole question of Marxism and monasticism. I suppose there are few people in the world more intimately involved in this question than the Dalai Lama, who is the religious head of an essentially monastic society. The Dalai Lama is very objective and open about this kind of thing. He is in no way whatever a fanatical anti-Communist. He is an open-minded, reasonable man, thinking in terms of a religious tradition. He obviously recognized the problem of a ruthless Communist takeover, a power move that had to get rid of monks, that had to drive monks out of Tibet. The Dalai Lama himself made every effort to coexist with Communism, and he failed. He said frankly that he did not see how one could coexist, in the situation in which he had been, with Communism—on an institutional level, anyway. He then went on to admit the blindness of the abbots and communities of the great, rich Tibetan monasteries, who had failed to see the signs of the times and had absolutely failed to do anything valid to meet the challenge of Communism. They refused to do anything, for example, about giving land to people who needed it. They simply could not see the necessity of taking certain steps, and this, he said, precipitated the disaster, and it had to happen.

I would like to add now, while speaking of the Dalai Lama, that he had some very interesting questions to ask about Western monasticism. He was extremely interested in it. He had seen a film of the Trappist monks of Sept-Fons,[7] and he was very much interested in everything they did in this film and wanted to know all about Trappist silence. Incidentally, the question of a married clergy amused him highly. He thought that the idea of priests of the West getting married was very funny. He knew he had some married monks in his outfit, but he was not exactly wild about married monks either.

But the questions he asked about Western monasticism were quite interesting. He started asking about the vows, and I did not quite know what he was getting at. Then he said: "Well, to be precise, what do your vows oblige you to do? Do they simply constitute an agreement to stick around for life in the monastery? Or do they imply a commitment to a life of progress up certain mystical stages?" I sort of hemmed and hawed a bit, and said: "Well, no, that's not quite what the vows are all about." But it was interesting to see that this is what he thought the vows *should* be about. When you stop and think a little bit about St. Benedict's concept of *conversio morum,* that most mysterious of our vows, which is actually the most essential, I believe, it can be interpreted as a commitment to total inner transformation of one sort or another—a commitment to become a completely new man. It seems to me that that could be regarded as the end of the monastic life, and that no matter where one attempts to do this, that remains the essential thing.

To get back to the lamas. I spoke to another Tibetan lama, a young one whom I consider a good friend of mine—a very

[7] Sept-Fons is a Trappist (Cistercian) monastery in the diocese of Moulins, Dompierre-sur-Besbre, in France.

interesting person indeed. Chogyam Trungpa Rimpoche is now about thirty-one or thirty-two years old—a Tibetan lama, a rimpoche, that is to say, a reincarnation, who got the complete reincarnation treatment: a thorough formation in Tibetan science, monasticism, and everything.[8] He had to escape from Tibet to save his life, like most other abbots.

When he was faced with the decision of leaving his country, he did not quite know what to do. He was absent from his monastery on a visitation to some other monastery, and he was caught out in the mountains somewhere and was living in a peasant's house, wondering what to do next. He sent a message to a nearby abbot friend of his, saying: "What do we do?" The abbot sent back a strange message, which I think is very significant: "From now on, Brother, everybody stands on his own feet."

To my mind, that is an extremely important monastic statement. If you forget everything else that has been said, I would suggest you remember this for the future: "From now on, everybody stands on his own feet."

This, I think, is what Buddhism is about, what Christianity is about, what monasticism is about—if you understand it in terms of grace. It is not a Pelagian statement, by any means, but a statement to the effect that we can no longer rely on being supported by structures that may be destroyed at any moment by a political power or a political force. You cannot rely on structures. The time for relying on structures has disappeared. They are good and they should help us, and we should do the best we can with them. But they may be taken away, and if everything is taken away, what do you do next?

The Zen people have a saying that has nothing directly to do with this, but is analogous in a certain sense: "Where do you go from the top of a thirty-foot pole?" You see? Well, in a certain way the answer has something in common. Where do you

---

[8] It should be noted that Thomas Merton, in telling Chogyam Trungpa's story, is relying on his memory, and hence certain of the details are not quite correct. For Chogyam Trungpa's life, see *Born in Tibet,* especially pages 115–16 and 192.

go from the top of a thirty-foot pole—which is where we all now sit? I think it is useful in this conference to take account of the fact that that is where we are.

Trungpa Rimpoche, then, on this advice to stand on his own feet, said: "O.K. I'm going to India." He had with him his cellarer (and this will be amusing to anybody who has lived in terms of abbots and cellarers). His cellarer had a whole train of about twenty-five yaks loaded with all kinds of provisions, and the abbot said to his cellarer: "Listen, Father, we aren't going to be able to take all those yaks. We're going to have to ford rivers and swim rivers, and we're going to have to travel light." The cellarer said: "Listen, we've got to take these yaks, we've got to eat." So they started off on their journey. The first thing that happened was that the Chinese Communists saw this train of yaks going down the road and got them. But the abbot didn't happen to be right there; he had gone on ahead, and was swimming a river somewhere, and he escaped.

I think there is a lesson in there somewhere, too. We can ask ourselves if we are planning for the next twenty years to be traveling with a train of yaks. It probably is not going to work. The ultimate end of Trungpa Rimpoche's story—which is, of course, still being lived out in full force—is that he got a degree from Oxford, speaks excellent English, has a thorough knowledge of both Western and Eastern civilization, and is now running a Tibetan monastery in Scotland, which is quite a good place. It is incidentally a place where you can temporarily be a monk. It is a place where you can make a three-year Buddhist retreat in total silence, and so forth. I hope to visit him there.[9]

Coming now toward a sort of conclusion, it is obvious that we have to plan the future. Let us look forward to the worst. Supposing that we are totally destroyed as an institution. Can

[9] Chogyam Trungpa Rimpoche now lives in the United States and has established several meditation centers here as well: Dharmadhatu in San Francisco; "Tail of the Tiger" in Barnet, Vermont; and Karma Dzong near Boulder, Colorado.

we continue? It is the same question: Where do we go from the top of that thirty-foot pole?

What is essential in the monastic life is not embedded in buildings, is not embedded in clothing, is not necessarily embedded even in a rule. It is somewhere along the line of something deeper than a rule. It is concerned with this business of total inner transformation. All other things serve that end. I am just saying, in other words, what Cassian said in the first lecture on *puritas cordis*, purity of heart, that every monastic observance tends toward that.[10]

Incidentally, I would say that the question of Asian monasticism for Christians should not be interpreted in terms of just playing an Asian part or an Asian role. It is not that we want to look like Asians; it is not sufficient simply to present an Asian image. Too often it seems to resolve itself into that. I think we have to go much deeper than this. For a Christian—as also, I believe, for a Buddhist—there is an essential orientation that goes beyond this or that society, this or that culture, or even this or that religion. When I said that St. Paul was attacking religious alienation, I meant that really he meant very seriously what he said about "There is no longer Jew or Greek, there is no longer Jew or Gentile." There is no longer Asian or European for the Christian. So while being open to Asian cultural things of value and using them, I think we also have to keep in mind the fact that Christianity and Buddhism, too, in their original purity point beyond all divisions between this and that.

So you respect the plurality of these things, but you do not make them ends in in themselves. We respect these things and go beyond them dialectically. The kind of thing I am saying is that in Christianity you have a dialectical approach to this, and in Buddhism you have an essential dialectic called the Madhyamika, which is the basis of Zen, and so on. All these dialectical approaches (Marxism, of course, is also dialectical) go beyond the thesis and the antithesis, this and that, black and white, East

10 See *Conferences of John Cassian,* Migne, P.L. 49, Conference 1, Chapter IV, "De Monachi Intentione et Fine," column 486.

and West. We accept the division, we work with the division, and we go beyond the division.

I will close with a remark on Buddhist iconography, on one of those traditional representations of the Buddha in which with one hand he is pointing to the earth (he is seated in the lotus posture) and in the other hand he holds a begging bowl. This is quite relevant for monasticism. It is a kind of summary of Buddhism, too. The Buddha's gesture of pointing to the earth is made in response to an accusation on the part of the devil, Mara. Mara is not quite the devil, but the tempter, the one who represents all illusion, and so forth. Mara came to Buddha where he was sitting when he had obtained enlightenment, and said: "You have no business sitting on that little square of earth where you're sitting, because it belongs to me." And the Buddha pointed to the earth and called it to witness that it did not belong to Mara, because he had just obtained enlightenment on it.

This is a very excellent statement, I think, about the relation of the monk to the world. The monk belongs to the world, but the world belongs to him insofar as he has dedicated himself totally to liberation from it in order to liberate it. You can't just immerse yourself in the world and get carried away with it. That is no salvation. If you want to pull a drowning man out of the water, you have to have some support yourself. Supposing somebody is drowning and you are standing on a rock, you can do it; or supposing you can support yourself by swimming, you can do it. There is nothing to be gained by simply jumping in the water and drowning with him.

The begging bowl of the Buddha represents what Father Amyot was talking about this morning. It represents the ultimate theological root of the belief not just in a right to beg, but in openness to the gifts of all beings as an expression of the interdependence of all beings. This is the most central concept in Buddhism—or at least in Mahayana Buddhism.

The whole idea of compassion, which is central to Mahayana Buddhism, is based on a keen awareness of the interdependence of all these living beings, which are all part of one another and all involved in one another. Thus when the monk begs from the layman and receives a gift from the layman, it is not as a selfish person getting something from somebody else. He is simply opening himself in this interdependence, this mutual interdependence, in which they all recognize that they all are immersed in illusion together, but that the illusion is also an empirical reality that has to be fully accepted, and that in this illusion, which is nevertheless empirically real, nirvana is present and it is all there, if you but see it.

I think, by way of closing, that this kind of view of reality is essentially very close to the Christian monastic view of reality. It is the view that if you once penetrate by detachment and purity of heart to the inner secret of the ground of your ordinary experience, you attain to a liberty that nobody can touch, that nobody can affect, that no political change of circumstances can do anything to. I admit this is a bit idealistic. I have not attempted to see how this works in a concentration camp, and I hope I will not have the opportunity. But I am just saying that somewhere behind our monasticism, and behind Buddhist monasticism, is the belief that this kind of freedom and transcendence is somehow attainable.

The essential thing for this, in the Buddhist tradition, is the formation of spiritual masters who can bring it out in the hearts of people who are as yet unformed. Wherever you have somebody capable of giving some kind of direction and instruction to a small group attempting to do this thing, attempting to love and serve God and reach union with him, you are bound to have some kind of monasticism. This kind of monasticism cannot be extinguished. It is imperishable. It represents an instinct of the human heart, and it represents a charism given by God to man. It cannot be rooted out, because it does not depend on man. It does not depend on cultural factors, and it does not depend on sociological or psychological factors. It is something much deeper.

I, as a monk—and, I think, you as monks—can agree that

we believe this to be the deepest and most essential thing in our lives, and because we believe this, we have given ourselves to the kind of life we have adopted. I believe that our renewal consists precisely in deepening this understanding and this grasp of that which is most real. And I believe that by openness to Buddhism, to Hinduism, and to these great Asian traditions, we stand a wonderful chance of learning more about the potentiality of our own traditions, because they have gone, from the natural point of view, so much deeper into this than we have. The combination of the natural techniques and the graces and the other things that have been manifested in Asia and the Christian liberty of the gospel should bring us all at last to that full and transcendent liberty which is beyond mere cultural differences and mere externals—and mere this or that.

I will conclude on that note. I believe the plan is to have all the questions for this morning's lectures this evening at the panel. So I will disappear.

APPENDIX VIII

Letter to Abbot Flavian Burns

December 11, 1968
Sawang Kaniwat, Bangkok

Dear Dom Flavian,

The news of the sudden and unexpected death of your beloved son, Father Louis, has already been conveyed to you. However, we the undersigned, as the Trappist delegates to this historic conference, wish to convey to you, and through you to all our brethren at Gethsemani, the information that we know you would be anxious to know.

In the first place we wish to extend to you and your community our deep heartfelt sympathy in your great loss of a son and brother, a loss which is also an intimate one for each of us. We know that you too will also feel that it is an occasion of great happiness with the realization that Father Louis has attained that goal that we all seek, eternal union with the Godhead.

This conference, with its coming together of some of the most outstanding figures in the monastic life of the present era, is in the main a public witness of the honor and respect that Benedictine monks as a whole wish to pay to Thomas Merton.

With one accord every delegate here and the hundreds represented by these delegates appreciate your own kindness and generosity in allowing Father Louis to attend this conference.

It was his presence here that drew us, and from the very moment of his arrival he was the center of all proceedings. Some had already met him, most of us were meeting him for the first time person to person. He was known to us through his writings and by his reputation, but now that we have had the privilege to meet and live with him we know just how truly great a monk he was. He endeared himself to everyone by his simplicity, his openness to all, his eagerness to give of all that he had, and above all by the fact that here indeed was a true monk.

On the morning of his death he had delivered to us the paper that he had prepared, and all were eagerly looking forward to the evening session when he was to answer questions on his paper and on matters dealing with monasticism in general.

After lunch he retired to his room, and on his way he commented to one of us that he was looking forward to his meridian as he had been unable to have it the day before due to an organizing meeting that he had had to attend.

Not long after he retired a shout was heard by others in his cottage, but after a preliminary check they thought they must have imagined the cry.

He was found at the end of the meridian and when found was lying on the floor. He was on his back with the electric fan lying across his chest. The fan was still switched on, and there was a deep burn and some cuts on his right side and arm. The back of his head was also bleeding slightly.

One of the nuns who had medical experience was quickly at his side, but it was evident that he was already dead.

A Thai doctor came, and later another Thai doctor arrived. It is difficult to determine at this stage just exactly what was the cause of his death.

It is believed that he could have showered and then had a heart attack near the fan, and in falling knocked the fan over against himself; or again that being in his bare feet on a stone floor he may have received a fatal electric shock.

As soon as the police had finished their investigation we asked permission to dress the body in his robe and scapular, and this permission they readily gave.

The body was toweled and then dressed and laid out on his bed. We then kept constant vigil beside his body, reciting the rosary and then the psalter until officials from the American army arrived to remove his body. The vigil was kept from 6 P.M. until approximately 1:30 A.M. this morning.

The American Consulate had been informed, and one of the secretaries, Miss Berry, had come out to claim his possessions and arrange for the transfer of his body.

Dom Joachim and Father Anselm together with the Primate Dom Weakland checked his personal belongings and made sure that all were gathered together. The Primate had been making every endeavor to contact you from the very first moment of the discovery of the fatality.

During the vigil all the other delegates came and paid their respects, and all took their turn in reciting the psalms.

In death Father Louis' face was set in a great and deep peace, and it was obvious that he had found Him Whom he had searched for so diligently.

The American army took his body to their hospital in Bangkok.

This morning at 10 A.M. we celebrated Requiem Mass for the repose of his soul. The Abbot Primate Dom Weakland was the principal celebrant and was assisted by the Apostolic Delegate of Thailand and Dom Joachim of Kopua. The Archbishop of Bangkok and his secretary were also present. All the priests concelebrated, assisted by the other delegates. The vestments were white to testify to our belief that this was indeed an occasion of great happiness as we rejoiced in the knowledge that our brother had truly gone to God.

Fortunately a tape had been made of his talk to the conference, and a movie film was also taken. Dom de Floris has informed us that a copy of the tape will be forwarded to you and that if you are interested in obtaining a copy of the film you should contact the Italian T.V. Company at their office in New York. More than any tape or film could attain there has been imprinted in our hearts and minds the living image of one whom we all fondly call brother.

Again extending to you and all our brothers at Gethsemani our heartfelt sympathy and an assurance of a continued remembrance of Father Louis in our Masses and prayers that his soul may rest in peace.

Your brothers and sisters in Christ,

(Signed by the six Trappist delegates at the Bangkok Conference)

DOM ANSELM PARKER, O.C.S.O., Australia
DOM JOACHIM MURPHY, O.C.S.O., New Zealand
DOM SIMEON CHANG, O.C.S.O., Hong Kong
MOTHER CHRISTIANA, O.C.S.O., Japan
DOM M. F. ACHARYA, O.C.S.O., India
DOM M. FRANS HARDJAWIJATA, O.C.S.O., Indonesia

APPENDIX IX

The Significance of the *Bhagavad-Gita*

by Thomas Merton

The word *gita* means "song." Just as in the Bible the *Song of Solomon* has traditionally been known as "The Song of Songs" because it was interpreted to symbolize the ultimate union of Israel with God (in terms of human married love), so the *Bhagavad-Gita* is, for Hinduism, the great and unsurpassed song that finds the secret of human life in the unquestioning surrender to and awareness of Krishna.

While the *Vedas* provide Hinduism with its basic ideas of cult and sacrifice and the *Upanishads* develop its metaphysic of contemplation, the *Bhagavad-Gita* can be seen as the great treatise on the "Active Life." But it is really something more, for it tends to fuse worship, action, and contemplation in a fulfillment of daily duty which transcends all three by virtue of a higher consciousness: a consciousness of acting passively, of being an obedient instrument of a transcendent will. The *Vedas,* the *Upanishads,* and the *Gita* can be seen as the main literary supports for the great religious civilization of India, the oldest surviving culture in the world. The fact that the *Gita* remains utterly vital today can be judged by the way such great reformers as Mohandas Gandhi and Vinoba Bhave[1] both spontaneously based their lives and actions on it, and indeed commented on it in detail for their disciples. The present translation and commentary[2] is another manifestation of the living importance of the *Gita*. It brings to the West a salutary reminder that our highly activistic and one-sided culture is faced with a crisis that may end in self-destruction because it lacks the inner depth of an authentic metaphysical consciousness. Without such depth, our moral and political protestations are just so much verbiage. If, in the West, God can no longer be experienced as other than "dead," it is because of an inner split and self-alienation which have characterized the Western mind in its single-minded dedication to only half of life: that which is exterior, objective, and quantitative. The "death of God" and the consequent death of genuine moral sense, respect for life, for humanity, for value, has expressed the death of an inner subjective quality of life: a *quality* which in the traditional religions was experienced in terms of God-consciousness. Not concentration on an idea or concept of God, still less on an image of God, but a sense of *presence*, of an ultimate ground of reality and meaning, from which life and love could spontaneously flower.

It is important for the Western reader to situate the *Gita* in its right place. Whereas the *Upanishads* contemplate the unconditioned, formless Brahma, the Godhead beyond created existence and beyond personality, the *Gita* deals with brahman under the conditioned form and name of Krishna. There is no "I-Thou" relationship with the unconditioned Brahma, since there can be no conceivable subject-object division or inter-

[1] Vinoba Bhave (1895–), founder of the Bhoodan land reform movement. A saintly, Gandhi-like figure, Bhave walks through the Indian countryside, accompanied by his followers, attempting to persuade landowners to give part of their holdings to the peasants who have no land.

[2] This essay by Merton on aspects of Hindu philosophy was first published as the preface to *The Bhagavad Gita, As It Is,* with an introduction, translation, and authorized purport by Swami A. C. Bhaktivedanta (New York, Macmillan, 1968).

personal division in him, at least according to Hindu thought. In Christianity, too, the Godhead is above and beyond all distinction of persons. The Flemish and Rhenish mystics described it as beyond all form, distinction, and division. Unconditioned Brahma, the Godhead, is not "what we see," it is "who sees." "Thou art that." Unconditioned brahman is pure Consciousness. Pure Act—but not activity. Conditioned brahman is the "Maker" and "Doer," or rather the "Player" and "Dancer," in the realm of created forms, of time, of history, of nature, of life.

Conditioned brahman, then, appears in the world of nature and time under personal forms (various incarnations for Hinduism, one incarnation only for Christianity). Realization of the Supreme "Player" whose "play" (*lila*) is manifested in the million-formed inexhaustible richness of beings and events is what gives us the key to the meaning of life. Once we live in awareness of the cosmic dance and move in time with the Dancer, our life attains its true dimension. It is at once more serious and less serious than the life of one who does not sense this inner cosmic dynamism. To live without this illuminated consciousness is to live as a beast of burden, carrying one's life with tragic seriousness as a huge, incomprehensible weight, (see Camus' interpretation of the myth of Sisyphus). The weight of the burden is the seriousness with which one takes one's own individual and separate self. To live with the true consciousness of life centered in Another is to lose one's self-important seriousness and thus to live life as "play" in union with a Cosmic Player. It is He alone that one takes seriously. But to take Him seriously is to find joy and spontaneity in everything, for everything is gift and grace. In other words, to live selfishly is to bear life as an intolerable burden. To live selflessly is to live in joy, realizing by experience that life itself is love and gift. To be a lover and a giver is to be a channel through which the Supreme Giver manifests His love in the world.

But the *Gita* presents a problem to some who read it in the present context of violence and war which mark the crisis of the West. The *Gita* appears to accept and to justify war. Arjuna is exhorted to submit his will to Krishna by going to war against his enemies, who are also his own kin, because war is his duty as a prince and warrior. Here we are uneasily reminded of the fact that in Hinduism as well as in Judaism, Islam, and Christianity, there is a concept of a "holy war" which is "willed by God," and we are furthermore reminded of the fact that, historically, this concept has been secularized and inflated beyond measure. It has now "escalated" to the point where slaughter, violence, revolution, the annihilation of enemies, the extermination of entire populations and even genocide *have become a way of life.* There is hardly a nation on earth today that is not to some extent committed to a philosophy or to a mystique of violence. One way or other, whether on the left or on the right, whether in defense of a bloated establishment or of an improvised guerrilla government in the jungle, whether in terms of a police state or in terms of a ghetto revolution, the human race is polarizing itself into camps armed with everything from Molotov cocktails to the most sophisticated technological instruments of death. At such a time, the doctrine that "war is the will of God" can be disastrous if it is not handled with extreme care. For *everyone* seems in practice to be thinking along some such lines with the exception of a few sensitive and well-meaning souls (mostly the kind of people who will read this book).

The *Gita* is not a justification of war, nor does it propound a war-making mystique. War is accepted in the context of a particular kind of ancient culture in which it could be, and was, subject to all kinds of limitations. (It is instructive to compare the severe religious limitations on war in the Christian Middle Ages with the subsequent development of war by nation states in modern times—backed of course by the religious establishment.) Arjuna has an instinctive repugnance for war, and that is the chief reason why war is chosen as the example of the most repellent kind of duty. The *Gita* is saying that even in what appears to be most "unspiritual" one can act with pure intentions and thus be guided by Krishna consciousness. This consciousness itself will impose the most strict limitations on one's use of violence because that use will not be directed by one's own selfish interests, still less by cruelty, sadism, and blood-lust.

The discoveries of Freud and others in modern times have, of course, alerted us to the fact that there are certain imperatives of culture and of conscience which appear pure on the surface and are in fact bestial in their roots. The greatest inhumanities have been perpetrated in the name of "humanity," "civilization," "progress," "freedom," "my country," and of course "God." This reminds us that in the cultivation of an inner spiritual consciousness there is a perpetual danger of self-deception, narcissism, self-righteous evasion of truth. In other words, the standard temptation of religious and spiritually minded people is to cultivate an inner sense of rightness or of peace, and make this subjective feeling the final test of everything. As long as this feeling of rightness remains with them, they will do anything under the sun. But this inner feeling (as Auschwitz and the Eichmann case have shown) can coexist with the ultimate in human corruption.

The hazard of the spiritual quest is of course that its genuineness cannot be left to our own isolated subjective judgment alone. The fact that I am turned on doesn't prove anything whatever. (Nor does the fact that I am turned off.) We do not simply create our own lives on our own terms. Any attempt to do so is ultimately an affirmation of our individual self as ultimate and supreme. This is a self-idolatry which is diametrically opposed to Krishna consciousness or to any other authentic form of religious or metaphysical consciousness.

The *Gita* sees that the basic problem of man is his endemic refusal to live by a will other than his own. For in striving to live entirely by his own individual will, instead of becoming free, man is enslaved by forces even more exterior and more delusory than his own transient fancies. He projects himself out of the present into the future. He tries to make for himself a future that accords with his own fantasy, and thereby escape from a present reality which he does not fully accept. And yet, when he moves into the future he wanted to create for himself, it becomes a present that is once again repugnant to him. And yet this is what he had "made" for himself—it is his karma. In accepting the present in all its reality as something to be dealt with precisely as it is, man comes to grips at once with his karma and with a providential will which, ultimately, is *more his own* than what he currently experiences, on a superficial level, as "his own will." It is in surrendering a false and illusory liberty on the superficial level that man unites himself with the inner ground of reality and freedom in himself which is the will of God, of Krishna, of Providence, of Tao. These concepts do not all exactly coincide, but they have much in common. It is by remaining open to an infinite number of unexpected possibilities which transcend his own imagination and capacity to plan that man really fulfills his own need for freedom. The *Gita,* like the Gospels, teaches us to live in awareness of an inner truth that exceeds the grasp of our thought and cannot be subject to our own control. In following mere appetite for power we are slaves of appetite. In obedience to that truth we are at last free.

BIBLIOGRAPHY

GLOSSARY

BIBLIOGRAPHY

Principal works quoted from by Thomas Merton, or quoted from or consulted for background by the editors in the preparation of the notes and glossary for this edition of *The Asian Journal*.

Definitions from *Webster's New International Dictionary*, Second Edition [indicated "Webster's II"], copyright © 1959, and *Webster's Third New International Dictionary* [indicated "Webster's III"], copyright © 1971, are used by permission of the copyright owners, G. & C. Merriam Co., publishers of Merriam-Webster dictionaries.

A number of descriptive passages in the glossary are reprinted from *The Columbia Encyclopedia*, Second Edition, edited by William Bridgwater and Elizabeth J. Sherwood, New York, Columbia University Press, 1950, by permission of the publisher.

Other acknowledgments to individual authors and the publishers of specialized works will be found at the end of the Editors' Notes on pages xi-xix.

Basham, A.L.: *The Wonder That Was India*, New York, Grove Press, Evergreen paperback edition, 1954.
Bhattacharya, Haridas, editor: *The Cultural Heritage of India*, Volume IV, The Religions; Calcutta, The Ramakrishna Mission, Institute of Culture, revised edition, 1956.
Bhattacharya, S: *A Dictionary of Indian History*, New York, George Braziller, 1967.
Blofeld, John: *The Tantric Mysticism of Tibet*, New York, A Dutton Paperback, 1970.
Conze, Edward: *Buddhism: Its Essence and Development*, New York, Harper Torchbooks paperback edition, 1959.
Conze, Edward: *Buddhist Meditation*, New York, Harper & Row, 1969.
Conze, Edward: *Buddhist Thought in India*, Ann Arbor, University of Michigan Press paperback edition, 1967.
Coomaraswamy, Ananda: *The Dance of Shiva*, New York, Noonday Press, 1957.

Cornford, F.M.: *The Unwritten Philosophy and Other Essays,* Cambridge, Cambridge University Press, 1950.

Critchfield, Richard: "Punjab, Bengal and the Green Revolution," in *The Nation,* New York, Volume 214, Number 5, January 31, 1972.

Dalai Lama: *Introduction to Buddhism,* New Delhi, Tibet House, 1965.

Daniélou, Alain: *Hindu Polytheism,* Bollingen Series LXXIII, New York, Pantheon Books, 1964.

Dasgupta, Shashi Bhushan: *An Introduction to Tantric Buddhism,* Calcutta, Calcutta University Press, 1958.

Dasgupta, Surendranath: *Indian Idealism,* Cambridge, Cambridge University Press, paperback edition, 1962.

Desjardins, Arnaud: *The Message of the Tibetans,* translated from the French by R.H. Ward and Vega Stewart, London, Stuart & Watkins, 1969

Dimock, Edward C., Jr. and Levertov, Denise: *In Praise of Krishna, Songs from the Bengali,* Garden City, A Doubleday Anchor paperback, 1967.

Dumoulin, Heinrich: *A History of Zen Buddhism,* New York, Pantheon Books, 1963.

Emmanuel, Pierre: *La Loi d'exode,* in Jules Monchanin: *De l'Esthétique à la mystique,* Paris, Casterman, 1967.

The Encyclopedia Britannica.

Engels, Friedrich: *Dialectics of Nature,* translated by Clemens Dutt, New York, International Publishers, 1940.

Esnoul, Anne-Marie: *Ramanuja et la mystique vishnouite,* Paris, Editions du Seuil, 1964.

Evans-Wentz, W.Y.: *The Tibetan Book of the Dead,* New York, Oxford University Press paperback, 1969.

Evans-Wentz, W.Y.: *The Tibetan Book of the Great Liberation,* New York, Oxford University Press paperback, 1969.

Evans-Wentz, W.Y.: *Tibetan Yoga and Secret Doctrines,* New York, Oxford University Press paperback, 1969.

Evans-Wentz, W.Y.: *Tibet's Great Yogi Milarepa,* New York, Oxford University Press paperback, 1969.

Frédéric, Louis: *The Art of Southeast Asia, Temples & Sculpture,* New York, Abrams, 1965.

Graham, Dom Aelred: *Conversations: Christian and Buddhist,* New York, Harcourt, Brace & World, 1968.

Hesse, Hermann: *Steppenwolf,* translated by Basil Creighton and Joseph Mileck, New York, Bantam paperback edition, 1969.

Humphreys, Christmas: *Buddhism,* Harmondsworth, Pelican paperback edition, 1952.

Jones, P.H.M., editor: *Golden Guide to South & East Asia,* Tokyo, Charles E. Tuttle Co., 1969.

Koestler, Arthur: *The Lotus and the Robot,* New York, Macmillan, 1961.

Lawrence, D.H.: *The Complete Poems of D.H. Lawrence,* edited by Vivian de Sola Pinto and F. Warren Roberts, 2 volumes, New York, Viking Press, 1964.

Lawrence, D.H.: *Twilight in Italy,* New York, Viking Compass paperback edition, 1962.

Lewis, Charlton T. and Short, Charles: *A Latin Dictionary,* Oxford, The Clarendon Press, 1966.

Lhalungpa, L.P.: "Tibetan Music: Sacred and Secular," in *Studies in Comparative Religion,* Bedfont, Middlesex, England, Spring 1969.

Massignon, Louis: *Essai sur les origines du lexique technique de la mystique musulmane,* Paris, J. Vein, 1954.

Merton, Thomas: *Conjectures of a Guilty Bystander,* Garden City, Doubleday, 1966.

Merton, Thomas: *The Seven Storey Mountain,* New York, Signet paperback edition, 1952.

Merton, Thomas: *The Way of Chuang Tzu,* New York, New Directions, 1965.

Mohan, G.B.: *The Response to Poetry,* New Delhi, People's Publishing House, 1968.

Monier Williams, M.: *Hinduism,* Calcutta, Susil Gupta, 1877.

Monier-Williams, M.: *A Sanskrit-English Dictionary,* revised edition, Oxford, The Clarendon Press, 1970.

Morgan, Kenneth W., editor: *The Path of the Buddha,* New York, Ronald Press, 1956.

Morgan, Kenneth W., editor: *The Religion of the Hindus,* New York, Ronald Press, 1953.

Murti, T.R.V.: *The Central Philosophy of Buddhism,* second edition, London, Allen & Unwin, 1960.

Murray's Handbook for Travellers in India and Pakistan, Burma and Ceylon, London, John Murray, 1953.

Nanasampanno, Ven. Acaiiya Maha Boowa: "Wisdom Develops Samadhi," translated from the Thai by Bhikkhu Pannavaddho, in *Visakha Puja,* Bangkok, The Buddhist Association of Thailand, 1967.

Nikam, N.A. and McKeon, Richard: *The Edicts of Asoka,* Chicago, University of Chicago Press, 1959.

Nin, Anaïs: *Under a Glass Bell,* New York, E.P. Dutton, 1948.

Nyanaponika Thera: *The Heart of Buddhist Meditation,* London, Rider & Company, paperback edition, 1969.

Pallis, Marco: "Considerations on Tantric Spirituality," in *The Bulletin of Tibetology,* Gangtok, Namgyal Institute of Tibetology, Volume II, Number 2, August 1965.

Pallis, Marco: "Discovering the Interior Life," in *Studies in Comparative Religion,* Bedfont, Middlesex, England, Spring 1968.

Pallis, Marco: "Is There Room for 'Grace' in Buddhism?" in *Studies in Comparative Religion,* Bedfont, Middlesex, England, August 1968.

Pallis, Marco: *Peaks and Lamas,* New York, Alfred A. Knopf, 1949.
Pallis, Marco: *The Way and the Mountain,* London, Peter Owen, 1960.
Radhakrishnan, Sarvepalli: *The Hindu View of Life,* New York, Macmillan, 1931.
Radhakrishnan, Sarvepalli and Moore, Charles A., editors: *A Source Book in Indian Philosophy,* Princeton, Princeton University Press, 1957.
Raghavan, V.: *The Indian Heritage,* Bangalore, Institute of Indian Culture, 1956.
Rahula, Walpola: *What the Buddha Taught,* New York, Grove Press, Evergreen paperback edition, 1962.
Rama IV: *His Majesty King Rama the Fourth Mongkut,* commemorative volume, edited by Phra Sasanasobhon, Bangkok, Mahamamakuta-Rajavidyalaya Foundation, 1968.
Ramakrishna: *The Gospel of Sri Ramakrishna,* translated by Swami Nikhilananda, New York, Ramakrishna-Vivekananda Center, 1942.
Renou, Louis: *Indian Literature,* translated by Patrick Evans, New York, Walker and Company, 1964.
Renou, Louis: *The Nature of Hinduism,* translated by Patrick Evans, New York, Walker and Company, 1962.
Revised Standard Version of the Bible (Roman Catholic).
Ross, Nancy Wilson: *Three Ways of Asian Wisdom,* New York, Simon and Schuster, 1966.
Rowland, Benjamin: *The Art and Architecture of India,* Baltimore, Penguin Books, 1953.
Sankaracharya of Kanchi: *Madras Discourses,* Madras, 1957–60.
Shankara (Sankaracharya): *The Crest-Jewel of Discrimination,* translated by Swami Prabhavananda and Christopher Isherwood, Hollywood, Vedanta Press, 1947.
Smith, Vincent A., translator and editor: *The Edicts of Asoka,* London, Essex House Press, 1909.
Suzuki, Daisetz T.: *Zen and Japanese Culture,* Bollingen Series LXIV, Princeton, Princeton University Press paperback edition, 1970.
Thomas, Edward J.: *The History of Buddhist Thought,* New York, Barnes & Noble, 1951.
Toukaram: *Psaumes du pèlerin,* translated into French by G.-A. Deleury, Paris, Gallimard, 1956.
Trungpa, Chogyam: *Born in Tibet,* as told to Esmé Cramer Roberts, London, Allen and Unwin, 1966.
Tucci, Giuseppe: *The Theory and Practice of the Mandala,* translated by A.H. Broderick, London, Rider & Company, paperback edition, 1969.
von Glasenapp, Helmuth: *Buddhism,* translated from the German by Irmgaard Schloegl, New York, George Braziller, 1971.
Wasson, R. Gordon: *Soma, Divine Mushroom of Immortality,* New York, Harcourt Brace Jovanovich, Harvest paperback edition, 1968.
Watts, Alan W.: *The Way of Zen,* New York, Pantheon Books, 1957.

West, Nathanael: *Miss Lonelyhearts* (combined with *The Day of the Locust*), New York, New Directions paperback edition, 1969.

Zaehner, R.C.: *Hinduism*, New York, Oxford University Press paperback, 1968.

Zimmer, Heinrich: *The Art of Indian Asia*, Bollingen Series XXXIX, New York, Pantheon Books, 1955.

Zimmer, Heinrich: *Philosophies of India*, edited by Joseph Campbell, Princeton, Princeton University Press paperback, 1969.

GLOSSARY

aardra darsanan: A Hindu puja (devotional service) which is performed
at the conjunction of the full moon and the star Aardra.

Abhidharma: a Buddhist metaphysical system; pure, intuitive knowledge
of the dharmas. Cf., in Pali, the *Abhidhammapitaka*, or third section
of the scriptures, the "Basket of the Supreme Doctrine," which contains a complete system of mind-training. Abhidharmika: one who
believes in this system.

abhimukhi: the sixth stage in the Buddhist progress toward bodhisattvahood.

acala: "immovable"; the eighth stage in the progress to bodhisattvahood.

(a-a-a-)achya: Bengali; an affirmative response to a question.

Advaita Vedanta: Sanskrit, in Hinduism, a school of Vedanta philosophy
which believes in the oneness of God, soul, and universe. Advaita:
monism. Vedanta: literally, "end of the *Vedas*." See pages 413–15.

advaya: (advaya-vada) "negation of both views or extremes of the real;
though almost the same as advaita [non-dual, not two ultimate reali-
ties], there is still some difference between them." (Murti; see pages
217–18)

Agama: the Sanskrit "tradition" in ancient Buddhist scriptures; thus the
Chinese Agamas are translations of Sanskrit originals at least as old
as the Pali canon (Nikaya), and it is thought that both descend from
the same collections of earlier recorded sayings. (See Murti, pages
113–15, for a discussion of the *Agama Sastra*.)

Agni: the Hindu god of fire.

Agra: the Indian city, about 120 miles south of Delhi, which the Mogul
emperor Akbar (1556–1605) made his capital, and where his grandson,
Shah Jehan, built the Taj Mahal, between 1630 and 1652, to commemorate his queen, Mumtaz Mahal.

Ahirbudhnya Samhita: a post-Upanishadic scripture in the Hindu Vaishnava school of thought. The samhitas are one of the three principal
categories of the *Vedas;* they are prayers, hymns, and mantras (words,
verses, or syllables whose sound invokes a god or supernatural power)
revealed by meditation or intuition and having salvatory benefit for

those who revere and repeat them. The samhitas are the basis of much later doctrinal elaboration and commentary.

akasa: in Madhyamika Buddhism, "empty space"; or simply "space" when the concept is used in the Hindu form of worship known as pratiko-pasana, in which a deity is worshiped not as a symbol, but through a symbol; here the intention is to find in the limited the presence of the all-pervading spirit which goes beyond all limitations of form or name. The pratika may be within the worshiper—his mind or soul—or external, as the mantra "om," akasa (space), or agni (fire).

alaya-vijnana: the abode of all mentation, the receptacle where everything is connected as effect, the prime cause in things. Alaya: "abode or support"; vijnana: "mentation." (Dasgupta: *An Introduction to Tantric Buddhism,* pages 27ff)

Allah: "Arabic *Allah,* contraction of *al-ilah,* the god. The Supreme Being of the Mohammedans." (Webster's II) See Islam and Moslem.

Amitabha: "A Buddha of the Great Vehicle who vowed to create a pure land, to be glorified as the Buddha of Boundless Light, and to save all having faith in his vows." (Webster's II) Also known, especially in Japan, as Amida. (See Humphreys: *Buddhism,* pages 161ff., for an account of Amida's vows (pranidhana) and the rise of the Pure Land school of Buddhism.)

Amritaratnavali: an ancient Sanskrit text on certain aspects of yoga in Tantric Buddhism. Amrita: "nectar," "ambrosia," whence, "seed of life," "deathlessness," "immortality." (mrita: "death"). *Ratnavali* is the title of one of the important works of Nagarjuna, one of the founders of the Madhyamika sect of Buddhism. Ratnavali: "collection of gems."

Ananda: a favorite disciple of the Buddha. As a philosophical term, in Hinduism, when applied to the god Krishna, ananda connotes "absolute bliss."

anapanasati: in Buddhism and yoga, one of the most popular techniques for developing the power to meditate, to free the mind from every other thought except the awareness of breathing in and out. When this concentration has been achieved, one is ready to move on to higher forms of meditation, such as dhyana, and thence to mystic experience. A high degree of concentration is necessary for penetrative insight into the nature of things, including the realization of nirvana. (See Walpola Rahula: *What the Buddha Taught,* New York, Grove Press, 1959, pages 69ff. for a simple account of how this form of meditation may be learned and practiced. The early Pali texts of the *Anapanasati Suttas* are one of the principal sources for the method. For a more scholarly exigesis, see W.Y. Evans-Wents: *Tibetan Yoga and Secret Doctrines,* Oxford University Press, 1958, Book II: "The Nirvanic Path; The Yoga of the Great Symbol." See also Nanasampanno: "Wisdom Develops Samadhi" in *Visakha Puja,* May 1967, Buddhist Association of Thailand, Bangkok, pages 75ff., the actual source from which Merton noted the term on page 16 of the holograph notebook.)

anatma(n): "Sanskrit term for the doctrine of non-ego; cf. anatta, the Pali term for the same concept, the denial of a permanent unchanging self." (Ross) Anatma-vada: "no-self (soul) theory; the basic Buddhist doctrine that all things lack substance or permanent identical reality; same as nairatmya-vada." (Murti) The Buddhist concept opposes the Hindu one of the atman as a personal, immortal soul. For a discussion of anatta as one of the "Three Signs of Being" in Theravada Buddhism, see Humphreys, *Buddhism,* Chapter 5, pages 78–89.

anatta: see anatma, above.

anicca: in Theravada Buddhism, the Pali term for impermanence or change; with anatta (see above) and dukkha (suffering) it is one of the "Three Signs of Being."

anushthana: certain religious devotional practices in Hinduism, particularly in South India. (Raghavan)

Anuttarantantras: one of the four groups of esoteric scriptures in Mahayana Buddhism known as the *Tantras,* which gives its name to the Tantric sect of Buddhism. "The *Anuttaratantras* are reserved especially for the creatures who sin the most." The four categories, which together make up the Vajrayana ("Thunderbolt Path") are the *Kriya-tantras, Caryatantras, Yogatantras* and the *Anuttaratantras.* (Tucci)

apana: a movement of the breath in Hindu Hathayoga (the school of yoga that concentrates on physical health and well-being). (Chakravarty). "There is a perfect parallelism between the physical processes of the universe and the biological processes in the body of man. With this idea in view, the Tantras try to locate the sun, the moon, the stars, the important mountains, islands and rivers of the exterior world within the human body; the time-element of the universe in all its phases of day and night, fortnight, month and year have often been explained with reference to the course of the vital wind (*prana* and *apana*). The implication seems to be that the human body, with its physical structure and biological processes, represents the manifestation of the same energy which is at play in the structure and processes of the vast cosmos. The human form is therefore the abode of truth of which the universe is a manifestation in infinite space and external time. . . . The important nerve on the right side, well known as *pingala,* through which flows the *apana* air or current, is said to represent the principle of Shiva, while the left nerve, known as *ida,* through which flows the *prana* air, is said to represent the principle of Shakti." (*The Cultural History of India,* Calcutta, 1956, Volume IV, pages 292–93 in the chapter "Some Later Yogic Schools.) See also "appana samadhi" in Nanasampanno: "Wisdom Develops Samadhi" in *Vishaka Puja,* May 1967. Buddhist Association of Thailand, Bangkok, page 84, the actual source from which Merton noted the term on page 16 of the holograph notebook. "The Samadhi that is subtle, firm, and unwavering, and in which one can remain concentrated for a long time. One may also remain concentrated in this state, or withdraw from it as one wishes."

The Apocalypse: the last book of the New Testament in the Christian Bible, also called *The Revelation of St. John the Divine.*

arcismati: "full of flames"; the fourth stage in the Buddhist progress toward bodhisattvahood.

arhat: "one who has reached the end of the fourfold way and attained nirvana." (Humphreys: *Buddhism*)

arigatai: "the religious sense of blessedness" in the Japanese Pure Land sect of Buddhism. (Reverend Kaneko in Aelred Graham: *Conversations: Christian and Buddhist*)

aropa: in Tibetan Buddhism, "the process of substitution from the psychophysical to the fully real personality." (Tucci) In Hindu Vedanta, the term has the sense of "superimposition," and is also "often used to describe the figurative, flattering language of eulogy addressed by court poets to their kings and by lovers to their mistresses." (Zimmer)

Arya Deva: 2nd–3rd centuries. The disciple of Nagarjuna who did much to develop and popularize the Madhyamika system of Buddhism.

Asanga: brother of Vasubandhu and disciple of Maitreya, founder of the Buddhist Yogacara school in either (scholars disagree: see Murti, page 107n and Thomas, page 237) the 3rd or 5th century A.D. See also Zimmer: *Philosophies of India,* page 529.

Ashoka: (Asoka, Asokavardhana, or, as he styled himself in his inscriptions, Devanamprya Pryadarsin, literally, in Prakrit, "beloved of the gods" and "one who sees to the good of others") (273–232 B.C.) The third emperor of the Maurya dynasty of Magadha founded by his grandfather, Chandragupta Maurya. Horrified by the slaughter of warfare, Ashoka was converted to Buddhism, and, like Constantine spreading Christianity throughout the Roman Empire, he imposed Buddhism on his own vast dominions, which stretched from Afghanistan to Mysore and Madras, also sending missionaries to Ceylon and other parts of Southeast Asia. Heinrich Zimmer has called Ashoka "one of the greatest conquerors and religious teachers of all time," while H.G. Wells, in his *Outline of History,* rated him one of the six greatest men of history (the others being Buddha, Socrates, Aristotle, Roger Bacon, and Abraham Lincoln). In *A Dictionary of Indian History* (New York, George Braziller, 1967) S. Bhattacharya writes that ". . . Nothing definite is known about the first twelve years of Asoka's reign except that during this period he was, like his predecessors, fond of convivial parties, hunting excursions, meat diet and tours of pleasure. . . . Eight years after his coronation, he embarked upon a war with Kalinga [modern Orissa] which lay along the coast of the Bay of Bengal from the [river] Mahanadi to the [river] Godavari. . . . Kalinga was conquered and annexed to Asoka's dominions, but the war had been extremely bloody in the course of which one lakh of persons were killed, one and a half lakhs were made captives and many lakhs of persons perished from famines, pestilence and other calamities that inevitably follow wars. Such widespread human suffering struck the conscience of Asoka. . . . Immediately afterwards Asoka began the study of what he calls in his edicts dhamma (dharma) which has been identified with Buddhism and which he soon afterwards embraced. After his conversion to Buddhism Asoka became a changed man. In Rock Edict XIII, which was probably issued four years after the conquest of Kalinga, Asoka declared that the loss of 'even the hundredth part or the thousandth part of all those people who were slain, who died, and who were deported . . . would . . . be considered very deplorable.' . . . He forswore war and never again did he fight a war during the long period of thirty-one years which intervened between his conversion and his death. . . . He went on tours of pilgrimage to Buddhist holy places . . During the course of these visits he deliberately contacted the ordinary people to whom he expounded the dhamma. For the purpose of permanently recording the doctrines of the dhamma he inscribed them on rocks and pillars . . ." (pages 67–68) To date, archaeologists have discovered some 35 rock inscriptions, written in the Brahmi and Karoshti scripts, located all over India from the foothills of the Himalayas to Mysore. For more background on the edicts see the note on page 242. There are many scholarly works on the edicts, but perhaps the most accessible in American libraries is *The Edicts of Asoka,* edited and translated by N.A. Nikam and Richard McKeon, Chicago, University of Chicago Press, 1959. The most detailed text and up-to-date interpretation of the edicts is to be found in *Asoka Maurya* by B.G. Gokhale, New York, Twayne Publishers, 1966.

ashram: from the Sanskrit *ashrama.* In Hinduism, "*a* A hermitage. *b* Any of the four stages of the Brahmanical scheme of life, which are: that of the student *(brahmachari),* of the householder *(grihastha)* of the hermit *(vanaprastha),* and of the homeless mendicant *(sannyasi).*" (Webster's II)

Asvaghosha (Ashvagosha): a 2nd-century Mahayana Buddhist Sanskrit poet and religious commentator, probably born in Ayodhya (Oudh), a protégé of the great Kanusa king, Kanishka, to whom tradition attributes far more literary works than it is likely one man could have written. But it seems certain that he did write the *Buddhanusmriti,* a hymn to the Buddha; two mahakavyas ("great poems"—minor epics with a lyrical quality); the *Buddhacharita,* a history of the Buddha's life up to the time of his enlightenment; and the *Mahayana Shraddhotpada Sastra,* of which the original Sanskrit text has been lost, but a Chinese version survives, translated by Suzuki as *The Awakening of Faith.* As a theologian, Morgan places him as "transitional from Sarvastivada to Mahayana, before Nagarjuna, Asanga, and Vasubandhu." Not to be confused with another writer of the same name who lived in the 5th

century. See Renou: *Indian Literature,* pages 60–61; Murti, page 79.
atman: in Sanskrit, ". . . breath, self, soul, Universal Self, Supreme Spirit.
. . ." In Hinduism, "the innermost essence of each individual; often: the supreme universal self." (Webster's III) The Pali term is atta, but Buddha taught the opposing doctrine of non-atman (Pali anatta) in which he showed that man possessed no permanent element, nor anything comparable to the unchanging, immortal "soul" of Christianity. Nevertheless, there is a concept of permanence in Buddhism, even though it does not pertain to the individual human being in himself. Thus Murti equates atman with dravya (substance), nitya (the permanent and eternal), svabhava (nature or self-being), sara (essence), and vastu (the real) in the Madhyamika doctrine. Atma: *"atma-vada,* the theory that the real is substance, permanent and eternal, and has a nature of its own." (Murti)
aucitya: propriety.
Aurangzeb: Mogul emperor of India, 1658–1707.
avidya: in Buddhism, the Sanskrit term for ignorance or nonawareness. (In Pali, avijja) See Humphreys: *Buddhism,* page 152; and for a detailed exigesis of the term, Murti, pages 238–42.
axis mundi: Latin, the center of the world, as in the symbolism of Tibetan mandalas. Cf. the Sanskrit, aksa.
Ayodhya: a mythical city in the ancient Sanskrit epic, the *Ramayana;* Rama, its hero, is prince of Ayodhya. The modern Oudh.
Ayyappan: a Hindu deity in South India. See Dr. V. Raghavan's note on Ayyappan on page 207.

Bab(-ud-Din): Mirza Ali Mohammed ibn-Radhik, founder of the Persian religious sect of "Babism" in 1844.
Baha'u'llah: Mirza Husayn Ali, founder of the Bahai religion.
baht: the silver coinage of Thailand.
Bana: a mythical king, enemy of Krishna, who was slain by the god.
Bardo Thödöl: the *Tibetan Book of the Dead.* Bardo: in Tibetan Buddhism, the period immediately following death. See W. Y. Evans-Wentz: *The Tibetan Book of the Dead,* Oxford University Press paperback, 1969.
Bhagavad-Gita: Sanskrit, "the discourse between Krishna and Arjuna that forms [perhaps the most famous] part of the Indian epic the *Mahabharata.*" (Ross) Many English translations are available, among them: that of Swami Prabhavananda and Christopher Isherwood, a Mentor paperback, 1954; that of Ann Stanford, New York, Herder & Herder, 1971; that of P. Lal, Calcutta, Writers Workshop, 1965; and that of Swami Nikhilananda, New York, Ramakrishna-Vivekananda Center, 1952. See "The Significance of the *Bhagavad-Gita,*" Merton's introduction to the book *The Bhagavad Gita, As It Is,* translated by Swami A. C. Bhaktivedanta, New York, Macmillan, 1968 (included as Appendix IX in this book).

bhakti: "Sanskrit, literally, portion, share . . . in Hinduism: religious devotion: love directed toward a personal deity." (Webster's III) The
Bhagavad-Gita gives three ways of reaching the life divine: bhakti
(devotional love), jnana (knowledge) and karma (action).

bhanita: Bengali, the signature line in Bengali Vaishnavite poetry.

Bhavaviveka (Bhavya): a 5th-century teacher who helped to develop the
Svatantrika school of Madhyamika Buddhism.

bhikkhu (Pali), bhikshu (Sanskrit): a Buddhist monk, mendicant holy
man or priest. "A fully ordained Buddhist monk. From the root
'bhik,' 'to beg.' While in Pali a bhikkhu is honorable, a beggar, in
English from the same root, is not so regarded." (Khantipalo) See also
thera.

bhutatathata: in Hinduism, "thatness, reality." (Surendranath Dasgupta)
Bhuta: "the principles of the five elements" and "physical-life." (Daniélou) The word can also mean "ghosts" or "evil spirits." (Daniélou)

Bodhgaya: the place in northeast India (near Gaya in Bihar State) where
the Buddha received enlightenment as he sat meditating under a bo
(or bodhi, actually a pipal) tree.

bodhi: "a term used in both Sanskrit and Pali meaning perfect wisdom or
enlightenment." (Ross) "The full perception of transcendental wisdom." (Blofeld)

Bodhicaryavatara: an 8th-century text by Santi Deva expounding the Madhyamika school of Buddhism.

bodhicitta: a key term in all sects of Buddhism. "The thought of enlightenment." (the Dalai Lama) "Human consciousness." (Tucci) "The Bud-
dha-mind, the Buddha-nature." (Morgan) "The mind of an Enlightened Being or 'Enlightened-mindedness.' " (Blofeld)

bodhipaksikas: in Buddhism, the thirty-seven virtues practiced in the arcismati (4th) stage of the progress toward bodhisattvahood. (S. B. Dasgupta)

bodhisattva: "in Mahayana Buddhism one who having attained enlightenment (bodhi) is on his way to Buddhahood but postpones his goal to
keep a vow to help all life attain salvation." (Ross)

bodhisattva-bhumis: the ten stages on the road to bodhisattvahood.

bodhi tree (or bo tree): see under Bodhgaya.

Bon-pa: "The indigenous religion of Tibet, some elements of which were
taken over by Tibetan Buddhism where it has influenced various
sciences of a cosmological order." (Marco Pallis in letter.)

bo tree: see under Bodhgaya

Brahma: in Hindu mythology, the creator god and chief in the triad of
classic Hindu gods: Brahma, Vishnu ("the preserver") and Shiva ("the
destroyer").

Brahma Kumari: a contemporary Calcutta cult leader.

brahman: in Madhyamika Buddhism, the absolute. But it is a far more
significant concept in Hinduism, especially Vedanta, in which it is the
metaphysical term for the supreme being, reality and principle of life.

369

Brahman is also one spelling for the name of the highest, priestly caste in the traditional Indian social system, though brahmin is perhaps more common. ". . . The chief duty of a brahman is the study and teaching of the *Vedas* and the performance of religious ceremonies. . . ." (Webster's II)

brahmanishtas: in Hinduism, devotees whose minds are fixed on god. (Chakravarty)

Brahma Sutra: written by Badarayana, it is one of the earliest source books of Hindu philosophy dealing with the nature of the godhead. (Chakravarty)

bramachari: in Hinduism, the student of a guru; one in the first of the four stages (ashramas) of the brahmanical scheme of life; one practicing continence.

Buddha: literally, an awakened or enlightened being, from the Sanskrit root "bodhati"—"he awakes or understands." The name usually refers to the "historic" Buddha, that is, Gautama Siddhartha (563–483 B.C.), born near Kapilavastu in India, a member of the Sakya clan, and hence called also Sakyamuni, the Sakya sage. He is also known as Tathagata, one who in following the path of dharma has come from and gone to tathata, the absolute, the unchanging real. But it is important to stress that Gautama was only one of many Buddhas who have existed before him and are destined to come after him, though all of the various sects of the present Buddhist religion derive from the teachings which Gautama gave his disciples.

Buddhapalita: a teacher, who probably lived in the first half of the 5th century A.D., who helped to develop the Prasangika school of Madhyamika Buddhism.

cakravartin: Sanskrit term for a universal sovereign in Hindu mythological tradition.

Candrakirti: a prolific commentator on Nagarjuna and the Madhyamika school of Buddhism. He probably lived at the turn of the 6th and 7th centuries A D.

caritas: (Latin) originally, "dearness" or "costliness"; thence, figuratively. "affection" or "love"; and later, in Church Latin, Christian love, or charity: "the virtue or act of loving God with a love which transcends that for creatures and of loving others for the sake of God." (Webster's III) Cf. the Sanskrit kama ("love, desire") and the Greek agape of the New Testament.

Caryatantras: one of the four groups of esoteric scriptures in Mahayana Buddhism known as the *Tantras,* which gives its name to the Tantric sect of Buddhism. "The *Caryatantras* are suited for the *rje rigs,* the nobleman, in whom a respect for ceremonial is accompanied by a capacity for spiritual meditation." (Tucci)

catechesis: "from Greek *katechesis* instruction . . . oral instruction of catechumens. . . ." Catechumen: ". . . one receiving rudimentary instruction in the doctrines of Christianity. . . ." (Webster's III) "Currently used to describe methods of teaching Christian doctrine." (Burton) Chaitanya: a 15th-century Bengali Vaishnava saint who wrote many commentaries and dialogues. See the index of *The Cultural Heritage of India* (Volume IV) for numerous references to his life and work.

chakra: Sanskrit for "wheel"; also a disk representing the sun and sovereignty (Cf. cakravartin); in the iconography of Indian art, a circular weapon carried by the god Vishnu; and in Tantric Hinduism, one of the six circles or centers of energy in the human body. (Based on Webster's II)

chedi: in Thailand, a pagoda or stupa (memorial shrine to the Buddha).

chorten: "[Tibetan *chorten*, alteration of *mchod rten*, from *mchod* offering + *rten* holder]: a Lamaist shrine or monument." (Webster's III) "A cenotaph in memory of Buddha or a canonized saint." (Murray) For a detailed explication of the symbolism of the chorten, see Evans-Wentz: *Tibet's Great Yogi Milarepa*, facing page 269 Cf. the stupa or chaitya in Indian Buddhism and the Sinhalese dagaba of Buddhism in Ceylon.

Cistercians: the Cistercian order of monks in the Catholic Church was founded at Citeaux, France, in 1098 by Robert de Molesmes. The Trappists are a reformed branch of the Cistercian order established in 1664 at the monastery of La Trappe in Normandy, France.

citta: the Pali term in Buddhism for "mind, pure consciousness . . . conceived as a stream or a series of momentary mental states without any abiding stratum." (Murti) In Hinduism, the Sanskrit cognate is "chit," with a similar meaning. "*Sat-chit-ananda:* existence, consciousness, bliss, constituting the nature of Absolute Reality." (Ross)

conversio morum: The vow of *conversio morum* (literally, in Latin, a "change of manners or will"), for St. Benedict, is a total commitment to Christ and His word, so that the monk tends toward perfection all his life according to the Rule of St. Benedict. Understood in this light, the vow includes within its scope the obligations of poverty and chastity.

dal masoor and dal moong; Hindi, varieties of an edible yellow split pea which is one of the staples of diet in northern India.

Dasara: in Hinduism, the festival of Ganga, goddess of the river Ganges.

Devadatta: Sanskrit, in Hinduism, a man's name which appears in Sankaracharya's *The Crest-Jewel of Discrimination*. It means "gift of God" and can also refer to the conch which, in the iconography of Hindu art, is one of the attributes of the god Indra.

Devaram: seven collections of Shaivite Sanskrit hymns, composed by saints of the 7th century A.D., which are often sung in Hindu religious processions along with the Vedic hymns.

dhamma (Pali), dharma (Sanskrit): "used in both Hinduism and Buddhism, meaning variously, according to context, the way, the law, righteousness, reality. 'The path which a man should follow in accordance with his nature and station in life.' " (Ross)

dharmakaya: the Sanskrit term for "the cosmical body of the Buddha, the essence of all beings." (Murti)

dharma-megha: "the clouds of dharma"; in Buddhism, the tenth and final stage in the progress to bodhisattvahood.

dharma-nairatmya: nairatmya: Sanskrit, "soullessness, substancelessness, unreality." dharma-nairatmya: in Buddhism, "the unreality of elements as separate ultimate existences; this contention of the Madhyamika is directed against the dogmatic acceptance of the reality of elements by the Hinayana Schools (Abhidharmika and Sautrantika)." (Murti)

dhikr: Arabic, in Sufism, the discipline of repeatedly mentioning the name of God. Cf. nembutsu in the Japanese schools of Buddhism, and Hindu Shaivite japa.

dhvani: in Sanskrit and Hindu poetry, the concept of "suggestion, evocation or resonance." (Mohan)

dhyana (Sanskrit), jhana (Pali): in both Buddhism and Hinduism, "Concentrated contemplation, same as Yoga or Samadhi." (Murti) " 'Trance,' recueillement, a state of mind achieved through higher meditation." (Rahula) It is from this Sanskrit word that comes the Japanese "Zen," which is a transliteration of the Chinese "Ch'an," the Chinese version of dhyana.

Diamond Vehicle: see the Vajrayana school of Buddhism.

Digha Nikaya: the first part, Collection of Long Discourses by the Buddha, many dealing with the training of disciples, in the Second Basket of the Pali canon of early Buddhist scriptures. Translated as Dialogues of the Buddha by Rhys Davids, Sacred Books of the Buddhists Series, London, 1899–1921.

ditthi (Pali), dristhi (Sanskrit): a "view, philosophical standpoint or speculative theory." (Murti)

Divali: the Hindu "Festival of Lights." "Dipali or Divali (properly Dipavali), 'the feast of lamps,' [is celebrated] on the last two days of the dark half of Asvina [the sixth month in the Hindu calendar] (September-October), and the new moon and four following days of Karttika [a son of Shiva; commander-in-chief of the army in heaven], in honour of Vishnu's wife Lakshmi, and of Shiva's wife Bhavani (Parvati)." (Monier-Williams)

divya: Sanskrit term in Tantric Buddhism for a soul which has attained divinity, one which has become fully realized and transcended samsara (the world of phenomena, the endless round of becoming, of birth and death).

dorje: the Tibetan equivalent of the Sanskrit "vajra"—"adamantine" or "diamond" (as to hardness), hence "pure" and "indestructible." Webster's II gives the Tibetan etymology as "rdo rje"—"stone lord." In the context of the quotation from Tucci, dorje is the thunderbolt scepter, symbol of "method" (the male principle), which with the tilbu, the handbell, symbol of "wisdom" (the female principle), is "married" to produce in the soul the "real Knowledge" which is "awareness" (remedy for ignorance) in Tibetan Buddhism. Both dorje and tilbu, held in the hands of a divinity, are frequently found in the iconography of Tibetan art, and lamas use the bell and scepter in their temple or altar rituals, the movements which they make with them symbolizing the union of wisdom and method, "method" here having also the connotation of "universal love" or "compassion." (Pallis) Many adepts in Tibetan Buddhism assume "Dorje" as part of their name. (Blofeld) Cf., in the iconography of Hinduism, the thunderbolt of the god Indra, which represents his power as a god who can bring thunderclouds and rain.

dorje phurpa: a magic dagger used in Tibetan mystery plays. See Evans-Wentz: *Tibetan Yoga and Secret Practices,* pages 289–94.

dukkha: the Pali term in the Abhidharma and other schools of Buddhism for "suffering" or "pain." (Murti) "Suffering, misery, unhappiness, pain. One of the three 'Signs of Being' with anicca [impermanence] and anatta [non-ego, substancelessness]." (Humphreys) "The true nature of existence." (Morgan)

durangama: literally, "going far away," the seventh stage in the Buddhist progress to bodhisattvahood.

Durga: see Kali.

dvaya-sunyata: Sanskrit, literally "duality-voidness"; the concept in the Vijnanavada ("consciousness only") or Yogacara schools of Buddhism that pure consciousness cannot have duality.

dzogchen: Tibetan, "great perfection." "Dzogchen—the Great Way of All-inclusiveness—is the esoteric tradition of the Nyingmapa order of Tibetan Buddhism. It is considered by Nyingmapas to be the highest esoteric system. Its origin goes back to the great Buddhist teachers such as Guru Padma Sambhava from the Swat Valley and Vimalamitra from India. Both of these teachers visited Tibet in the 8th century A.D. and laid the foundations of dzogchen teachings. The dzogchen tradition demands an earnest dedication and application of intensive preparation from its devotees in order that they may qualify themselves to receive dzogchen initation and secret instructions from a truly awakened teacher. Dzogchen may be defined as the simplest and most beneficial way to rediscover instantly for oneself the transcendental awareness that is within, whose all-inclusive qualities are either presently active or lying latent in human beings, thus dissolving in the process all discriminations such as ignorance and awareness. Ever present attentiveness holds the vital key to the degrees and tempo of one's attainment of illumination, instant and ultimate, leading to the All-inclusive Enlightenment through the total transformation of all forms of bondage including one's physical body into the perfectly illuminating form." (L. P. Lhalungpa, private letter)

Eucharist: ". . . from Greek Eucharist, giving of thanks, gratitude . . . the sacrament of the Lord's Supper . . . a central rite in many Christian churches in which bread and wine are consecrated by the officiating clergyman, shared with the people, and consumed as memorials of Christ's death or as symbols for the realization of a spiritual union between Christ and communicant or as the body and blood of Christ —called also *Communion, Holy Communion.* . . ." (Webster's III) "The Eucharist is the central act of worship of Roman Catholics." (Burton)

Ezekiel: The Book of Ezekiel in the Old Testament of the Judaeo-Christian Bible, attributed to Ezekiel, one of the Hebrew prophets of the 6th century B.C.

Feast of Christ the King: in the Roman Catholic Church calendar, "a church festival instituted by Pius XI in 1925 to honor Christ as the spiritual Lord of the world, and celebrated on the last Sunday in October." (Webster's II)

The Five Precepts: in Buddhism, not to kill, to steal, to do sexual wrong, to lie, or to use intoxicants or drugs.

Franciscan sisters: members of one of the orders of Roman Catholic nuns who follow the rule of St. Francis of Assisi. The first of these, known as the Poor Clares, was founded by Saint Clare (1193–1253), a devoted follower of St. Francis, who stressed the concept of dedication to poverty in forming the order. There are now many communities of Franciscan sisters throughout the world; some are contemplatives only, but many are teachers, nurses, or administrators of hospitals.

Gadong oracle: a Tibetan monk who was the medium for a spirit residing in a temple in a small town west of Lhasa. This oracle was frequently consulted by the leaders of the Tibetan lamaistic government prior to the Chinese intervention. The monk himself, still known as the "Gadong oracle," is now in exile near Dharamsala. (Sonam Kazi, private letter)

Gal Vihara;: "gal"—"black"; "vihara"—"temple." The site of three huge figures, two of Buddha and one of his disciple Ananda, carved in a natural rock wall at Polonnaruwa in Ceylon.

Gampopa: born in 1079 A.D., a disciple of the Tibetan poet-saint Milarepa and compiler of *The Precious Rosary,* also called *The Jewel Ornament of Liberation.*

gana: Sanskrit, in Hinduism, "category," or one of the "fundamental elements of existence." (Daniélou)

Ganapati: see Ganesha.

Gandavyuha Sutra: one of the "Nine Dharmas," an early and influential Sanskrit text of the Madhyamika school of Buddhism.

Gandhi: Mohandas Karamchand Gandhi (1869–1948), the Hindu nationalist leader who led the movement which culminated in independence for India from the British Empire; usually known as Mahatma Gandhi, "mahatma" meaning "great-souled" or "wise" in Sanskrit and still used as an honorific title in Hindi. "Gandhiji" was the affectionate popular name used by most Indians in referring to him. The Gandhi Samadhi is the name of the memorial built on the spot in Delhi where he was cremated, though the primary meaning of the Sanskrit term "samadhi" is "the supreme goal of yogic effort; superconsciousness." (Ross)

Ganesha: also called Ganapati, the Hindu god of wisdom and "remover of obstacles," usually depicted as a fat man with the head of an elephant."

Ganga: the Hindu goddess who is the personification of the river Ganges.

Gautama: the family name of the historic Buddha.

Gelugpa: the "Yellow Hats," one of the four principal sects of Tibetan Buddhism and the one to which the Dalai Lama belongs. It was founded in the late 14th century A.D. by Tsongkapa, one of the greatest Buddhist scholars of the period. Gelugpa derives from the "Three Stages" doctrines of the earlier sage, Atisha, and lays less emphasis on Tantric practices than most of the other Tibetan sects. For an excellent account of how the different sects developed in Tibet, see Chapter 6, "Buddhism in Tibet," coauthored by Merton's friend Lobsang Phuntsok Lhalungpa, in Kenneth W. Morgan: *The Path of the Buddha.*

geshe: in Tibetan Buddhism, a title of respect for a learned lama, roughly equivalent to the Western "Doctor of Divinity." (Pallis)

Gita: see *Bhagavad-Gita.*

gompa: in Tibet and the neighboring Himalayan regions, a Buddhist monastery; literally, "a solitary place." Ani gompa: a nunnery.

gopis: "cowherd girls in the stories of [the Hindu god] Krishna's life as a cowherd; enthralled devotees of Krishna." (Ross)

"The Great Vehicle": in Sanskrit, the literal translation of "Mahayana," one of the main schools of Buddhism.

Gtum-mo. See tum-mo.

guru; in Sanskrit and Hindi, a sage, teacher, or venerable holy man, particularly "a spiritual guide; one who takes disciples for religious instruction." (Ross)

gyeling: a Tibetan musical instrument like a shawm (reed pipe).

Hanuman: the monkey god of Hindu mythology who, in the *Ramayana* epic, rescues Sita, the wife of Rama, from the demon Ravana.

Hesychast: from the Greek for "hermit." "One of a sect of mystics or quietists, in the Eastern [Christian] Church, which originated among the monks of Mt. Athos, in the 14th century. They gave themselves up to protracted contemplation with the eyes fixed on the navel, holding that thus they were enabled to see or feel diffused through them an uncreated but communicable divine light, the same which shown on Mt. Tabor at the transfiguration of Christ." (Webster's II)

Himalayas: the great range of mountains, including the world's highest peak, Mount Everest, which are the dividing region between India and Tibet, and enclosed within the arms of the Indus and Brahmaputra rivers. From the Sanskrit "hima"—"snow" and "alaya"—"abode." Perhaps because their snows provide so much of the water for agriculture in India, the Himalayas have always been worshiped and personified as a deity in Hinduism. In mythology, the home of the god Shiva was the Himalayan Mount Kailasa, while both Durga, the great "Mother Goddess" and personification of shakti, the female principle, and Shiva's wife Parvati were daughters of the god of the Himalayas. Devout Hindus make pilgrimages to the Himalayas, as they do to the sacred river Ganges, and the most famous shrines are at Badarinath and Kedarnath, north of Hardwar.

Hinayana: literally, in Sanskrit, the "Lesser Vehicle." One of the major sects of Buddhism, earlier than Mahayana (the "Greater Vehicle"), based entirely on the Pali Canon of scriptures, and now surviving chiefly in Burma, Ceylon, and Thailand, where it is also often called Theravada, or "The School of the Elders," or "Southern Buddhism." In Tibetan Buddhism, Hinayana is the first of the "Three Stages" formulated by the Indian pandit Atisha who came to Tibet in 1042 A.D. Essentially, Hinayana is nontheistic and dominantly monastic. See the chapters on Theravada in *Buddhism* by Christmas Humphreys and *The Path of the Buddha,* edited by Kenneth W. Morgan.

Hindi: "an Indo-Aryan language, the chief vernacular of Northern India, spoken by over 300,000,000 people, mainly in the United and Central provinces and Central India." (Webster's II) It has many dialects, the most widespread of which is Hindustani. It is scheduled to become the official language of India, but the efforts of the central government to impose it on regions having their own indigenous languages have met with continued and sometimes violent resistance.

Hindu: properly, a believer in Hinduism, but the name is often, in the West, incorrectly applied to any member of one of the many races in India.

Hinduism: probably the oldest of the world's major religions, Hinduism is also the basic social system of India, rooted in the concept of function (dharma) and the observances of caste. It has many sects and no single creed; it has no single "founder" and a pantheon of many thousands of gods. It is now the predominant religion of India, its followers outnumbering the Indian Moslems, Sikhs, Jains, Parsis, Buddhists, Christians, and Jews. At the risk of oversimplification, it might be said that most Hindus believe in causality (karma), in the transmigration of the soul from life to life, and aspire to a final salvation (nirvana) which will release the soul from the succession of rebirths.

See the section on Hinduism in *Three Ways of Asian Wisdom* by Nancy Wilson Ross; *The Religion of the Hindus,* edited by Kenneth W. Morgan; *Hindu Polytheism* by Alain Daniélou; *The Nature of Hinduism,* by Louis Renou; and *Hinduism* by M. Monier-Williams.

Hrishikesa: "Lord of the Senses," one of the icons of the Hindu god Vishnu. (Daniélou)

Humayun: one of the 16th-century Mogul emperors of northern India.

Indre: a "département" (roughly the equivalent of an American state) in central France. It takes its name from the river Indre.

Islam: "meaning 'submission to the will of God'; a general term for the religion of the Muslim (Moslem) world." (Ross)

Isvara: in Hinduism, "the personal God." (Monier-Williams) " 'Lord,' beyond the world of the gods." (Renou) For a detailed discussion of the concept, see the subchapter " 'God' (Isvara) and the Illusion of Divine Unity" in Daniélou: *Hindu Polytheism,* pages 95–96.

Jainism: one of the minor religions of India with an estimated million adherents at the present time. It is an outgrowth of Hinduism, founded in the 6th century B.C., as a reformist movement, by Mahavira Jnatiputra, who constructed a "tradition" of twenty-three predecessor leaders of the movement who were called "jinas" ("conquerors"). Jains, like Hindus and Buddhists, believe in transmigration of the soul, and, as with certain sects of Buddhism and Hinduism, in severe asceticism intended to purge the body of its appetites for pleasure. But the religion is perhaps best known for its emphasis on ahimsa, the doctrine of nonviolence to all living creatures. Thus Jains will go out of their way not to kill insects or snakes, even if they bite. There are two major subdivisions of contemporary Jainism: the Digambaras, who believe that women cannot aspire to salvation, whose sacred images, as well as extreme ascetics, are naked; and the Svetambaras, who believe that women can achieve salvation and whose images are clothed. See Monier-Williams: *Hinduism,* pages 156–58. (Monier-Williams holds that Jainism is closer in origin and spirit to Buddhism than to Hinduism.)

Jama Masjid: one of the finest Mogul mosques in Delhi, built between 1644 and 1658.

Janissaries: Turkish infantry soldiers between the 14th and 19th centuries.

Jantar Mantar: the Mogul observatory in Delhi, built about 1725 A.D. by Maharaja Jai Singh II of Jaipur.

japa: Sanskrit, in Hindu Shaivite sects, particularly those of Kashmir, and also in Sikhism, as initiated by its founder, Guru Nanak, the repetition of a holy word as a form of prayer or devotion. Cf. dhikr in Sufism and nembutsu in certain schools of Japanese Buddhism, also the mantras of all Hindu and Buddhist sects, including the "Om mani padme hum" ("Hail to the jewel in the lotus") of Tibetan Buddhism.

Jesuit: member of the Company (or Society) of Jesus, a Roman Catholic religious order founded in 1534 by Saint Ignatius Loyola. Most Jesuits become either teachers or missionaries, and the Jesuits were among the first missionaries to explore North America after its discovery. The Jesuits have been active as missionaries in India since the time of Saint Francis Xavier, friend of Ignatius and one of the first members of the order, who came to Goa, the Portuguese enclave near Bombay, in 1542. In later years, Saint Francis moved eastward, continuing the work of conversion, in Ceylon, Malaya, Japan, and China, where he died, though his body was afterward returned to Goa, where it still reposes in a magnificent shrine.

Jesus: in Christianity, the Son of God. "The name *Jesus* is Greek for the Hebrew *Joshua,* a name meaning *Savior; Christ* is a Greek translation of the Hebrew *Messiah,* meaning *Anointed.*" (*The Columbia Encyclopedia,* Second Edition)

jhana (Pali): see dhyana (Sanskrit).

Jiva: Sanskrit, in Buddhism, "the empirical self, individual soul." (Murti) In Hinduism, "experience within consciousness . . . the nature of the living-being." (Daniélou) Sankaracharya of Kanchi personifies Jiva as Eve, and Atman as Adam, in his interpretation of the biblical Adam and Eve story as a degradation of a Hindu philosophical concept.

jivanmukta: in Hinduism, "one liberated from maya while living in the body." (*The Gospel of Sri Ramakrishna*)

jnana: Sanskrit, in Hinduism, the term for the transcendent knowledge through which the believer is aware of his identity with Brahman, the supreme being. Jnana-yoga (vichara), the path of knowledge, is one of the five principal yogas, or disciplines for achieving union with the absolute which is "God."

jnanasattva: Sanskrit, "jnana"—"knowledge" and "sattva"—"state of being"; hence, in Tibetan Buddhism, "ideal being . . . the 'projection' of the God (which corresponds to an essential archetype existing *ab aeterno*)" into a "regenerated being who has offered to the God all kinds of honour and worship." When jnanasattva comes to the devotee, carrying him beyond samsara, the worldly life, "he finds himself on another plane, on that of consciousness, upon which are projected the symbols of the Gods expressed in the *mandala.* This is not yet the supercosmic state, but one in which merely illuminated cognition takes possession, with its symbols, of the psyche, and substitutes itself for them. At this moment, the initiate, by the concentration of his mind, takes part, as actor, in the supreme consecration which will impose a definitive seal on his rebirth." (Tucci)

Kagyudpa (Kargyud-pa): from the Tibetan "ka"—"Buddha's teaching" + "gyu"—"transmission" + "pa"—"upholder." One of the four principal schools of Tibetan Buddhism, founded in the 11th century and sometimes called "the school of Successive Order." "The Order of

Lamas which Marpa and Milarepa founded on Earth is called Ka-gyudpa or Oral Tradition Order. It hands down, in golden succession, doctrines which perhaps represent the richest manifestations of the Tibetan spirit." (Pallis) See also the note on the two sects of Kagyudpa under Gyalwa Karmapa on pages 173–74.

Kali: also known as Durga, wife of the god Shiva. "One of the many forms of Shakti, the Divine Mother or Great Goddess of Hinduism." (Ross) In Bengal, devotees of Kali commemorate the myth of her victory over the buffalo-headed demon Mahishasur in a nine-day festival, Kalipuja (or Durgapuja), at the time of the autumnal equinox.

Kalighat: Bengali, a school of popular folk art which flourished in the 19th century, done by the patuas or bazaar artists in the market area near the great Kali temple of Calcutta who sold their work to the temple pilgrims. See W. G. Archer: *Bazaar Paintings of Calcutta, The Style of Kalighat,* London, Victoria & Albert Museum, 1953.

kalpa: Sanskrit, "in Hinduism, an eon, a vast period of time that encompasses the creation and dissolution of a universe. Each kalpa is divided in Indian reckoning into four *yugas,* or ages, of which mankind is now said to be living in the fourth, the last and darkest, the Kali yuga, at the end of which inevitable recurrent dissolution will take place. . . . the present Kali yuga is dated with startling certitude by some Indian sages as having begun as long ago as Friday, February 18, 3102 B.C." (Ross) An analagous concept of a succession of universes was carried over into Buddhism. ". . . the Buddha reduced this immense concept to singularly vivid terms. Imagine, he said, a mountain of the very hardest rock, a mountain much larger than any peak in the Himalayas, and suppose that a man, with a piece of the very finest, sheerest silk gauze from Benares comes just once every hundred years to touch that great mountain with the gauze ever so slightly. The time it would take him to wear away the entire mountain would be about the length of a kalpa." (Ross)

kama: Sanskrit, "desire, passion, physical love"; hence, Kama, the god of love in the Hindu pantheon; in his negative aspect, the god of lust —cf. Mara in Buddhism.

Kamalasila: an 8th-century Indian sage who helped to introduce the Madhyamika school of Buddhism into Tibet.

kamma (Pali): see karma (Sanskrit).

kammatthana: Pali, a "subject of meditation." Edward Conze, in his *Buddhist Meditation,* tells us that Buddhagosha, the 5th-century Indian monk who went to Ceylon to translate back into Pali the Sinhalese texts of the Buddhist canon (*Tripitaka,* the "Three Baskets"), which apparently had been lost in the decline of Buddhism in India, gives in his *Visuddhimagga* ("The Path of Purity") a standard list of forty kammatthanas suitable for meditation. They are: ten "devices": earth, water, fire, air, blue, yellow, red, white, light, and enclosed space; ten "repulsive things": a swollen corpse, a bluish corpse, a festering corpse, a fissured corpse, a gnawed corpse, a scattered corpse, a hacked and scattered corpse, a bloody corpse, a worm-eaten corpse, and a skeleton; ten "recollections": the Buddha, the dharma ("the path"), the Sangha (the order of Buddhist monks), morality, liberality, devas ("the shining ones," angels, divine beings), death, what belongs to the body, respiration, and peace; four "stations of brahma": friendliness, compassion, sympathetic joy, and evenmindedness; four "formless states": the station of endless space, the station of unlimited consciousness, the station of nothing whatsoever, and the station of neither perception nor nonperception; one "perception": the disgusting aspects of food; and one "analysis": consideration of the four elements, that is, of the body as a compound of the four primary elements (earth, water, fire, and air), which promotes the understanding of emptiness and gives insight into the absence of a self.

Kancheepuram (Conjeeveram): a town south of Madras which was the capital of the Pallava dynasty which controlled the southeast coast of India in the 7th and 8th centuries; it is famous for its great Hindu Kailasanath (Shaivite) temple, built by Rajasimhavarman about 700 A.D. It is considered by the Hindus as one of the seven sacred cities of India.

Kanchenjunga (Kinchinjanga): one of the most spectacular peaks of the Himalayas, 45 miles north of Darjeeling and 28,146 feet in elevation.

Kandy: the capital of the Central Province of Ceylon, a city of about 40,000, once the capital of an ancient kingdom of the same name. During the wars with the Portuguese and the Dutch, the city was so often burned that few ancient buildings, except for some of the temples, remained when the British took it over in 1815. For a description of Kandy's most famous monument, see the note on the "Temple of the Tooth" on page 240.

Kangyur (Kanjur) (Kagyur): (Bhah-hgyue—"Translations of the Precepts"). The Tibetan versions, translated from Sanskrit for the most part, of the basic Buddhist canonical scriptures. The collection runs to slightly more than a hundred volumes and corresponds to the Pali Canon (*Tipitaka*) and Sanskrit scriptures (*Tripitaka*—the "Three Baskets") of Theravada and Mahayana Buddhism. It is supplemented by the *Tangyur,* a collection of 225 voumes of commentaries on the Tantras and the Sutras by Indian and Tibetan scholars. See Morgan: *The Path of the Buddha,* pages 268–72; Conze: *Buddhism: Its Essence and Development,* page 32; and Humphreys: *Buddhism,* pages 202–3 for detailed lists of the contents of the two collections.

Kapaleeswara: the Hindu Shaivite temple in the Mylapore district of Madras. Daniélou states that the *Shiva Purana* gives over a thousand different names for Shiva, most of them descriptive epithets, though some may be descended from the names of the deities of various pre-Aryan peoples. One may speculate that "Kapala" in the name of this temple comes from the epithet Kapala-malin—"Wearing-a-garland-of-skulls."

karma (Sanskrit) kamma (Pali): one of the central doctrines of Hinduism which was carried over into Buddhism. "Literally 'action'; the law of cause and effect, sometimes interpreted personally as punishment or reward for deeds performed in former lives." (Ross) "While the individual and the social sides of karma are inseparably intertwined, the theory of *varna* or caste emphasizes the social aspect, and that of *ashrama* or stages of life the individual aspect." (S. Radhakrishnan: *The Hindu View of Life,* page 59) See under ashram for the "stages of life." In Hinduism, karma has also the meaning of ritualistic worship. See Humphreys: *Buddhism,* pages 100–3; Renou: *The Nature of Hinduism,* pages 64–66.

karuna: "the Mahayana Buddhist term for compassion; a trait of bodhisattvas." (Ross) Among the mythic bodhisattvas, Samantabhadra is the classic exemplar of karuna, "representing the love aspect of the Buddha-principle." (Humphreys) "He has vowed to serve all sentient beings by guiding them to a happy life which is attained by the profound intention to be free from all attachment and resistance to things. In him, action is identical with his vow." (Morgan) In Theravada Buddhism, karuna is the second of the four Brahma viharas, or sublime states of consciousness. (See Humphreys: *Buddhism,* pages, 125–26.)

Kashmir: one of the most beautiful regions of India, famous for its lakes and views of the mountains of the Himalayas and Karakorams, Kashmir is a high oblong valley, about 85 miles long and 20–25 miles wide, situated north of India and east of West Pakistan. Formerly an independent principality, ruled by a Hindu maharaja, although the majority of its 4,000,000 inhabitants are Moslems, it is claimed, and partially dominated, both by India and Pakistan, while the Chinese Communists occupied a small part of Kashmir, Ladakh, in 1959.

Kasyapaparivarta: an ancient Sanskrit text of Madhyamika Buddhism. (Kasyapa—a Buddha of the past; "parivarta"—"revolving.") A part of the *Ratnakuta Sutra.* (Ratnakuta—a bodhisattva.)

Kham: a district in eastern Tibet, on the Chinese border, inhabited by the fierce and valorous Khambas who put up a strong though finally futile resistance to the Chinese Communist take-over of Tibet. In his *Peaks and Lamas,* Marco Pallis wrote that "Kham seems from all accounts to be a romantic country of seers and brigands, artists and armourers, hermits and Homeric heroes. The Khambas are the most warlike as well as the handsomest of the Tibetan races and are noted for their raiding propensities, their victims being usually the caravans of wealthy merchants trading between China and Lhasa." The Khambas are Buddhists, and the seat of their government was the large monastery of Chiamdo.

khandha (Pali): see skandha (Sanskrit).

khanika samadhi: Pali, one of the three kinds of samadhi ("by name and nature calmness"), along with upacara samadhi and ap(p)ana samadhi, which Nanasampanno singles out for discussion in "Wisdom Develops Samadhi." (in *Visakha Puja,* May 1967, Buddhist Association of Thailand, Bangkok, pages 74–85) ". . . [it is the kind] in which the heart becomes unwaveringly fixed and calm for a short time, after which it withdraws." Bhikkhu Pannavaddho, who translated the work from the Thai original, glosses the term khanika as "momentary, changeable."

kirtan: "praise," religious singing, often done in processions, and particularly among the Hindu Vaishnavite sects. (Chakravarty) Cf. sankirtana.

klesa: Sanskrit, literally, "pain, affliction, distress, anguish." In Buddhism, "defiling forces, passion" (Murti); "karmic defilement, any of the hindrances to Enlightenment caused by desire, passion and delusion." (Blofeld)

koan: "a term used in Zen Buddhism describing a problem which cannot be solved by the intellect alone." (Ross) See Ross: *Three Ways of Asian Wisdom,* pages 177ff.; Humphreys: *Buddhism,* pages 183–84; Miura and Sasaki: *The Zen Koan,* New York, Harcourt Brace Jovanovich, paperback edition, 1965.

Koran: Arabic, "Qur'an" from "qara'a"—"to read." "The scriptures of the Mohammedans [Moslems] containing the professed revelations to Mohammed. By Mohammed the name *Koran* was given to a single revelation or to a collection of revelations, but after his death, when his various utterances had been collected in writing, this name was applied to the whole book. The *Koran* is in Arabic, is divided into 114 suras, or chapters, and is the basis for the religious, social, civil, commercial, military, and legal regulation of the Mohammedan world." (Webster's II)

Krishna: one of the most important gods in the Hindu pantheon, the eighth avatar (earthly incarnation) of the god Vishnu. He figures prominently in innumerable episodes in Hindu mythology, and in the *Bhagavad-Gita* it is he who discourses with Arjuna, the hero of the *Mahabharata,* for whom he acts as charioteer and counselor. Legend has it that he was brought up near Vrindaban as a cowherd and later fell in love with Radha, most beautiful of the gopis (cowherd girls), a subject which is much celebrated in Indian art and poetry. He is worshiped particularly at the Holi festival in March, when his devotees spray his images—and themselves—with colored water and powders. His images are to be found in many Shaivite and Vaishnavite temples; he is usually shown standing on the coiled body of the serpent Kaliya, whom he slew, and playing a flute, which symbolizes "the call of the infinite . . . leave all and follow me." See Morgan: *The Religion of the Hindus,* pages 58ff., also the passages devoted to Krishna in Ross, Renou, and Monier-Williams, as well as

Dimock and Levertov: *In Praise of Krishna,* a collection of translations of Bengali Vaishnavite songs and love poems commemorating the amours of Krishna with Radha and the other gopis.

Kriyatantras: one of the four groups of esoteric scriptures in Mahayana Buddhism known as the *Tantras.* See page 80 for Giuseppe Tucci's explanation of the ritual function of the *Kriyatantras.*

Kumari puja: Sanskrit, literally "the worship of a virgin." "A ritualistic worship prescribed by the Tantra [in Hinduism] in which a virgin is worshipped as the manifestation of the Divine Mother of the Universe." *(The Gospel of Sri Ramakrishna)*

Ladakh Buddhi Vihara: Ladakh: the eastern parts of the former Indian principalities, now states, of Jammu and Kashmir. Buddhi: "Sanskrit, literally, understanding, from *bodhati,* he awakes, understands . . . the faculty of intuitive discernment or direct spiritual awareness in the beliefs of Hinduism and Buddhism." (Webster's III) Vihara: "Sanskrit, from *viharati,* he spends time, he walks about for pleasure . . . in ancient India, a pleasure garden, especially the precincts and grounds of temples and monasteries devoted to the Buddhist and Jain religions; hence, a monastery; in modern Ceylonese usage, a Buddhist temple." (Webster's II & III)

lakh: in Hindi, the word for 100,000 (from the Sanskrit "laksa"—'mark, sign").

Lakshmi: in the Hindu pantheon, the wife of Vishnu, and in her own right, goddess of beauty and wealth; mother of Kama, the god of love. Also ". . . the luck or fortune personified of a king or kingdom . . ." (Webster's II)

lama: "a title applied in the Tibetan world to any spiritual figure of unusual eminence, notable to those dynasties of abbots (such as the Dalai Lama) through which a recognized spiritual influence has perpetuated itself by successive 'incarnations.' The same word can be applied to any teacher dispensing esoteric instruction under the seal of initiation; thus used, 'lama' becomes the equivalent of the Indian word 'guru.' Literally, 'lama' means 'exalted.' A lama need not be a monk, though many are so. Some of the most revered lamas are best described as 'consecrated laymen'; the word itself indicates a spiritual qualification, not a social function." (Pallis)

Lamaism: "a loose term coined by foreigners to describe that branch of Mahayana Buddhism found in Tibet, Mongolia, and the cis-Himalayan principalities; Tibetans never use the term, however. The original foundation out of which Tibetan Buddhism developed dates from the 7th century, when the Indian teacher Padmasambhava was invited by the reigning king of Tibet to come and preach the dharma." (Pallis)

Lankavatara Sutra: (Saddharma-lankavatara) Sanskrit, "the entrance of the good doctrine into Lanka." One of the "Nine Dharmas" and most influential early scriptures of the Yogacara sect of Mahayana Buddhism; it is also revered in Zen Buddhism. Authorship and date unknown, but it already existed as a composite work when it was translated into Chinese about 430 A.D. "Lanka" refers to the name given to what is now Ceylon in the *Ramayana*, but more specifically to the ten-headed rakshasa (man-eating demon) Ravana. In the sutra, the Buddha discourses with Ravana and convinces him of two basic principles of the doctrine of subjective idealism: "that everything external is due to a wrong interpretation of inner experience, and . . . that the apprehension of reality is reached by a sudden revulsion in which the truth bursts upon the yogi (by which is meant the bodhisattva) in his contemplation." (E.J. Thomas: *The History of Buddhist Thought*, pages 230 ff.)

Lauds: the religious service which is usually performed at dawn in most Roman Catholic monastic communities.

lila: Sanskrit, "play, sport, diversion, amusement, pastime"; hence, in Hinduism, the concepts "of all nature seen as *lila*, the creative activity of the Divine in playful or sportive mood." (Ross) "The free, sportive, playful will of God." (Morgan)

lingam: "Sanskrit *linga* . . . literally, mark, characteristic . . . a stylized phallic symbol often depicted in conjunction with the yoni, connoting, maleness, vitality, and creative power, and being an emblem of the Indian god Shiva. . . ." Yoni: "Sanskrit, vulva: a figure representing the female genitals serving as the formal symbol under which Shakti is worshiped. . . ." (Webster's III) See Morgan: *The Religion of the Hindus*, pages 64–65.

lokavidu: Sanskrit, "loka"—"world" or "heavenly abode"; "vid"—"to know." Merton found the term in Ven. Nanasampanno's "Wisdom Develops Samadhi," where it is glossed by the translator of the work (from the Thai), Bhikkhu Pannavaddho, as: "one who knows the worlds. In other words someone who has investigated and seen all the realms of existence. The Buddha was sometimes referred to as Lokavidu," but it may have come originally from the *Maitrayani Samhita*, one of the early collections devoted to the canons of Hindu Vaishnavism. (Monier-Williams: *Sanskrit-English Dictionary*) Cf. the concept of the "Six Lokas" in Tibetan Buddhism, which relates to "bardo," the translation of the soul after death. See Evans-Wentz: *The Tibetan Book of the Dead*, pages lxxvii–viii.

lucernarium: Latin, "the time when the lamps are lighted." (Lewis and Short: *A Latin Dictionary*)

Madhava: Sanskrit and Bengali, the third icon, as "Lord of Knowledge," of the Hindu god Vishnu. (Daniélou, *Hindu Polytheism*, page 154) See also Daniélou's discussion (pages 316–19) of the Hindu Seers (". . . although represented as human sages, they are considered eternal powers who appear every time a new revelation is needed . . .") There was also a Madhava who was one of the seven seers of the fourteenth manvantara (cycle of creation). Later, in Bengali Vaishnavite lyrics, Madhava is an epithet for the Hindu God Krishna, himself an avatar of Vishnu.

Madhyamika: the "Middle Path" school of Buddhism, based largely in the teachings of Nagarjuna, who probably lived in the 2nd or 3rd centuries A.D. Its doctrine drew heavily on the *Prajnaparamita Sutras,* and it was the forerunner of the more extensive Mahayana school of Buddhism. The definitive scholarly work on Madhyamika, which Merton studied closely during his Asian journey, is T.R.V. Murti: *The Central Philosophy of Buddhism, A Study of the Madhyamika System,* London, Allen & Unwin, 1955. See also Heinrich Zimmer: *The Philosophies of India,* New York, Meridian Books, 1964, pages 509–10, 521–24.

Madhyamika Karika Vritti: a religious text of the Madhyamika school of Buddhism by Candrakirti, who lived in the early part of the 7th century A.D.

Mahabharata: one of the two great Sanskrit epics of India. See note on page 44.

mahakaruna: "the great compassion of the Buddha." (Chakravarty)

Mahayana: "Sanskrit . . . from *mahat* great + *yana* vehicle . . . A branch of Buddhism made up of various syncretistic sects that are found chiefly in Tibet, Nepal, China, and Japan, have vernacular scriptures based on a Sanskrit canon, believe in a god or gods, and usually teach the bodhisattva ideal of compassion and universal salvation—called also *Great Vehicle.* . . ." (Webster's III) "The later, theistic form of Buddhism, developed in northern India from the 2nd century A.D. . . ." (Webster's II) Mahayana also survives, in various modified forms, in Mongolia and Korea; essentially, it is the "Northern School" of Buddhism, as against Hinayana (the "Lesser Vehicle," also known as Theravada), the "Southern School," which is followed today in Burma, Ceylon, and Thailand.

Mahayanasutralankara: an important text of the Abhidarma ("consciousness only") school of Buddhist Mahayana philosophy, written by Asanga, who lived in the 4th century A.D.

Mahinda (Pali), Thera Mahendra (Sanskrit): either the son or the younger brother of the Indian emperor Ashoka, who brought Buddhism to Ceylon in the 3rd century, B.C.

maithuna: Sanskrit, "sexual union."

Maitreya: Sanskrit, from "maitri"—"benevolence"; Pali: Metteya, from "metta"—"lovingkindness." "The Buddha of the Future." (Ross) In Tantric Buddhism, the "human Buddha" form of Amoghasiddi, one of the five Dhyani Buddhas. (See S.B. Dasgupta: *An Introduction to Tantric Buddhism,* pages 84ff.) Also Maitreya(natha) (280–360 A.D., according to Murti; 420–500 A.D., according to Thomas) one of the founders of the Yogacara school.

Majjhima Nikaya (Pali), *Madhyamagama* (Sanskrit): the second section of the *Sutta Pitaka,* the second of the three "Triple Baskets," *Tipi-taka* (Pali), *Tripitaka* (Sanskrit), one of the principal texts in the Pali Canon of Buddhism which recorded, first through oral tradition and then written by later Buddhist sages, the discourses of the Buddha with his disciples. See Morgan: *The Path of the Buddha,* pages 68ff.; Thomas: *The History of Buddhist Thought,* pages 265ff.

manas: Sanskrit, "mind." In Hinduism, one of the "Four Inner Organs" of perception: manas (mind), buddhi (discernment, the discriminating faculty), chitta (mind-stuff, pure consciousness), and ahamkara (I-consciousness). "The mind . . . regarded as an internal organ of perception, volition, and action." (Monier-Williams)

mandala: Sanskrit, in both Buddhism and Hinduism, "a diagrammatic picture used as an aid in meditation or ritual; sometimes a symbol of the universe, or a representation of a deed of merit." (Ross) "Mystic symbols made on the ground usually with powders of five different colors: worshiped by the initiated as representing any of the deities." (Morgan: *The Religion of the Hindus*) In Buddhism, particularly in Tibetan Buddhism where the use of the mandala is most frequent, the symbolic design usually represents the cosmic nature of the principal Buddhas who have existed, the list perhaps varying from sect to sect, but who stand for the five jinas or wisdom-energy-aspects of the Buddha principle. Thus in Tantric Buddhism ("The Diamond Vehicle"), the Buddhas most often represented in tanka paintings of the mandala are Vairocana ("The Brilliant One"), Akshobya ("The Unshakable"), Ratnasambhava ("The Matrix of the Jewel"), Ami-tabha (Amida in Japanese "Pure Land" Buddhism, "The Infinite Light"), and Amoghasiddhi ("The Infallible Realization"). In Tantrism, there are special liturgies for the initiation of devotees into the use of the mandala for worship, and the elements of the mandala are believed to be reproduced in the parts of the human body. One of the definitive works on the mandala, which Merton studied closely, is Giuseppe Tucci's *The Theory and Practice of the Mandala,* but see also John Blofeld: *The Tantric Mysticism of Tibet* and J. & M. Arugelles: *Mandala.*

mandapa(m): Sanskrit, a cave temple dedicated to a Hindu god.

Manjusri: "the bodhisattva of Meditation whose image—as personification of Supreme Wisdom—is usually seen in Zen meditation halls." (Ross) But veneration of Manjusri is common to other Mahayana sects of Buddhism as well.

mantra: "a Sanskrit term used in Hinduism signifying a sacred word, verse or syllable which embodies in sound some specific deity or super-natural power." (Ross) "A sound symbol which, when repeated and reflected on, frees the soul from bondage." *(Cultural Heritage of India)* In Buddhism, the comparable term is dharani.

Mara: Sanskrit, the spirit or personification of evil, enemy of the Buddha, who tried to tempt him from the path of enlightenment by promising to make him a universal king, and to drive him from his seat of meditation under the bodhi tree, claiming that the place was his. Cf., in Hinduism, the negative aspects of Kama, as god of lust. For a detailed discussion of the origin and extensions of the Mara myth in the various Buddhist scriptures, including the Jataka stories of the Buddha's previous existences, see Thomas: *The History of Buddhist Thought,* pages 145ff.

Marathi: the language of the Maharastra region of west-central India.

Marpa: often called "the translator." Marpa (1012–96), the pupil of the sage Naropa, and in turn the master of the poet-sage Milarepa, was one of the chief founders of the Kagyudpa school of Tibetan Buddhism. See Morgan: *The Path of the Buddha,* pages 244ff; Blofeld: *The Tantric Mysticism of Tibet,* page 128.

math: "Hindi *math,* from Sanskrit *matha,* literally, hut: a Hindu monastery." (Webster's III)

Mathura: now Muttra, on the banks of the river Jumna in north-central India; in Hindu mythology, the city whose inhabitants the god Krishna protected by slaying the serpent Kaliya, and to which he went after his stay among the gopis at Vrindaban. Now the site of a beautiful temple, a place of pilgrimage for devotees of Krishna

maund: "Hindi *man,* from Sanskrit *mana:* any of various Indian units of weight; especially: a unit equal to 82.28 pounds." (Webster's III)

maya: "Sanskrit *maya.* 1. an extra-physical wonder-working power in the Vedas; 2a. the illusion-creating power of a god or demon; b: the powerful force that creates the cosmic illusion that the phenomenal world is real. . . ." (Webster's III) In Hinduism, "magic; nature as opposed to pure being; the power by which the phenomenal world is manifested or created; also, magic as the means by which a magician produces his effects. b: the power of manifestation inherent in the deity, personified as the supreme goddess, Devi, or any of her forms. c: Maya, the mother of the Buddha." (Webster's II) "Sankaracharya's 'primal cause'; in part reality, in part illusion." (Chakravarty)

mela: Hindi, from Sanskrit, melaka, mela: a meeting or assembly: a religious festival or fair, sometimes attended by hundreds of thousands of Hindu pilgrims at such sacred places as Hardwar, Allahabad, Ujjain, Nasik, and others. (from Webster's III & Morgan)

"Middle Path," "Middle Way": "Buddhism's description of the path lying between all extremes as, for instance, asceticism and self-indulgence; advocated by the Buddha as the proper path for many to follow." (Ross) More specifically, the "Middle Path" of the Madhyamika school of Buddhism as it descended from Nagarjuna's sunyata, "the Silence of the Middle Way." (Murti)

Milarepa: (1040–1123) also called Jetsun ("the holy"), Milarepa was Tibet's greatest poet, considered a saint, and one of the founders of the Kagyudpa sect of Tibetan Buddhism. See W.Y. Evans-Wentz, editor: *Tibet's Great Yogi Milarepa,* being the *Jetsun-Kahbum* ["kahbum"—

"100,000 words"], translated from the Tibetan by Lama Kazi Dawa-Samdup, Oxford University Press, 1928, now available as a Galaxy paperbook; *The Hundred Thousand Songs of Milarepa,* translated and annotated by Garma C.C. Chang, New York, Harper & Row, 1962, available as a Colophon paperback.

Mizos: tribesmen of northeast India in the region near Assam.

Mogul (or Mughal): "Moslem empire of India, 1526–1857. The name Mogul, a variant of Mongol, stems from the claim of descent from Jenghiz Khan made by Baber, who founded the Mogul empire with the capture of Delhi [in 1526]. Not until near the end of the reign of Akbar was the empire, then occupying the vast territory from Afghanistan south of the Godavari river, free from divisive wars. Shah Jehan and Aurangzeb brought the Mogul territory to its greatest extent, but even at its zenith the empire suffered the blows of the Sikhs and the Marathas who later had brought it to near ruin by the late 18th century. When Great Britain occupied Delhi in 1803 the empire actually came to an end, but the British maintained puppet emperors until 1857. . . ." (*The Columbia Encyclopedia,* Second Edition)

monsoons: the rainy seasons in India, which vary in different parts of the country, brought on by periods of strong, prevailing wind, coming usually from the southwest.

Moslem (or Muslim): a believer in Islam, the religion and social system established by the Arabian prophet Mohammed (570?–632 A.D.)

mudra: from Sanskrit "seal" or "token"; "a mystic or symbolic gesture of the hand and fingers." (Ross) Mudras are used in the iconography of art works, in religious rituals, in some forms of yoga, and in various Indian dance forms, particularly Bharata Natyam. In all Buddha rupas (images) the hands are done in one of the formalized mudra positions.

mukti: (Sanskrit) mutti (Pali): spiritual freedom; liberation from the captivity of worldly things, which is the goal of religious activity both in Buddhism and Hinduism. Cf. nirvana.

Muzak: trade name for the product of an American company which for some forty years has been providing, by means of direct wire electric transmission "functional background music in factories, offices, and public areas." The Musak Company is now a subsidiary of Teleprompter, Inc., a worldwide organization.

"My Param Dham (Brahmlok)": from a religious cult poster which Merton saw in Calcutta; probably Bengali spellings from Sanskrit roots: "paramdam"—"supreme abode"; brahmlok: from Brahma (the creator god) and "loka"—"heavenly abode."

Nagarjuna: an Indian sage of the 2nd or 3rd century A.D. who was one of the principal founders of the Madhyamika school of Buddhism.

nama dhamma: Pali, "Nama Dhamma includes Vedana, Sanna, Sankhara, and Vinnana, these four being the second group of the five Khandas [Sanskrit, Skandhas] but they are more subtle than the Rupa Khanda which is the body. One cannot look into them with one's eyes, but one can come to know them by way of the heart." (Venerable Acariya Maha Boowa Nanasampanno: "Wisdom Develops Samadhi") See page 267 for the text from which Merton drew the list of terms on page 24 of the holograph notebook, which more fully elucidates the above terms.

namaste: the traditional form of greeting in India (in lieu of shaking hands) by joining one's palms together.

Jawaharlal Nehru: (1889–1964) Prime Minister of India from 1947 to 1964.

nembutsu: in Zen Buddhism, the repetition, as a form of prayer, of the name of the Buddha Amitabha. (Watts: *The Way of Zen*) Also, in the "Pure Land" (Jodo) school of Buddhism in Japan, invocation of the formula "Namu Amida Butsu" ("Hail to Amitabha Buddha") is a constant means of grace. (Pallis: "Is There Room for 'Grace' in Buddhism?") Cf. dhikr in Sufism, and, in Vaishnavite Hinduism, the constant repetition of the name of a god, such as Rama, for the cultivation of bhakti; japa in Hindu Shaivism, and similar practices in Guru Nanak's original formulation of Sikhism.

Nepal: the small independent kingdom, with a population of about 7,000,000, lying between northern India and Tibet. In religion, about half the people are Mongoloid Buddhists, and the other half Hindus. The population is divided into many tribes which speak various Tibeto-Burman dialects, most important of which, politically, are the Gurkhas. Nepal first had treaty relations with Great Britain in 1792, and after a border war in 1814–16 came under British protection, though retaining an independent monarchy. A similar relationship now exists between Nepal and India. Nepal supplied many Gurkha troops for the British Indian army in both world wars. Except for the well-populated Valley of Nepal in the eastern part of the country, Nepal is largely mountainous and includes Mount Everest, the world's highest mountain, 29,141 feet, and many other Himalayan peaks. The capital city is Katmandu.

Nikaya: Pali, "collection." In the Pali Canon of Buddhist scriptures, the *Tipitaka*, or "Three Baskets," the Second Basket, known as the *Sutta Pitaka* ("Basket of Discourses"), is made up of five Nikayas of discourses which the Buddha gave at various times. For a description of these collections, see Morgan: *The Path of the Buddha,* pages 69–70.

nirvana (Sanskrit), nibbana (Pali): "the attainment of final enlightenment; freedom from rebirth." (Ross) "The ultimate stage of realization according to the teachings of the Buddha." (Chakravarty) The general concept is common both to Buddhism and Hinduism, but in Hinduism it is more likely to be called moksha or mukti (deliverance). In

The Gospel of Sri Ramakrishna, the 19th-century Hindu teacher and saint, it is defined as: "final absorption in Brahman, or the All-pervading reality, by the annihilation of the individual ego."

nivritti: Sanskrit, "the negation or control of passion, as opposed to pravritti (passion)." (Chakravarty) In Tantric Buddhism, as in Hindu Tantrism, the terms have somewhat more basically metaphysical connotations; thus, "matter as the ultimate substance has two modes which are called pravritti and nivritti, action and rest, dynamic and static, concrete and abstract," and the terms may be related, respectively, to prajna an upaya, and, in Hindu Tantrism, to the union of Shiva and Shakti. (S.B. Dasgupta: *An Introduction to Tantric Buddhism,* pages 97ff.)

Nizamuddin: a 14th-century Sufi poet and saint whose tomb is in Delhi.

Nyingmapa: one of the four major, and oldest, sects of Buddhism in Tibet, colloquially known as the "Red Hat" lamas. It is sometimes called the "Old Translation" school, as it traces its origins back to the "Great Guru," Padma Sambhava, who came to Tibet about 747 A D., translated many works of Tantrism into Tibetan, and founded the first Buddhist monastery in Tibet at Samye. Not all Nyingmapa lamas take monastic vows; they wear a special habit, but are permitted to marry and need not reside in monasteries. See the chapter "Buddhism in Tibet" by Lobsang Phunstock Lhalungpa in Morgan: *The Path of the Buddha.*

Octave of All Saints: in the Roman Catholic Church, the special liturgy for the eighth day after the Feast of All Saints, which was observed on November 1.

om (aum): Sanskrit, first in Hinduism and then carried over into Buddhism and Sikhism, a sacred syllable for chanting, in invocation or meditation, dating back to the *Vedas.* "Originally a syllable denoting assent; later a mantra representing the triple constitution of the cosmos. The three component parts (a + u + m) of the sound are the Absolute, the Relative, and the relation between them." (Webster's II) In Hinduism, it stands for both the personal and impersonal god.

om mani padme hum: the extended form of the mantra om most used by Tibetan Buddhists. "The literal translation of the formula is '*Om, the jewel in the lotus, Hum!*' In a general way it may be described as an act of assent to the divine aim. *Om* (derived from the Sanskrit *aum*) stands for Brahma, 'the one without second' or 'the inexpressible Absolute.' As one writer has put it, '*Om* is the ultimate word that can be uttered, after which there remains nothing but silence.' In it, therefore, are summed up prayer and praise and worship. *Om* is also the sound of all sounds, audible to the initiated ear, which is produced by the act of Manifestation or, as we would say, of Creation, which produces and nourishes this and other Universes. It might also be compared with Pythagoras' music of the Spheres. *Mani* means 'jewel';

therefore a precious thing, the Doctrine. *Padme* means 'in the Lotus'; it may refer to the world which enshrines the doctrine of Buddha (the jewel), or to the spirit in whose depths he who knows how to take soundings will discover Knowledge, Reality, and Liberation, these three really being one and the same thing under different names. Or possibly the lotus, the usual throne of divinities and saints, is simply attached as a divine attribute to the gem of doctrine. *Hum* is an ejaculation denoting defiance. Its utterer hurls a challenge, as it were, at the enemy, at the passions such as lust, hatred and stupidity, the poisons that drug beings into submitting to the tyranny of the Round of Existence. Or, viewed in yet another way, the adversary is no other than the cherished belief in an indissoluble 'myself,' and the desire for individual recompense." (Pallis: *Peaks and Lamas,* page 162.)

Ovid: Publius Ovidius Naso, the Roman poet (43 B.C.–17 A.D.), author of the *Amores, Heroides, Metamorphoses,* and other works.

Padma Sambhava: the "Great Guru," who came from India to Tibet about 747 A.D., translated many works of Tantrism into Tibetan, established the first Buddhist monastery in Tibet at Samye, and is considered the principal founder of Nyingmapa, one of the four major schools of Tibetan Buddhism.

Pali: the language, now "dead," in which many of the earliest scriptures of Buddhism were recorded in writing; a member of the Indic group of the Indo-Iranian subfamily of Indo-European languages. It probably descended from Vedic Aryan, but some early commentators refer to it as the language of the Maghada kingdom region of India. "Sanskrit, *pali* row, line, series of Buddhist texts : an Indic language found in the Buddhist canon and used today as the liturgical and scholarly language of Hinayana Buddhism." (Webster's III) For a discussion of its origins and the relationships among the various languages in which Buddhist scriptures exist, see Thomas: *The History of Buddhist Thought,* pages 261ff.

palingenesis: "Greek *palin* again + Latin *genesis* birth . . . renewal by or as if by rebirth as *a* : Christian baptism *b:* the doctrine of continued rebirths. . . ." (Webster's III)

Pancakrama: a text of Tantric Buddhism, dealing chiefly with the concept of sunyata (the void, or emptiness), written in the 7th century A.D. by Nagarjuna-pada, who should not be confused with Nagarjuna, one of the founders of the Madhyamika philosophy, who lived in the 2nd or 3rd century A.D. See S. B. Dasgupta: *An Introduction to Tantric Buddhism,* pages 43ff.

panna (Pali): see prajna (Sanskrit)

papakamma: Pali, "evil action." (Khantipalo)

paramatman: Sanskrit, in Hinduism, and particularly in Vedanta, "the Supreme Soul," as contrasted with jivatman, "the personal individual soul of living beings." Paramatman is also sometimes called brahman or purusha. (Monier-Williams)

Parvati (Bhavani): in Hindu religion and mythology, one of the wives of the god Shiva; she was a daughter of the god who personifies the Himalayas, and also considered an embodiment of the Divine Mother Goddess, Kali (Durga), or, more abstractly, Shakti, the female creative power.

Pascha Christi: Latin. In Christianity, the Easter season: but coming originally, by way of Greek, from the Hebrew "pasah"—"to pass over." Passover: ". . . from the phrase *pass over;* from the exemption of the Israelites from the slaughter of the first-born in Egypt, Exodus 12:23–27 . . . an annual religious and spring agricultural festival of the Jews that commemorates the liberation of the Hebrews from slavery in Egypt. . . ." (Webster's III) In Christian scripture and commentary, Christ is sometimes called the "Paschal Lamb," who is sacrificed for man's redemption.

Pelagian: relating to the theories of Pelagius, a heretical British monk who died *circa* 428 A.D. "His distinctive teachings . . . are: (1) There is no such thing as original sin; consequently, (2) there is no baptismal regeneration. . . . (3) Man has perfect freedom of the will and has no absolute need of God's grace to set him right. (4) Man, though aided in various ways by divine grace, is virtually the author of his own salvation." (Webster's II)

Perak: one of the small independent states, each ruled by a sultan, on the Malay peninsula; formerly British protectorates but now part of the Federation of Malaysia.

Periyalvar: a 9th-century South Indian Tamil poet who wrote two collections of Vaishnavite hymns called the *Tiruppallandu* and the *Tirumoli.*

pho-va: a term in Tibetan Yoga denoting the "transference of the consciousness." (Evans-Wentz: *Tibetan Yoga,* page 172n.)

Phra Pathom Chedi: one of the most important of the Buddhist temples in Thailand, at Nakorn Pathom, about 50 miles west of Bangkok. It is said to be the largest pagoda in Southeast Asia. Legend has it that it was first built in the 5th century to mark the spot where missionaries sent by the Indian emperor Ashoka first preached Buddhism in Siam, but it was restored in its present large bell-shaped form by King Rama IV Mongkut, who ruled from 1851 to 1868. The word "phra" is now often used as an honorific, preceding the name of a learned, or particularly saintly, Buddhist monk, roughly equivalent to the more common "bhikkhu." Chedi: temple or pagoda.

pice: Hindi, paisa; a small Indian coin, equal to the old ¼ anna of the British regime; since India went on the decimal system there are now 100 pice to a rupee. The rupee now exchanges at about 12½ U.S. cents.

Pokhara: a small city and valley in Nepal, about 100 miles west of Katmandu.

Poya day: in Ceylon, the weekly holiday, related to the quarter phases of the moon, which has replaced Sunday as the day of rest in the time of British rule.

prabhakar: the third stage in the Buddhist progress to bodhisattvahood.

prajna: Sanskrit; Pali, panna: in Buddhism, supreme knowledge or wisdom; spiritual awakening; wisdom which brings liberation.

Prajnaparamita Sutras: Sanskrit, in Buddhism, one of the most important early texts of the Mahayana and Madhyamika philosophies; a collection of many sutras, often called "The Perfection of Wisdom." The core of the sutras, which describes the emptiness of all form, is called the *Prajnaparamita Hridaya,* and is recited daily in thousands 'of monasteries in Asia. As a concept, prajnaparamita is "the Highest Reality identified with the Buddha" (Murti) and the "perfect wisdom that destroys all illusions and brings one to the world of the Awakening." (Morgan)

prajna-sunyata. Merton's own combination of terms: "prajna"—"liberating wisdom"; "sunyata"—"the void, emptiness."

prajna-upaya: Pallis's combination of terms in his essay "Considerations on Tantric Spirituality": "prajna"—"wisdom"; "upaya"—"process, method or means." "The method of arriving at supreme knowledge in Buddhism." (Chakravarty)

Prakrit: from Sanskrit, "prakrita"—"original, usual, vulgar." "The Aryan (Indo-Iranian) vernacular dialects of India as distinguished from Sanskrit. . . . Three stages of Prakrit are: the *Primary,* including Pali and other vernaculars developed from Vedic Aryan as early as 250 B.C.; the *Secondary,* or medieval Aryan vernaculars of India; the *Tertiary,* or modern vernaculars, developed from the latter, approximately since the 10th century." (Webster's II) A great part of the literature of Jainism is written in Prakrit. See *The Columbia Encyclopedia* for a good brief sketch of which other religious texts were written in Prakrit.

prakriti: Sanskrit, in Buddhism, particularly in the Sankhya system, "the primordial ground of phenomena." (Murti) "The ultimate material cause of the universe; unconscious primal matter; ultimate cosmic energy." (Morgan) "World substance . . . passive objectivity." (S.B. Dasgupta) The term is also basic in Hinduism: "Indian cosmology usually postulates, as the starting point of creation, *prakriti,* or primitive matter . . . a material continuum filling all space and bearing in itself the three factors called *gunas* ('qualities' or 'substances') *sattva,* the good, luminous principle, *rajas,* the impure principle, mingled with affectivity, and *tamas,* the principle of darkness; the phenomenal world, both physical and psychological, being built up of different combinations of these factors. From this mixture are born the five original elements (ether, air, fire, water, earth) constituting what is known as 'the egg of Brahman,' namely the universe." (Renou: *The Nature of Hinduism,* pages 58–59) In Hinduism, prakriti also has the connotation of nature or matter conceived as feminine, and, personified as an abstract deity, is equivalent to Shakti (Maya, Devi), the supreme goddess.

pramudita: the first stage, that of "delight or joy," in the Buddhist progress toward bodhisattvahood.

Prasangika: with Svatantrika, one of the two main subsects of Madhyamika Buddhism in its second main phase of development. Buddhapalita (*circa* 5th century A.D) was the principal formulator of Prasangika teachings. See Murti, pages 87ff.

pratibha: Sanskrit, "poetic sensibility, intuition, inventiveness, genius. The ability to create novel works. *Pratibha* is a form of direct perception. It has been divided into creative (*karayitri*) and receptive (*bhavayatri*)." (Mohan: *The Response to Poetry,* page 161)

prema: Sanskrit, in Tibetan Buddhism, "the spiritual sublimation of love." (Tucci) In Hinduism, "ecstatic love, divine love of the most intense kind." *(The Gospel of Sri Ramakrishna)* Also sometimes called priti.

Prex Eucharistica IV: one of the four versions of the principal part of the Roman Catholic Mass. See Eucharist. Prex: Latin, "prayer."

priti: see prema, above.

pudgala-nairatmya: pudgala (Sanskrit), puggala (Pali): in Buddhism, "the empirical individual, ego." Nairatmya: Sanskrit, "soullessness, substancelessness, unreality." (Murti)

pudgalatman: Sanskrit, in Buddhism, particularly in the Vatsiputriya and Sammitiya sects, a concept that pudgala (the individual self) is "a quasi-permanent entity, neither completely identical with the mental states, nor totally different from them." (Murti)

puja: ". . . Sanskrit *puja,* probably of Dravidian origin; akin to Tamil *pucu* to anoint, besmear. . . ." (Webster's III) In Hinduism, ". . . *a* Worship, office or devotional service of a deity in the presence of his or her icon. *b* Hence, loosely, a religious festival: as, the Durga *puja.*" (Webster's II). The term did not carry over into Buddhism, though Humphreys does gloss it as "a gesture of worship or respect, usually that of raising the hands, palms together, the height of the hands indicating the degree of reverence. Cf. namaste.

purusha: Sanskrit, in both Buddhism and Hinduism, the term stands for consciousness, as opposed to prakriti, matter. In Sanskrit, "purusa" literally means "man," and in Hindu philosophy the term also refers to the male or static principle in the godhead. In Buddhism, particularly in the Sankhya system, "the separate existence of the soul as a transcendental entity." (Murti) "The universe evolves from the union of Prakriti and Purusha." *(The Gospel of Sri Ramakrishna)* "Divine original being." (Von Glasenapp: *Buddhism*)

Purushottama: Sanskrit, "supreme being." In Hinduism, the seventeenth of the twenty-four icons of the god Vishnu, "Best of Men." (Daniélou)

Qutb Minar: the red sandstone "Tower of Victory," 238 feet high, built by the Moslem conquerors of Delhi in the early years of the 13th century.

ra'fah: Arabic, "meekness."

rahbaniya: Arabic, "monasticism."

rahmah: Arabic, "compassion."

Raj: Hindi, "reign, rule." Thus the British imperial rule in India was commonly called the "(British) Raj," and the term still survives since independence in the name of certain government buildings, as "Raj Bhavan," the former governor's mansion in many Indian cities.

rajas: Sanskrit, a term common to both Hinduism and Buddhism. In Hinduism, "the principle of activity or restlessness." *(The Gospel of Sri Ramakrishna)* See also Renou's interpretation under prakriti, above. Rajas is one of the three gunas, the elements which make up primal matter. "The element which is of the nature of pain, is active and stimulating," (Morgan) In Buddhism, it has the same sense of restless activity, but also that of "passion as passionate anger. One of the 'Three Fires' with *Dosa* (Pali, 'hatred, anger, ill-will') and *Moha* (Pali, 'mental dullness, infatuation, stupidity; the philosophical doctrine of Maya applied to the human mind') . . . which cause *Dukkha* (Pali, 'suffering')." (Morgan) There is also Raja Yoga: "one of the four schools or disciplines of Hindu yoga teaching the highest self-realization." (Ross) And the title of rajah, a prince or ruler, also comes from the same Sanskrit root-word: "rajan"—"king."

Raj Ghat: the memorial to Gandhi in Delhi.

Rajput: Hindi, but originally from the Sanskrit "rajaputra"—"king's son." The name of a people or tribe, numbering now about 700,000, who took over the northwest region of India in the 7th century A.D., giving it the name of Rajputana. The Rajputs are of the warrior, or Kshatriya caste, they claim divine origin, and are divided into three groups (Solar, Lunar, and Fire) and thirty-two exogamous clans. The Rajputs held off the Moslem invaders from their hillcrest fortresses, but were overrun in the 18th century by the Marathas, then, in the 19th century, taken under the protection of the British, who maintained the semi-independent princely states of the Rajputana. After Indian independence, in 1949, Rajupatana became a part of the state of Rajasthan. Merton's reference is to the highly sophisticated art of miniature painting which developed at the courts of the Rajput princes.

Rama: the protagonist of the great Sanskrit epic, the *Ramayana;* he is also worshiped in Hinduism as a divine incarnation of the god Vishnu.

Shri Ramakrishna: (1836–86) the Bengali teacher and saint for whom the Ramakrishna movement in Hinduism was named. He did not institutionalize a religion himself but developed doctrines centered on the concept that God-Consciousness is worshiped as the Mother of the Universe. See *The Gospel of Sri Ramakrishna.*

Ramanuja: (1017–1137) a Tamil (South Indian) religious scholar who put the Vaishnavite school of Hinduism on a solid philosophical basis with his doctrines of "Qualified Nondualism," or "Qualified Monism." See Morgan: *The Religion of the Hindus,* pages 39–40; Renou: *Hinduism,* pages 117–18.

Ramayana: one of the two great Sanskrit epics of India, which narrates the life and adventures of Rama, incarnation of the Hindu god Vishnu. With the *Mahabharata,* these ancient myths are so central to and vital in the Indian culture that they have taken on the character and stature of scripture.

rangjung Sangay: Tibetan; "rang"—"itself" or "by itself," hence, "natural"; "jung" (or "chung")—"born," "coming into being"; "Sangay" —a Tibetan name for the Buddha. In complimenting Merton as a "natural Buddha," Chatral Rimpoche did not imply that Merton was a Buddha, but that he had attained through meditation a condition of spirit which might enable him to achieve the final enlightenment.

rasa: Sanskrit, in Hinduism, "essence, fluid, the sap in trees, living water, amrita [ambrosia, whence: seed of life]." In Hindu aesthetics, "flavor, taste, that which distinguishes a work of art from a mere statement." (Webster's II) Rasa can also have the sense of "love," as symbolized by the god Krishna. (*Cultural Heritage of India*) See also the discussion of bhakti-rasa in the same work.

rasadhvani: Sanskrit, "suggestion of rasa." (Mohan)

Raso vai sah: Sanskrit, "he is the essence"; from Chapter II of the *Taittiriya Upanishad."* (E. C. Dimock, Jr., private letter) "The divine rasa identified with the Brahman (the absolute) in Hinduism." (Chakravarty)

rath: a monolithic rock carved in bas-relief dedicated to a Hindu god. Ratha: a wooden chariot, used by a god, or a temple float-car, such as the huge one which carries the image of Jagannath (Vishnu) in the festival at Puri.

repa: Tibetan, "cotton"; hence, the name of the poet-saint Milarepa, "clad in one piece of cotton." Cf. "tummo," psychic heat.

rgyal rigs: Tibetan, "royalty, royal person." (Tucci)

rimpoche: Tibetan, "the precious one." In Tibetan Buddhism, "it is the deferential title given to the religious elite, spiritual masters and ecclesiastical dignitaries." (Desjardins) ". . . accorded to high Lamas and Tulkus or recognized incarnations." (Blofeld)

Rishikesh: a holy pilgrimage city for Hindus on the upper reaches of the river Ganges.

rje rigs: Tibetan, a nobleman.

roshi: Japanese, "in Rinzai Zen Buddhism, a Roshi is specifically one who has finished his entire training with a teacher, and the teacher considers him qualified to be a teacher in turn. 'Zen Master.' Of the many men who spend some years in Zen Monasteries, only a few actually receive permission to teach by the koan method. Of course other Zen priests are free to write books, give lectures, or teach in various ways,

but taking disciples and teaching them by means of koans is limited
to the Roshi class alone. 'Dharma-heir' means he finished his studies,
received the o.k., from that man. It is not, then, an honorific, but more
like a professional degree or license. As for the Soto sect of Zen, the
term Roshi seems to be given in a more honorific way, to distinguished older priests." (Gary Snyder in a private letter)

Rudrayamala Tantra: an ancient text of Tantrism. Rudra was an early
name for the Hindu god Shiva in Vedic times, "The Lord of Tears,"
personifying the concept of destruction that balances creation.

rupa: Sanskrit and Pali, in Buddhism and Hinduism, "matter, material
forms or elements." (Murti) "Body, corporeal processes." (Nyaponika
Thera) "Body, form. As the physical body and personality, one of the
five *Skandhas* (Pali, khandhas)—a collection of parts forming a whole.
The elements of existence. The components of the so-called 'self' being Rupa, Vedana [feeling, sensation], Sanna (perception, recognition), Sankhara [mental conformation, innate tendencies], and Vinnana (Sanskrit, vijnana; literally, 'without knowledge,' consciousness;
in some sense the reincarnating entity)." (Humphreys) A "Buddha
Rupa" is an image of the Buddha. Rupa is also the name of one of
the chief disciples of the 15th century Hindu Vaishnavite saint, Sri
Chaitanya. (See page 267 for further interpretations of the skandha
terms based on Nanasampanno's "Wisdom Develops Samadhi.")

rupa dhamma: Pali, "means seeing in a true way everything within the
body and coming to the end of all doubts with regard to the body."
(Nanasampanno: "Wisdom Develops Samadhi") "The way, the facts
or the teaching as it applies to Rupa. Although Rupa literally means
"form," in practice it nearly always refers to the physical body. . . ."
(Bhikkhu Pannavaddho's gloss on the above)

rupee: the chief unit of currency in India today, now exchanging at about
12½ U.S. cents.

sadhaka: Sanskrit, in Hinduism, "an aspirant devoted to the practice of
spiritual discipline." (*Cultural Heritage of India*) A devotee.

sadhana: Sanskrit, in Hinduism, spiritual discipline, or a course of spiritual training.

sadhu: Sanskrit, an Indian ascetic or holy man.

sadhumati: Sanskrit, the ninth stage, that of "good will," in the Buddhist
progress toward bodhisattvahood.

sahaja: Sanskrit, in Buddhism, "the term essentially means a state of equi-
librium between one's self and the world; it later came to mean a state
of suspended particular consciousness, the ultimate condition of bliss."
(E. C. Dimock, Jr. in a private letter)

sahrdaya: "man of sensibility." (Dimock: *In Praise of Krishna*)

Sakya: Tibetan, the name of the monastery in Tibet which was the center
of the Sakyapa school of Buddhism. But, earlier, the Sakyas were a
clan who inhabited the foothills of the Himalayas, and to which the

historic Buddha belonged, his father being the clan's king. Thus, Buddha is sometimes called Sakyamuni. Later, after the Sakyas had been converted to Buddhism and abandoned warfare, they were obliterated when an enemy tribe attacked and they put up no resistance. See Pallis: *Peaks and Lamas,* page 249. The Sakya Monastery, which was founded in 1071 A.D., was called the "Gray Earth Monastery," because it was built on ground that was gray-colored (sa-kya). Presumably, the name of the clan would have had a similar origin.

Sakyapa (Sas-kya): one of the four major sects of Tibetan Buddhism. It was founded in the 11th century by Koncho Gyepo Khon as a reform movement to correct the "debauchery" which had become prevalent in Nyingmapa ("Old Translation" school) communities, and also to resist the corruptive teachings of yogins who were coming up to Tibet from India and Kashmir. The Sakya masters stressed study of the Buddhist scriptures rather than development of the yogic powers of the physical being. By the 13th century, the Sakya school was dominant, both philosophically and politically in Tibet, and when the Mongols threatened Tibet, the Sakya leaders, Kunga-Gyetsen and his nephew, Phakpa, were invited to Mongolia, where their learning so impressed Kubla Khan that Mongolia was converted to Buddhism. Phakpa was made ruler of Tibet and thus began the tradition of lamaistic rule. One of the greatest achievements of the Sakyapas was the compilation, in the 14th century, of the scriptures of Tibetan Buddhism, the *Kangyur* and the *Tangyur,* in a total of 329 volumes. The doctrines of the Sakyapas are based on their own recension of the Pali *Tipitaka* canon together with certain Tantras taken over and re-interpreted from the already existing Tibetan sects. See Morgan: *The Path of the Buddha,* pages 247ff. (With respect to the conversion of Mongolia to Buddhism, it should be noted that Christmas Humphreys gives a slightly earlier date for the event and attributes it to a Sakya master named Dro-gon, who served as tutor to Kubla Khan when he was a boy. See Humphreys: *Buddhism,* page 194.)

samadhi: Sanskrit and Pali, profound meditation. The term and concept are common to both Hinduism and Buddhism, though, of course, with variations of interpretation and practice in each. In Hinduism, samadhi is the final stage in the practice of yoga, in which "the mind is so deeply absorbed in the object [of meditation] that it loses itself in it and has no awareness of itself. . . . This state of perfectly concentrated thought is known as the trance of meditation. . . ." (S. C. Chatterjee in Morgan: *The Religion of the Hindus*) "Ecstasy, trance, communion with God." (*The Gospel of Sri Ramakrishna*) In Buddhism, samadhi is the final step in the Noble Eightfold Path, the Middle Way, which leads to the liberation from all evil and dukkha (suffering) and the achievement of nirvana (final enlightenment and freedom from rebirth). "With the mental discipline achieved by the practice of right efforts and right mindfulness the practitioner sets himself to the attainment of a state which transcends the normal discursive understanding, he seeks to reach a mystic state of mind known as samadhi." (J. Kashyap in Morgan: *The Path of the Buddha*) See also the three sections entitled "Samadhi" in Nanasampanno's "Wisdom Develops Samadhi," from which Merton took many notes.

Samkhya-prakriti: Sanskrit. Samkhya (or Sankhya) is one of the six orthodox schools, or darsanas, of Hindu philosophy. (The others are: Nyaya, Vaiseshika, Yoga, Mimamsa, and Vedanta.) Its origin is "attributed by tradition to the Sage Kapila" and it "is a system of dualistic realism which is the basis of a religion without belief in God. For it, there are two ultimate realities which exist independently of each other; a plurality of selves (purusha) on the one hand and infinite matter (prakriti) on the other The self, purusha, is pure consciousness without any activity in it, while primal matter, prakriti, is unlimited energy and activity but has no consciousness or intelligence in it. . . . The process of the world's evolution is started by the contact between self, or purusha, and primal matter, or prakriti." (S. C. Chatterjee in Morgan: *The Religion of the Hindus*, pages 208ff. See also pages 36–37 and 273–74 in the same work.)

samsara: Sanskrit, transmigration of the soul, metempsychosis. "The ceaseless round of becoming; the life of phenomena; opposite of Nirvana." (Ross) The concept originated in Hinduism and was carried over into Buddhism, and is one of the central beliefs of both philosophies.

samskara (Sanskrit), sankhara (Pali): in both Hinduism and Buddhism, the innate tendencies of a person, and what in terms of karma is carried from one life to the next. "The forces, mental and material, that condition existential (phenomenal) entities." (Murti) One of the five skandhas (Pali, khandhas), the groups of elements into which all existences were classified in the early schools of Buddhism.

Sangay dorje: Tibetan; "Sangay"—a Tibetan name for a Buddha; "dorje" —here, in an honorific accorded distinguished lamas, probably the sense of "diamond," rather than "thunderbolt" or "scepter."

Sangha: Pali and Sanskrit. "The Buddhist monastic order." (Ross) It was founded by the historic Buddha himself and still continues in the Theravada sect. Symbolically, the Sangha is the third of the "Three Jewels" and of the "Three Refuges." The first two are the Buddha himself and the dharma (Pali, dhamma), the "path" or "way."

Sanghamitta (Arhat Theri): the daughter of the Indian emperor Ashoka and sister of Mahinda, who brought Buddhism to Ceylon. Legend has it that she brought a cutting from the Buddha's bo tree at Bodhgaya, which is still growing at Anuradhapura.

Sankara(charya): author of *The Crest-Jewel of Discrimination (Viveka-Chudamani)*, founder of the Advaita Vedanta doctrine of nondualism, and one of the most influential of all Hindu theologians. He lived in India in the 8th century A.D. Not to be confused with the contemporary South Indian sage and teacher, Sankaracharya of Kanchi.

sankirtana: Sanskrit, a form of devotion in Hinduism in which groups of
people march through the streets chanting religious songs, mantras,
or the names of gods. Cf. kirtan.
sanna (Pali), samjna (Sanskrit): in Buddhism, "ideation; apprehension of
determining marks, i.e., judgement; one of the Five Groups (Skandhas)." (Murti) Merton's source for the term was in the section entitled "Wisdom" of Nanasampanno's "Wisdom Develops Samadhi,"
where it is explained as one of the five khandhas (Pali, spelling of
skandha), meaning "remembering (recollecting)—for example, remembering names, sounds, objects and, or verses in the Pali language, etc."
(*Visakha Puja,* May 1967, Bangkok, page 87)
sannyasin (or, sannyasi): from Sanskrit "samnyasin"—"abandoning." In
Hinduism, a monk, a wandering religious mendicant, or any person
who has renounced the material world and thus entered into the
fourth and final stage of human life as Hinduism conceives it.
Sanskrit: from "sam"—"together" and "kri"—"to make." "The ancient
Aryan (*Indo-Iranian*) language of the Hindus of India, including the
language of the Vedas, often termed *Vedic Sanskrit,* as well as the
later *classical Sanskrit,* which is essentially a literary language, given
rigid form by early grammarians, above all by Panini (probably 4th
century B.C.), preserved in a great and varied literature of religion,
philosophy, lyric, epic, fable . . . and even today a sacred and learned
tongue in India." (Webster's II)
santa: Sanskrit. In Buddhism, "quiescent, tranquil." (Murti) In Hinduism,
"one of the five attitudes cherished by the dualistic worshipper toward his Chosen Ideal. It is the attitude of peace and serenity, in
contrast with the other attitudes of love, which create discontent and
unrest in the minds of the devotees. Many of the Vaishnavas do not
recognize the attitude of santa, since it is not characterized by an intense love of God." (*The Gospel of Sri Ramakrishna*)
Santaraksita: (705–62 A.D.) one of the teachers who brought the Madh-
yamkia philosophy of Buddhism into Tibet.
Santi Deva: (691–743 A.D.) one of the most important early formulators
of the Madhyamika school of Buddhism.
sapientia: Latin, "wisdom."
Sariputta: (Sariputra in Sanskrit) one of the Buddha's chief disciples.
sarva-kalpana-ksayo hi nirvanam: Sanskrit, "Freedom is the total cessation
of imagination." (Murti)
Sarvastivada: an early Buddhist sect of philosophical realists, its doctrines
fairly close to those of Theravada, which once flourished in the northwestern part of India. "The Buddhist School which holds that all the
elements (dharmas) exist in all the three times (sarvada asti); another
name for the Vaibhasika." (Murti)
sastras (shastras): from Sanskrit "sas"—"to instruct"; in Hinduism, "the
four classes of scriptures sruti, smriti, purana, and tantra; technical
treatises on religious or other subjects such as law, medicine, archi-

tecture, etc." (Webster's II) The term also is used in Buddhism, where the sastras are introductions to or commentaries on the sutras, such as those composed by the sages Vasubandhu and Dinnaga.

sat: Sanskrit, in Hinduism, the concept of reality or being. "Absolute existence." (*Cultural Heritage of India*) "One might therefore describe Vedanta as a method of instruction and practice leading to a personal experiencing of the living Reality which lies behind the world of appearances. This Absolute Reality is Brahman or *sat-chit-ananda,* pure Existence-Consciousness-Bliss." (Ross, page 53)

Satan: from Hebrew "shatan"—"adversary." "The great adversary of man in Christian theology; the Devil, or Prince of Darkness; the archfiend. . . . According to the Talmud he was once an archangel but was cast out of heaven with his followers for disobedience and pride." (Webster's II)

satipatthana (Pali), smritupasthana (Sanskrit): in Buddhism, "right mindfulness." "One of the Five Aggregates . . . the Setting-up of Mindfulness." (Rahula: *What the Buddha Taught,* page xii) "Right mindfulness, the seventh step [of the Noble Eightfold Path taught by the Buddha] is based on a constant awareness which the disciple is taught to develop within himself, an unfailing vigilance over the states of his own personality. . . . The Maha Satipatthana Sutta of the Dighu Nikaya describes in full how this mindfulness must be developed and perfected. The four steps in right mindfulness . . . are reflection on the states of the body, on the states of feeling, on the states of mind, and on the states of things." (J. Kashyap in Morgan: *The Path of the Buddha,* page 30) See Appendix II of this book for Bhikkhu Khantipalo's notes on the conversation which he had with Merton in Bangkok on the concept of mindfulness. See also page 132 of Ross: *Three Ways of Asian Wisdom,* for an account of satipatthana training in Burma based on E. H. Shattock: *An Experiment in Mindfulness.*

satori: Japanese, in Zen Buddhism, "awakening, illumination, enlightenment." "The state of consciousness, known in the Zen vocabulary as *satori,* is held to be comparable to that special level of insight attained by the Buddha while seated in deep meditation under the sacred Tree of Enlightenment in the sixth century before the birth of Christ." (Ross, page 140)

Shaivism (Shivaism): the major sect of Hinduism which concentrates its worship on Shiva, the third in the Hindu trinity of gods, the Trimurti. Renou states that Shaivism came to prominence in India during the Gupta dynasty, largely displacing Vaishnavism (the worship of Vishnu) from about the 6th century A.D. on. There are many close connections between Shaivism and Shaktism, since the cult of the Mother Goddess and the exaltation of the female principle emanate from Shiva.

shakti: Sanskrit, "sakti"—"energy, force." A basic concept in Hinduism. When the term is capitalized, Shakti, it relates to the Divine Mother or Great Goddess of Hinduism (Durga, Parvati, Kali), and Shaktism, whose devotees worship the divine Female Principle, is one of the three main sects of Hinduism. "The feminine essence of the universe embodied in a consort of Shiva." (Ross) "Power; the Phenomenalising Aspect of the Absolute, Shiva." (Murti) Shaktism: "a religious movement which conceives the power that moves the world as feminine." (von Glasenapp) See Marco Pallis's note on Shakti, page 72. The first traces of Shaktism (or shakta) date back to Vedic times; later it was to become closely involved with Tantric ritual, but Shaktism and Tantrism are *not* synonymous. (Renou)

shawm: ". . . one of a family of early double-reed straight-bodied woodwind instruments preceding the oboe family. . . ." (Webster's III)

Shiva (Siva): with Brahma and Vishnu, one of the three gods of the classic Hindu triad of deities. See the footnote on Shiva on page 42. "The Personal Absolute of the Tantra philosophy; as an adjective, it means 'benign,' 'blessed.'" (Murti) See Shaivism, above. Another aspect of Shiva is as ". . . the great ascetic, the worker of miracles by virtue of penance and meditation. . . ." (Webster's II)

Shivasamhita: Sanskrit, an ancient teratise on Tantra; date of composition uncertain, but since the samhitas are the first portion of the *Vedas,* consisting of collections of mantras, it is likely that this work may date back beyond 1000 B.C.

Siddhartha: Sanskrit, literally "he who has attained his aim." The given name of Gautama Buddha. Also the name of the formulator of one of the Samkhya schools of Vaishnavite Hinduism. And the title of the well-known novel by Hermann Hesse, the Swiss Nobel Prize winner, which is based on the life of the Buddha.

Sikhs: from the Hindi for "disciple." "[A] religious community of India and Pakistan, numbering some 5,500,000 persons. They are concentrated in the Punjab. The religion was founded by Nanak (born 1469), the first guru ['teacher' of the sect]. He taught a monotheistic creed and the fundamental identity of all religions . . . opposed . . . a priesthood and the caste system. Angad, the third guru, separated the ascetics (udasis) from the laity and eliminated most features of Hinduism. Under the fourth guru, Ram Das, Amritsar was founded as a sacred city . . . Govind Singh . . . was installed in 1676 as the 10th and last guru. His policy was to raise all Sikhs to the warrior caste. This was accomplished by a military ceremony, after which the initiate took the name Singh (lion). He introduced the Sikh practices of wearing a turban, carrying a dagger, and never cutting the hair or beard. Under his authority there was made the final rescension of the Sikh scriptures, the *Granth* (Sanskrit—'treatise'), which contains hymns, hortatory tales, and ritual injunctions, all in verse. He welded the Sikhs into a military community which adopted the caste practices and the polytheistic beliefs typical of Hinduism. The Sikhs conquered most of the Punjab by the 18th century and established a number of feudal states. Their greatest leader in the 19th century was Ranjit Singh, who conquered much territory. After his death, conflict with the British caused the Sikh Wars and the subjugation of the Punjab. Sikh soldiers were a large element of the British armies in India. In 1947, in the partition of India, the Sikhs' territory there was divided [with Pakistan] despite their protest." (*The Columbia Encyclopedia, Second Edition*) See Khushwant Singh: *History of the Sikhs*, Princeton University Press, 1963–66.

Siksasamuccaya: an early text of Madhyamika Buddhism by Santi Deva. "The entire work is a string of excerpts from important Sutras, most of which are now lost in the original. Santi Deva supplies 27 verses [karikas] that serve as the chapter headlines under which the citations from the Sutras are arranged. Santi Deva's preoccupation, in this and the *Bodhicaryavatara,* is with spiritual discipline, the cultivation of the Bodhicitta. These two works are our chief sources for the Madhyamika path of spiritual realisation." (Murti, page 101) Karika: "a verse that is used for embodying philosophical ideas; the word was made famous by Gaudapada in his Vedantic treatise called *Gaudapada-Karika.*" (Chakravarty)

sila: Sanskrit, in Buddhism, the "practice of moral virtues." (Murti) See the section on sila in Nanasampanno's "Wisdom Develops Samadhi" in *Visakha Puja,* Bangkok, May 1967, which is Merton's chief source for his notes on the term. In the same work, Bhikkhu Pannavaddho, who translated it from the Thai original, glosses the term thus: "Sila means 'morality' . . . but it also has a wider connotation in its higher and more subtle levels, for it includes all bodily actions and speech, which are assessed as right or wrong, depending on whether they make one's heart less or more passionate."

sitar: Hindi, "a Hindu guitar with a long neck and a varying number of strings." (Webster's III) Cf. the earlier Persian setar.

skandha (Sanskrit), khandha (Pali): "the (Five) Groups of Elements (dharmas) into which all existences are classified in Early Buddhism. The Five are: Rupa (matter), Vedana (feeling), Samjna (ideation), Samskara (forces or drives), Vijnana (pure consciousness or sensation)." (Murti) Not to be confused with the Hindu god Skanda.

"The Small Vehicle": in Sanskrit, the literal translation of "Hinayana," one of the main schools of Buddhism, which is also known as the Theravada, or "Southern" school. Cf. "The Great Vehicle"—"Mahayana."

soma: Sanskrit, an East Indian vine (*Sarcostemma acidum,* family *Asclepiadaceae*) from which, it is believed, the ancient Indians made an intoxicating drink which produced "higher consciousness," and was used in sacrificial rites in honor of Indra and other gods. "The term is also used in regard to the deity who provided this inspiring, exhilarating experience, who, personified, becomes the presiding power of Soma. See R. C. Zaehner: *Hinduism,* pages 20–22 in the Oxford

University Press 1968 paperback edition, for a detailed account of Soma/soma, as deity and psychedelic drug, in Vedic times. In the passage from Mohan's *The Response to Poetry* which Merton quotes on page 285, it seems clear that Mohan simply intends to identify the juice of the soma plant, which produces exhilaration (or 'blessedness') with the perfect rasa, the essential flavor of deep artistic experience." (Chakravarty) See also R. Gordon Wasson: *Soma, Divine Mushroom of Immortality,* New York, Harcourt Brace Jovanovich, 1971. Wasson, who has done extensive search for and research in hallucinogenic plants all over the world, believes that the ancient soma of Vedic times should be identified with the mushroom *Amanita muscaria,* popularly known in English as the fly agaric.

soongkhor: Tibetan, a fence, in this case of barbed wire, which was built around the Dalai Lama's house near Dharamsala to discourage intruders. (Sonam Kazi in a private letter)

stupa: Sanskrit, in Buddhism and Hinduism, "originally a mound for relics, in particular the Buddha's; [later] developed into elaborate architectural forms: chortens, dagobas, pagodas." (Ross) Renou credits a Kushana king, Kanishka, with building the first stupas in the middle of the 2nd century A.D.

sudurjaya: the fifth stage in the Buddhist progress to bodhisattvahood.

Sufi, Sufism: from the Arabic: "suf"—"wool" or a "man who wears garments of wool," hence, an ascetic. The Sufis are the mystic ascetics of Islam. "The theories connected with the genesis of Sufism are varied and even contradictory. . . . (1) It represents the esoteric doctrine of Prophet Mohammed. There exist some stray references in the *Qur'an* [*Koran*] and the *Hadis* (Traditions) to the Prophet saying, 'I was a hidden treasure and I desired to be known; therefore I created Creation that I might be known,' and 'Whosoever knoweth himself, knoweth his God.'. . . (2) It must be regarded as the reaction of the Aryan mind against a Semitic religion imposed upon it by force. There are, no doubt, some resemblances between Sufi doctrines, in their more advanced forms, and the Vedanta, which can be referred to their common origin in India. It is an established fact that, as early as Naushirwan's time, cultural contacts were established between India and Iran by exchange of scholars and envoys. Even earlier than that, Buddhism extended its sway over Iran and Afghanistan, through the efforts and missionary zeal of the Indian emperor, Ashoka [who reigned from 268 to 224 B.C.] The pacifism, contentment, and nonviolence which gained ground in Sufism can claim their origin in Buddhism. (3) It was due to neo-Platonist influence. Plotinus himself is stated to have visited Iran with seven neo-Platonist philosophers, who were driven out from their home and compelled to flee to Iran in the times of Naushirwan. (4) It has an independent origin. Because Sufism meets the requirements and satisfies the cravings, of a certain class of minds, existing in all ages and in most of the civilized communities, the evolution of this system of thought should be regarded as a phenomenon of spontaneous, independent, and indigenous growth, recurring in many similar and unconnected forms, wherever the human mind continues to concern itself with the problems of the wherefore, the whence, and the whither of the Spirit." (*The Cultural Heritage of India,* Volume IV, pages 593–94. See the whole chapter on Sufism in the same work for a detailed exposition of the history and tenets of the sect in India.) Sufism developed an elaborate symbolism which had a profound influence on Persian and other poets. Basically, its objective is to gain knowledge of and communion with God through contemplation and the trancelike ecstasy which such meditation produces in its adepts. For a good general study of the movement, see A.J. Arberry: *Sufism, An Account of the Mystics of Islam,* London, Allen & Unwin, 1950; New York, Hillary House, 1956.

Sumeru (Mount Sumeru): symbolically, the center of the Cosmos in the mandalas of Tibetan Buddhism. Its origins go back to "the sacred Mount Meru of Hindu mythology, around which all the planets are said to revolve." (*The Gospel of Sri Ramakrishna*) See Tucci: *The Theory and Practice of the Mandala,* pages 23–35 and 109.

sunya, sunyata: Sanskrit, "emptiness, the Void." A basic concept in certain schools of Buddhism, particularly Madhyamika and Zen. The term goes back to Nagarjuna's sunyata, the "Silence of the Middle Way," and continued to evolve, in depth and complexity, finally to reach its maturity in the sunya doctrines of the Madhyamika school. "The terms are used in two allied meanings: (i) the phenomena are sunya, as they are relative and lack substantiality or independent reality; they are conditioned (pratitya-samutpanna), and hence are unreal; (ii) the Absolute is sunya or sunyata itself, as it is devoid of empirical form; no thought-category or predicate ('is,' 'not-is,' 'is and not-is,' 'neither is nor not-is') can legitimately be applied to it; it is Transcendent to thought (sunya)." (Murti) S.B. Dasgupta, in his *Introduction to Tantric Buddhism,* page 9, defines sunyata as "enlightenment of the nature of essencelessness" and points out that when it was combined with karuna (universal compassion) as the two chief elements of bodhicitta (enlightened-mindedness) this "perfect commingling . . . had far-reaching effects in the transformation of the Mahayanic ideas into the Tantric ideas." Christmas Humphreys relates sunya with tathata (suchness or thusness), while the Dalai Lama, in his pamphlet *Introduction to Buddhism,* calls sunyata "the knowledge of the ultimate reality of all objects, material and phenomenal."

sursum corda: Latin, "lift up your hearts"; a versicle in the Roman Catholic liturgy.

sutra (Sanskrit), sutta (Pali): "Buddhist scriptures, meaning a discourse by the Buddha, or a disciple, accepted as authoritative teaching; literal meaning—'A thread on which jewels are hung.'" (Ross) See Morgan, Thomas, Humphreys, et al. for detailed analyses of the various principal sutra texts. See *Suttapitaka* under *Tripitaka*.

svarupa: Sanskrit, a rather recondite term, meaning "man's essential divine nature," which, according to Tucci, came originally from the ancient Hindu treatise on Tantra, the *Shivasamhita,* and was then carried over to Tibetan Tantric Buddhism. The term also appears again in the 16th century in the Hindu worship of the god Krishna which was promulgated by the great reformer and teacher Chaitanya, where it is coupled with the concept of shakti (the female principle) in relation to the lilas (divine play) of Krishna. See *The Cultural Heritage of India,* Volume IV, pages 192–93.

Svatantrika (Svatantra): Sanskrit, in Buddhism, one of the schools of Madhyamika, that of "Bhavaviveka and others which adduced arguments and examples of their own in refuting their opponents; this is opposed to the other Madhyamika school (the Prasangika) of Buddhapalita, Candrakirti, etc., which strictly adhered to the method of *reductio ad absurdum.*" (Murti; see pages 95ff. and 132)

Taittiriya Upanishad: Sanskrit, one of the more important *Upanishads,* the ancient Indian speculative treatises which are part of the corpus of Vedic literature, but, in most cases, commentaries or refinements on earlier *Vedas.* The exact date of its composition is uncertain, but some of these writings date back to the 8th century B.C. The *Taittiyira* belongs to the group known as "Black Yajus," which are part of the *Krishna Yajurveda,* dealing mainly with early Hindu rites of sacrifice. The first part of the *Taittiriya* is concerned chiefly with the pronunciation of earlier Vedic terms, but the second part deals with substantial metaphysical concepts from which certain essential elements of the doctrines of Vedanta were derived. Brief selections from it, with commentary, will be found in Morgan: *The Religion of the Hindus,* pages 303–7. See also the introductions to standard translations of the *Upanishads,* such as E. Roer: *The Twelve Principal Upanishads,* Theosophical Publishing House, Adyar, Madras, 1931; F. Max Müller: *The Upanishads,* originally published 1879–84 in the Oxford University Press "Sacred Books of the East" Series, and now available here in a Dover paperback; Swami Nikhilananda: *The Upanishads,* 4 volumes, New York, Harper, 1949–59, but now distributed by the Ramakrishna-Vivekananda Center, 17 East 94, New York, 10028.

talelo: Tamil, the refrain in a lullaby to put the baby god Krishna to sleep; used by Periyalvar, a 9th-century South Indian poet.

tamas: Sanskrit, in Hinduism, one of the three gunas, the element in nature that embodies ignorance, indifference, or inertia. "According to the Samkhya philosophy, Prakriti (nature), in contrast with Purusha (soul), consists of three gunas (qualities or strands) known as sattva, rajas, and tamas. Tamas stands for inertia or dullness, rajas for activity of restlessness, and sattva for balance or wisdom." *(The Gospel of Sri Ramakrishna)*

Tamil: one of the largest branches of the Dravidian race who have inhabited South India since ancient times; some Tamils are also to be found in northern Ceylon. The Tamil language is the most highly developed of the Dravidian languages and possesses an extensive and varied literature, including the *Shilappadikaram* ("The Ankle Bracelet") by the 3rd-century Ilango Adigal, which is perhaps the earliest "novel" in Indian literature, and the 6th-century *Kural* by Tiruvalluvar, "a collection of one thousand three hundred stanzas on virtue, material prosperity and love, written in the form of epigrams that are irreproachably pertinent and concise." (Renou) Many Tamils call it the "Holy Kural" or speak of it as the "fifth *Veda*." Very ancient Tamil used the "round writing" (vatteluttu) alphabet, but modern Tamil, which has both a literary and an ordinary form, makes use of an alphabet derived from the Brahmi character which was originally a Semitic script.

Tangyur (Tanjur: Bstan-hgyur—"Translation of the Commentaries"). The Tibetan versions, translated for the most part from the Sanskrit, of a collection of 225 volumes of commentaries on the *Kangyur,* a group of over a hundred volumes of translations of the chief Buddhist canonical writings. Together, the *Kangyur* and the *Tangyur* make up the basic scriptures of Tibetan Buddhism.

tanka: Tibetan, "thanka"—"picture"; in the art of Tibet, the painting of a religious subject, often a god or demon, or one of the Buddhas surrounded by bodhisattvas or famous sages, executed on silk or brocade. Tankas are used as aids to meditation, for the invocation of deities, or carried in religious processions. (Not to be confused with the Japanese tanka, a strict form of poetry having five lines, the first and third of which have five syllables and the others seven.)

Tantra, Tantras, Tantrayana, Tantrism: Sanskrit, literally "woven." "A body of esoteric Hindu religious literature said to have been revealed by the god Shiva for man's guidance in the present age, *i.e.* the Kali Yuga. These scriptures place emphasis on the worship of the female essence of the universe, the Divine Mother or Shakti." (Ross) In India, Tantric thought moved toward yoga and even into areas of magic. Thus when the Tibetan king Trisong-Detsan ("Fair-Throne," "Powerful-Key"). who reigned in the 8th century, invited the great Indian guru Padma Sambhava to come to Tibet to help spread Buddhism, it was partly because Padma Sambhava "possessed great supernatural powers by means of which he is said to have subdued many powerful spirits." (Lhalungpa in Morgan) Padma Sambhava translated many Sanskrit works of Tantrism into Tibetan and founded the Nyingmapa ("Red Hats," "Old Tantric," "Old Translation") school of Buddhism. He shrewdly integrated elements from the pre-Buddhist Bon-pa (animist) religion of Tibet into Tantrism, creating, as it were, positions as minor Tantric guardian deities for many of the old gods and goddesses of Bonism. But he did replace the Bon-pa animal sacrifices and rituals of black magic with true Buddhist doctrines of spiritual purification. Tantrism and the Shakti concepts thus became an integral part of Tibetan Buddhism, as evidenced in Nepalese and Tibetan art by the bronze figures in positions of coupling, symbolic of the Tantric "union of the opposites" (yah-yum). (See plate 71, page 106 in Ross) Thus Tantrayana, also known as Vajrayana, became firmly embedded and an important factor in Tibetan Buddhism. Its esoteric doctrines were transmitted orally from master to pupil, and the meditation it taught put heavy emphasis on "symbolic rites consisting of gestures, postures, breathing, and the use of powers of sounds and secret, mystic formulas." (Lhalungpa in Morgan) See Tucci: *The Theory and Practice of the Mandala;* Blofeld: *The Tantric Mysticism of Tibet;* S. B. Dasgupta: *An Introduction to Tantric Buddhism;* W.Y. Evans-Wentz: *Tibetan Yoga and Secret Doctrines.*

tathata: Sanskrit, "suchness, thisness or thusness, reality." In Buddhism, "Suchness, Thatness; the Real that stays unmodified; Absolute." (Murti) Cf. sunya.

thanatos: Greek, "death." Cf. the Sanskrit "adhvanit"—"vanished."

thera: Pali, "the elders." "An old and revered monk." (Conze: *Buddhist Meditation*)

Theravada: Pali, "the doctrine or teaching of the elders." The "Southern" school of Buddhism, now dominant in Burma, Thailand, and Ceylon. Also called the Hinayana (Sanskrit, the "Lesser Vehicle") school See the chapters on Theravada Buddhism in Christmas Humphreys: *Buddhism,* and that by the Venerable Balangoda Ananda Maitreya in Morgan's *The Path of the Buddha.*

tierce: the service or office for the third of the Roman Catholic canonical hours, or 9 A.M.

tilbu: Tibetan, the bell which is used in certain ceremonies of Tantric Buddhism.

Tipitaka (Pali): see *Tripitaka* (Sanskrit).

Tirumoli: a 9th-century Tamil hymn in praise of the Hindu god Krishna by Periyalvar.

Tiruppallandu: a 9th-century Tamil hymn in praise of the Hindu god Vishnu by Periyalvar.

Titan: ". . . one of a family or race of earth giants in ancient Greek mythology whose power was destroyed by the Olympian gods and who are usually held to have been characterized by gigantic size, immense brute strength, and primitive force and appetite rather than intelligence or morality. . . ." (Webster's III)

trapa: Tibetan, a "cleric, schoolman, or monk." (Pallis)

Trappist: ". . . a member of a reformed branch of the Roman Catholic Cistercian Order established in 1664 at the monastery of La Trappe in Normandy and united with the Cistercians since 1892." Cistercian: '. . . a member of an austere order founded on the Benedictine rule as adapted by Robert de Molesme at Citeaux, France, in 1098, the order being now divided into a group that follows a mitigated rule and a group that follows a more strictly interpreted rule. . . ." (Webster's III) Merton's community, the Abbey of Gethsemani near Bardstown, Kentucky, established in 1848, belongs to the Cistercians of the Strict Observance (O.C.S.O.). Its rule still maintains silence, isolation, fasts, restricted diet, and manual labor, but many of its former austerities have been somewhat relaxed in recent years.

Trimsika (Trimsakakarika): Sanskrit, "Thirty Verses," an important work on disputed aspects of Yogacara Buddhism by Vasubandhu, brother of Asanga, who lived near Peshawar in Gandhara either in the 3rd and 4th centuries (see Murti, page 107n) or in the 5th century (see Thomas, pages 238–40).

Tripituku(s) (Sanskrit), Tipitaka (Pali): the "Three Baskets" of the Buddhist scriptures. "Pitaka" is "basket" in Sanskrit. These main divisions are the Vinayapitaka, the "Basket of Discipline"; the Suttapitaka, the "Basket of Discourses"; and the Abhidhammapitaka, the "Basket of Metaphysics." See U Thittila in Morgan: The Path of the Buddha, pages 68ff.; E.J. Thomas: The History of Buddhist Thought, pages 265ff.

Tsongkapa: Born in 1357, Tsongkapa was the founder of the Gelugpa school of Tibetan Buddhism and builder of the Gadan monastery. For a detailed account of his life and teachings, see L.P. Lhalungpa's chapter, "Buddhism in Tibet," in Morgan: The Path of the Buddha, pages 249–52; Humphreys: Buddhism, pages 193–95.

Tukaram: (1598–1650) a Hindu poet and religious teacher, one of the Maharastra saints. See Toukharam: Psaumes du pèlerin, translated and edited by G.-A. Deleury, "Connaissance de l'orient" Series, Paris, Gallimard, 1956; Louis Renou: Indian Literature, New York, Walker, 1964, pages 111–12. Renou points out that the teaching of Tukaram marks the culmination of the bhakti influence in western India.

tulku: Tibetan, one who is recognized as the reincarnation of someone who had advanced far on the path to enlightenment in his earlier incarnation. ". . . the kind of succession which seems especially to belong to Tibetan Buddhism is that of those masters who are chosen in their earliest years and are called tulkus. The word tulku has been translated to mean a 'living Buddha.' If Buddha means awakened or enlightened, fortunately for human kind there have always been living Buddhas on our planet, outside as well as inside that form of religion which is called Buddhism, whether that condition is theirs by birth or whether they have obtained to it in the course of this life. Tulkus, whether abbots of monasteries, or abbots general of some religious order, are recognized as such at about the age of two.

"Many books and magazine articles have told how the present Dalai

Lama, like his predecessors, was sought for a long time and then discovered. An oracle had directed the search toward the east of Tibet and given certain indications as to the appearance of the house. There a small boy recognised at once that the man dressed in civilian clothes who came toward him was a religious personage, and cried out 'Lama, Lama!' then he triumphantly passed the test of the certified true copies: he was shown several objects (such as a tea-bowl), and in each case there were three exactly alike, though only one had belonged to his predecessor, 'the thirteenth incarnation.' Each time the child chose without hesitation the one 'which had been his in his preceding existence.' But the Dalai Lama is not the only Tibetan dignitary or pundit discovered by this system of 'reincarnations'; the custom has been tending to spread more and more widely. This rather baffling system requires some further explanation if it is to be clearly seen in the Tibetan perspective.

"Our words reincarnation, metempsychosis, transmigration, are highly inadequate translations of the Buddhist idea, which does not recognise any stable and permanent principle capable of passing from body to body and from century to century. Tibetans speak rather of predecessor and successor, or simply of continuation. . . . This method of recruitment to such ranks is highly impartial, not to say democratic, since the *tulkus,* far from always being recognised among the families of the nobility, may be discovered in humble surroundings and in any part of the country.

"The surprising thing is that this custom of recognising great men before they have, for obvious reasons, been able to give any proofs of greatness, generally affords excellent results. Many of the present-day Tibetan gurus, of whose wisdom and Realisation I have had no doubt, were set aside for the veneration of their disciples from their early childhood. I think particularly of Gyalwa Karmapa and Dudjom Rimpoche." (Desjardins: *The Message of the Tibetans,* pages 42–43) See also: Chogyam Trungpa: *Born in Tibet,* London, Allen & Unwin, 1966, and Shambala, Berkeley, for the account of how the eleventh Trungpa Tulku was "selected" for his station while still a baby.

tummo (gtum-mo): Tibetan, "psychic heat." The yogic discipline by which adepts of Tantric Buddhism are able to generate heat within their bodies. See Evans-Wentz: *Tibetan Yoga and Secret Doctrines,* page 172n.

Udanavarga: Pali, one of the canonical scriptures of Tibetan Buddhism. A translation by W.W. Rockhill was published in London in 1883. A group of selected precepts from the *Udanavarga* will be found on page 260 of Evans-Wentz: *Tibetan Yoga and Secret Doctrines.* Udana: one of the five "vital winds" in esoteric Yoga. (See S.B. Dasgupta: *An Introduction to Tantric Buddhism,* pages 167–68.) Varga: a group or category.

upacara samadhi: Pali, one of the three kinds of samadhi (profound meditation), along with khanika samadhi and ap(p)ana samadhi, which Venerable Nanasampanno singles out for discussion in "Wisdom Develops Samadhi." (in *Visakha Puja*, May 1967, Buddhist Association of Thailand, Bangkok, pages 74–85) ". . . [it is the kind] of which the Lord said, that it is almost the same, but it lasts longer than khanika samadhi. Then the citta [heart] withdraws from this state. . . . In upacara samadhi, when the citta has dropped into a calm state it does not remain in that state, but partially withdraws from it to follow and get to know about various things which have come into contact with the heart." Bhikkhu Pannavaddho, the translator of Nanasampanno's essay, glosses upacara as "approaching or getting close to (the object)." In Hinduism, the term upacara has a different meaning, that of "offerings" in the worship of a deity. This in turn is related to the highly complicated concept of the pancopacara (five offerings). See *The Cultural Heritage of India*, Volume IV, the chapter on "Rituals of Worship," pages 461–63.

Upanishads: Sanskrit, "the word . . . is derived from *upa*, near *ni*, down, and *sad*, to sit. Groups of pupils sat near the teacher to learn from him the truth by which ignorance is destroyed." (Radhakrishnan and Moore, *A Source Book in Indian Philosophy*, page 37) ". . . the third section of the sacrosanct *Vedas* which form the basis of Hinduism's highest spiritual concepts." (Ross) These treatises are for the most part commentaries or refinements on earlier *Vedas;* some of them probably date back to the 8th century B.C. See under *Taittiriya Upanishad* for reference to source material and available translations.

upaya: Sanskrit, "The free phenomenal activity of the Absolute manifesting itself as Karuna [compassion]." (Murti) Upaya (or karuna) and prajna (wisdom) form the dualistic basis of Tantric Buddhism, a dualism which may be compared to the shakti and shiva concepts in Hindu Tantrism. See Murti, page 284. In Zen Buddhism upaya (Japanese, hoben) may refer particularly to the "skillful means" which the Buddha, or a Buddhist master, uses to bring any being to a state of enlightenment and happiness. See D. T. Suzuki: *Zen and Japanese Culture*, page 425 n3.

Urdu: Hindi, "an Indic language that is an official literary language of Pakistan and widely used particularly by Indians in India, has a colloquial basis very similar to that of Hindi but has developed under strong Persian rather than Sanskrit influence, and is generally written in Persian script." (Webster's III) There is a considerable body of literature in Urdu, most of it concentrated in poetry, although it was not widely used until the 17th century by the court poets of the Mogul empire. Later there was a school of Urdu poetry at Lucknow that also wrote plays. The most famous poet of the 19th century under Mogul patronage was Ghalib (d. 1869). Iqbal of Sialkot (1876–1938), the most notable writer in Urdu in this century, is considered "the national poet, and a kind of spiritual father, of Pakistan." See Renou: *Indian Literature,* pages 107–8. Two books by Iqbal, *Javid-Nama* and *Mysteries of Selflessness* are available in English translations by A.J. Arberry.

Uttar Pradesh: Hindi, one of the largest states in North India, known as the United Provinces under the British regime, which took over the region from the Moguls in 1764. At present the population is about 88,000,000. Uttar Pradesh lies below the kingdom of Nepal, and its northern part is in the foothills of the Himalayas. But most of the state is fertile plain, watered by the Ganges, Jumna, and Gogra rivers, supplemented by extensive irrigational systems, which make it one of the most productive agricultural areas of India, with cotton as a leading crop. Lucknow is the capital of the state, but the holy cities of Benares (Banaras) and Allahabad on the Ganges attract millions of Hindu pilgrims. The Buddha lived in the eastern part of the state and in Bihar; sacred sites such as Bodhgaya, where he attained enlightenment, Sarnath, where he preached his first sermon, and Sanchi, with its many early Buddhist stupas, are still important places of Buddhist veneration. But since the decline of Buddhism in India, around the beginning of the Christian era, Hinduism has been the predominant religion of the region, except during the period of Mogul domination from the 12th to 18th centuries.

Vaccha(gotta): a wandering ascetic who became one of the Buddha's chief disciples. Many of the most important tenets of the Buddha's teachings are recorded in the form of conversations between Buddha and Vacchagotta, as handed down in such early works of the Buddhist Pali canon as the *Samyutta-nikaya* (sometimes called the *Vacchagotta Sutta,* translated by Davids and Woodward as *The Book of Kindred Sayings,* London, Pali Text Society, 1918–30). See Murti, pages 44ff., and Thomas, pages 126–27.

vada: Sanskrit, doctrine or philosophy; often attached as a suffix to the name of a particular author or work to indicate its nature.

Vaibhasika: one of the early subsect schools of Buddhism in northern India, taking its name from the *Vibhasha,* a commentary on the principles of Abhidharma which survives in a Chinese text. See Sarvastivada, which is the more common name of this school of philosophical realism. See the indexes of Murti and Thomas for references to detailed explications of the school's doctrines. Vaibhasika flourished particularly in Gandhara and Kashmir.

vaikuntha: Sanskrit, in Hinduism, particularly the Vaishnavite sects, the "heavenly abode" of the God Vishnu. Daniélou, describing the icons of Vishnu, writes that "the parasol, emblem of the royalty of Vishnu, represents the Land-of-No-Hindrance (Vaikuntha), the heaven of Vishnu, the land where there is no fear." While at the philosophical level the principal Hindu sects believe in the theory of karma, that is, of the transmigration of the soul after death to another body, a process which is repeated until deliverance from the round of birth and death is achieved, at the popular level there is often fear of a day of judgment not too different from that in Christianity: that after death the soul will be judged by Yama, the god of death, and be sent either to a heaven such as vaikuntha, or to the summit of Mount Meru, the abode of other gods, or to a hell for punishment. But neither heaven or hell are thought to be eternal for mortals; there is, after a time, mortal rebirth in another person. See Renou: *The Nature of Hinduism*, pages 63–64.

Vaishnava, Sanskrit (Vaishnavite when Anglicized): pertaining to the Hindu god Vishnu, with Brahma and Shiva, one of the three deities of the classic triad. Thus Vaishnavism, one of the major Hindu sects, is made up of devotees of Vishnu, who, for the most part, believe that bhakti, the intense love for a personal deity, provides the only path to liberation and immortality. See the index of Morgan, Renou, Ross, *The Cultural Heritage of India*, Volume IV, and *The Gospel of Sri Ramahrishna* for references to detailed discussions of the Vaishnavite schools and doctrines.

Vajrayana: Sanskrit, "vajra"—"thunderbolt" or "adamantine, invincible" and "yana"—"vehicle, body." Also called Tantrayana, Vajrayana is the name of the Tantric school of Tibetan Buddhism. See under "Tantra" for details on its basic tenets, many of which are set forth in the *Vajracchedika*, or "Diamond Sutra," one of the most important works in the Mahayana canon of Buddhist scriptures, parts of which are available in English translation in the collection *Buddhist Mahayana Texts*, Oxford, 1894, 1927. In addition to the reference sources listed under "Tantra," see *The Cultural Heritage of India*, Volume IV, pages 267–70; A.L. Basham: *The Wonder That Was India*, New York, Evergreen paperback, 1954, pages 265 and 279 81.

Vatsiputriya: Sanskrit, one of the subsects of the Sammatiya school of early Indian Buddhism. None of its scriptures now survive, but from references to them in those of other sects scholars have established that the Vatsiputriya doctrine (or heresy?) centered on the concept of pudgalavada, that a person's consciousness is more than the sum of its parts, and that it is this total entity which is the basic element of metempsychosis. See the indexes of Morgan, Murti, and Thomas for references to this school.

vedana: Sanskrit, "feeling, sensation." "The second of the Five Groups (Panca Skandhas)." (Murti) The skandhas are the groups of elements into which all existences are classified in early Buddhism. See Nanasampanno: *Wisdom Develops Samadhi*, page 87, the source from which Merton is quoting the term: "Vedana means those things (feelings) which are experienced by the heart that are sometimes pleasant, sometimes painful, and sometimes neutral."

Vedanta: Sanskrit, literally "end of the *Vedas*," i.e., the *Upanishads* and

413

the later commentaries on them, from which was derived what Renou describes as a form of "mystical ontology," that led to the classical school of monistic philosophy which is one of the six major systems of orthodox Hinduism. Among the earliest texts of Vedanta are Vyasa's *Brahma-Sutra* and the sutras of Vedanta attributed to Badarayana; the *Bhagavad-Gita* was also an influence; but the most intense development of the doctrine came in the 8th century A.D. in the teachings of Sankaracharya (from whose *The Crest-Jewel of Discrimination* Merton quotes frequently in this volume), who formulated the nondualistic concepts of Advaita Vedanta. As the importance of Vedanta increased over the centuries, many variant sects were developed—elements of bhakti and other theories from Shaivism and Vaishnavism were introduced—and theologians such as Ramanuja (11th century) and Chaitanya (15th century) contributed to its evolution, as did Swami Vivekananda (late 19th century), the disciple of Sri Ramakrishna, who founded Vedanta Societies in Europe and America which are still very active. See the indexes of Morgan, Renou, Ross, Zaehner, *The Cultural Heritage of India,* Volume IV, and *The Gospel of Sri Ramakrishna* for references to extensive discussions of the many aspects of Vedanta. See also the anthology, *Vedanta for the Western World,* edited by Christopher Isherwood, Hollywood, Marcel Rodd Co., 1945

Vedas: Sanskrit, "knowledge" from "I know"; "the sacred, primary scriptures of Hinduism, held to have been 'born of the very breath of God.' " (Ross) As a language, Vedic was the Aryan precursor of Sanskrit, and Vedism, a religion having its sources in ancient Indo-Iranian cults, came into northwestern India with the Aryan invasions between 2000 and 1500 B.C., gradually spreading its influence through the rest of the subcontinent in the various sects of Hinduism which proved stronger than Buddhism, and became the dominant religious and social force of India. ". . . comprising more than one hundred extant books and including in addition to the four Samhitas [collections of hymns] to which they are individually attached, works of exegesis, legend, ritual, and religio-philosophical speculation [such as brahmanas, aranyakas, upanishads and sutras] . . . the four canonical collections of hymns, prayers and liturgical formulae . . . the *Rig-Veda,* the oldest and most important, comprising more than a thousand hymns; the *Yajur-Veda,* comprising liturgical and ritualistic formulae in verse and prose; the *Sama-Veda,* hymns, many of which occur in the Rig-Veda, for which musical notation is added or indicated; and the *Atharva-Veda,* in verse and prose, comprising charms, prayers, curses, spells, etc., as well as some theosophic and cosmogonic hymns, and written in a cruder and more popular style than the preceding. . . ." (Webster's II) A selection of translations of brief but representative passages from the *Vedas,* made by Prof. V. Raghavan, who was

Merton's friend and guide in Madras, will be found in Morgan: *The Religion of the Hindus,* pages 277–323.

veritas: Latin, "truth."

v.g.: verbi gratia, Latin, "for example"

vidya: Sanskrit, "knowledge," specifically, in Hinduism, the kind which can lead to the soul's liberation through knowledge of ultimate reality In the Lingayata (idealistic) sect of the Virashaivite school of Hinduism, largely formulated by Basava in the 12th century A.D., vidya is one of the "pure road" group of the thirty-six principles which form the axis of the sect's doctrines. See the chapters on Virashaivism by Shri Kumaraswamiji, pages 98–107 in Volume IV of *The Cultural Heritage of India.*

Vidyapati: a 15th-century Vaishnavite poet at the court of the Bengali king of Mithila. See Dimock: *In Praise of Krishna,* page 82.

vihara of Dambulla: vihara, Sanskrit, "place of recreation"; hence a temple, usually a Buddhist shrine, as that of Dambulla in Ceylon. In ancient India a vihara could also be a pleasure garden or the precincts of a Buddhist or Jain temple or monastery. Today a vihara may as well be a teaching center for Buddhist monks, and there are Theravada viharas in London and a number of European countries. The word is also a religious term in Theravada Buddhism, which teaches four Brahma viharas, or sublime states of consciousness: love, compassion, joy, and equanimity. (See Humphreys: *Buddhism,* pages 125–26.)

vijnana (Sanskrit), vinnana (Pali): in Buddhism, "consciousness or pure awareness without content; the last of the Five Groups (Skandhas)." (Murti) "Mentation." (S.B. Dasgupta) See Nanasampanno: *Wisdom Develops Samadhi,* page 87, the source from which Merton is quoting the term: "Vinnana means awareness (sense awareness)—of forms, smells, tastes, or things which touch us, and of mental objects, just at that moment when these things come into contact (Samphassa) with the eye, ear, nose, tongue, body, or heart respectively." In Hinduism, the term has the sense of "Special Knowledge of the Absolute, by which one affirms the universe and sees it as the manifestation of Brahman." (*The Gospel of Shri Ramakrishna*)

Vijnanavada: Sanskrit, one of the later sects of Mahayana Buddhism, founded by Dignaga and Dharmakirti, which lays stress on the fundamental consciousness as the void. It is sometimes called the "Consciousness Only" sect, and most authorities consider it a branch of the more comprehensive Yogacara school. "In Vijnanavada the absolute becomes 'mind only,' which in its highest and true form is beyond the opposition of subject and object, whereas in its lower form it manifests itself as a kind of derived, half-real truth." (von Glasenapp: *Buddhism,* page 117) See also the indexes of Morgan and Murti for many references to different aspects of Vijnanavada.

415

vijnapti-matrata: Sanskrit, "pure consciousness."

vikalpa: Sanskrit, in Madhyamika Buddhism, "conceptual construction; the subjective activity of thought interpreting the object." (Murti)

vimala: Sanskrit, the second stage, "free from defilement," in the Buddhist progress toward bodhisattvahood.

vina: Sanskrit and Hindi, one of the classical musical instruments of India, which is still in popular use. It usually has four main strings and movable frets on the fingerboard, producing a sound somewhat like that of a guitar but which is made to resonate by gourds at each end of the fingerboard.

vinaya: Sanskrit and Pali, "discipline." The rule or code which governs the life and training of the Sangha, the Buddhist monastic orders. The *Vinaya Pitaka* is one of the most important works in the Pali canon of Abhidarmika Buddhism.

vipassana: Pali, in Theravada Buddhism, the meditation which brings insight, the step in realization which follows samatha, the meditation which brings tranquility. (See Morgan, page 144). Merton extracted the term from Nanasampanno's *Wisdom Develops Samadhi,* where it is glossed by Bhikkhu Pannavaddho, the translator, as "'insight,' of such a type as is deep and effective in 'curing' the defilements. It is insight which arises out of Samadhi, and not just an intellectual exercise."

Dr. Raghu Vira: founder of the International Academy of Indian Culture in New Delhi and once head of the Jan Sangh party.

Vishnu: "one of the three great gods of Hinduism; a member of the classic triad: Vishnu-Shiva-Brahma or Vishnu-Shiva-Shakti." (Ross) The religious sect of Hinduism which centers on Vishnu is called Vaishnavism.

Swami Vivekananda: (1863–1902), the leading disciple of Sri Ramakrishna and founder of Vedanta societies in Europe and America.

wat: Thai, from the Sanskrit "vata"—"enclosed ground." A Buddhist temple or monastery in Thailand.

Yadavas: a clan living in the Mathura region which figures prominently in the *Mahabharata* epic of ancient India. It is believed that, in his earthly incarnation, the Hindu god Krishna was born into this tribe.

yak: Tibetan, a large wild ox of the highland regions of Tibet and central Asia which is domesticated for use in farming or to carry loads in caravans.

Yamala: a group of writings important in the development of Tantric Buddhism, perhaps composed around 1000 A.D., and thought to have been written by bhairavas, "human teachers who had attained complete spiritual emancipation and had almost become Shiva." For details, see *The Cultural Heritage of India,* Volume IV, pages 216–17.

Yasoda (Yasodhara): in Hindu mythology, the foster-mother of the God Krishna when he was incarnated as a mortal.

Yellow Hats: see Gelugpa school of Tibetan Buddhism.

Yin-yang: "Chinese (Pekingese) *yin*, dark, feminine principle: the feminine and negative principle (as of passivity, depth, darkness, cold, wetness) in nature that according to traditional Chinese cosmology combines with its opposite, *yang*, to produce all that comes to be." (Webster's III)

Yoga: Sanskrit, "literally to unite (or be yoked with) God." (Ross) In Hinduism, "mental discipline consisting in the direction of attention exclusively upon any object, abstract or concrete, with a view to the identification of consciousness with the object; attainment of this end is *samadhi*. The object of attention may be, but need not be, the deity. Yoga includes various physical disciplines such as controlled breathing and posture. The yogi should also be an ascetic, or, at least, continent. By yoga it is sought to gain control over specific natural forces, and over one's own body, and to gain occult powers; also to attain union with the universal spirit, Brahma. The chief yogas are the *bhakti* (devotional) *jnana* (intellectual), *karma* (work), and *hatha* (physical) yoga. The three stages of yoga trance are *dharana* (fixed attention), *dhyana* (contemplation), and *samadhi* (concentration)." (Webster's II) See the indexes of Monier-Williams, Morgan, Renou, Ross, *The Cultural Heritage of India,* Volume IV, and *The Gospel of Sri Ramakrishna* for references to detailed discussions of various aspects of yogic doctrine and practices.

Yogacara: Sanskrit, "yoga"—"yoke" and "acara"—"custom, conduct." "One of the two major philosophical systems of Mahayana Buddhism agreeing with Madhyamika that external objects are unreal but holding that mind is real and that objects which appear to be external and material are in fact ideas or states of consciousness." (Webster's III) See also under Vijnanavada, another name frequently associated with this sect.

Yogatantras: Sanskrit, in Hinduism, one of the four main groups of Tantras. See under Tantra for details about these scriptures and the religious practices which derived from them, in Buddhism as well as in Hinduism.

Zen: Japanese. "One of the main schools of Japanese Buddhism, original Japanese pronunciation of the Chinese ideograph Ch'an, derived from Sanskrit *dhyana* [concentrated contemplation]." (Ross) ". . . a Japanese school of Mahayana Buddhism that teaches self-discipline, deep meditation, and the attainment of enlightenment by direct intuitive insight into a self-validating transcendent truth beyond all intellectual conceptions and characteristically expresses its teachings in paradoxical and nonlogical forms. . . ." (Webster's III) These forms include the koan, "a problem which cannot be solved by the intellect alone," mondo, "a rapid-fire question-and-answer technique employed to overcome conventional conceptual thought patterns," and lead to satori, "the state of consciousness . . . comparable to that special level of insight attained by the Buddha. . . ." (Ross) "There are two chief schools of Zen teaching extant in Japan today—the Rinzai School, known as the 'sudden' school and the Soto or 'gradual' School." (Ross) "In the Rinzai sect we find the dynamic character of the daring *koan* experiment and of lightninglike enlightenment, while the Soto School is characterized by a preference for silent sitting in *zazen* meditation and the quiet deeds of everyday life. . . ." (Heinrich Dumoulin, S.J.: *A History of Zen Buddhism,* as quoted in Ross) Zen came to Japan from China, and in ancient times the Zen or Ch'an school of Buddhism was classified into the "Five Mountains, the Ten Schools"; but, with time, some of these subdivisions disappeared or were merged into others until, by the date when Zen was transmitted to Japan, there remained only the two major sects, Rinzai and Soto.

PICTURE CREDITS

All photographs by Thomas Merton in this book are reproduced by courtesy of The Trustees of The Merton Legacy Trust; photographs from *A Hidden Wholeness* by Thomas Merton and John Howard Griffin (Boston, Houghton Mifflin, 1970; Copyright © 1970 by John Howard Griffin, Copyright © by The Trustees of The Merton Legacy Trust) are reproduced by courtesy of The Trustees of the Merton Legacy Trust, John Howard Griffin, and Houghton Mifflin; all other photographs by John Howard Griffin are reproduced by the courtesy of John Howard Griffin.

Frontispiece, page iv, by John Howard Griffin, *A Hidden Wholeness;* pages xii–xiii, courtesy of The Trustees of The Merton Legacy Trust, page xxii, Philip Stark, *A Hidden Wholeness;* page xxv, Griffin; page xxvi, Griffin, *A Hidden Wholeness;* page xxix, Thomas Merton, *A Hidden Wholeness;* pages 11 and 12, Merton; page 32, courtesy of The Trustees of The Merton Legacy Trust; page 33, courtesy of Kathy De Vico; page 36, courtesy of The Victoria and Albert Museum (London); page 41, courtesy of Mahamakuta-Rajavidyalaya Foundation (Bangkok); page 55, Merton; page 58, mandala, item B63 D13+, courtesy of The Center of Asian Art and Culture, The Avery Brundage Collection (San Francisco, California); page 62, from The Collection of The Newark Museum (Newark, New Jersey); page 65, Merton; page 83, courtesy of Stuart & Watkins (London); page 89, Merton, *A Hidden Wholeness;* page 98, Merton; page 101, from *A Hidden Wholeness;* page 106, Merton, *A Hidden Wholeness;* page 109, courtesy of The Victoria and Albert Museum (London); page 120, courtesy of The Newark Museum (Newark, New Jersey); page 122, courtesy of The Trustees of The Merton Legacy Trust; page 127, Merton, *A Hidden Wholeness;* page 128, Merton; page 139, Merton; page 142, courtesy of The Trustees of The Merton Legacy Trust; page 144, courtesy of The Trustees of The Merton Legacy Trust; page 145, Merton; page 149, Merton; page 152, Merton; page 156, Merton, *A Hidden Wholeness;* page 164, Merton; page 193, courtesy of Dr. V. Raghavan; pages 199, 200, and 201, Merton; page 217, Merton, *A Hidden Wholeness;* page 232, Merton; pages 234 and 235, Merton; page 249, Merton; page 251, Merton.

INDEX

INDEX

437

440

New Directions Paperbooks

Walter Abish, *Alphabetical Africa.* NDP375.
Ilangô Adigal, *Shilappadikaram.* NDP162.
Alain, *The Gods.* NDP382.
G. Apollinaire, *Selected Writings.*† NDP310.
Djuna Barnes, *Nightwood.* NDP98.
Charles Baudelaire, *Flowers of Evil.*† NDP71.
 Paris Spleen. NDP294.
Gottfried Benn, *Primal Vision.*† NDP322.
Eric Bentley, *Bernard Shaw.* NDP59.
Wolfgang Borchert, *The Man Outside.* NDP319.
Jorge Luis Borges, *Labyrinths.* NDP186.
Jean-François Bory, *Once Again.* NDP256.
Kay Boyle, *Thirty Stories.* NDP62.
E. Brock, *Invisibility Is The Art of Survival.*
 NDP342.
 Paroxisms. NDP385.
 The Portraits & The Poses. NDP360.
Buddha, *The Dhammapada.* NDP188.
Frederick Busch, *Manual Labor.* NDP376.
Ernesto Cardenal, *In Cuba.* NDP377.
Hayden Carruth, *For You.* NDP298.
 From Snow and Rock, from Chaos. NDP349.
Louis-Ferdinand Céline,
 Death on the Installment Plan. NDP330
 Guignol's Band. NDP278.
 Journey to the End of the Night. NDP84.
Blaise Cendrars, *Selected Writings.*† NDP203.
B-c. Chatterjee, *Krishnakanta's Will.* NDP120.
Jean Cocteau, *The Holy Terrors.* NDP212.
 The Infernal Machine. NDP235.
M. Cohen, *Monday Rhetoric.* NDP352.
Cid Corman, *Livingdying.* NDP289.
 Sun Rock Man. NDP318.
Gregory Corso, *Elegiac Feelings American.*
 NDP299.
 Happy Birthday of Death. NDP86.
 Long Live Man. NDP127.
Edward Dahlberg, *Reader.* NDP246.
 Because I Was Flesh. NDP227.
David Daiches, *Virginia Woolf.* NDP96.
Osamu Dazai, *The Setting Sun.* NDP258.
 No Longer Human. NDP357.
Coleman Dowell, *Mrs. October Was Here.*
 NDP368.
Robert Duncan, *Bending the Bow.* NDP255.
 The Opening of the Field. NDP356.
 Roots and Branches. NDP275.
Richard Eberhart, *Selected Poems.* NDP198.
Russell Edson, *The Very Thing That Happens.*
 NDP137.
Wm. Empson, *7 Types of Ambiguity.* NDP204.
 Some Versions of Pastoral. NDP92.
Wm. Everson, *Man-Fate.* NDP369.
 The Residual Years. NDP263.
Lawrence Ferlinghetti, *Her.* NDP88.
 Back Roads to Far Places. NDP312.
 A Coney Island of the Mind. NDP74.
 The Mexican Night. NDP300.
 Open Eye, Open Heart. NDP361.
 Routines. NDP187.
 The Secret Meaning of Things. NDP268.
 Starting from San Francisco. NDP 220.
 Tyrannus Nix?. NDP288.
Ronald Firbank, *Two Novels.* NDP128.
Dudley Fitts,
 Poems from the Greek Anthology. NDP60.
F. Scott Fitzgerald, *The Crack-up.* NDP54.
Robert Fitzgerald, *Spring Shade: Poems
 1931-1970.* NDP311.
Gustave Flaubert,
 Bouvard and Pécuchet. NDP328.
 The Dictionary of Accepted Ideas. NDP230.
M. K. Gandhi, *Gandhi on Non-Violence.*
 (ed. Thomas Merton) NDP197.
André Gide, *Dostoevsky.* NDP100.
Goethe, *Faust,* Part I.
 (MacIntyre translation) NDP70.

Albert J. Guerard, *Thomas Hardy.* NDP185.
Guillevic, *Selected Poems.*† NDP279.
Henry Hatfield, *Goethe.* NDP136.
 Thomas Mann. (Revised Edition) NDP101.
John Hawkes, *The Beetle Leg.* NDP239.
 The Blood Oranges. NDP338.
 The Cannibal. NDP123.
 The Innocent Party. NDP238.
 The Lime Twig. NDP95.
 Lunar Landscapes. NDP274.
 Second Skin. NDP146.
A. Hayes, *A Wreath of Christmas Poems.*
 NDP347.
H.D., *Helen in Egypt.* NDP380
 Hermetic Definition NDP343.
 Trilogy. NDP362.
Hermann Hesse, *Siddhartha.* NDP65.
Christopher Isherwood, *The Berlin Stories.*
 NDP134.
Gustav Janouch,
 Conversations With Kafka. NDP313.
Alfred Jarry, *Ubu Roi,* NDP105.
Robinson Jeffers, *Cawdor and Medea.* NDP293.
James Joyce, *Stephen Hero.* NDP133.
 James Joyce/Finnegans Wake. NDP331.
Franz Kafka, *Amerika.* NDP117.
Bob Kaufman,
 Solitudes Crowded with Loneliness. NDP199.
Hugh Kenner, *Wyndham Lewis.* NDP167.
Kenyon Critics, *Gerard Manley Hopkins.*
 NDP355.
P. Lal, *Great Sanskrit Plays.* NDP142.
Tommaso Landolfi,
 Gogol's Wife and Other Stories. NDP155.
Lautréamont, *Maldoror.* NDP207.
Denise Levertov, *Footprints.* NDP344.
 The Jacob's Ladder. NDP112.
 O Taste and See. NDP149.
 The Poet in the World. NDP363.
 Relearning the Alphabet. NDP290.
 The Sorrow Dance. NDP222.
 To Stay Alive. NDP325.
 With Eyes at the Back of Our Heads.
 NDP229.
Harry Levin, *James Joyce.* NDP87.
García Lorca, *Five Plays.* NDP232.
 Selected Poems † NDP114.
 Three Tragedies. NDP52.
Michael McClure, *September Blackberries.*
 NDP370.
Carson McCullers, *The Member of the
 Wedding.* (Playscript) NDP153.
Thomas Merton, *Cables to the Ace.* NDP252.
 Emblems of a Season of Fury. NDP140.
 Gandhi on Non-Violence. NDP197.
 The Geography of Lograire. NDP283.
 New Seeds of Contemplation. NDP337.
 Raids on the Unspeakable. NDP213.
 Selected Poems. NDP85.
 The Way of Chuang Tzu. NDP276.
 The Wisdom of the Desert. NDP295.
 Zen and the Birds of Appetite. NDP261.
Henri Michaux, *Selected Writings.*† NDP264.
Henry Miller, *The Air-Conditioned Nightmare.*
 NDP302.
 *Big Sur & The Oranges of Hieronymus
 Bosch.* NDP161.
 The Books in My Life. NDP280.
 The Colossus of Maroussi. NDP75.
 The Cosmological Eye. NDP109.
 Henry Miller on Writing. NDP151.
 The Henry Miller Reader. NDP269.
 Remember to Remember. NDP111.
 Stand Still Like the Hummingbird. NDP236.
 The Time of the Assassins. NDP115.
 The Wisdom of the Heart. NDP94.
Y. Mishima, *Confessions of a Mask.* NDP253.
 Death in Midsummer. NDP215.
Eugenio Montale, *Selected Poems.*† NDP193.

Complete descriptive catalog available free on request from
New Directions, 333 Sixth Avenue, New York 10014.   † Bilingual.